ISSUES IN
AMERICAN
ECONOMIC
HISTORY

ISSUES IN AMERICAN ECONOMIC HISTORY

Selected Readings

Third Edition

Edited by
GERALD D. NASH
The University of New Mexico

D.C. HEATH AND COMPANY
Lexington, Massachusetts   Toronto

International Standard Book Number: 0–669–02480–5

Library of Congress Catalog Card Number: 79–89005

PREFACE

The great activity in American economic history during the past four decades and the succession of new interpretations provide a justification for this book of readings, which is designed to introduce the novice to the subject. Significant developments since 1972 in the field, as well as notable changes in the courses taught, made it desirable to revise the book for a third edition.

The aims of the book are fourfold. First, it is designed to provide supplementary readings in American economic history from a variety of secondary sources. Second, it seeks to acquaint its readers with some of the controversial issues in the field. Third, it presents challenging reinterpretations of these problems. Finally, it can serve as a basis for discussions, since selections have also been chosen for their clashing and contrasting opinions.

The readings in this book focus upon the theme of economic expansion. Thus the topics and selections relate to the historical development of factors responsible for economic growth. These factors include population and labor, government policies, technology, entrepreneurship, and crises. Materials in the book bear upon conflicting assessments of the influence that these forces have had upon the evolution of the American economy.

In this third edition, several modifications have been made to preserve the usefulness of the work as a teaching tool. The book has been shortened to make it more compact. In addition, I have added several new issues that seem particularly relevant to changing student interests.

The making of the book has been a cooperative endeavor. The authors whose selections are included have made the major contribution. The students who have used the book in previous editions at American and Canadian colleges and universities have taught me much about their needs for such a book. Finally, I wish to thank the following colleagues for their advice in preparing this edition: Jeremy Atack, University of Illinois at Urbana-Champaign; August Giebelhaus, Georgia Institute of Technology; and Harold Livesay, SUNY at Binghamton.

Gerald D. Nash

CONTENTS

ISSUES IN AMERICAN ECONOMIC HISTORY

1

THE NEW
ECONOMIC
HISTORY

PROBLEM: *What is new in the New Economic History?*

The 1960's witnessed exciting advances in the field of American Economic History, many of them by economists who were advocates of the New Economic History. Their prime objective was to apply economic theories to historical data and to develop models of economic behavior in a historical context. As practitioners of econometric history they were frequently preoccupied with quantification and statistical analysis, usually with the aid of sophisticated mathematical techniques. By 1970 this extraordinary outburst of activity had resulted in an impressive spate of works embodying the new approach. If the New Economic Historians achieved somewhat less than what they had hoped—to revolutionize major conclusions of traditional qualitative historians—nevertheless they exercised an important influence in the revision of various points of view. And they demonstrated the utility of economic and mathematical theories in rigorous historical analysis. Yet, dispute still abounds over the precise nature of their contributions. Professor Robert Fogel, an economist who was a leading representative of the New Economic Historians in the 1960's, argues that an emphasis on measurement, the use of theory, and the application of statistical inference to historical data constitute the gist of their contributions. Not so, argues Professor Fritz Redlich, one of the elder statesmen in the field of economic history, whose background has been

1

oriented toward a wide range of the social sciences. Redlich
notes that economic historians have always emphasized quantification and the use of theory. The newness of the New
Historians lies in their neglect of institutions and processes
in favor of statistical formulations, and the construction of
artificial or hypothetical models. Both of these selections provide a stimulating introduction to one of the most controversial contemporary issues in the field of American Economic
History. Can "new" and traditional approaches be reconciled?
What are the unique contributions of quantitative and qualitative methods in economic history? Which topics in American Economic History have undergone revision because of
the work of the New Economic Historians?

"New" and Traditional Approaches to Economic History and Their Interdependence

FRITZ REDLICH

The purpose of this paper is to analyze the various new or current
approaches to economic history. In so doing I reluctantly use the now
widely accepted terms "new" economic, or "econometric," history considered by some authors as synonymous. In fact, however, there is both
a broader and a narrower application of the phrase "new economic history." In the broader sense, the term embraces the work of the various
authors who have in common as their aim theoretically underpinned
quantitative economic history; in the narrower, it refers only to what I
shall call the "model builders." Moreover the terminology seems to be in
process of change.[1]

I

The new approaches, to use a neutral term, are both the phenomenon of a
generation and a matter of *Weltanschauung*. When I speak here of genera-

Reprinted by permission from *Journal of Economic History*, XXV (December, 1965),
pp. 480–495.

[1] Papers and Proceedings of the Seventy-seventh Annual Meeting of the American
Economic Association, Chicago, December 1964. The *American Economic Review*,
LV (1965), pp. 90, 91, 98.

tions I mean, of course, historical generations, which in distinction from biological ones can also be called groups of coevals. Men born and maturing at the same time are, under the pressure of the particular historical situation in which they grow up, molded into a community of problems. In the present case, men like Parker, North, Conrad, Fogel, Davis—all born within eight years of one another—belong to such a group. But already there is a younger generation coming along which proceeds farther on the road blazed by the former.

Secondly, the new approaches are based on a particular *Weltanschauung*. By this term I mean a certain articulate outlook on the world which is in itself consistent but neither provable nor disprovable. Research in this area has been badly neglected since the death of Wilhelm Dilthey, the great Berlin philosopher of history. In his time, the late nineteenth and early twentieth centuries, one could still distinguish between three *Weltanschauungen:* positivism; the *Weltanschauung* of freedom; and that of harmony, the latter having been held by Leibniz, by Adam Smith, and (deteriorating almost into a cartoon) by Bastiat. Two world wars have shown it to be untenable, and it has died out. Today one has to distinguish between two: positivism and antipositivism "according to their peculiar combination of ontological and epistemological components."[2]

The new approaches to economic history are definitely positivistic, in that for positivism nothing matters unless it can be counted, measured, or weighed. But the age-old empiricism also roots in positivism. Consequently the lines are strangely drawn. The new approaches, while positivistic at their roots, are antiempiricistic through their reliance on economic theory. Thereby they come closer to analytical economic history as practiced by some antipositivistic traditionalists than to the empiricistic approach to which they are related on the basis of the underlying *Weltanschauung*.[3]

II

Two elements are constitutive for the new approaches to economic history: one is the overruling interest in quantification, the other is the use of economic theory manifested by the reliance on hypotheses and figments, as will call for our attention later. The first element, quantification,

[2] Don Martindale, "Limits of and Alternatives to Functionalism in Sociology," in The American Academy of Political and Social Science Monograph No. 5, *Functionalism in the Social Sciences* (Philadelphia: The American Academy, 1965), pp. 149 ff.

[3] See also the illuminating remarks on the role of figures in the Enlightenment and in bourgeois society in Max Horkheimer and Theodor W. Adorno, *Dialektik der Aufklärung* (Amsterdam: Querido, 1947), pp. 17, 18. I stress that the new economic history is not empiricistic, since I have found the statement that it is "coming close to what a modern empiricist might demand of it." See George G. S. Murphy, "The 'New' History," in *Explorations in Entrepreneurial History*, 2d ser., II, No. 2 (1965), p. 132.

is by no means new. Fogel pointed out in his Boston address of 1963 that the effort "to discover and present numerical information relating to historical processes" is not new; and Hughes's brilliant bibliographical article in the *Journal of Economic History* bears out that contention.[4] Yet between December 1963 and December 1964 Fogel changed his emphasis: now "the novel element in the work of the new economic historians is their *approach* [italics mine] to measurement and theory." Formerly, so Fogel goes on, one simply located and classified numerical information; now, however, the emphasis is on "reconstructing measurements . . . no longer extant," on combining primary data with measurements never made before, and on indirect measuring where direct measuring is impossible. It does not appear to me that these aims are held in common by the exponents of all the various new approaches.[5]

It is agreed that the quantitative approach to economic history is not new; it has been pointed out that Fogel's *specific approach* is not shared by all pertinent members of the young generation; finally, reliance on economic theory, where it was sufficiently developed to be useful, characterizes also the work of older analytical economic historians, for example in price, monetary, and banking histories and some other fields. Yet actually there is something new in what goes under the name of "new economic history" in the term's broader connotation, so that one must look for those elements which really distinguish between the traditional and the new approaches. In so doing I again disagree with Fogel.

The matter is rather complicated, as we will see, but one difference between the traditional and the new approaches can be characterized as follows: the old approach deals essentially with institutions, and with processes only to the extent that the latter took place within institutions. (Incidentally, the introduction of the *process* into economic history, or into historical economics if you prefer, was the work of Gustav Schmoller.) The new approach, in contrast, often goes directly at macroeconomic processes, thus disregarding institutions. If one wanted to put it pointedly, though by oversimplifying the problem, he could say: Traditional economic history deals primarily with the development of economic institutions and secondarily with processes taking place therein. The new approaches tend to deal primarily and directly with economic processes while more or less neglecting economic institutions.

This switch in approach became possible only in about the last twenty years when a genuinely dynamic theory, that is, a theory of economic development, rose beside the traditional static theory, largely useless for

---

[4] Robert William Fogel, "A Provisional View of the 'New Economic History,'" in *American Economic Review*, LIV (1964), p. 377; J. R. T. Hughes, "Measuring British Economic Growth," in *Journal of Economic History*, XXIV (1964), p. 60 ff.

[5] *American Economic Review*, LV (1965), p. 92.

the economic historian, whose subject matter is dynamic. Now in consequence of new theoretical goals essentially akin to historical ones, more economists than before are taking an interest in economic history. Now, through that increased interest, quantification and reliance on theory are growing in this field; now, these scholars are gaining a greater influence on its development. Thus, the trend toward quantification with the help of refined mathematical and analytical methods is not due only to the prevailing *Weltanschauung* and to the bias of a young group of coevals. To the extent that its exponents started in economics it is largely due to their training; for economics, according to Milton Friedman, presumably speaking for many of his colleagues, is "a disguised branch of mathematics."[6] The economists devoting themselves to historical topics apply what they have learned. The trouble is only that the mathematical and the historical bents, except for a few extraordinary men like Schumpeter, do usually not go together, a difficulty which can only be partly overcome by appropriate training; and this means more than being steeped in economics and then taking a few courses in history for a year or so. Anyway, the key to the new development in economic history is, besides the evolution of refined economic analysis, the emergence of a new economic theory, the theory of economic development.

The quantitative approach to economic history has been recognized as nothing essentially new, and the application of refined mathematical and analytical economic methods would have come automatically with progress in these fields. Yet the genuinely new elements in the recent movement should not be underestimated. Beside the component already pointed out before, the younger researchers' neglect of institutions, there is another equally important one. The "new" economic historians actually *specialize*, that is on the "purely 'economic' problems of economic history," to quote from a letter of J. R. T. Hughes. Finally the introduction of modern methods of economic analysis into the quantitative approach to economic history has brought in its wake another fresh element, never used before in this area, namely, statistical inference. That is, "quantitative evidence may be used to verify a qualitative historical hypothesis." Conrad and Meyer, whose book containing the quotation will be analyzed in more detail later, refer as an example to an article by Michael C. Lovell. He infers from certain time series that the Bank of England became a lender of last resort in the crises of the eighteenth century. The qualitative hypothesis that the Bank of England came to stand for a central bank as early as that century was tested by statistical means against the actual numerical data and thus verified.[7]

---

[6] *Essays in Positive Economics* (Chicago: University of Chicago Press, 1953), p. 12.

[7] As to the book of Conrad and Meyer, see . . . footnote 14. The article by Lovell, "The Role of the Bank of England as Lender of Last Resort in the Crises of the Eighteenth Century," is in *Explorations in Entrepreneurial History*, X (1957/58), p. 8 ff.

The last statement has already brought us to another characteristic feature of the new approaches to economic history, but one which is only partly new—namely the use of hypotheses and figments. Test hypotheses have been used extensively by traditional analytical historians; but historians in general have shied away from the use of figments as leading to conjectural history which is generally held in disrepute. But we shall need to change our opinion to some extent, since the application of figments may provide useful tools for analytical economic history.

Hypotheses and figments are in fact two very different things, but it is a common error to confound them. Hypotheses are based on assumptions which are held to have a counterpart in reality, while figments are assumptions having no such counterparts or at least known to be irrealistic. While hypotheses reflect and are derived from reality, figments are mere "as if" constructs, without parallels in reality. A hypothesis cries for verification or, if one prefers the more modern way of thinking, for falsification. Figments as mental constructs are neither verifiable nor falsifiable. They demand justification by their usefulness. With the help of hypotheses we gain knowledge, with that of a figment we obtain a tool for the acquisition of knowledge. Scholarly work based on figments is comparable with industrial roundabout production since, as we shall see later, it leads to models.[8] To be sure, what in line with the German philosophical (that is, the Herbarth-Lotze-Vaihinger) tradition I have called "figment," has recently appeared in America under the name of "counterfactual or subjunctive conditional."[9]

III

If we make the use or nonuse of hypotheses or figments, respectively, the criterion, we are able to distinguish between economic historians and the builders of historical models, and we can point to essential characteristics of the various new approaches which, on the other hand, are held together by a common aim: the extensive use of modern economic analysis, concentration on the purely economic aspects of economic history, and quantification along with refined mathematics.

If with such ends in mind the researcher works with the help of a hypothesis, the outcome tends toward analytical quantitative economic

[8] My thinking is based on the famous book by Hans Vaihinger, *Die Philosophie des Als Ob.* I have used the third edition (Leipzig: F. Meiner, 1918). An English translation by C. K. Ogden appeared under the title, *The Philosophy of 'As-if'* (London: K. Paul, Trench, Trubner & Co., 1924). See especially the Introduction, ch. iii, and Part IA, ch. ii. The English author translates the German word *Fiktion* as fiction. I prefer the term figment.

[9] Conrad and Meyer have taken the term into their book already mentioned and to be cited in footnote 14.

history, and Douglass North's achievement is representative of the approach. On the first page of his much-discussed book, *The Economic Growth of the United States, 1790–1860*,[10] he has been articulate about the hypotheses underlying his presentation: "The gist of the argument is that the timing and pace of an economy's development has been determined by (1) the success of its export sector, and (2) the characteristics of the export industry and the disposition of the income received from the export sector." This is clearly hypothetical as opposed to fictitious, nothing is postulated that is unrealistic. North assumes what he considers correct. Using the established method of the analytical economic historian or for that matter any social scientist, he proceeds to prove his hypotheses on the basis of available material, yet emphasizing quantification. What is new in the book is neither the method nor the far-going quantification, but the subject matter. As he himself states, he emphasizes economic growth as a total phenomenon whereas it has been traditional "to provide separate treatments of the various sectors in the economy . . . with only superficial linkages between them." It should be understood that I do not analyze or criticize the content of the book but deal with the *method* he uses. It is essentially related to the historical quantitative tradition. The result is history beyond any doubt.

Yet regardless of the fact that North starts from hypotheses and not from a figment, there is a fictitious element implied in his work, as in that of all scholars who identify economic development with some set of figures, whatever their character. He states in the preface of his book[11] that due to the preoccupation with description and institutional change, there is "no comprehensive, integrated analysis of United States Development." Economic historians have, according to North, "only incidentally discussed the process of economic growth." The content of this statement is granted to be correct, in fact entirely correct. But if North thinks that he has filled the gap, I should have to object as a matter of principle. His integrated discussion of American economic development was made possible by his bringing every phenomenon on a quantitative level; and while he gained integration thereby, he lost touch with reality. Figures are not identical with any process whatsoever. Figures are quantitative symbols which stand for something, in this case for the *result* of a process. By lining those symbols up in the form of a time series, we incorrectly create the impression that they actually represent a process, whereas they merely act as yardsticks, measuring a process. Or to express it differently, they represent a process only by the introduction of a figment, an as-if construct, and so furnish a good example of how useful figments can be in research and why their use is a widely accepted scholarly convention.

[10] *The Economic Growth of the United States, 1790–1860* (Englewood Cliffs, N.J.: Prentice Hall, Inc., 1961), p. vi.

[11] *Ibid.*, p. vi.

We now turn to those scholars who *base* their research on figments and begin with Fogel's work.[12] Here the fictitious character of the assumptions is beyond any doubt. Fogel investigates what would have happened to American economic development if there had not been any railroads. Now, as every schoolchild knows, there were railroads. That is, Fogel investigates what would have happened in the event that something else had happened which could not have happened. I emphasize now the phrase, which *could not have happened*. Technological development follows its own logic. Once the atmospheric engine had been developed into an efficient steam engine and the steam engine had successfully been put into boats, making steamers out of them, it was only a question of when the steam engine would be put on wheels, particularly as the railroad minus locomotive had existed for a long time. Having started from a figment, Fogel did not produce history, he produced what my friend Arthur Johnson has called quasi history, which in professional terms must be characterized as a historical model. Based on a figment it does not cry for verification—which is, of course, impossible—but for justification. Now some young friends of mine, who are by no means "new" economic historians, tell me how useful as an eye-opener Fogel's book is in teaching when used, of course, beside the standard presentations on railroad history by Chandler, the Hidys, Jenks, Overton, and others. So it is actually justified, but this does not make Fogel's product history.

Previously I have described Fogel's program of "reconstructing measurements no longer extant," of constructing yardsticks, and of measuring indirectly what cannot be measured directly. This program implies figments all the way through, because for the execution one must rely on the dependence of some figures on others, dependences which econometric theory establishes. This by necessity must be done in disregard of the historical situation in which a theoretically established interdependence of magnitudes may not come into play, because other causal factors impinge. What in theory is entirely correct becomes fictitious in the application, the result being a model rather than something related to reality. But we are not yet at the end.

There are additional elements which characterize Fogel's presentation as an as-if construct, a historical model. He himself states that he has omitted "many conspicuous aspects" because they were "too important" and "too complex" to be treated in this context. He himself knows that the validity of his findings is "not absolute" and nevertheless thinks that he has corrected unwarranted assumptions. This claim is epistemologically untenable, since one *cannot correct anything* by using a figment. As a

[12] Robert William Fogel, *Railroads and American Economic Growth: Essays in Econometric History* (Baltimore: Johns Hopkins Press, 1964).

matter of fact, one can thus only point to tendencies, a term introduced into economics by John Stuart Mill if I am correctly informed.[13]

But I am afraid that I must criticize Fogel also for not having asked the most fruitful question. Everyone who knows French economic history in the eighteenth and early nineteenth centuries knows that then there was economic development under way without the railroad. The fruitful question, if one wished to work in this area with figments, seems to be: At what point would economic development, under way by 1800, have become an arrested development for lack of adequate transportation? The stop would have come rather late in England, because there ore and coal were available in close proximity and because of the easy access to the sea, providing a kind of unpaid-for road or canals system, if you please. The United States development would have come to a halt much earlier, or several national economies might have developed.

✓So much for Fogel's work. The most representative model builders besides Fogel are Alfred H. Conrad and John R. Meyer, and they are less extreme. These coauthors have made it easy for the analyst, in that they have published an elaborate methodological introduction to their collection of papers, its title being "Economic Theory, Statistical Inference, and Economic History."[14] They have elucidated the difficult subject with unusual clarity, and, while I would have used other language and while I have objections to a good many details, I can accompany them almost all the way through.[15] Specifically, I agree with them that there can be generalization in historiography to a point and that hypotheses can be tested by historical research. As to the former, if generalization is the goal, I prefer comparative history as a means toward it rather than working with hypotheses. And as to the latter, the authors themselves have indicated the difficulties involved (pp. 24 ff.), while I myself think of qualitative testing as standing on the same level as quantitative.

Now let us see how the methodological prescriptions are applied in actual research and take as representative the paper "The Economics of Slavery in the Antebellum South," first published in the *Journal of Political Economy*, Vol. LXVI (1958). We begin by comparing the basis of the article with those of the books by North and Fogel. The former, as we

---

[13] Introduction, pp. vii, viii.

[14] *The Economics of Slavery and Other Studies in Econometric History* (Chicago: Aldine, 1964).

[15] I wish to register my objection to one minor point only: namely, their juxtaposition of the view that everything in history is unique, with extreme determinism. They are not sufficiently familiar with European history teaching and writing to know that since the turn of the last century outstanding historians have taken a stand which represents the middle ground. These are Jacob Burkhard in Basel, Otto Hintze in Berlin (whose student the author was), and the now-living Theodor Schieder of Cologne. One could also point to Karl Lamprecht in Leipzig, who had an approach of his own.

remember, begins with hypotheses, the latter with a figment. Conrad and
Meyer (p. 45) start from a hypothesis; according to them, American
Negro slavery was characterized by two production functions—namely,
that of southern staples ("inputs of Negro slaves and the materials required
to maintain them to the production of the southern staple crops, particularly cotton") and that of slave labor. This is what they "postulate."
Analyzing the execution of this program, one finds that parts II and III
of the paper use different methods. In Part II about a dozen additional
assumptions are heaped on the basic one. As a matter of fact, the authors
were forced to do this. Their primary quantitative material was not only
shaky but also was not collected for their specific purposes. They had to
make it suitable and this could only be done by introducing more assumptions. Tables 10 and 11 are each based on three of these; and as to Table 9,
their number is "untold."[16] If one looks at the assumptions as such, one
finds that some are hypothetical, others fictitious, such as the life ex-
pectancy of slaves and the fertility of field wenches. These are mere
guesses. Under these circumstances, that is, because of the large number of
assumptions and the mixture of hypothetical and fictitious ones, I must
contend that the whole Part II of the paper is fictitious even though the
basic assumption is hypothetical. Things look different in Part III; the
figures are much better, the assumptions (estimates) very few and not
basic. This part looks much more like history than Part II, and is in fact
historically interesting and useful.

Nevertheless I am reluctant to consider the paper as a whole a work of
history. In the original discussion over it, one speaker blamed the authors
for disregarding the interrelations of economic and other social factors.
The authors agreed, but the objection is in fact crucial from our point of
view. Both the isolating theorist and the narrative historian (who on principle refuses to ask and answer the question, Why? and, as a true empiricist, asks only: What has happened and when?) are in one boat. They
can—to be sure, for different reasons—legitimately present one side of a
development only. The analytical historian cannot afford to do so; for then
his presentation becomes a one-sided exaggeration—that is, a model.

Yet during the discussion the authors made another important statement: namely, that the purpose of their paper was to test "hypotheses
about the profitability [from the economist's point of view] of slavery
and the efficiency of the slave labor market." This program poses another
question: Is this actually a historical question? An economic question, as
this undoubtedly is, does not become *ipso facto* a historical one simply
because the problem investigated is of yesterday or before yesterday. An
economic problem becomes one of economic history only when a specifically historical element is added. As history is essentially changed over

---

[16] "Various hypothesized conditions"; p. 61.

time, the economic problem must be seen as changing in order to be a subject for the historian. Otherwise, if the test is unspoiled by figments, it may stand at best on the level of a historical case study.

At the time when Conrad and Meyer were working on their paper, they were aware that they were constructing a model. On page 67 they speak of "our model," on page 73 of the "validity of the model"; on page 82 we read "our model of the antebellum southern economy"; and when they first presented their paper, one discussant accepted their own characterization of the work and cited it (*ibid.*, 93). If they had stuck to that perfectly sound description, I would have had no fault to find. Historical models have been used earlier; we have been articulate about them ever since the days of Max Weber, and their refinement by mathematical means or otherwise deserves praise. But at some point, the authors changed their minds and they are now trying to sell their work as "history." And this and this alone is the reason for my protest. A model is never a piece of history, because it is conjectural or subjunctive or, in Max Weber's language used for all ideal types, a distortion of reality. This position I can not abandon even if a qualifying adjective, be it "new" or "econometric," is added. If we were to accept it as history, the piece would be bad history. It is based entirely on secondary sources without any source criticism whatsoever. In their methodological paper (p. 18), they stress the necessity of hunting for quantitative material which they consider "likely to be found." In fact, as experts in southern history have told and even shown me, it can be found in their case. If the authors wanted to write "history" they were by professional standards obliged to search for primary material; if they wanted to build a model, they were free from that obligation. As "history," most professional historians, in contrast to economists with an interest in history, will reject the piece. As a historical model it might be very useful, as only those can decide who work with the tool, for a tool it is and not a consumers' good.

I have tried to show that the result of the scholarly endeavors of both Conrad and Meyer and of Fogel is not history but quasi history. One can express this also in other terms, as has been done. These men do not write history but produce historical models. Now when one distinguishes between models by reduction and models by construction, the latter also called nonempirical models, one recognizes that there is a difference between Conrad and Meyer's Part II and Fogel's book, on the one hand, and the formers' Part III, on the other. The first named are models by construction, the last named one by reduction in that it abstracts only from the noneconomic determining factors. But models they are, so that we are cautioned against reifying them, against misplacing concreteness of them, to use the expressions of Morris Cohen and T. N. Whitehead. I am afraid the architects of the models in question and their admirers are not free from these errors. As far as I can see, the applause comes from economists rather than historians, from men never exposed to methodology and often not even to history.

IV

The so-called new approach to economic history has revealed itself as consisting of different movements. One, as represented for example by the data-processing jobs of Davis and Hughes or by Fishlow's paper, "The Trustee Savings Banks 1817-1861,"[17] is close to the tradition of quantitative economic history but uses much more refined mathematical tools. The second, exemplified by North, is based both on quantification and on clearly defined hypotheses which are tested. The product is economic history. The third, typified by Fogel as well as Conrad and Meyer, again emphasizes quantification but is simultaneously based on figments. The result is quasi-economic history, or as-if economic history, if you please, or more exactly a historical model.

A final question remains to be asked and answered: namely, What is the relationship of the traditional economic history to the new approaches? What makes it a little difficult to answer is the fact that, like the "new" economic history in the wider sense of the term, the traditional economic history is by no means uniform. Some is microeconomic history; some corresponds to macroeconomics. One branch emphasizes figures, another institutions. Some is empiricistic, some analytical. Or, focusing on the method applied, we can distinguish between a branch using the positivistic from another using the hermeneutic, that is, the interpretative "understanding" method.

Under these circumstances it is quite impossible to confront the two approaches and characterize them with a few concise words. Yet it is not far from the truth to say that the best traditional-yet-modern economic history, beside emphasizing the study of institutions, is well aware of the role of noneconomic factors and of imponderables which the "new" economic historians specializing in the purely economic aspect of the field disregard. To the extent that traditional economic history stresses institutions, noneconomic factors, and imponderables, it might draw for theoretical support on sociology and anthropology rather than on economics; whereas the "new" economic historians rely exclusively on the latter. T. C. Cochran's interest in the cultural element in economic development, or mine in the personal element therein, simply does not interest the exponents of the new approaches. But I am sure nothing is further from their thought than a scientific ostrich policy. Their *interests* lie in a different direction.

Once new approaches have come into existence and are here to stay, the traditional and the "new" economic history become interdependent, but

---

[17] *Journal of Economic History*, XXI (1961), p. 26 ff.

interdependent in different ways since they are not uniform phenomena. To the degree that the new approach simply implies quantification with refined mathematical methods, it will probably be the successor of the traditional quantitative approach to economic history. To the extent that the "new" approach is quantitative and analytical, as in the case of North's work, the old-line empiricists will take the result and the old-line analytical economic historian will take it also, once he becomes convinced that the underlying hypothesis is tenable and the analysis correct. More interesting is the question how the traditional analytical economic history will be related to the "new" analytical economic history as practiced by Conrad and Meyer or Fogel.

It has been pointed out earlier that on the basis of figments one arrives at quasi history or models. These the traditional analytical economic historian will use as he will use any other suitable model—namely, as a flashlight. He will *compare* his empirical material with the model and, if he sees something which he otherwise would not have seen, he will recognize the model's usefulness and be grateful to the model builder. If it does not help him, he will reject it as unsuitable in the particular case, although this will not exclude the possibility of its being valuable for other research purposes. Yet there are also specific interdependences of the traditional and the "new" approaches. A new approach may be based on the work of the traditionalists or, vice versa, it may make the latter's research possible. Let me give an example for each case.

Historians have long known that early English savings banks were founded with a view to helping the poor. But there we were. We did not know whether or not that goal was reached, until Fishlow came and subjected the material to modern statistical analysis.[18] This showed clearly that in fact the British savings banks originally served the lower middle classes rather than the poor. This finding will be adopted in any presentation of savings banking by traditional economic historians.

Now the other case: in a painstaking study by L. E. Davis and J. R. T. Hughes, "A Dollar-Sterling Exchange 1803-1895,"[19] the authors, members of the Purdue faculty, have shown by applying very refined mathematical analysis that "the exchange rate stability commonly associated with the pre-1914 gold standard was a characteristic of the dollar-sterling exchange only after the early 1870's," a conclusion which no economic historian can afford to disregard. But right here, where the "new" economic historians stopped, the traditionalist would start with his research. I myself was tempted to ask a few years ago: Why did the gold-point mechanism work after the 1870's and not earlier? My answer would have been sought in a study of the development of communication and of business administra-

[18] *Ibid.*

[19] *Economic History Review*, XIII (1960), p. 52 ff.

tion, and I am sure it is to be found in these areas. This example shows very well where the shortcomings of both the traditional and the new approaches lie which, in turn, result from different goals. The "new" men emphasize measuring, and comprehending by measuring; the old nonempiricistic economic historian stresses comprehending and "understanding." They are certainly now interdependent.[20]

I have found in some pieces by leading exponents of the "new" approach remarks which indicate their consciousness of the fact that they are standing on the shoulders of traditional economic historians. In their programmatic statements they were not always fortunate, so that these can be misconstrued.[21] A still younger group now coming out of their seminars with the arrogance which is the privilege of youth seem to believe that their approach will take the place of the traditional one, that they will rout economic history as practiced by the old fogies. They will in time mature and learn, or so it can be hoped.

But there comes a point where I stop. A few years ago Bulletin 64 of the Social Science Research Council seemingly wanted to merge history into the social sciences. I do not think that the attempt was a success. Now Fogel wants to "reunify" economic history with economic theory, presumably a *societas leonina* in which economic history would cease to exist, after all traditional economic historians have committed hara-kiri. First, Fogel's concept of reunification is out of order. He does not realize that economic history, created by historians, goes back independently to the eighteenth century, as does modern economics, both being coeval, and that what he presents as the history of a separation of economic history from economic theory is neither factually correct nor correctly interpreted.[22] Moreover a merger, as Fogel plans it, would mean that economic history is dropped in favor of model building, as the economist learns in class. I would not expect many genuine historians to be willing to take that road, and it seems to me that resistance would come even from some of the exponents of the "new" approaches of different persuasion. At all events, since as before a sizable portion of American economic historians will come from history rather than from economics, there is no fear that model building will outgrow historiography or that measuring in economic history will entirely replace the understanding variety.[23] On the other hand

[20] Although speaking only on a related problem, R. L. Basman, in his article, "The Role of the Economic Historian in Predictive Testing of Proffered 'Economic Laws,'" in *Explorations in Entrepreneurial History*, 2d ser., II (1965), p. 159 ff., points in the same direction. He seems to plead for the use of realistic assumptions to be provided by professional historians. I wonder if he means to take a stand against the model builders and the use of figments as the basis of historical research.

[21] See, for example, *American Economic Review*, LV (1965), p. 92 ff.

[22] *Ibid.*, pp. 94, 95.

[23] A high-class discussion of the methods of measuring as against those of compre-

I feel strongly that the day of empiricistic historiography is gone and I wholeheartedly agree with Rondo Cameron that the choice is not between theory or no theory in economic history but between consciously and professionally formulated theory and unconscious amateurish theorizing, because the historian is unavoidably guided by some ideas somehow absorbed.[24]

The Reunification of Economic History with Economic Theory

ROBERT WILLIAM FOGEL

In the brief time allotted to me I want to outline two provisional propositions concerning the new economic history.

The first proposition is that one can observe in the work of the new generation of economic historians a departure from the past sufficient to justify a title like new economic history.

The departure is not to be found in the realm of subject matter. The new generation has not turned away from the traditional theme of its discipline. The central interest of the new economic historians is still the description and explanation of economic growth. This continuity with the past holds in the small as well as in the large. The specific research projects of the new generation focus on such familiar issues as the developmental impact of railroads and canals, the effect of changes in supply and demand on the growth of the iron industry, the profitability of slavery, the factors affecting the growth of productivity in agriculture, the effect of federal land policy on the distribution of income, the influence of foreign trade on the creation of a market economy, the sources of the capital required for industrialization, the explanation of urbanization, and the causes of economic fluctuations.

The novel element in the work of the new economic historians is their approach to measurement and theory. Economic history has always had a quantitative orientation. But much of the past work on economic data was

---

hending and understanding took place at a meeting of the Verein für Sozialpolitik. See its *Schriften*, new ser., No. 25, *Diagnose und Prognose als Wirtschaftliches Methodenproblem* (Berlin: Duncker and Humblot, 1962). Especially pertinent here is p. 178, a remark by Georg Weippert.

[24] *American Economic Review*, LV (1965), p. 112.

Reprinted by permission from American Economic Association, *Papers and Proceedings of the Seventy-Seventh Annual Meeting*, LV (December, 1964), pp. 92–98.

limited to the location and the simple classification of the numerical information contained in government and business records. While continuing this pursuit, the new economic history places its primary emphasis on reconstructing measurements which might have existed in the past but are no longer extant, on the recombination of primary data in a manner which enables them to obtain measurements that were never before made, and on finding methods of measuring economic phenomena that cannot be measured directly.

In performing these tasks, the new economic historians draw on virtually the whole gamut of the theoretical and statistical models of economics. William Whitney uses input-output analysis in his attempt to measure the effect of tariffs on the rise of manufacturing during the post-Civil War period. Eugene Smolensky and D. Ratajczak employ location theory to explain the growth of San Diego. Paul David relies on a constant elasticity of substitution function to infer the growth of the capital stock in Chicago during the nineteenth century. James K. Kindahl applied an extension of the hypergeometric distribution to estimate the number of nonnational banks in existence after the Civil War. The theory of rent has proved to be relevant to the analysis of problems as diverse as the economic viability of slavery and the estimation of the social saving of canals. Even so rarefied a construct as the Von Neuman-Morgenstern utility index proved to be of practical value in quantifying the effect of risk on the financial enervation of the Union Pacific Railroad.[1]

The measurements obtained through the application of economic theory and statistics have yielded considerably more precise information than has hitherto been available. For example, Paul MacAvoy, combining regression analysis with a theory of cartel stability, has been able to date the onset and duration of the rate wars among the trunk-line railroads, to identify the initiators of these wars, to measure the intensity of the conflict and to estimate certain of the gains and losses of the participants. Stanley Engerman, applying regression analysis to a body of cross-sectional data on the iron industry that has lain fallow for more than a century, has been able to produce remarkably detailed time series on the growth of the capacity of blast furnaces by state and type for the years from 1800 through 1856.

Such improved information has frequently resulted in dramatic re-evaluations of the economic impact of past events and institutions. Thus capital theory has been used by Alfred Conrad and John Meyer, Yasukichi Yasuba, Robert Evans, Jr., and Richard Sutch to show that slavery was a profitable system. Richard Easterlin's construction of estimates of the regional distribution of income combined with Robert Gallman's new series on gross national product imply that between 1840 and 1860 per

---

[1] Other statements on the redirection in measurement characteristic of the new economic history and the role which theory plays in this redirection, [have been made.]

capita income in the slave South grew at approximately the same rate as the long-term average for the United States as a whole.[2] The last finding is in startling contradiction to the traditional view that the antebellum South was economically stagnant. Other traditional views that have been upset or at least seriously challenged by the new economic history include the hypothesis that railroads were built ahead of demand, the view that the lag of wages behind prices during the Civil War led to unusually great prosperity for northern manufacturing interests, and the proposition that the development of the Bessemer process was of transcending significance for the rapid emergence of a modern iron and steel industry in the United States.[3]

My second proposition is that the new economic history represents a reunification of economic history with economic theory and thus brings to an end the century-old split between these two branches of economics.

Economic history emerged as a distinct discipline during the course of the mid- and late-nineteenth-century revolt against the deductive theories of classical economics. Led by Roscher, Knies, Hildebrand, and Schmoller in Germany and by Leslie, Ingram, and Ashley in England, the original aim of the historical school (or schools) was to replace what they believed to be the unrealistic theories of deductive economics by theories developed inductively through the study of history. Yet despite a half century of programmatic proclamations and despite the many fine historical monographs produced by the school(s), no alternative theory emerged.

In a 1901 review of the accomplishments of the historical school(s), Thorstein Veblen called their effort to supplant classical theory a "failure." "There seems," he continued, "no reason to regard this failure as less than definitive." Veblen's judgment was reaffirmed three decade later by J. H. Clapham who wrote, "Most scholars are now agreed that such an attempt failed even in the hands of Schmoller."

Recognition of this failure led neither to the disappearance of economic history nor to its reunification with economics proper. When Ashley ascended to the first chair of economic history at Harvard shortly before the turn of the century, he called for a truce between the warring factions. He disclaimed any desire to compete with deductive economics in the formulation of rival theories of value and distribution, asking only that

---

[2] If slaves are included in southern society, the average annual rate of growth of southern per capita income is 1.3 percent per annum. If slaves are treated as inputs in the production of final products rather than as consumers of final products, the rate of growth of per capita income rises to a little over 1.4 percent per annum. The average rate of growth of per capita income for the U.S. as a whole between 1834–43 and 1944–53 was 1.5 percent per annum.

[3] Because of the limitation of time and because the topic assigned to me specified the field of American economic history, this brief survey omits important contributions by scholars in the United States and abroad whose field of research is the economic history of other nations.

economic history "be let alone." Ashley believed that conflict was avoid-
able because in his view economics proper and economic history focused
on different problems: the former on the static properties of modern
economies; the latter on the evolution of economic societies or—as we
now call it—economic growth. To J. M. Keynes's contention that "famili-
arity with economic theory is essential to the interpretation of industrial
phenomena such as it falls within the province of the historian to give,"
Ashley replied: economic theory revealed little about the connections of
economic phenomena that could not be understood through the application
of "plain common sense."

The truce for which Ashley called lasted for more than a half a century.
During this time intellectual enmity abated. Within economic history,
scholars such as Callender, Heckscher, Cole, Hamilton, and Rostow effectively applied economic theory and statistics to the study of history.
Within economics proper, empirically- and historically-oriented analysis
developed far more extensively than Ashley foresaw. One of the centers of
such work, although not the only one, was the National Bureau of Economic Research where Wesley Mitchell, Simon Kuznets, and others applied
theory and statistics in massive empirical studies of the development of
the American economy.

Still, as late as 1941, the relationship between economic history and
economics proper was essentially one of truce. In that year Edwin F. Gay,
on the occasion of his election as the first president of the Economic History Association, both gave recognition to the breach that remained and
called for its elimination. "Full cooperation," he said, "is not yet easy or
intimate and one of the first tasks of the economic historian today is to
open the way to a more complete connection of the two disciplines."

In the years following World War II, the movement toward the reunification of economic history with economic theory accelerated. Among
the factors that led to the quickened pace, two may be singled out. One
was the substantial increase in the range and subtlety of the models encom-
passed by economic theory. The other was the widespread experimentation, in many fields of economics, with the adaptation of general models
to specific (historical) situations—an experimentation stimulated by the
upsurge in econometrics and other forms of applied mathematics.[4] With
such developments Heckscher's isolated plea of the 1920's for a greater
use of theory in the study of economic history became a relative commonplace in the 1950's. Post-World War II texts announced their reliance on
the "framework of economic analysis to elucidate the historical narrative"
and treated their "emphasis on economic principles" as a mark of distinction.

[4] An experimentation, it might be pointed out, that has increased awareness, not only
of the usefulness, but also of the limitations of existing models in the explanation of
economic growth.

However, the reunification of economic history with economic theory could not have been brought about merely by the interjections of theory in textbooks. Reunification required the utilization of economic theory as an integral tool in the basic research on which the discipline of economic history rests. This condition has been met, as I tried to illustrate in the first part of my comments, by an outpouring of studies published or initiated during the past half-dozen or so years.

The effort to improve the precision of measurement in economic history has been a powerful catalyst in transforming desire into reality. For as Simon Kuznets (whose work, perhaps more than that of any other scholar, inspired the new economic history) has frequently pointed out, there is an intimate connection between economic measurement and economic theory. Hence the emphasis placed on theory in the work of the new economic historians is neither an irrelevant, popular affectation nor a stilted superimposition. Rather it is the logical consequence of their desire to quantify the contribution of various changes in economic institutions, in factor supplies, and in technology to the rate and direction of economic growth.[5]

It is probably too soon to attempt a generalized evaluation of the quality of the output of the new economic history and of its contribution to our knowledge of the economic past. Much of this output is still in the pre-publication stage or has only recently been published. And many of the debates it has touched off are in full flush.

Yet I cannot resist making one observation. N. S. B. Gras concluded his 1930 survey of the status of economic history in the United States on a gloomy note. "The universities," he wrote, "have generally neglected the study of economic history, apparently regarding it as a very special subject. There has been a lack of controversy, even of intellectual resilience, in the field."

The situation today is quite different. Controversy abounds; and the level of the debate is, in my opinion, quite high. Imaginative applications of theory and statistics have brought to the fore evidence which until recently was considered unobtainable. Moreover, the hiatus in recruitment into the field appears to have come to an end. Meetings of the Economic History Association which just a few years ago were peopled almost exclusively by scholars who received their training before or during World War II are now marked by the attendance of a large corps of young people who entered economic history during the last half-dozen years or so. And the rate of entry seems to be rising. At the same time

---

[5] In this connection mention should be made of the Purdue Seminar on Quantitative Methods in Economic History. Convened for the first time in December, 1960, the Seminar has met annually since that date. It brings together twenty to thirty scholars for three days of intensive discussion on problems encountered in the adaptation of theory and statistics to the requirements of historical analysis.

several leading departments of economics have for the first time appointed teachers in economic history, while other departments have expanded or are in the process of expanding their appointments in this area. Vibrant is the word that best describes the present atmosphere in economic history.

FOR FURTHER READING: The literature is surveyed in Harry N. Scheiber, "On the New Economic History—And Its Limitations: A Review Essay," *Agricultural History*, XLI (October, 1967), pp. 383–395. For examples, see Lance David and Douglas North, "Institutional Change and American Economic Growth: A First Step Towards a Theory of Institutional Innovation," *Journal of Economic History*, XXX (March, 1970), pp. 131–149. Convenient collections are Robert W. Fogel and Stanley L. Engerman (eds.), *The Reinterpretation of American Economic History* (New York, 1971) and Peter Temin (ed.), *New Economic History: Selected Readings* (Hammondsworth, 1973). Enlightening is John Kenneth Galbraith, "The Broad Approach to Economics," *Journal of Economic Issues*, XI (June, 1977), pp. 185–200.

2

COLONIAL
AGRICULTURE

PROBLEM: *Was colonial agriculture profitable?*

As the major industry of Colonial America, employing more
than 90 per cent of the population, agriculture constituted the
basis of economic life in the seventeenth and eighteenth centuries. But was it a profitable venture for most farmers? Students of Colonial agriculture still disagree over this issue. Impressed by the relative decline of farm income in more recent
times they have traced contemporary problems such as over-
production, foreign market fluctuations, and falling prices to
the Colonial era. Lewis C. Gray, perhaps the foremost agricultural historian of the first half of the twentieth century,
expertly traces the problems of Southern tobacco growers in
the seventeenth century. Already by 1638 tobacco farmers
faced mounting surpluses and declining profits. Gray thus
seriously questions the profitability of one of the most important segments of Colonial agriculture. A more optimistic
appraisal of the profitability of agriculture in the north during
the later eighteenth century is presented by William Sachs.
Utilizing sophisticated techniques of economic analysis Sachs
notes that despite continuous complaints about hard times by
northern farmers, price statistics indicate that they were generally prospering. While the ramifications of agricultural surpluses in the history of American agriculture are complex,
these authors introduce important issues that need to be considered in examining the problem. How did foreign market

21

fluctuations affect farmers in the New World? Were the promotional and regulatory policies of colonial legislatures adequate to aid farmers to overcome existent obstacles? Why have American farmers complained about their condition even during times of prosperity?

The Market Surplus Problems of
Colonial Tobacco

LEWIS C. GRAY

I have been moved to select the subject of this paper because of the paramount interest of the present problem of market surpluses, and because in the history of colonial tobacco may be found many analogies and parallelisms with the present-day aspects of the problem.

EARLY ARTIFICIAL LEVEL OF PRICES AND ITS COLLAPSE

At the time it first began to be planted by the Virginia colonists in 1610–1611 tobacco in the English market was essentially a luxury product. In the seven years preceding 1622 there had been imported from Spain an annual average of about 60,000 pounds of high-grade tobacco produced in the West Indies, with probably about as much more introduced by smugglers. In 1619 it was stated that the Spanish product customarily sold for eighteen shillings sterling per pound, an enormous price considering the high value of sterling in that period. Virginia tobacco as made in these earlier years was of much poorer quality than the Spanish product, and though it was assessed in the English "Book of Rates" at ten shillings the pound, actually sold at less than half this amount in the latter part of 1619. However, in 1620 it sold as high as eight shillings in the London market. Under these conditions it is not surprising that tobacco was mainly used by the wealthy and was retailed on the London streets by the pipeful.

On the basis of these prices the Virginia Company in 1618 authorized its representatives in the Colony to allow three shillings for the best grades and eighteen pence for that of second quality in trade at the company's warehouse. Naturally such prices stimulated a frenzy of activity in colonial tobacco planting comparable with the feverish spirit of a mining camp. The volume of production and of exports was rapidly expanded. From 1615 when the first colonial shipment reached England

Reprinted by permission from Lewis C. Gray, "The Market Surplus Problems of Colonial Tobacco," *Agricultural History*, II (January, 1928), pp. 1–34.

until 1622 the exports had increased to 60,000 pounds, and six years later to 500,000 pounds, or more than eight times the amount of official imports of England a little more than a decade earlier. The next decade witnessed a three-fold increase, the annual exports averaging 1,395,063 pounds for the four years, 1637–1640, inclusive.

Prices fell precipitately from their unnatural levels, in spite of frantic efforts by the Crown and the Company to maintain them. By 1630 Governor Harvey was complaining that the merchants were buying tobacco in Virginia for less than a penny per pound.

THE BEHAVIOR OF PRICES, 1630–1774

From this time forward prices never returned to their original high levels, but until the outbreak of the Revolutionary War ranged between about three pence per pound as a maximum down to a half penny or less. Indeed at times even this minimum price was purely nominal, for tobacco was practically unsalable. It was rarely higher than two pence.

I shall not attempt in this paper to trace the course of prices year by year, but it is desirable to devote some attention to the behavior of prices for longer periods.

The data indicate not only fluctuations from year to year, reflecting the seasonal variations in yield and consequently in volume of production, but also the periodical emergence of long periods of acute depressions. It is desirable to trace briefly the record of these depressions. As already noted, the precipitate fall of prices from the original high levels had brought tobacco by 1630 to what then appeared to be an absurdly low price. For several years thereafter prices were ruinously low, and various legislative attempts were made to deal with the problem.

The crop of 1638 was two and a half times as large as the average for the other years from 1637 to 1640, inclusive, and being thrown into an already sagging market, caused prices again to collapse. In 1638–9 prices were so low that planters could not subsist by them, and there resulted a series of attempts at legislative price-fixing which will be described later. The probability is that in spite of the rather generous official rates placed on tobacco during the next two or three years, prices did not recover until the situation was relieved by the short crop of 1644.

While the outbreak of the civil war in England appears for a short time to have depressed prices, the activity of the illicit trade with the Dutch tended to sustain prices fairly well, with only occasional years of low prices until after the Restoration. In the latter part of the sixth decade there began a period of depression which, excepting a slight improvement in 1663, continued until 1667. It is probable that the acreage planted to tobacco had become excessive by reason of the rapid migration to the colonies induced by the disturbances of the period of the Civil War and the Protectorate. Probably another factor was the extension and more rigid application of the navigation policy in 1660 and the following years and the restrictions on Dutch competition. The situation was further complicated by the unusually large yield of the crop of 1666, and by the demoralization of the market due to the plague in London, which was so severe that in 1665 the tobacco fleet did not go to the colonies at all. The depression was relieved by the great storm of 1667 which destroyed from two-thirds to four-fifths of the crops in Virginia and by the destruction of twenty tobacco ships by the Dutch.

For about a decade conditions appear to have been somewhat improved, but with a tendency for prices to sag to very unprofitable levels in particular years, as in 1671, 1673, 1678. Apparently throughout this period the tobacco acreage was so large as to permit reasonably good prices only following years of small yield with a constant tendency toward entirely unprofitable prices in years of good crops.

The enormous crop of 1677, said to be in Virginia as large as the total production of three normal years and in Maryland the largest "ever heard of" precipitated another crisis. In 1680 Governor Culpeper, of Virginia, wrote the French authorities that the low price of tobacco "staggered" him and that its continuance would prove "the fatal and speedy ruin of this once noble Colony." The crop of that year, however, proved again unusually large, and added to an already abnormal carry-over so glutted the market that tobacco became practically worthless. For several years the depression continued, leading in 1682 to plant-cutting riots in New Kent, Gloucester, and Middlesex counties, Virginia. As a result of the destruction of about 10,000 hogsheads of tobacco by the rioters, the price of tobacco was improved in 1683.

From this time forward until after the outbreak of the war of the Spanish Succession in 1702 there was a period of generally favorable tobacco prices. It was a period of expanding demand, and years of poor yields occurred with sufficient frequency to prevent the accumulation of an abnormal carry-over.

One of the most desperate periods of depression in the history of the industry began to make its influence felt in 1703 and continued for a decade. The good prices just preceding the war had stimulated production and a gradually increasing carry-over. The war cut off the tobacco trade to Spain, France, Flanders, and part of the Baltic States, leaving only Holland as the principal foreign market. Since the Dutch preferred the brighter variety of Oronoke, the Dutch market had been glutted with the brown type. The depression grew worse as the war continued. In 1704 several thousand hogsheads of consignment tobacco brought the planters no return whatever, and the returns from some of it were not sufficient to pay the freight. In 1705 complaints were made of "the extraordinary low price of tobacco of this year beyond what hath been known for several years past." Conditions continued to get worse. In 1710 it was said that the merchants in Maryland would make no advance on tobacco. In Virginia tobacco was nominally rated at a penny per pound, but large quantities were actually unsalable. Toward the close of the war William Byrd wrote that poor people could not make enough to clothe themselves, while the larger planters were getting deeper and deeper in debt. Many had been forced to sell part of their lands and negroes to meet debts, while still others had emigrated to the Carolinas and elsewhere.

Good prices continued for four years after the close of the war. This relief, however, was but temporary, and merely served to stimulate expansion of production, which again brought low prices in 1720, continuing until 1724, when a crop failure brought temporarily good prices. Then followed a decade of severe depression. Thus the industry appears to have suffered from extreme depression for a period of fourteen years with the exception of one year, and during a period of thirty-two years depression had prevailed except for one interval of four years and another of one year of good prices.

After 1734 there ensued a period of a quarter of a century free from a serious and protracted price depression, although there were occasional years of low prices. Even the War of the Austrian Succession and the Seven Years War did not bring serious price depression, such as had prevailed during the War of the Spanish Succession, for the tobacco trade had become so important both to England and to France that during the two later wars an indirect and informal arrangement was made between England and France whereby tobacco ships, whether British or neutral, engaged in carrying tobacco from England to France were given special passes exempting them from capture, very curious instances of the deliberate continuance of trade relations by belligerent nations. An examination of trade statistics indicates that neither of the later wars seriously affected the volume of the tobacco trade; and prices do not appear to have been abnormally affected, with the exception of the last two years preceding the peace of Paris. The inflation of the Virginia currency which accompanied the course of the war began to manifest itself in a general rise of prices in 1760, which continued until 1764. However, tobacco appears to have lagged behind in the general advance. It appears probable that in spite of the higher nominal prices paid for tobacco there was a period of almost continuous depression from about 1760 or 1761 until about the beginning of the eighth decade, followed in turn by several years of good prices.

I shall not undertake to say how much the behavior of tobacco prices, as revealed by this summary of the experience of a century and a half, is characteristic of the price history of other agricultural products and of other periods, nor to what extent the conditions responsible for it have prevailed elsewhere. To some extent, probably, these conditions are generic in a sense, but to some extent they were peculiar to the production and marketing of colonial tobacco. . . . .

ATTEMPTED SOLUTIONS OF THE PROBLEM

Many attempts were made to deal with the problem of marketing the tobacco surplus more effectively so as to bring greater advantages to the producer, including a vast amount of legislation, probably more than has ever been devoted to any other crop, with the possible exception of sugar.

Attempts at monopoly. In an earlier part of this paper it was shown that the first decade of tobacco growing in the American colonies was on the basis of an abnormally high price level. It was an age of monopoly, and, consequently, the attempts to uphold this abnormally high level took the form of a series of monopolistic concessions calculated to maintain unity of control in merchandizing the product. There was also sufficient practical recognition of the laws of supply and demand to lead to provisions in the earlier proposals for restricting the quantity brought to market from the colonies and from Spain, and later to restrict the quantity grown in the colonies.

I shall not undertake to trace in this paper the various negotiations in connection with the proposed contract with Henry Somerscales in 1619; the contract with Sir Thomas Rowe and his associates in the following year; the Jacobs contract arranged in 1621-2; the long negotiations by the Virginia Company itself for an exclusive monopolistic privilege in marketing tobacco, which contract was finally nullified through the factional controversies in the Company itself; the Ditchfield contract of 1625, which failed because of the determined opposition of the Virginia planters; the Anis contract of 1627, which also met the strong opposition of the colonies; and finally the negotiations in 1638 for the Goring contract, in which the proponents attempted to popularize their proposal by suggesting the revival of the Virginia Company, a scheme which did not break down the determined resistance of the colonists.

While the colonists opposed these various attempts at monopolistic concessions, except that of the Virginia Company, which was a matter of controversy both in the Company itself and in the Colony, this opposition was due less to antagonism to the monopolistic solution than to the fact that the various proposals were made largely for the benefit of the Crown and of a persistent group of courtiers who sought to fatten their purses at the expense of the planters. . . .

Legislative price-fixing. In the early decades of the industry some attempts were made at crude legislative price-fixing. Two such acts were passed in 1632, two others in the following year, and other acts in 1639 and 1640. These were acts fixing the general price level for tobacco and prohibiting by penalties its exchange at a lower price. They are to be distinguished from the numerous rating acts, necessitated by the use of tobacco as currency, to determine the ratio of tobacco to sterling in payment of taxes, fees, quitrents, tavern rates, and ferry charges. In 1641 a royal ordinance inspired by the merchants put an end to these attempts at legislative price determination.

Our forefathers are not to be charged with complete ignorance of the laws of economics in the passage of these acts fixing the general price level of tobacco. In the first place, the several acts were associated with attempts at stinting or restricting the volume of production. In the second place, they were more or less justified by the uncertain conditions of marketing and the imperfection of marketing machinery. At a time when no general price level had as yet developed and when the individual planter was largely at the mercy of the merchant who chanced to call for his crop the legislative enactments served to define crudely the limits of bargaining and to supply a price criterion for the application of the laws against engrossing, forestalling, and regrating.

Restriction of volume of production or of exports. As suggested above, from an early period attempts were made to solve the surplus problem by stinting or restricting production, usually by allowing so many plants for each household, for each tithable or other unit of labor. Various arrangements for stinting were included in the later monopolistic contracts, as well as in connection with the price-fixing acts just described. In the legislation of 1639–40 designed to restrict production and fix prices, it became apparent that such legislation would be largely futile without an inter-colonial agreement with Maryland. This was the beginning of a succession of attempts to achieve such agreements.

There is evidence that Virginia legislation for stinting existed in the latter part of the seventeenth century and the early part of the eighteenth. The depression beginning in 1725 resulted in renewed attempts at control of volume of production. Virginia renewed an act in 1727, which had expired in 1725, for improving the staple of tobacco, probably involving destruction of inferior grades and stinting. A stinting act passed at the special session of the Maryland Assembly in 1726 encountered the opposition of the council because of the provision for scaling fees and debts by reason of the expected rise of prices. Another attempt in 1727 in which a compromise was effected on the scaling problem was vetoed by the proprietor. The continuing distress, which culminated in an outbreak of plant-cutting riots in Maryland, finally led to the successful passage of a stinting act in 1730, which, however, lapsed in 1732. The currency act of 1733 provided for the enforced destruction of 150 pounds per taxable during each of the two succeeding years. During this period also negotiations were carried on between Maryland and Virginia looking to mutual legislation for restricting the latest date of planting tobacco, in the interest of curtailing production.

The restriction of volume of production was also intrinsic in numerous acts passed from time to time in both colonies, partly for the purpose of improving quality, such as prohibitions against the packing of ground leaves and suckers, the tending and packing of second growth crops ("seconds"). In some of these acts it was provided that viewers should annually inspect the fields in their respective localities and insure the destruction of second growth tobacco. To some extent restriction of quantity was also achieved by the various acts against packing inferior tobacco and the destruction of such tobacco found in tobacco hogsheads. Restriction of quantity was also involved in the practice of stemming tobacco, which was strongly opposed by the British government because of resulting loss of revenues and prohibited in 1722 by an act of Parliament. However, the act led to vigorous protest by the colonies, Virginia sending John Randolph to London especially to obtain repeal of the act, which he succeeded in achieving.

The aim of restricting the quantity of tobacco was also more or less present in the various acts in the early colonial period requiring the production of food crops (the two-acre acts), acts to exempt new settlers from taxation for a time on condition that they refrain from tobacco cultivation, and certain temporary legislation against the importation of slaves.

ATTEMPTS AT STANDARDIZATION AND IMPROVEMENT OF MARKETABILITY

Probably more effective than the attempts at direct control of price and restriction of output were the efforts to improve the marketability of the product.

Prohibition of shipments in bulk. Among these measures we may include the long struggle to restrict the shipment of tobacco in bulk instead of in the hogshead. The former custom increased greatly in the latter part of the seventeenth century and early decades of the eighteenth by reason of the expansion of the industry into frontier regions where facilities for prizing in hogsheads were lacking, and by reason of the practice of pioneer farmers trading small miscellaneous lots of tobacco at neighborhood stores in exchange for goods brought by the outport ships.

The practice of shipping in bulk, which had increased rapidly with expansion of the industry into the back country, was strongly opposed by the administrative authorities, by the old-time commission merchants, and by the larger planters, because it was favorable to smuggling; because it was an obstacle to the standardization of quality; because a smaller number of ships for transportation were required, which did not appeal to the mercantilist ideals of the period; and because the earlier arrival of the bulk tobacco tended to disorganize the market, besides lending itself to cut-throat competition by small and irregular dealers. We may suspect that in part the opposition grew out of the general resistance of the old-line commercial agencies to the encroachments of the aggressive outport merchants, whose new and vigorous methods were tending to displace them in the trade.

The practice was defended on the ground of smaller cost of transport and because it was essential to the welfare of the poorer classes on the frontier and to the profits of the small outport merchants; and for many years this democratic resistance defeated attempts at prohibition in the colonies. The practice was prohibited by Parliament in 1698, but there was much evasion until the practice was prohibited by the inspection acts hereafter mentioned.

Attempts to regulate size and shape of hogsheads. There was also a long struggle to regulate the size and shape of the hogshead and the time of shipment. Both of these points were of special concern to the merchants, for hogsheads of irregular shape and size were costly to transport because requiring an undue amount of cargo space. Carelessly made hogsheads came to pieces or warped apart in transit. Maryland long held out for a larger hogshead than was specified by Virginia laws on the ground that the character of Maryland tobacco did not admit of such close packing as in Virginia, while the Virginians attributed the difficulty to slovenly methods of packing in Maryland. Even an order by the Queen annulling the Maryland act and requiring that the Maryland specifications be made identical with those of Virginia did not settle the problem. . . .

Provisions for official inspection before shipment. It early became apparent that none of these measures for improvement of quality would be effective without a system of standardization by thorough inspection before shipment. As early as 1619 there was developed the practice of employing sworn viewers to inspect tobacco. From this time forward various temporary or partial measures for inspection were provided for, which cannot be traced in the present paper. No permanently effective system was achieved until the passage of the Virginia act of 1730, which marks an important milestone in the evolution of agricultural marketing machinery and practice.

The foundation for this important measure was laid by the warehouse act of 1712, which provided for the establishment of public warehouses at convenient points not more than one mile from navigable water. Though these warehouses might be privately owned they were made public utilities. The rates and conditions of storage were fixed by law.

An inspection law was also passed in 1713 providing for licensed inspectors to enforce certain minimum standards, issuing warehouse receipts against tobacco. However, the measure excited tremendous opposition, including that of such important merchant planters as William Byrd (II), who reflected the attitude of the conservative consignment merchants, such as Micajah Perry, of London. These influences obtained in 1717 the royal veto of the measure.

Fortunately, the warehouse act, slightly amended in 1720, still remained to serve as a nucleus, and the serious and protracted depression beginning in 1725 brought public sentiment to the support of the act of 1730. Variously amended from time to time, this act and the cognate warehouse act constituted the backbone of the colonial system of marketing until the Revolutionary War.

I cannot undertake here a detailed description of the system. Briefly, it involved several licensed and bonded inspectors stationed at public warehouses. They were authorized to open each hogshead; with the consent of the owner to sort out and destroy inferior tobacco, and lacking his consent to destroy the entire hogshead. The class and grade of the tobacco was then marked on the repacked hogshead. For the purpose of issuing warehouse receipts a distinction was made between "transfer" tobacco and "crop" tobacco. Against the former, general negotiable receipts were issued which did not entitle the owner to any particular hogshead, while the receipts for "crop" tobacco were specific in character, representing largely the consignment tobacco. When the receipts in course of circulation reached the hands of the exporter, he could demand delivery and at that time require a second opening and inspection of the hogshead, and in case the tobacco was found below the standard, could enforce judgment against the inspector for compensation and costs. A scale of allowances for shrinkage was provided, and tobacco stored in public warehouses was publicly insured against loss by fire and other causes.

This was probably the most constructive type of marketing legislation passed in the colonial period, and its influence was profound. It contributed to improving the average quality of exports, standardized the commodity as a medium of exchange and of public payments and as a standard of deferred payments, and improved the system of customs administration. It gave Virginia growers and merchants a great advantage over those of Maryland. In 1743 Daniel Dulaney wrote that Maryland factors were moving to Virginia where they could buy better tobacco, though at a higher price. The French "regie" buyers also were turning more and more to Virginia to obtain their supply. The Council and governor of Maryland informed the proprietor that unless Maryland took similar action the whole trade in tobacco would be lost to Virginia.

Maryland experimented for about a quarter of a century with a vacillating policy comprising acts against tending of seconds, suckers, and ground leaves, and acts imposing heavy penalties for false packing, enforced by the offer of rewards to informers. Finally, in 1747, the colony was forced to adopt the Virginia solution by the adoption of an inspection law closely modelled after that of the sister colony.

Summary. Through more than a century and a half great progress was made in the marketing of tobacco along the lines of more complete commercial organization and greater standardization. It is probable this progress accounts in part for the comparative freedom from protracted depression during the last three or four decades of the colonial period; but the market surplus problem, as we know it today, remained unsolved in spite of the numerous and varied efforts at solution which have been described. It continues as one of the outstanding economic problems of our own time.

Agricultural Conditions in the Northern Colonies Before the Revolution

WILLIAM SACHS

I

Many writers treating the late colonial period have touched upon the subject of economic fluctuations, but no agreement is found as to the duration, intensity, and amplitude of these alterations of good and bad times. Nor has any investigation as yet assembled all the available data necessary to an understanding of this phenomenon. Since agriculture constituted an important aspect of the colonial economy, some light may be shed upon these economic vicissitudes by an examination of Northern agricultural conditions in the two decades preceding the Revolution.

Although contemporaries depicted the period of the French and Indian War as one of great prosperity, the benefits that farmers derived from the war were not strikingly impressive. From 1755 to 1759 inclusive, prices of agricultural products remained almost stationary, while prices of almost all other commodities climbed steadily. Meanwhile, as provincial governments commenced to raise and outfit regiments, taxes began to mount. Thus, while farmers' outlays were unmistakably increasing, the evidence of price data indicates a lag in farm income. Admittedly, an exact computation of agricultural income for this period is impossible, since we do not know how much farmers produced. Nevertheless, price data together with other available information can provide a rough approximation of how the agricultural classes fared.*

In 1759 and 1760, prices of agricultural products exhibited a significant upward movement for the first time since the beginning of the war. This relatively short period of farm prosperity came to an abrupt end in 1761

Reprinted by permission from William Sachs, "Agricultural Conditions in the Northern Colonies Before the Revolution," *Journal of Economic History*, XIII (Summer, 1953), pp. 274–290.

* Wholesale prices in Philadelphia for wheat, corn and pork, major staple crops, generally declined until 1758 when they began a steady rise that continued till the end of the Seven Years' War. [Editor's note]

when a severe drought laid waste the crops. Governor Bernard of Massachusetts proclaimed a day of public prayer to the end that God "would visit us with refreshing showers, as may still preserve the remaining fruits of the earth, and bring forward the withered grass, that there may be fruit for man and beast." The supplications went unanswered, no rains came to moisten the parched earth, and crops withered before they were ripe.

The next year the colonists again suffered from unrelenting droughts and serious crop failures. Complaints of distress were heard from every quarter—from the lower classes in the cities who found wages out of line with famine prices and from farmers who saw their income shrinking while debts mounted. Frontier communities, especially hard hit, flooded legislatures with petitions for relief. Pontiac's Revolt in 1763 added further hardships to frontier counties, particularly in Pennsylvania. However one may impute material gains made from war, certain it is that farmers, for whom the war years were not years of exceptional prosperity, emerged from the war in serious economic plight.

At about the same time that poor harvests brought economic hardship to the farm population, merchants also were complaining of depressed trade and financial stringency. The agricultural depression contributed directly to this business slump. At a time when English merchants were pressing their American debtors for settlement of balances outstanding, payments from rural areas to urban merchants were not forthcoming; exports of farm products to foreign ports, an important source of remittance for American merchants, were drastically curtailed; and rural buying shrank when other markets also were contracting. On the other hand, the postwar business depression, although aggravating the situation, did not produce any striking effect upon the economic fortunes of agriculture. Following a lively speculation in real estate, land values seem to have been generally depressed by 1763. For most farmers, however, what was derived from the land and what possible improvements could be made upon it were matters of greater significance than the money rating imputed to land. With the first abundant harvest, prices of farm products dropped from their famine peaks. The fundamental question in relation to prices is, however, how severe was the decline?

TABLE 1

AVERAGE PRICES OF THE FOURTH QUARTER
OF THE YEAR AT PHILADELPHIA

Product	Unit	1756	1757	1758	1759	1760	1763
Wheat	S—bu.	3.36	3.44	4.10	5.42	5.16	5.42
Flour	S—cwt.	11.33	11.11	12.67	16.31	15.16	14.42
Corn	S—bu.	2.11	1.70	2.13	3.41	3.06	3.69
Beef	S—bbl.	50.00	44.50	47.50	50.00	51.93	68.73
Pork	S—bbl.	60.50	61.63	59.17	69.53	71.17	93.33

By referring to Table 1 . . . , we can compare prices of agricultural commodities in 1763 with those that farmers obtained during the war years. Philadelphia has been selected because it was the most important colonial market for provisions, because price data for that port are most adequate, and because Pennsylvania currency, in which prices are measured, was relatively stable. Since the heaviest trading in farm products took place during the fall months, the last quarter of each year has been selected for comparison.

Excluding the famine years of 1761 and 1762, a period when farm income was much reduced, quarterly averages in 1763 were even slightly above those of the prosperous years of 1759 and 1760, except for flour. In comparison with the remainder of the war years, prices of all important agricultural commodities were substantially higher in 1763.

By the end of 1763, prices of farm produce still hovered at relatively high levels, while shortages, particularly of animal products, made themselves felt. Unable to procure provisions on the Continent for the army garrison at Nova Scotia, John Hancock was forced to turn to Ireland for supplies. Similarly, John Watts ordered a shipment of pork from Ireland, as that commodity was "excessively dear" at New York. In December of 1763 John Van Cortlandt instructed his various agents to remit in wheat to New York as the demand for that article was brisk. On January 14, 1764, John Watts informed his correspondent at Madeira that he would try to ship wheat from Philadelphia, for "here [New York] it is not to be had without an advanc'd price and scarcely then." At Philadelphia, however, the produce market was no more favorable to such operations than at New York. "Corn @ 5/ not 300 Bushels to be got— flour @ 19 to 20/—pork 5 pounds. Few barrels to be had, bought up months past," wrote Thomas Riche of Philadelphia in response to an order for provisions from the West Indies. The new army contractors of the Pittsburgh district, finding themselves unable to secure sufficient provisions for fulfilling the terms of their contracts, effective as of April 13, 1764, requested that the army administration sell them the surplus food supplies obtained from the previous contractors.

Yet in 1764 American merchants complained persistently of poor markets abroad. Why then should prices of provisions in home markets remain at moderate levels when exports constituted the main outlet for farm surpluses? The answer is to be found in trade statistics. With the cessation of privateering, production of large crops, and a fall in freight and insurance rates after the war, the volume of overseas commerce expanded rapidly. American importers found it decidedly more profitable to send out their ships full-freighted than empty while vessels bringing goods to America sought return freight. In turn, the augmented volume of trade created a strong demand for agricultural products.

II

Farmers' difficulties immediately following the termination of war were the result of financial liabilities incurred when crop failures had reduced their income. Debts, both public and private, weighed heavily upon them, while in every province postwar taxes were taking a larger chunk out of farm income than they had before the war.

In New England particularly, postwar taxes were extremely heavy, while public creditors further aggravated the situation by adding their weight to a policy of rapid currency contraction. It is little wonder that in an area of relatively low agricultural productivity, yet experiencing the heaviest taxation and most marked currency appreciation north of the Potomac, debts constituted the one great complaint of farmers. Shortly after the end of the war, however, Connecticut and New Hampshire eased tax burdens considerably by using the Parliamentary grant to liquidate their liabilities, and with the appearance of good harvests both of these colonies realized improved economic conditions more rapidly than elsewhere in New England.

Although rural taxes in New York were higher after 1763 than before the war, it can hardly be said that they were burdensome. In Pennsylvania, taxes on rural real estate were relatively light in the postwar years. Of a total annual assessment of £34,855, about one half came from Philadelphia and Chester Counties and the city of Philadelphia. Although times were hard immediately after the war, farmers of the middle colonies did not seem to have been heavily involved in debt litigation, foreclosures, or in other types of legal action indicating financial disabilities. Quite in contrast with New England, complaints of such a nature were conspicuously absent from newspaper columns, legislative journals, reports of government officials, and other media of public expression. In these colonies, where taxes were relatively low, agricultural productivity high, and currency contraction slow, it did not take farmers long to emerge from hard times once large crop yields succeeded those of the drought years. German farmers, enjoying flourishing conditions, took no part in the agrarian disturbances that occurred in Pennsylvania in 1764. More significant still, the economic grievances of the disaffected western sector pertained mainly to Indian affairs, land speculation, and disbursements of public funds—they did not include complaints of economic distress or demands for debtor relief. Similarly, the tenants' revolt in New York in 1765–1766 was not connected with depressed agricultural conditions; it was essentially an attempt of farmers to extricate themselves from a landholding system that denied them secure tenure. It would be strange indeed that men who so copiously poured forth their economic complaints, real or imagined, and who were ready to secure their demands by force of arms should be so negligent as to omit any reference to hard times if they were suffering from an economic depression.

Not only were crop yields large in the years after 1763, but prices which farmers received were excellent. Students of price history have pointed out the divergence in the movement of imported- and domestic-commodity prices at New York. A similar divergence seems to have taken place at Philadelphia; while domestic-commodity prices moved rather upward, prices of imported commodities seemed to oscillate around a horizontal trend.

With prospects of an abundant harvest, agricultural prices at Philadelphia declined somewhat in 1764. From the last quarter of that year, however, prices of farm products began a steady and uninterrupted rise which was not arrested until the middle of 1768. The price of wheat, Pennsylvania's major crop, rose from a monthly relative of 125 to 230 (1741–1745 = 100), surpassing the famine peak of 1763! In 1769 the price of wheat turned definitely downward but still stood substantially above the price levels of 1764. The average price of the lowest quarter of 1769 was still above the highest quarterly average of 1764, and 28 per cent over the lowest quarterly average. The price movement of flour strongly paralleled that of wheat, while prices of corn, beef, and pork displayed a similar tendency.

On the other hand, prices of salt, rum, and molasses, like those of agricultural commodities, dropped drastically after the war. But unlike farm-commodity prices, prices of this group of products fell well below the base or prewar period and, except for the brief period of nonimportation in 1765–1766, failed to rise much above the depressed price levels of 1764. The lowest quarterly average price of New England rum in 1769 was but 9 per cent above that of 1764, molasses only 8 per cent higher, while salt dipped to 11 per cent below. From evidence of scattered prices—mainly those of osnaburgs, a representative coarse linen fabric—Anne Bezanson and her associates have indicated the course of prices of British imported textiles as falling after the Peace of Paris and fluctuating around a horizontal trend from about 1764 to 1775. Although prices of farm implements and finished metal products are nonexistent for this period, the available evidence affords reasonable ground for belief that this group of products fell in price during the 1760's. For what amounts or in what proportions farmers exchanged their surpluses for salt, molasses, rum, iron products, and dry goods we do not know, since consumption statistics are unavailable. However, since these commodities constituted rather important single items of farmers' budgets in the eighteenth century, the conclusion is almost inescapable that farmers' per unit expenditures decreased in relation to farm revenue per unit of output.

After 1769 merchants once again began to enjoy a period of political calm and generally improved business conditions, at least until the latter part of 1772 or early 1773. Farmers, too, shared in the general prosperity. Prices of agricultural products again began to climb, reaching even higher peaks than before, and not until the eve of the Revolution did any significant decline occur from the new high levels. Meanwhile, prices of salt, molasses, and rum remained fairly constant at the levels of the preceding decade.

III

The prevailing high prices of agricultural produce from 1764 to 1775 were mainly the result of an expansion in demand from abroad. Beginning in 1764, a series of poor crops converted England from a grain exporting to a grain importing nation. European ports formerly supplied with English grain immediately turned to the British colonies in America to supply the deficit. On February 19, 1766, the British Parliament modified its corn laws to allow the importation of American grain duty free. British merchants sought American foodstuffs not only for their home markets but also to fulfill their contracts with foreign mercantile houses. Poor crops in scattered parts of Europe in 1766 and more serious crop failures beyond the Atlantic the next year further augmented the demand for American provisions.

TABLE 2

TONNAGE CLEARED FROM PHILADELPHIA, NEW YORK, AND BOSTON

| | Philadelphia | | New York | | Boston | |
Year	West Indies	Southern Europe	West Indies	Southern Europe	West Indies	Southern Europe
1764	—	—	7,340	1,882	—	—
1765	13,494	4,455	8,385	3,190	7,806	1,075
1768	12,019	7,255	6,981	2,360	10,095	1,333
1769	11,114	12,040	5,466	3,278	8,995	1,081
1770	13,842	10,940	7,005	2,920	8,248	813
1771	13,449	7,110	7,708	2,029	9,171	1,113
1772	15,674	8,415	8,076	2,449	10,703	555

Source: Harrington, *The New York Merchant*, pp. 356–68.

Table 2 represents tonnage cleared annually from the three major ports of the Northern colonies to the two most important foreign markets for American agricultural staples. This record, while it does not show particular commodities shipped, provides a rough, over-all indication of quantity change and of the direction of trade to specific areas. The strong demand for American foodstuffs is especially noticeable in the tonnage statistics of Philadelphia, the largest colonial mart for provisions. From 1765 to 1769 tonnage clearing to the West Indies declined absolutely, but that to southern Europe increased almost threefold, surpassing exports to the West Indies for the first time in colonial history. Improved markets in the

West Indies after 1769 further augmented the demand for Pennsylvania grain and flour but reversed the movement of exports. For the entire period, however, the major increase in Philadelphia's export trade, as measured by tonnage, was with southern Europe. Exports of New York, ranking next to Philadelphia as a grain-exporting port, followed a somewhat similar course to that of the Quaker City. Boston, however, lacking a highly productive hinterland and a prominent staple having a strong demand abroad, witnessed its foreign-export trade develop in a different direction from that of its sister ports to the south. From 1765 to 1769, tonnage cleared from Boston to southern Europe remained almost stationary, while a 15 per cent increase took place in tonnage cleared to the West Indies. By 1772 exports to the West Indies, on the basis of tonnage, had grown by an additional 19 per cent. But while these markets offered Boston traders strong allurements, exports to southern Europe dwindled to insignificant proportions.

IV

An analysis of the consensus of contemporary opinion reinforces the conclusions drawn from the preceding data. Unfortunately, farmers left no letters, carefully kept diaries, or other written records from which the historian might form some judgment about what they thought their economic position to be. Thus, our conclusions must be based on different types of evidence coming from people who were not tillers of the soil and whose interests were at times diametrically opposed to those of farmers.

During the early political controversies with Great Britain, colonial agitators advanced the argument of the "poverty of the people" and predicted the most dire results for the rural population as a consequence of British legislation. Some even insisted that these grim forebodings were actually taking place. Such contentions had as their purpose the creation of a favorable opinion in order to secure modification of specific Parliamentary legislation regarded by the colonists as inimical to their interests.

After the Sugar Act was modified and the Stamp Act repealed, all utterance on agricultural distress practically ceased. In fact, the complaints came only from urban quarters and were concerned not with farm distress but with soaring prices, food shortages, and rising costs of living. As early as the Stamp Act controversy, "Colbert" argued that a policy of conducting no business without stamps would hurt Britain because large orders of grain were "bought up or shipped by orders from home, and if it should remain here now it will be sold at a cheaper rate to our increasing manufacturers."

With the continuing high prices of food, complaints emanating from the cities mounted. One writer depicted farmers as literally rolling in wealth and urged that more people take up farming in order to increase the supply of wheat and to reduce its price. Another New Yorker accused farmers of getting rich at the expense of city people. "In Consequence of the Scarcity and Dearness of Provisions in Europe . . . upwards of Twenty sail of European ships arrived last Week in different Ports of America, in order to purchase Wheat," he wrote. "This must of Consequence raised the Price of Wheat and other Provisions upon us, already too high for the Poor of this City . . . If those Ships get their Loads of Wheat, it will benefit Farmers that have it to sell, but it must impoverish the Citizens, in advancing the Price of Provisions."

By 1766 a persistent agitation developed in New York City to prohibit the exportation of provisions until prices should fall to "reasonable levels." "Flour has risen to the enormous price of twenty four shillings per [cwt], which . . . is higher than it rose in the last war, and considering the prodigious scarcity of money . . . how can we afford to pay for bread even to the price which it is now risen?" When prices have risen to a point at which people cannot possibly pay, the author argued, "it must demonstrate the strongest reason" to embargo exportation of food supplies. "The price of wheat and provisions are . . . already too high for the poor of this city," claimed another, while advocating similar measures. Colonial legislatures, however, took no effective steps to halt the rising prices of food, and protests from city dwellers continued.

By no means were such protests against high food prices motivated by humanitarianism, or by a purely philanthropic desire to ease the burdens of the "deserving poor." The mercantilist mind, regarding low costs of production as beneficial and wages as directly related to the cost of living or the level of subsistence, naturally viewed with hostility a rise in the price of indispensable necessities. Taxpayers did not relish a rise in poor rates which mounting prices might occasion. Merchants generally looked upon high prices of commodities earmarked for exportation with disfavor, and some exporters were not slow in accusing farmers of cupidity and outright profiteering. Benjamin Fuller, a Philadelphia merchant, informed his correspondent that "wheat is now at 5/6, but its a kind of nominal price—the farmers are Rich and are loth to part with it at that." ". . . tho' the last Crop is said to be a tollerable good one yet the Farmers having been used a long time to great prices the most of them are become wealthy, and therefore will keep back their supply unless they can obtain what they call a good price," another Philadelphia merchant reflected in 1773. Nevertheless, artisans and mechanics, small shopkeepers, and common laborers, finding it ever more difficult to make ends meet, fully supported the publicists who urged legislative action to beat down climbing prices of food. John Woolman's "Conversation between a thrifty Landholder, and a Labouring man" posed the problem confronting the lower urban classes as follows:

Labouring Man: I observe of late years that when I buy a bushel of grain for my family, I must do more work to pay for it than I used to do twenty years past. What is the reason of this change?

Landholder: Towns and villages have a gradual increase in these provinces, and the people now employed in husbandry bear, I believe, a less proportion to the whole inhabitants . . . but the main cause is that of Sending So much grain & flower abroad.

Massachusetts offered bounties for the production of wheat and flour, among other reasons, to free itself of outside dependence for food supplies for its maritime towns. However, it was the city governments which, possessing a large degree of control over local consumption and more amenable to the pressure of a grumbling and resentful citizenry, attempted in many ways to alleviate the disabilities of their consumers. New York City, frustrated in 1763 from assizing provisions in its public markets at rates lower than those current, turned to other stringent regulatory practices aimed at depressing retail prices. Boston followed closely in the footsteps of New York in strengthening its code regulating public markets. Nevertheless, the continuation of a seller's market provided incentives to speculation and temptations for traders to buy up supplies before they ever reached the markets, frequently causing serious food shortages. By 1769 the situation at Boston had become so serious that a town meeting appointed a committee "to investigate and propose methods for the General Court to prevent forestalling of the markets." A petition to the Pennsylvania Assembly in 1772 from the inhabitants of Germantown, made up largely of artisans, claimed that butter and middling flour were being bought up before reaching the public market and requested legislation to prevent "engrossing and forestalling." It is not at all strange that mercantilist regulations regarding prime necessities were strengthened by city administrations at the same time all other types of mercantilist enactments were disintegrating.

The validity of the claims and denials, charges and countercharges, accusations and vindications of those who partook of the heated arguments over food prices, trading practices, and government regulation is of no concern here. What is relative to this study is the fact that complaints of hard times emanated almost wholly from urban groups and did not picture farmers as victims of depressed economic conditions. When it is considered that over 90 per cent of the population made their living directly from agriculture, the years from the Peace of Paris down to the Revolution may be viewed as fairly prosperous for the major body of income receivers.

FOR FURTHER READING: Lewis C. Gray's views are more fully elaborated in his *History of Agriculture in the Southern United States to 1860* (Washington, 1933). Factual surveys are Percy W. Bidwell and John I. Falconer, *History of Agriculture in the Northern United States, 1620–1860* (Washington, 1925), and Philip A. Bruce, *Economic History of Virginia in the Seventeenth Century* (2 vols., New York, 1895). William B. Weeden, *Economic and Social History of New England* (2 vols., Boston, 1891) and Theodore Saloutos, "Efforts at Crop Control in Seventeenth Century America," *Journal of Southern History*, XII (February, 1946), pp. 45–66, are enlightening. World conditions affecting American agriculture are surveyed in George E. Mingay, "The Agricultural Depression, 1730–1750," *Economic History Review*, Second Series, VIII, No. 3 (1956), pp. 323–338. Aubrey C. Land, "The Tobacco Staple in the Planter's Problems, Technology, Labor, Crops," *Agricultural History*, XLIII (January, 1969), pp. 69–81, considers profitability as affected by colonial use of capital and labor.

3

LABOR
IN THE
COLONIAL
ERA

Received passage for labors.

PROBLEM: *What were the social origins of indentured servants in the Colonial Era?*

During the seventeenth and eighteenth centuries, white indentured servants constituted a significant proportion of the American labor force, which also included free workers and slaves. Without indentured servants the chronic shortage of labor in the colonies would have been even more acute. The nature of this work force has been the object of considerable dispute among historians. According to the traditional view, as developed by Marcus W. Jernegan, a distinguished historian of Colonial labor, the social origins of indentured servants could be found among the lowest strata of English society, including criminals and vagrants. Moreover, he argued that in view of such backgrounds, indentured servants usually tended to be unskilled. This traditional view has been challenged in recent years by historians and economists such as Walter Galenson, who have subjected existing records concerning indentures to statistical analysis. On the basis of limited case studies, Galenson concluded that indentured servants were as likely to be of middle class as lower class origins and that they brought a variety of skills. Both writers raise significant issues about the composition and skills of the Colonial labor force. What were the motivations of indentured servants? Was the productivity of forced labor restricted? What were the advantages of indentured servants for employers?

British Servants and the Colonial Indenture System in the Eighteenth Century

DAVID W. GALENSON

The past decade has seen a major resurgence of interest in the study of the American institution of slavery. But despite the intensive research devoted to that system, another system of forced labor that looms large in American history has been curiously neglected. Inextricably intertwined with the origins and progress of slavery in the American colonies, indentured servitude initiated the colonies' use of bound labor. Its quantitative importance is of the first order: one authority has estimated that "More than half of all persons who came to the [North American] colonies south of New England were [white] servants"; another, "that nearly half of the total white immigration to the thirteen colonies came over under . . . [indenture]." As is the case with slavery, much is known of the functioning of the system, but, also as with slavery, less is known of those who worked under the system. The main focus of this paper will be on these people, the servants. The evidence used will be from eighteenth-century British records. The specific questions asked will concern the personal characteristics of the servants and the choices they made within the constraints imposed by the system. Where did they go? What were their skills? How long did they serve, and what determined the length of service? All these will aim toward constructing composite answers to two more general questions: who were these early immigrants and how did they fare in America's first system of forced servitude?

No definitive answers are possible at present because of the scarcity of information about the indentured servants of the seventeenth and eighteenth centuries. Anonymous to most contemporaries, few records were kept either of their departure from Europe or their arrival in the New World, and fewer survive today. Since the lack of a large number of sources rules out the possibility of a truly quantitative study of the servants from available information, this paper will instead attempt to infer more general answers from a close study of one particular source, a collection of over three thousand indenture records for the years from 1718 to 1759 preserved at the Guildhall in London.

This set of indenture papers owes its existence to a clause of an act of Parliament of 1717 designed to protect the English merchants who signed

Reprinted with permission from *The Journal of Southern History*, XLIV (February, 1978), pp. 41–52, 65. Copyright 1978 by the Southern Historical Association. Footnotes omitted.

servants to indentures. The clause made it lawful for merchants to transport minors provided the potential servants were brought before a magistrate of London, or two magistrates elsewhere, in order to acknowledge that they went of their own accord. A contract was to be signed and a record of it kept; when this had been completed the merchant was then safe from prosecution for kidnapping. As a result of this act registration of servants of all ages, previously done only sporadically, became more systematic for some time. Many of the recorded contracts have apparently been lost, but over 2,800 survive for the years from 1718 to 1739, then, after a gap from 1740 to 1748, more than 100 remain from 1749 to 1759. These form the source for this inquiry.

The indentures were written on printed forms. In blank spaces were written the date of issue, the name of the servant, his parish and county of origin, his age, the name of the agent, the length of the indenture, the servant's destination, the signature (or mark) of the servant, as well as the signature of the magistrate. About half the contracts also recorded the servant's occupation. A few failed to give the length of the contract, while over 150 failed to record the age of the servant. Only those which did contain these last two pieces of information were used in this investigation; the total number of cases considered was 2,955. Of these, 2,792 were men, 163 women.

TABLE 1

AGE OF EMIGRATION OF SERVANTS

	Number of Servants Aged:							
---	Under 15	15–19	20–24	25–29	30–34	35–39	40–44	45–49	Total
Men	35	1391	938	274	98	39	13	4	2792
Women	3	106	41	9	3			1	163

Source: This and all other tables in this paper, except where noted, are based on indenture records in the Guildhall, London, transcribed by Jack aand Marion Kaminkow, *A List of Emigrants From England to America, 1718–1759* (Baltimore, 1966).

TABLE 2

AGE OF EMIGRATION OF SERVANTS
LESS THAN 21 YEARS OLD

	Number of Servants Aged:							
---	Under 13	13	14	15	16	17	18	19	20
Men	4	3	28	135	207	243	365	441	457
% of Total Men	0.1	0.1	1.0	4.8	7.4	8.7	13.1	15.8	16.4
Women	1	1	1	4	12	26	24	40	27
% of Total Women	0.6	0.6	0.6	2.5	7.4	16.0	14.7	24.5	16.6

All the indentures were entered in London, and apparently all the servants thus registered sailed from London. The fewer than three thousand records involved represent only a small fraction of the hundreds of thousands of servants who traveled to the colonies between the initiation of indentures in the early seventeenth century and the American Revolution. They are studied here for lack of more comprehensive sources and for the unusually complete information they give for those individuals covered. Since little is known of the overall population of servants, no real argument can be made about the representativeness of this sample, aside from the observation that there is no obvious reason for systematic bias when the origin of the records is considered. They represent only English servants, for all sailed from England and all but a few were English by birth.

Almost 95 per cent of the sample consisted of men. Table 1 shows the age of emigration of the servants, separately for men and women. The relative youth of the servants is clear: 94 per cent of the men were under thirty years old, as were 98 per cent of the women. About two-thirds of the men and four-fifths of the women were minors; Table 2 gives a more complete breakdown of their ages. It shows a heavy concentration of both men and women in ages fifteen to twenty, with 66 per cent of all male servants and 82 per cent of all the women in that age group.

Tables 3 and 4 show the number of men and women sent to each destination in the colonies, broken down by five-year periods. The principal destinations in the Caribbean during the period were Antigua and Jamaica, and these are enumerated separately; the principal mainland destinations, Maryland, Pennsylvania, and Virginia, are also listed separately. No other single destination received more than thirty-five servants from the sample in the period.

TABLE 3

DESTINATION OF MALE SERVANTS BY DATE

Destination

Date	Antigua	Jamaica	Other Islands	Maryland	Pennsylvania	Virginia	Other Mainland	Other	Total
1718–19	—	11	11	116	3	15	40	3	199
1720–24	6	132	122	264	37	84	48	4	697
1725–29	28	125	10	143	80	31	24	2	443
1730–34	18	470	18	120	62	25	35	5	753
1735–39*	16	341	8	109	49	9	45	2	579
1749*	1	12	—	—	1	3	—	—	17
1750–54	2	30	1	26	9	21	3	1	93
1755–59	1	3	—	—	—	—	—	7	11
Total	72	1124	170	778	241	188	195	24	2792

* No records of indentures remain from the years 1740–48.

TABLE 4

DESTINATION OF FEMALE SERVANTS BY DATE

Destination

Date	Antigua	Jamaica	Other Islands	Mary-land	Penn-sylvania	Virginia	Other Main-land	Total
1718–19	—	—	2	10	5	6	4	27
1720–24	1	2	5	16	7	13	8	52
1725–29	—	—	—	3	11	4	3	21
1730–34	—	13	1	9	6	—	4	33
1735–39	—	6	—	5	5	1	6	23
1749–56	1	2	—	—	—	3	1	7
Total	2	23	8	43	34	27	26	163

The two tables contrast sharply. While the men divided almost evenly between the Caribbean islands and the mainland colonies—49 per cent to the former, 50 per cent to the latter—the few women in the sample overwhelmingly went to the mainland; 80 per cent went there against 20 per cent to the islands. It is likely that relatively high mainland demand for women was reinforced by the female servants' own preferences. Similarly, in the case of the men the breakdowns cannot be taken strictly to represent the patterns of colonial demand; they also reflect to some etxent the preferences of the servants themselves.

Table 5 shows a breakdown of the male servants' destinations by age. The servants emigrating to the mainland colonies were generally younger than those emigrating to the islands: 60 per cent of those who went to the mainland were less than twenty years old, and 90 per cent were under twenty-five, compared to 42 per cent and 80 per cent, respectively, of those who went to the Caribbean. Relatively, Jamaica received

TABLE 5

DESTINATION OF MALE SERVANTS BY AGE

Destination

Age	Antigua	Jamaica	Other Islands	Mary-land	Penn-sylvania	Virginia	Other Main-land	Other
Under 15	1	7	2	12	2	4	7	—
15–19	38	424	105	438	136	112	123	15
20–24	19	448	45	249	75	52	46	4
25–29	9	152	12	54	23	12	9	3
30–34	3	59	4	15	5	3	8	1
35–39	1	27	—	6	—	4	—	1
40–44	—	5	2	3	—	1	2	—
45–49	1	2	—	1	—	—	—	—
Total	72	1124	170	778	241	188	195	24

the fewest servants under twenty; only 38 per cent of the men who went there were nineteen or less. All the mainland colonies received substantially higher proportions of young servants; Pennsylvania had the lowest proportion, with 57 per cent of its male servants under twenty, while 58 per cent of Maryland's and 62 per cent of Virginia's indentured men were in that age group.

A similar tabulation for women, not shown, indicates a similar pattern, but with a smaller difference. While 55 per cent of the female servants who went to the islands were less than twenty years old, 70 per cent of those who emigrated to the mainland colonies were under twenty.

Unfortunately, the information given on the indenture records tells little of the servants' personal characteristics. Two pieces of information are directly relevant: the trade of the servant, if entered, and the literacy of the servant, measured approximately by whether the servant signed or marked the paper. Trades were entered in only about half the cases: 56 per cent of the men's and none of the women's indentures listed occupations. The occupations listed are extremely diverse, running from the more common trades of smith, cooper, and cordwainer to schoolmasters and apothecaries, and even one dancing master. Table 6 shows the number of servants who recorded occupations on their indentures, broken down by age. The numbers rise sharply as a percentage of all male servants in the appropriate age group after the age of sixteen: 23 per cent of the seventeen-year-old servants recorded occupations, rising steadily to 67 per cent of the twenty-year-olds and 89 per cent of those twenty-one and over. Unfortunately, it is not clear exactly what this implies about the age at which the servants entered occupations, for there is no indication of how much experience was necessary before men considered themselves to have a trade.

It is difficult to assess the significance of the occupational entries, for the information seems to have been optional. Therefore, it does not seem to be

TABLE 6

NUMBER OF MALE SERVANTS
RECORDING OCCUPATIONS BY AGE

Age	Number of Servants	As % of Total Servants In Each Age Group
14	1	4
15	4	3
16	16	8
17	56	23
18	119	33
19	240	54
20	308	67
Over 20	812	89

a fair conclusion that if a man recorded no occupation he necessarily had no trade. Rather, it appears the number that recorded trades should be taken as a lower-bound estimate of the number that actually had occupations. Marcus Wilson Jernegan's judgment that "Most of the servants were unskilled laborers . . ." does not seem apt for this sample. In fact, only another 6 per cent of the men were described as "laborers" on the forms. Mildred Campbell noted that to contemporaries "the laborers' status was the lowest in the social hierarchy"; clearly, laborers played a small part in the Guildhall sample.

A tentative conclusion from the foregoing discussion might be that at least 62 per cent of the men were in the British labor force at the time they were indentured. Whether they were currently employed cannot be determined. Nonetheless, 62 per cent of the men is equivalent to the number of male servants in the Guildhall sample over the age of eighteen. Less than one tenth of these men were laborers. If this tentative conclusion is warranted and the entering of occupations on the papers was meaningful, it would cast significant doubt on Abbot Emerson Smith's contention that the servants were drawn "mainly from the lower strata of the population, the most ignorant and idle of the inhabitants of the metropolis . . . ."

Though an imperfect measure of literacy, the ability to write one's name is the measure most often used by historians. Tables 7 and 8 show the numbers of servants who signed their indentures, broken down by age and sex. The men's literacy rates rise steadily up to the age of eighteen, then level off until twenty; those over the age of twenty-one had a considerably higher rate. The overall literacy rate for men was 69 per cent. The women's table shows no such progression: no major increase in literacy seems to have occurred after the age of seventeen, and the overall rate is a much lower 34 per cent.

TABLE 7

LITERACY RATES FOR MALE SERVANTS BY AGE

Age	Marked	Signed	% Signed
Under 13	3	1	25
13	2	1	33
14	17	11	39
15	71	64	47
16	101	106	51
17	97	146	60
18	127	238	65
19	158	283	64
20	145	312	68
Over 20	155	754	69
Total	876	1916	83

TABLE 8

LITERACY RATES FOR FEMALE SERVANTS BY AGE

Age	Marked	Signed	% Signed
Under 13	—	1	—
13	1	—	—
14	1	—	—
15	4	—	—
16	9	3	25
17	17	9	35
18	16	8	33
19	26	14	35
20	17	10	37
Over 20	16	11	41
Total	107	56	34

The patterns of literacy found here have some interest for their implications concerning English education in the early eighteenth century. The results tell something quite concrete about how late many boys and girls learned to write, and perhaps to read. By contrast, in a recent study Kenneth Alan Lockridge assumes that in colonial New England male children learned to write by age ten.

The evidence of large increases in the literacy rate, particularly among the men in the sample, between the ages of fourteen and twenty-one begs

TABLE 9

LITERACY RATES FOR MALE SERVANTS
BY AGE AND OCCUPATION

(% Signed)

Age	Laborers	Tradesmen	Others
14	—	—	37
15	—	(75)	47
16	(22)	62	52
17	(57)	73	56
18	68	73	61
19	58	71	56
20	50	71	66
21	82	82	100
22–5	72	83	100
26–9	83	80	(100)
30–4	(60)	84	(100)
35–9	(66)	91	—
40–9	—	87	—
Totals	61	77	57

(Note: percentages recorded for minimum of 3 cases; for less than 10 cases, percentages in parentheses.)

the question of the mechanism involved. If many boys were learning to write beyond school age, how were they learning?

While these data contain no conclusive answer, breaking down the data on men's literacy offers some evidence. In Table 9 literacy rates are given separately by age for laborers, men with trades, and others. The highest literacy rates are for men with trades: the majority were literate at every age. Some increase occurred between ages sixteen and twenty-one. Thus, apprentices might have been taught to write by their masters in the course of training. There is no apparent trend in the rates for laborers. However, the strongest and steadiest trend appears for the men in the third category, those with no occupational entry. While only about one-third of the fourteen-year-olds were literate, two-thirds of the twenty-year-olds signed, and all of the adults. The source of education of these men cannot be determined, though the trend suggests the existence of one for men in their teens; it appears possible that for many Englishmen of the eighteenth century who had not received formal training or education as children the passage into adulthood may nonetheless have been accompanied by the acquisition of skills, such as literacy, that helped them cope with an increasingly complex society.

What do these rates tell us of the servants? Were the servants "the most ignorant and idle," as Smith would have it? The servants whose indentures are recorded in the Guildhall records were not. Two separate studies of English marriage registers for the years from 1754 to 1760 and from 1754 to 1762 "found that about 51 per cent of those who contracted marriage were able to sign their names." If the Guildhall sample had been evenly divided between the sexes and the literacy rates by sex had remained the same, its overall literacy rate would have been 51.5 per cent. The literacy rate for all men in the Guildhall sample, 69 per cent, was well above the 64 per cent and 48 per cent found by the two studies for adult males in rural areas. The mean age of the men in the Guildhall sample was 20.48 years, that of the women 19.29. The mean age of those marrying in England was apparently considerably higher. In one study of parish registers, E. A. Wrigley found the mean age of men at first marriage from 1720 to 1749 to be 26.2 years, and that of women 27.2. The mean ages for all marriages are obviously higher. In addition, the Guildhall sample includes a higher proportion of very young people than the marriage rolls. Thus, it would appear that literacy rates among the servants in the Guildhall sample were considerably higher than for the English population at large.

The evidence of occupation and literacy together points toward a higher level of skills and education among indentured servants than many historians in the past have believed. While the Guildhall servants were a small proportion of the total, they do not generally seem to have been Smith's "ignorant and idle," nor Thomas Jefferson Wertenbaker's "poor

TABLE 10

LENGTH OF INDENTURE OF MALE SERVANTS, BY AGE

(Number of servants by age)
Years indentured

Age	2	3	4	5	6	7	8	9	Mean years
Under 13						3		1	(7.5)*
13						1	2		(7.66)
14			1	1		13	13		7.29
15			8	17	15	68	27		6.65
16		1	28	51	61	59	7		5.82
17		4	79	79	52	28	1		5.10
18		4	198	112	27	22	2		4.65
19	1	4	299	107	28	2			4.37
20		3	382	65	3	4			4.18
21 and over	1	4	865	33	4	1	1		4.05

* Parentheses in this table and elsewhere indicate means based on less than ten observations.

wretches . . . willing to sell their liberty to go to the New World" in order to save themselves from "lives of drudgery and misery" at home. They seem rather to have been the young, the "middling people" of Mildred Campbell and "the restless, skilled men and women" of Warren M. Billings, anxious for a new life and better opportunity in the colonies. Seen in this light, the active role of the servants in shaping the system of indentured servitude is less likely to be overlooked, and a more fruitful reinterpretation of the institution is possible.

*   *   *

This investigation . . . has asked who the servants were. For the nearly three thousand servants whose indentures were examined, it has established certain characteristics. Their literacy rate was apparently higher than that of the English population at large. Their rate of entry into occupations appears to have been high. This partial evidence clearly cannot provide a conclusive answer to the question, but the tentative answers it has given for the servants in the sample constitute challenges to much of the received knowledge on the issue and provide a stimulus to further research on the whole population of servants. . . .

Economic and Social Influence of the Indentured Servant

MARCUS W. JERNEGAN

Could we draw the curtain which conceals the life of prehistoric people, we should see that the servant problem is as old as the human race. Indeed, if it were possible for extremes to meet, cave-dwellers and denizens of twentieth-century skyscrapers would doubtless converse sympathetically on this never-ending problem. Its existence is due to the universal desire of man to use the strength of others for his own profit and pleasure—an unchangeable trait of human nature.

During the colonial period of our history, service was performed in the main by two classes—the Negro slave and the indentured white servant. The white servant, a semi-slave, was more important in the seventeenth century than even the Negro slave, in respect to both numbers and economic significance. Perhaps the most pressing of the early needs of the colonists was for a certain and adequate supply of labor. It was the white servants who supplied this demand and made possible a rapid economic development, particularly of the middle and southern colonies. In 1683 there were twelve thousand of these semi-slaves in Virginia, composing about one-sixth of the population, while nearly two-thirds of the immigrants to Pennsylvania during the eighteenth century were white servants. Every other colony made greater or less use of them, and it is likely that more than a quarter of a million persons were of this class during the colonial period.

Such a widespread and important institution has great significance for the social and economic history of Europe and America in the seventeenth and eighteenth centuries. Moreover, the story is full of human interest because of methods used to supply the demand, similar to methods in the slave-trade: the classes of people from which some servants were drawn—convicts, paupers, and dissolute persons of every type; the stormy life of many servants, and the troublesome moral and social problems which their presence engendered, such as intermarriage with Negro slaves; the runaway criminal servants, and their influence on moral standards and on other phases of life in the colonies.

White servitude developed rapidly because of favorable conditions—a large demand for servants coupled with a large supply. The economic theory of European states in the seventeenth century called for a large population in their colonies, in order that trade and commerce might develop rapidly. The colonists were to supply food and raw materials, and the home country was to develop manufactures. Means, therefore, must be devised, first, to attract settlers who would develop the economic resources of the colonies, and, second, to provide them with an adequate supply of labor. There were vast areas of rich virgin lands, which, in the southern and middle colonies, were usually granted in a manner to promote rapid increase of population and extension of cultivated tracts. This method was known as the "head-right" system. Anyone emigrating was rewarded with a gift of land—about a hundred and fifty acres. Since labor was needed to clear and work this land, anyone importing a servant was entitled to an additional allotment, a "head right." To induce laborers to emigrate, a similar allotment was promised to them after each had served a term of years as a servant. Thus free land solved the two most pressing problems mentioned above.

Fortunately, the enormous demand for white servants came when economic conditions had created a large supply. In the sixteenth century, English agriculture was giving way to sheep-raising, so that a few herders often took the place of many farm laborers. As a result, the unemployed, the poor, and the criminal classes increased rapidly. Justices, who were landowners, had the power to fix the maximum wages of farm laborers. Sometimes they made them very low, hardly a shilling a day; for the lower the wage the greater the profits of the tenant farmer, and, therefore, the greater his ability to pay higher rents demanded by the landowner. Thus, while wages remained practically stationary, wheat multiplied in price nearly four times in this period, 1500–1600. In other words, a man worked forty weeks in 1600 for as much food as he received in 1500 by working ten weeks. To prevent scarcity of farm laborers, the statute of apprentices (1562) forbade anyone below the rank of a yeoman to withdraw from agricultural pursuits to be apprenticed to a trade. Moreover, the poor laws passed in this period compelled each parish to support its poor, and provided penalties for vagrancy. Thus the farm laborer had no chance to better himself. Conditions were almost beyond description, and in dear years people perished from famine. Sheffield in 1615, with a population of 2,207, had 725 relying on charity, 37.8 per cent of the population. As a result, the colonies were regarded as a convenient dumping-ground for undesirable citizens. Velasco, the Spanish minister in England, wrote his sovereign, 1611, "Their principal reason for colonizing these parts is to give an outlet to so many idle, wretched people as they have in England, and thus prevent the dangers that might be feared of them."

It is evident that if this surplus population could be transferred to the American colonies, both the mother country and the colonists would profit. One of the earliest proposals was made by Sir George Peckham, 1582. He declared that there were such great numbers living in penury and want that they might be willing to "hazard their lives and serve one year for meat, drinke, and apparell only without wages, in hope thereby to amend their estates." It was natural for men and women, in order to secure free transportation to America, to bind themselves by written contract, called an indenture, to serve some individual for a term of years.

There were three main classes of servants. One who entered into such a contract with an agent, often the shipmaster, was called an indentured servant. The shipmaster reimbursed himself, on arrival in America, by selling the time of the servant to the highest bidder. The second class included the "redemptioners," or "free-willers." They signed no contract beforehand, but were given transportation by the shipmaster with the understanding that on arrival they were to have a few days to indenture themselves to someone to pay for their passage. Failing this, the shipmaster could sell them himself. The free-willer then was at a great disadvantage. He had to bargain in competition with many others, and was so much at the mercy of the buyer or shipmaster that laws were passed by several colonies limiting his time of service and defining his rights.

The third class consisted of those forced into servitude, such as convicts, felons, vagrants, and dissolute persons, and those kidnapped or "spirited" away by the so-called "spirits" or "crimps." Convicts were often granted royal pardon on condition of being transported. For example, Charles I, in 1635, gave orders to the sheriff of London to deliver to Captain Thomas Hill or Captain Richard Carleton nine female convicts for removal to Virginia, to be sold as servants. At an early date judges imposed penalties of transportation on convicted criminals and others. Thus Narcissus Luttrell notes in his diary, November 17, 1692, that the magistrates had ordered on board a ship lying at Leith, bound for Virginia, fifty lewd women out of the house of correction and thirty others who walked the streets at night. An act of Parliament in 1717 gave judges still greater power by allowing them to order the transportation of convicts for seven years, known as "His Majesty's seven-year passengers," and, in case the penalty for the crime was death, for fourteen years. Those agreeing to transport convicts could sell them as servants. From London prisons, especially Newgate and the Old Bailey, large numbers were sent forth, the latter alone supplying not far from 10,000 between 1717 and 1775. Scharf, the historian of Maryland, declares that 20,000 felons were imported into that colony before the Revolution. At least nine of the colonies are known to have received felons as servants, so that the total number sent was not far from 50,000. Lists of felons ordered transported were often printed in the *Gentleman's Magazine*; one of May, 1747, numbering 887. Remembering this, perhaps, Dr. Johnson said in 1769, "Sir, they are a race of convicts, and ought to be content with anything we may allow them short of hanging."

The colonists became alarmed as early as 1670. At that date Virginia passed an act prohibiting the importation of convicts. The preamble speaks "of the great nombers of felons and other desperate villaines sent hither from the several prisons of England." Later, communications which appeared in the newspapers show great indignation. One writer speaks of the practice as a "vile importation" and comments particularly on the bad moral effects of such persons. Even at an earlier date Lord Bacon had commented on the injustice and fallacy of this policy as follows: "It is a shameful and unblessed thing to take the scum of people and wicked, condemned men to be the people with whom you plant." And Benjamin Franklin, in reply to the arguments of British authorities that it was necessary to get rid of convicts, asked whether Americans for the same reason would be justified in sending their rattlesnakes to England! For a brief period Great Britain listened to the complaints of the colonists, confirmed the Virginia Act of 1670, and made it apply to other colonies. But in 1717 Parliament in effect repealed it by the act of that date mentioned above, and, throughout the eighteenth century, convicts were a never-failing source of supply for white servants. In this connection it has been suggested that American genealogists in search of missing data to complete their family tree would find a rich mine of unexplored material in the archives of Newgate and Old Bailey, the latter filling 110 manuscript volumes!

The reasons for sending so many convicts were several. It is obvious why Great Britain was particularly anxious to rid herself of this class of her population. Criminals were not only unproductive but entailed a great expense on the country. Economists urged their transportation, while others argued that in a new country many criminals would forsake their old habits and become good citizens. Some of the colonists were certainly not averse to convicts as servants, since their term of service was longer. The committee of trade for New York even petitioned the authorities, 1693, to send them all the prisoners who were to be transported from Newgate. It should be remembered, too, that the word felon in the seventeenth and eighteenth centuries conveyed a different meaning from that at present. The penal code of England in 1600 provided a death penalty for hundreds of offenses, many of which were of a trivial nature, and even just before the American Revolution Blackstone states that there were some one hundred and fifty capital crimes. Thus many persons called "felons" were less objectionable as servants than might be supposed, and there was good reason to expect that a number would become respectable when transported.

One of the most interesting sources of supply was kidnaping. The profits gained by such practices were so great that this developed as a regular business in London and seaport towns like Bristol. "Spirits" would pounce on all classes of persons and entice them on board ships bound for the colonies, and even children were induced to go by offers of sweet-meats. The county court records of Middlesex give evidence of this practice. A record for November 7, 1655, states that Dorothy Perkins accuses Christian Chacrett, alias Sacrett, "for a Spirit, one that taketh upp men and women and children and sells them on a shipp to bee conveyed beyond the sea, having entised and inveagled one Edward Furnifull and Anne his wife with her infant to the waterside and put them aboard the shipp called *The Planter* to be conveyed to Virginia." Parliament passed an act in 1671 providing a death penalty for this crime.

Analogous to the spirits were the "newlanders," or "soul-sellers." The great German immigration to America in the eighteenth century developed this class of agents, who traveled up and down the Rhine Valley, persuading peasants to sell their belongings and migrate to the colonies. They pretended that they were rich merchants from Philadelphia, dressed in costly clothes, and wore wigs and ruffles. They would seek acquaintance with a merchant in Holland and agree with him upon a sum for every person persuaded to remove. They described Pennsylvania as a land of Elysian fields flowing with milk and honey, where gold and silver could be picked up on the hills, and servants could become independent and live like noblemen. The simple German peasant would often sell his belongings and trust himself to the mercy of the soul-seller. Many were forced to become servants by indenture, because the excessive charges imposed for transportation from the Rhine Valley to the port of departure used up their small capital.

The voyage over often repeated the horrors of the famous "middle passage" of slavery fame. An average cargo was three hundred, but the shipmaster, for greater profit, would sometimes crowd as many as six hundred into a small vessel. Picture to yourself several hundred people of all ages with only six feet by two feet allotted between decks for one adult person, with no privacy whatever, wearing the same clothing for the whole voyage—from four weeks to four months or even more—and often lying flat for whole days at a time when the ship was tossed by terrific storms. Imagine the vile atmosphere in an unventilated space containing hundreds of people, many ill with all manner of contagious diseases, living and dead side by side, without medical attendance, moaning and shrieking, praying and crying, and perhaps crazed by famine and thirst. John Harrower, an indentured servant, describing in his diary a scene between-decks during a storm, says, "There was some sleeping, some daming, some blasting their leggs and thighs, some their liver, lungs, lights, and eyes, and for to make the scene the odder, some curs'd Father, Mother, Sister, Brother." When food ran short it was doled out at the rate of three ounces of bread a day. Mittelberger, an eyewitness, says that spoiled biscuit were given the passengers, "dirty and full of red worms and spiders' nests." When such vile stuff called food was lacking, rats and mice were eaten.

The mortality under such circumstances was tremendous, sometimes more than half of the passengers dying of hunger and privation. Children from one to seven rarely survived. Mittelberger says he saw thirty-two little children thrown into the ocean during one voyage. It must be remembered, of course, that a safe, short passage of thirty days was not uncommon. Still, conditions were so terrible that several colonies passed laws regulating food, the number of passengers to be carried, and care of the sick. Philadelphia and other ports were exposed to constant dangers from contagious diseases. Sickness continued after landing, so that much legislation was necessary respecting quarantine, inspection of vessels, and the building of pesthouses.

When the vessel finally made her port, no one was permitted to leave unless the passage had been paid for. The sick and old always fared worst, the very ones whose misery ought to have been relieved first. Parents were forced to sell their children to service, perhaps never to see them again. Husband and wife were often separated. Children under five were sometimes given away to serve until they were twenty-one. "Soul-drivers" would purchase fifty or more servants from the captain of one of these ships, and drive them through the country like a drove of cattle, offering them for sale to the highest bidder. They were protected, in part, however, first by their indenture, which specified the term of service, lodging, food, and apparel; and, second, by "freedom dues," which were provided for by law, and included such things as clothing, corn, a gun, and sometimes a fifty-acre tract of land.

Most of the servants were unskilled laborers.

FOR FURTHER READING: The views of Marcus Jernegan are further elaborated in the excellent volume of Abbot E. Smith, *Colonists in Bondage: White Servitude and Convict Labor in America, 1607–1776* (Chapel Hill, 1943), and in his article, "Indentured Servants: New Light on Some of America's 'First' Families," *Journal of Economic History*, II (1942), pp. 40–53. Mildred Campbell, "Social Origins of Some Early Americans," in James M. Smith (ed.), *Seventeenth Century America: Essays in Colonial History* (Chapel Hill, 1959), pp. 63–89 stresses the middle class character of indentured servants. Richard B. Morris, *Government and Labor in Early America* (New York, 1946) focuses on the attitude of colonial courts towards indentured workers. Richard Hofstadter, *America at 1750: A Social Portrait* (New York, 1971), emphasizes regional differences to explain variations in the social background of indentured servants.

4

COLONIAL
FINANCE

PROBLEM: *Did monetary policies of colonial governments stimulate expansion?*

Deficit financing in America is not an innovation of the twentieth century. Over three hundred years ago colonial legislatures embarked on the issuance of paper money to stimulate economic development. Although the practice was quite common, it aroused much controversy, then as later. Contemporaries often clashed over the issue: "Was paper money or hard specie best to promote economic expansion?" Historians too have not agreed on this question. Writing at the close of the nineteenth century, C. J. Bullock attacked the issuance of fiat currency because he believed that it would inevitably depreciate, and so impede growth of the economy. In a more recent and favorable appraisal, perhaps conditioned by theories of deficit spending advocated by the British economist John M. Keynes, Professor E. James Ferguson of the University of Maryland finds that Colonial issues of paper money were not always subject to depreciation, and that they provided needed investment funds for exploitation of the undeveloped economy. Both authors use cogent arguments to sustain their respective views and raise broad questions. Why do advocates of hard money find deficit financing evil? What were the results of cheap money in the Colonial Era? What were some strengths and weaknesses of the paper money policies of colonial legislatures?

Colonial Paper Money

CHARLES J. BULLOCK

Soon after the colonies commenced to advance the ratings of their current coins, there began a series of attempts to establish private banks. It must be remembered that, during the entire colonial period, the word "bank" meant simply a batch of paper money, a conception that has disappeared only gradually during the present century as the functions of deposit and discount have assumed greater importance in modern banking. During the seventeenth century, more especially during its closing decades, public and private credit had been developed in the countries of northern Europe upon a scale that was previously unknown. Naturally enough the real nature and precise limitations of the great agency thus created were not clearly understood. It was perceived that credit increased enormously the control over capital enjoyed by a person or a company; but it was not realized so readily that credit is not the same as capital, and that capital cannot be directly created by credit, although its efficiency may be greatly increased. John Law's projects, the Mississippi Scheme in France, the English Land Bank Scheme, and the South Sea Bubble were no isolated phenomena: many other fallacious enterprises grew out of the misunderstandings that prevailed concerning the nature and proper uses of credit. Theories and plans of a paper currency began to appear in England as early as 1650, when William Potter published "The Key of Wealth, or A new way for Improving of Trade." Other schemes followed, all of which proposed to find some other medium than metallic money for a basis of paper credit. For this purpose deposits of merchandise or pledges of land were commonly suggested. In England the existence of more settled industrial conditions and the possession of a larger supply of capital facilitated the growth of sounder views concerning the true nature and proper basis of credit, but these lessons were not learned until much sad experience had been gained from unsafe banking ventures; while, as late as the period of restriction from 1797 to 1819, all the forces of unreason had to be most vigorously combated before it was generally admitted that the premium on bullion was due to the depreciation of the paper currency, and not to an alleged scarcity of gold. In the American colonies, however, the economic conditions were precisely the reverse of those which prevailed in the mother country; and all circumstances favored the persistence of erroneous ideas.

At some time previous to 1652, "paper bills" seem to have circulated

Reprinted with the permission of the Macmillan Company from *Essays on the Monetary History of the United States* by Charles J. Bullock (New York, 1900), pp. 29–59.

in some parts of Massachusetts, and there is a record of projects "for raiseing a Banke." William Potters's "Key of Wealth," or some similar publication, may have come to the attention of Governor John Winthrop, of Connecticut; for, in 1661, he is found to be entertaining "some proposalls concerning a way of trade and banke without money." A few years later, the Rev. John Woodbridge submitted a project "for erecting a Fund of Land, by Authority, or private Persons, in the Nature of a *Money-Bank* or *Merchandise-Lumber*." In 1671, 1681, and 1686, private banks were actually established in Massachusetts; and bills were issued, probably upon the security of "such Real Estates of Lands, as also personal Estates of goods and Merchandizes not subject to perishing or decay." These projects, however, proved to be short lived. In them can be distinctly traced the influence of theories that were then prevalent in England. In 1690, Massachusetts, followed shortly by other colonies, emitted its first public bills of credit. Such issues soon became so common as to divert attention, in a great measure, from private banking enterprises. Yet in 1700, 1714, 1733, 1739, and 1740, private banks were projected in Massachusetts, and were finally suppressed with great difficulty. In some cases, however, these associations actually placed a considerable quantity of their bills in circulation. The great Land Bank of 1740 issued about £35,000 of notes, and made a most vigorous struggle to maintain its existence. In New Hampshire, Connecticut, and South Carolina, associations were formed, between 1732 and 1738, for the purpose of engaging in similar ventures; and at a later date we hear of other attempts in Pennsylvania and Virginia. But Parliament interfered, in 1741, by extending to the colonies the provisions of the "Bubble Act," which had been passed twenty-one years earlier in order to suppress such swindles as had occurred during the time of the South Sea Company.

The paper money that so long cursed the American colonies was issued by acts of the several legislatures. Massachusetts had led the way, in 1690, with an issue of bills that were used to defray the expenses of a disastrous military expedition. Her example proved contagious; and, by 1712, New Hampshire, Rhode Island, Connecticut, New York, New Jersey, North Carolina, and South Carolina had issued quantities of bills of credit in order to meet the outlays occasioned by Queen Anne's War. In subsequent years bills were emitted as a regular means of defraying the current expenses of government; and, as the volume of paper accumulated, a great depreciation ensued. Sooner or later all the plantations were deeply involved in the mazes of a fluctuating currency, for the burdens attending the various wars of the eighteenth century were so great as to induce even the most conservative colonies to resort to this easy method of meeting public obligations. Virginia succumbed last, in 1755, but made large issues in the ensuing years.

A second excuse for issuing bills of credit was found at an early date.

In 1712, South Carolina created a public loan bank, and issued bills that were loaned to its citizens at interest, upon real or personal security. This expedient was followed sooner or later by nearly all of the other colonies. Rhode Island easily distanced all competitors in the readiness and facility with which she created loan banks; while Pennsylvania, New Jersey, and Delaware followed a more conservative course than most of the other plantations.

The abuses attending both forms of paper currency were usually of the most flagrant sort. Bills were issued for the payment of current expenses or extraordinary outlays, and taxes would be voted for the purpose of redemption. Then subsequent assemblies would extend the period during which the paper money should be current, or would neglect to levy sufficient taxes for its withdrawal. Thus the currency tended always to accumulate, and its depreciation increased. Sometimes a legislature would resolve that the bills in circulation should not exceed a certain sum, but such a declaration would prove utterly worthless. In almost every colony the first issues were to remain current for a short time only, and were to be redeemed speedily by taxes; but the periods were gradually lengthened to twelve, sixteen, or twenty-five years. Laws were often passed providing for the emission of new bills to replace worn or mutilated issues. Then the new money would frequently be placed in circulation without withdrawing and cancelling the old, while bills that had been withdrawn for the original purpose of destroying them would often be reissued for current expenses. In some colonies it happened that paper issued upon loan would not be repaid at the stated periods, and interest payments were commonly in arrears. When this occurred, the legislature would frequently extend the time of the loans, and sometimes a large part of both principal and interest would never be repaid. In this respect Rhode Island was probably the worst offender. Her loan banks were placed in the hands of a few favored persons, called "sharers," who happened to possess the requisite "pull." The "sharers" then proceeded to lend out the money at a rate of interest that was, for the first ten years, five per cent higher than that which they were obliged to pay to the colony. In some cases the fortunate "sharers" would sell their privileges for premiums that sometimes amounted to as much as thirty-five per cent. The results of such performances can readily be imagined.

Although the colonial bills of credit were not always made a legal tender, they were usually given a forced circulation. Most of the advocates of paper money would have agreed with the New York legislature that bills not legal tender were useless. The direct penalties—fines, imprisonment and confiscation—were imposed upon those evil-disposed persons who should dare to discriminate in favor of specie; but such forcing laws were as ineffectual in supporting the credit of the paper money as they have proved in all other cases. When older issues had depreciated hopelessly, "bills of a new tenor" were often emitted; and these were sometimes followed by others of a newer tenor. Thus it happened that issues of the "old tenor," "middle tenor," and "new tenor" circulated concurrently at different rates of depreciation, the legislature usually undertaking to fix the relative values of the three classes of currency. In order to prevent depreciation some of the issues bore interest, but this was a provision that was readily repealed by subsequent assemblies.

As has always been the case, the appetite for paper money increased with the issues of bills of credit. Complaints of the scarcity of money almost invariably followed each emission, and one pretext after another was found for issuing larger quantities of paper. Trade was said to be decaying, public buildings had to be constructed, fortifications were needed, and dozens of other things must be done by setting the printing presses at work. The experience of the colonies demonstrates conclusively the impossibility of satisfying the desire for "more money" by issuing a paper currency. Depreciation commenced at an early date, and tended to increase as time went on. In New England sterling exchange was 133 in 1702, a rate corresponding exactly to the rating of the dollar at 6s. In 1713, it rose to 150, and had reached 550 by the year 1740. The climax was reached in Massachusetts and Connecticut in 1749 and 1750, when exchange was quoted at 1100, indicating a depreciation of nearly 9 : 1. In Rhode Island, the old tenor bills finally sank to 23 for 1. In the middle colonies the depreciation never reached such figures. In Pennsylvania exchange once reached 180, while the par of exchange for specie was not higher than 166½. In Maryland exchange rose from 133 to 250. In North and South Carolina the paper currencies finally sank to one-tenth the value of sterling. Such fluctuations in the standard of value wrought intense hardships. . . .

Currency Finance: An Interpretation of Colonial Monetary Practices

E. JAMES FERGUSON

The accepted view of the financial and monetary history of the American colonies needs revision. It owes too much to the influence of nineteenth-century scholars who were themselves partisans in currency disputes. In

Reprinted by permission from E. James Ferguson, "Currency Finance: An Interpretation of Colonial Monetary Practices," *William and Mary Quarterly*, X (April, 1953), pp. 153–180.

their own day, William G. Sumner, Albert S. Bolles, Charles J. Bullock, and Andrew M. Davis stood for "sound money" against inflationist movements. One of their chief aims was to show the disastrous effects of wandering off the straight line of a sound-money policy.[1] Hence, they studied those colonies whose money depreciated and relied on the opinions of such eighteenth-century controversialists as Dr. William Douglass, Thomas Hutchinson, and others in whose views they concurred.[2] With the notable exception of Andrew M. Davis, who did a scholarly work on Massachusetts,[3] they were interested in the colonies chiefly as background to the financial history of the Revolution. Their works in the latter field incorporated study in primary sources and were generally accepted as authoritative.

The pattern they stamped on historical interpretation still survives in its major outlines. Recent books sometimes modify their harsher judgments and bring in new material, but the interpretation rests largely on the story they told of paper money in Massachusetts, Rhode Island, and the Carolinas. These were the provinces where depreciation created a

[1] See a review by Curtis Nettels of Richard A. Lester, *Monetary Experiments, Early American and Recent Scandinavian* (Princeton, 1939), in *English Historical Review*, LVI (1941), 333.

[2] The treatment of the colonies in William Graham Sumner, *A History of American Currency* (New York, 1874) is hardly a serious effort, and the same can be said of the earlier work of William M. Gouge, *A Short History of Paper Money and Banking in the United States, Including an Account of Provincial and Continental Paper Money*, 2nd ed. (New York, 1835). Of considerably greater merit are two studies of particular colonies: Joseph B. Felt, *An Historical Account of Massachusetts Currency* (Boston, 1839) and Henry Bronson, "An Historical Account of Connecticut Currency, Continental Money, and the Finances of the Revolution," New Haven Historical Society, *Papers*, I (1865), 1–192 (separate pagination following page 170). Early works displaying another bias are Henry Phillips, *Historical Sketches of the Paper Currency of the American Colonies, Prior to the adoption of the Federal Constitution* (Roxbury, Mass., 1865–1866) and John H. Hickcox, *A History of the Bills of Credit or Paper Money Issued by New York from 1709 to 1789* (Albany, 1866). The book by Phillips includes surveys of several colonies, written by different authors.

The case against paper money as drawn by nineteenth-century historians rested heavily on the data and opinions supplied by William Douglass, *A Discourse Concerning the Currencies of the British Plantations in America* (Boston, 1740). This treatise came out of a bitter controversy and was highly partisan. A careful reading shows how deeply the local situation in New England colored Douglass's attitudes and his judgment of the situation in other colonies. Even in the case of New England, he correctly attributed depreciation to the uncontrolled emissions of one province, Rhode Island. His observations on other colonies are not reliable.

[3] Andrew M. Davis, *Currency and Banking in the Province of Massachusetts-Bay*, American Economic Association, *Publications*, 3rd ser., I (1900), no. 4. Davis was a careful and honest scholar, but his main concern was to expose the evils of fiat money. He relied, for example, on the testimony of Thomas Hutchinson and Douglass, although his chapter on sources listed without comment works by Franklin and Thomas Pownall, as well as secondary accounts, which gave quite another view of colonial currency. It must be said, however, that these sources related to provinces outside New England and therefore lay beyond the immediate scope of his study. See *ibid.*, I, 413–435.

The same year that Davis's essay came out, Charles J. Bullock published *Essays in the Monetary History of the United States* (New York, 1900) which included a general survey of colonial currency and more detailed treatment of North Carolina and New Hampshire. The latter studies were based on research in primary sources and are of value.

major problem. Neglect of other colonies whose experiments were more fortunate conveys the impression that paper money typically depreciated and was harmful to the community.

A correlated idea is that paper money was significant mainly as a ground of conflict between colonial debtors and creditors. No doubt this view is more readily accepted because it fits in with the Turner hypothesis. Here again, Massachusetts furnishes the prime example. The land bank controversy of 1740 is portrayed as a struggle of creditors against debtors, coastal merchants against back-country farmers. Other instances can be found in the early history of South Carolina.

While the debtor-creditor thesis has logical probability and a foundation in fact, it is nonetheless inadequate when viewed in a perspective embracing the whole development of the American colonies. Historians generally concede, for example, that in most provinces, a propertied aristocracy dominated the government. The debtor-creditor thesis, broadly considered, affords no sufficient explanation for the fact that in the half century before the Revolution, these aristocratic bodies regularly and persistently issued paper money. The thesis is also at odds with the fact that in the middle provinces, at least, mercantile groups strongly opposed the act of Parliament which prevented the colonies from making paper money a legal tender in private transactions. On the assumption that serious internal conflict existed between debtor and creditor, the stand taken by merchants would be inexplicable.

Several accounts of individual provinces appearing in the last few decades appraise the fiat money methods of the colonies in their setting. As the authors have stayed close to primary sources and have extended their range beyond New England, they depict a more successful use of paper money. The collective influence of these works has not been as great as one might suppose. Curtis P. Nettels has added a general study of monetary affairs; unfortunately, it covers only the period before 1720, when the colonies were just beginning to employ paper currency.

There are signs, however, that the dogmas which have prejudiced research are giving way. Fiat money is now the rule, and most economists have ceased to believe that currency must be convertible into gold or silver. Governments freely manipulate currency, as a means of economic control. In this frame of reference, the ways of the American colonies acquire new significance. An economist, Richard A. Lester, explores their use of paper money in the attempts to curb economic depression. He finds that their tactics were analogous to those of the New Deal and bore some ancestral relationship to present-day Keynesian doctrine. The most promising effort, however, is an unpublished doctoral dissertation by Leslie Van Horn Brock, which displays a grasp of colonial usages and attitudes seldom found in older studies. When such works as these attract

more notice, other scholars may be persuaded to explore a field which
is rich in implications for social and economic history.

Until more evidence is brought together, any general conclusions must
be tentative. The formulations attempted in this paper are, therefore, ex-
ploratory and subject to correction. It seems possible, however, to qualify
older interpretations and point out the tendency of future research. An
effort will be made to show that in the middle colonies, from New York
to Maryland, paper money was successful. Secondly, it will be argued
that except in New England and the Carolinas, paper money did not
engender any great conflict between broad classes of the population.
Finally, the system of paper money will be described in general terms and
an attempt made to define the essential features of "currency finance."

In judging the success of paper money, the first question is whether it
depreciated. The answer cannot always be explicit. Different authors do
not mean exactly the same thing by the word depreciation. Older historians were inclined to go by the rate of exchange. If currency passed
below its legal rate in trade for hard money or in the purchase of bills of
exchange, they considered that it had depreciated and inferred that too
much had been issued or that people lacked confidence in fiat money.
This was certainly true in colonies like Rhode Island, Massachusetts, and
the Carolinas, where currency sank to low levels. In colonies where
fluctuations in the value of money were only moderate, however, a discount on currency in exchange for specie or sterling bills did not necessarily imply that the currency was unsound. Historians of such provinces
refer to paper money as stable, even though its value sometimes sank in
relationship to specie.

It was normal to discount currency somewhat in exchange for hard
money. First of all, the colonies sought to attract foreign coin by giving
it a high legal value. They fixed such rates that hard money equivalent to
£100 British sterling was legally worth from £133 to around £175 in
the currency of different provinces. This was the legal rate. But hard
money ordinarily commanded a premium beyond this, for it had more
uses than paper. It was more negotiable in payments to foreigners and in
inter-colonial transactions.

Besides a general preference for hard money, other factors sometimes
worked to bring about a further discount on paper money. Detailed information on the processes of colonial trade is lacking, but it appears that
most payments to Britain were made in bills of exchange, that is, drafts
payable in Britain which the colonists procured largely by shipments of
cargoes. The availability of sterling bills in America depended on the
condition of trade. When British purchases fell off and the colonies
shipped less than would pay for their imports, sterling bills became
scarce and expensive, and people sought hard money to make payments
abroad. Specie and bills of exchange rose in value relative to paper money.

On the other hand, there were times during the French and Indian War when the colonies enormously increased the volume of their domestic currency, yet the exchange with specie remained constant or even improved because large British expenditures, decreased importations, and a greater supply of specie at hand reduced the need for hard money. Circumstances beyond the control of colonial governments affected the rate of exchange, regardless of how scrupulously the colonies managed their paper money or how good its credit was at home.

The most accurate test of the stability of paper money would be its value in exchange for commodities sold in colonial markets. An adequate price study exists for Pennsylvania, and there is some information for a few other colonies. Unfortunately, this kind of data is fragmentary, and historians usually have to depend on scattered figures and the casual remarks found in contemporary letters.

The weight of evidence suggests, however, that in the middle colonies fluctuations were not great enough to impair the credit or utility of paper money. Historians agree that Pennsylvania "maintained the system without fear of repudiation and to the manifest benefit of the province." It appears that for the half century before the Revolution, the domestic price level was more uniform than in any succeeding period of equal length. The emissions of New Jersey and Delaware are said to have been stable and to have passed usually at par with that of Pennsylvania. New York's currency was highly regarded, and the colony's ability to keep its bills at par was a "subject for special commendation."

Maryland's first emission of 1753 depreciated, even though well-secured, apparently because tobacco remained the primary medium of exchange. Later her bills rose in value and by 1764 were reported "locked up in the Chests of the Wealthy" for the sake of the interest falling due on them. Thereafter, in spite of heavy additions, the bills held their value. "As a colony," writes a modern scholar, "Maryland had solved the problem of a paper currency."

The provinces further south had trouble with their currency. Until 1755, Virginia supplemented the hard money in circulation with tobacco notes, which passed in local exchange and payment of taxes. But the coming of the French and Indian War forced the colony to emit paper money. The bills held their value until 1760, when a sharp break in tobacco prices marked the onset of a long and severe depression. For the next several years, planters could hardly sell their crops, and prices stayed very low. A shortage of the planter balances ordinarily arising from tobacco sales in Britain caused bills of exchange and specie to grow scarce, and their value rose in terms of the currency offered by planters obliged to make payments to British creditors. Virginia currency was discounted as much as 50 per cent to 60 per cent in purchase of bills of exchange. Although specie was extremely scarce, the colony did not put aside its plans to retire war-time paper emissions, and it probably contributed to the easement of conditions that the treasurer of the province, John Robinson, restored some £100,000 to circulation through secret loans to hard-pressed planters. Robinson's defalcations probably occurred in 1765 and 1766. It appears, however, that the decline in Virginia's currency in these and preceding years owed little to Robinson's private emissions, but was rather the result of trade depression. In the last years of the decade, the value rose, and by 1771 it was reported that the British merchants who had formerly complained of paper money were among its warmest advocates.

In the Carolinas, depreciation was severe, though it occurred for the most part early in the eighteenth century, when these colonies were thinly populated and undeveloped. Clearly, however, the legislature of North Carolina did little to sustain its first emissions, and the bills steadily depreciated. In 1748, they were called in to be exchanged for new bills at the rate of 7½ to 1. The new bills fluctuated thereafter around a point considerably below their nominal value, but were rising towards the end of the colonial period, when the British government kept the legislature under close rein.

A different situation prevailed in South Carolina, where all the depreciation occurred before 1731. The infant colony was then under heavy financial strain resulting from war. Debtor elements found the depreciation to their liking, however, and tried to maintain the downward trend. They were overcome after a bitter struggle. The currency was stabilized in 1731 at the rate of 7 to 1 of sterling, which remained unchanged until the Revolution. During its maturity, the province had a stable currency and a record of successful management.

Constancy of value was not, in many minds, the sole test of a currency. Another criterion is suggested by the remark of Thomas Pownall, that in spite of the depreciation in New England, "it was never yet objected that it injured them in trade." Thomas Hancock, one of the greatest merchants in America, seems at one time not to have been altogether convinced that paper money was an unmitigated evil, though he had dealt in a depreciated medium all his life. Of the legislation which placed Massachusetts on a sound money basis, he said: "This d——d Act has turn'd all Trade out of doors and it's Impossible to get debts in, either in Dollars or Province Bills." No study has been made of the economic effects of depreciation in the provinces where it occurred. It is possible that a steady and continuing inflation was not wholly injurious to an expanding country whose people seldom had fixed incomes or large stores of liquid capital.

Even if stability is taken as the sole rule in judging the success of colonial currency, the record is not entirely black. The depreciation in New England was mainly the fault of Rhode Island, whose emissions flooded the unitary economy of that area and undermined the currency of her neighbors. Elsewhere, North Carolina was the leading offender. The colonies, it must be said, did not have complete freedom to act. Each of them felt, in varying degree, the weight of British authority, which was always cast on the side of moderation in the use of currency. Nevertheless, the predominating fact was not the failure of paper money but its success and good credit—in the colonies from New York to Maryland, and in Virginia, as well as in South Carolina during its later development.

Serious conflicts between debtors and creditors did not arise when paper money stayed near par value. Ideally, perhaps, men of property would have preferred a circulation of coin or a currency backed by precious metals. Practically, however, most of them shared the popular belief that there was no alternative to the existing system. "Contrary to the traditions that historians have perpetuated," writes a modern student of economic thought, "a critical analysis of the contemporary literature indicates that the proponents as well as the critics were not poor debtors or agrarians, but for the most part officials, ministers, merchants, and men of substance and learning in general."

Pennsylvania's currency was esteemed by all classes and regarded as having contributed to the growth and prosperity of the colony. In his widely read work on colonial affairs, Thomas Pownall wrote that there "never was a wiser or a better measure, never one better calculated to serve the uses of an encreasing country . . . never a measure more steadily pursued, nor more faithfully executed for forty years together." Merchants and traders of Philadelphia formally opposed the restraining act of 1764 which prevented the colonies from making paper money legal tender. As colonial agent in England, Benjamin Franklin fought the enactment of the law and afterward wrote pamphlets urging its repeal. Franklin joined other colonial representatives and English merchants to argue the case for repeal before British ministers and members of Parliament. By 1767, the American agents planned to secure the introduction of a repealing act into Parliament. They gave up the idea only when it became known that Parliament would very likely insist that the price of such a concession must be the surrender by the colonies of permanent revenues to the crown.

Franklin told the House of Commons that restrictions on paper money were among the leading reasons why the American provinces had become alienated from the mother country. In 1774, the First Continental Congress cited the restraining act among the violations of colonial rights.

New York merchants also protested the restraining act. The assembly appointed a committee of New York county members, whose duties included corresponding with other provinces and the colonial agent with respect to the act. Governor Moore espoused the cause and repeatedly

asked the Board of Trade to sanction an emission on the terms desired
by the province. The assembly refused aid to British troops unless the
crown approved a currency bill, and, according to Carl Becker, opposition to the Townshend Acts had one of its sources in this grievance.
Popular unrest was stilled not only by the repeal of the duties, but also
by a special act of Parliament which allowed the colony to issue paper
money.

Public opinion in Maryland, according to historians of the province,
was nearly unanimous in favor of paper money. Among the beneficiaries
of the currency system were many of the most prominent men of the
colony, who received loans from the government. The list included a
"surprising number" of merchants. After Parliamentary restrictions were
laid down in 1764, all classes concurred in the need for further emissions,
and Maryland's agents in London tried to get the act repealed.

In spite of the notorious depreciation which afflicted North Carolina's
emissions, paper money does not seem to have been a major factor in the
sectional antagonisms of that colony. Both houses of a legislature presumably dominated by the "court house ring" petitioned the crown in
1768 to approve paper money legislation. At a time when the Regulator
Movement in the backcountry had begun to split the colony into warring
factions, Governor Tryon added his pleas to those of the legislature. His
letters to the Board of Trade repeated familiar arguments, which, coming
from less responsible sources, have often been dismissed as the pretence
of debtors trying to evade their obligations. He said a larger circulating
medium was necessary and that much distress arose from the lack of it.

In South Carolina, the early struggle between debtors and creditors
was never quite forgotten, but in time the memory grew so dim that the
contemporary historian, David Ramsay, could write: "From New-York
to Georgia there had never been in matters relating to money, an instance of a breach of public faith." On the basis of his personal recollec-
tion, no doubt, he wrote that the use of paper money "had been similar
from the first settlement of the colonies, and under proper restrictions
had been found highly advantageous." Another historian of the province,
Alexander Hewatt, an extreme foe of paper money at the time he wrote,
acknowledged the benefit of currency emissions to a "growing colony"
like South Carolina, provided they were kept within bounds.

Virginia's treasurer, Robert Carter Nicholas, expressed the view of a
conservative planter. In a public defense of the government's conduct in
emitting paper money, he declared that the outbreak of the French and
Indian War had made it absolutely necessary. Sufficient funds could be
obtained in no other way, and, though hesitant at first, the assembly
found no other course open. Nicholas himself knew well the dangers of a
paper medium and was conversant with the arguments against it, including the pamphlet of William Douglass, its ardent foe in New England.

But Nicholas believed that the evils discovered in some places did not arise from paper money as such. "They have been chiefly, if not totally owing," he wrote, "either to these Bills of Credit not being established upon proper Funds, or to a Superabundance of them or to some Mismanagement." Granting a risk was involved, Nicholas believed that many countries had derived great benefit from paper money. He thought it had been helpful to Virginia.

Nicholas's opinion was much like that of a conservative New York merchant, John Watts, who was highly critical of the restraining act of 1764. Like many others, Watts thought the act would virtually put an end to paper money. "The use of paper money is abolished as an evil," he complained, "when, properly treated, it is the only medium we have left of commerce and the only expedient in an exigency. Every man of estate here abominates the abuse of paper money, because the consequences fall upon himself, but there is just the same difference in the use and abuse of it as there is in food itself . . ."

The writings of the post-Revolutionary era contain many allusions to the success of paper money in colonial times and the esteem in which it was then held. In 1786, a correspondent to a New York newspaper recalled how easily the provinces had maintained their paper money systems:

Before the commencement of the late war, when public faith was still in possession of vestal chastity, divers of the states, then provinces, had large sums in circulation at full value, depending on funds calculated to redeem only five to ten per centum per annum of the amount issued; consequently it must be from ten to twenty years before the whole would be redeemed; and yet, tho' the money drew no interest . . . it circulated freely and at its full nominal value on a perfect equality with specie . . .

As this article appeared, the New York Chamber of Commerce made the same point in declaring its opposition to a paper money issue contemplated by the legislature. The Chamber of Commerce acknowledged that paper money had worked well in colonial times, but argued that this should not be taken as evidence that it would succeed under changed conditions.

An observation frequently made in these times was put down by David Ramsay in his *History of the American Revolution*. Noting that Continental currency held its value during the first year or two of the war, even though it had no security behind it, Ramsay explained: "This was in some degree owing to a previous confidence, which had been begotten by honesty and fidelity, in discharging the engagements of government." Alluding to the same fact, Financier Robert Morris observed: "There was a time when public confidence was higher in America than in any other country."

The inflation of the Revolution destroyed that confidence, at least among propertied men, for they believed that paper money could never be a reliable instrument in an era when the whims of the people dictated, as they said, the policy of the government. A great proportion of the people, however, never lost the old affection for paper money. "From the earliest settlement of America," declared a petition composed in 1785 for presentation to the Pennsylvania legislature, "most of our improvements have been aided by the medium of paper currency . . . and your petitioners are persuaded that . . . public faith might be restored, and the ancient system revived, to the great ease of the inhabitants and emolument of the community." Such an appeal invoked common knowledge.

It becomes clear that paper money occupied an important place in colonial affairs not because it embodied the aims of a particular class, but because it rendered important services to the community.

The circumstances which led to the adoption of paper money are well known. There was not enough hard money to provide a medium of trade for domestic transactions. Gold and silver coins flowed outward in purchase of British commodities and while in the colonies circulated mainly among merchants. Much business was done on the basis of book credits and debits, but specie was nearly always in short supply. Economic depression intensified the problem, for when cargoes did not raise enough to meet debts owed abroad, specie had to be shipped. Domestic trade became almost wholly barter. People who had specie could get an exorbitant premium, and those forced to make payments in hard money faced difficulty. Provincial governments could not collect taxes. The inhabitants felt the need of a medium of exchange which, unlike specie, would not "make unto itself wings and fly away."

The colonies, therefore, adopted paper money. It was issued by two different processes. The first method, in point of time, was the direct emission of fiat money by the government to pay expenses, particularly the costs of war. The other method, which we shall consider immediately, was the emission of money through a loan-office or "land bank."

The land bank was the primary social legislation of colonial America. It was a method of putting currency into circulation and at the same time affording loans to farmers which they could scarcely obtain from other sources. Provincial governments set up loan offices which advanced currency to farmers at low rates of interest, taking mortgages on real property as security. An individual could usually get only a limited sum. He repaid the loan in annual installments over a period of years. Frequently, though not always, the bills were legal tender in private transactions; in any case, they were almost always accepted in payments to the government for taxes, land, etc. As the annual installments due on the principal came back into the loan office, the bills were cancelled and retired, though they were often reissued, or successive banks established to keep up a continuous flow of loans. The colonies thus developed a medium of exchange out of "solid or real property . . . melted down and made to circulate in paper money or bills of credit."

The land banks of the middle colonies were, from all accounts, markedly successful. Pennsylvania managed one almost continuously after 1723 without mishap. For more than twenty-five years before the French and Indian War, the interest received by the government from money out on loan supported the costs of provincial administration, without the necessity of direct taxes. Relative freedom from taxation probably contributed to Pennsylvania's remarkable growth.

Other middle colonies also obtained good results. New Jersey enacted three separate loans up to 1735, and the interest enabled the government to exist without direct taxation for sixteen years before 1751. Delaware issued land bank notes from 1723 to 1746, with apparent benefit to the province. New York extended its land bank of 1737 until the last installment of the principal fell due in 1768, at which time all classes demanded its renewal. The bank was reinstituted in 1771 by virtue of the special act of Parliament, of which mention has already been made. Governor Tryon's report in 1774 showed that the interest from loans comprised about half the revenue of the province, an amount which nearly matched expenses in time of peace.

The notes which Maryland issued on loan in 1733 fell considerably below par, but later rose to nominal value. A modern historian writes:

Considering the peculiar benefits to grain and tobacco culture, the conveniences offered to trade, the exceptionally high exchange that the bills maintained throughout most of their life, and the faithful redemption of every shilling at face value, it is hardly too much to say that this was the most successful paper money issued by any of the colonies.

A new bank was instituted in 1769, and the notes stayed at par until the Revolution.

Virginia never adopted a land bank. In North and South Carolina, land banks figured in the early depreciation of paper money, and it became the settled policy of the British government to disallow acts for their establishment. Similarly, as is well known, the land banks of the New England colonies, particularly those of Rhode Island, contributed to the decline of currency in that area and brought on the first statutory regulation of paper money by Parliament.

This system of agricultural credit so widely practiced in the colonies would seem to be a subject of considerable importance for social and economic history, yet it has not received the attention it deserves. The economist, Richard A. Lester, offers a general view of the use of land bank emissions to curb depressions, and it may be added that such a background of experience explains why even after the financial chaos of the Revolution, the common people still looked to paper money for relief from hard times. But the subject has further ramifications. Agriculture's need for credit facilities has been a constant factor in American history and a source of political unrest. Banks have served commerce and industry; until lately, agriculture remained at a disadvantage. It should be an interesting fact that colonial governments loaned money to farmers at low rates of interest. But no analysis has been made of the effects of land bank loans in the domestic economy, nor has anyone yet approached the general subject with sufficient breadth of view to place it in its relationship to the main currents of American development.

The revenue problems of colonial governments were lessened by land bank emissions; taxes were more easily collected when citizens had access to money. During the frequent wars of the eighteenth century, however, the provinces developed another use of paper money. They emitted it to pay governmental expenses. The procedure became a rationalized system of public finance.

Provincial revenues were normally small and inflexible. Officials drew fees rather than salaries, and the few public services were performed mainly by local government. Such provinces as Pennsylvania and New York spent no more than £5,000 a year apart from war expenses. Taxation was adjusted to limited needs. Imposts and excise taxes usually afforded a maintaining fund, while direct levies on polls and property raised what else was needed. None of these revenues could be freely expanded. Heavy duties on imports tended to drive off trade or cause smuggling. Direct taxes were often hard to collect and slow coming in.

Colonial governments found it difficult or impossible to borrow money from their own citizens. Private capital was tied up in lands or commodities. No banks or business corporations existed with liquid capital which could be enlisted in the public service. When a war or other emergency required large outlays, colonial governments knew no alternative but to issue paper money. Massachusetts hit upon this device in 1690, and eventually all the colonies took it up. "Currency finance" became the regular mode of financing government during war and often, as well, in time of peace.

Practice varied in details, but over the period in which the colonies experimented, they regularized their procedure in something like a system conducted on the basis of known principles. The one exception was Massachusetts, which went on a sound money basis in the 1750's. Elsewhere, methods fall into a pattern that can be described in general terms.

The essential feature of the system was that it avoided dealing in hard money. During a war, for instance, colonial legislatures printed, from time to time, the money needed to pay their expenses. Usually, the act which authorized the emission also appropriated sufficient taxes to withdraw the money from circulation. If expenses were large, the taxes for several years ahead might be pledged to the redemption of money issued during a single year.

The credit of the bills depended on several interrelated factors. Regardless of any promise on the face of the notes, the basic security was the fund assigned to withdraw the money. The holder had to be certain that all taxes and payments to the government taken together would be enough to create a general use for the bills and ensure a demand for them. He must rest easy in the knowledge that withdrawals would be continuous and that future governments would have the ability and the will to collect taxes. As this money was created and upheld by political acts, confidence in government was essential to its value.

Meanwhile, the value of the money was sustained by its current usages, as in paying fees, buying land from the province, or use in ordinary trade. So long as there was no great reason to question it, the people accepted currency in day-to-day transactions because it was the recognized medium of exchange. Colonial legislators, however, knew something about the quantity theory of money and understood that the amount must not exceed too far the requirements of trade at existing price levels, else depreciation would occur regardless of guarantees.

The system appears to have worked against the accumulation of public debt. The debt at any particular time consisted of bills of credit in circulation; to retire it, the government levied taxes payable in the certificates of indebtedness themselves. If the debt was large, paper money was apt to be correspondingly plentiful and widely distributed. The people were taxed in a medium readily accessible to them. As withdrawals reduced the supply of currency and it became concentrated into fewer hands, the debt was by that token rendered less onerous, until at some point the taxes imposed to cancel it could be discontinued and the remaining currency left in circulation. Under the benign operation of currency finance, the facility with which the public debt could be retired was in rough proportion to its size.

Other means than currency were used to anticipate future income. Colonial governments, and to a much greater extent the state governments of the Revolution, issued various kinds of warrants and certificates which, though often given an extensive circulation, did not serve as a medium of exchange to the same degree as paper money. With certain exceptions, however, these notes were issued and redeemed on the same terms as currency. In spite of variations, therefore, it is possible to trace a basic pattern in the financial methods employed by the colonies. They met expenses by issuing a paper medium, whether currency or certificates, directly to individuals in payment for goods and services. They redeemed this paper not by giving specie to those who held it, but by accepting it for taxes or other payments to the government. This was the system of currency finance.

It was not a system which would stand the strain of a prolonged and expensive war. Nonetheless, it sufficed for the wars in which the colonies engaged. During the French and Indian War, for example, New York emitted £535,000. Pennsylvania, whose currency normally stood at £80,000, issued £540,000. Virginia authorized £440,000. Other colonies made extraordinary contributions. The Board of Trade estimated that the North American provinces spent £2,500,000 sterling beyond their ordinary costs of government. About £800,000 of this represented expenditures of Massachusetts, the sound money colony. The remainder of £1,700,000 sterling consisted almost entirely of currency or certificates issued in the expectation that they would be retired only by acceptance for taxes and other payments to the government. In spite of the volume of this paper, little or no depreciation appears to have resulted in most provinces. The colonies benefited from expenditures of the home government, and from large British subsidies which put specie in their hands.

Debt retirement was rapid after the war. Virginia's currency was down to £206,000 by 1767, according to the treasurer's report, and though two small post-war emissions restored some money to circulation, only £54,391 was afloat in 1773. Pennsylvania, no longer tax free, made regular withdrawals until the Revolution. In New York, an acute shortage of currency existed by 1768. Elsewhere, the provinces quickly freed themselves of their debts. A speaker in the House of Commons observed in 1766 that they had already retired £1,755,000, and that most of the remaining debt of £760,000 could be written off within two years.

How much this happy situation was due to British subsidies is hard to know. During the war, Parliament granted over £150,000 sterling for distribution among the American colonies, a sum which was nearly half of the £2,500,000 estimated as their war expenses. Even so, when one compares their real expenditures during the war with the sums involved in their ordinary fiscal operations, it appears that they made what was for them a most unusual effort, and the ease with which they retired their debts must in some measure be attributed to the peculiar facility offered by the methods of currency finance.

British policy on matters pertaining to colonial currency is a subject which has scarcely been touched. No doubt it was a factor of greater importance in imperial relations than is commonly understood. From the one considerable treatment available, it appears that most of the time the British government acknowledged the necessity of colonial emissions. Before 1740, the Board of Trade was "reluctantly sympathetic and essentially reasonable" in sanctioning both land bank loans and direct emissions. The Board, however, always opposed making currency a legal tender in private transactions, even though it approved laws for this purpose. Generally speaking, the Board tried to regulate colonial issues by ensuring that the amounts were reasonable, that funds for redemption were adequate, and that emissions were withdrawn within a limited period of time. Control was exerted largely through instructions to governors, who were ordered to refuse assent to laws which did not have a clause suspending their execution until approved by the crown.

Supervision was not effective and lapsed almost completely during frequent periods of war. As currency emissions were the only way the provinces could furnish aid, governors were permitted to approve acts without a suspending clause, provided the Board's other stipulations were satisfied. The colonies took advantage of their bargaining position, however, to procure the governors' assent to laws which did not comply with the Board's requirements. Neither governors nor the crown could afford to scrutinize too closely the modes by which assistance was rendered.

War still hindered the enforcement of policy, but British control tightened after 1740. Rhode Island's emissions were a flagrant abuse. The Board also appears to have been more susceptible to complaints of British merchants, some of whom claimed injury from legal tender laws. The same mercantile and creditor interests carried their appeals to Parliament, with the result that after 1750 the standing instructions of the Board of Trade were given statutory effect.

The act of 1751 applied only to New England. It did not abolish the paper money system even in that area, as is sometimes supposed, but merely established rules for carrying it on. Bills already in circulation were to be retired in strict accord with the terms of the issuing acts. When these were withdrawn, no paper money was to be legal tender. The provinces were allowed to emit bills from year to year to pay governmental expenses, provided they committed taxes sufficient to redeem them within two years. This clause was flexible enough to accommodate a moderate expansion of currency. In event of war or other emergency, all curbs were relaxed as to the amount which could be issued, provided enough taxes were appropriated to redeem the bills within five years. The act of 1751 left the colonies outside New England undisturbed. Within New England, its major effect was to prohibit legal tender laws and to rule out land banks.

The restraining act of 1764 came at the end of the French and Indian War, when the colonies had large sums outstanding. As first drafted, it would have placed all the provinces under the curbs imposed on New England. In its final form, it merely prohibited legal tender laws and required that existing legal tender currencies be sunk at their expiration dates. Many colonies protested, in the belief that the legal tender feature was an essential prop to their money. Experience was to show, however, that the restriction did not materially impair the workings of the currency system.

There is more than a hint that by this time Britain's policy as to paper money was subordinated to the larger purpose of securing a permanent civil list, and that attempts were being made to trade approval of colonial emissions for the grant of a fixed revenue to the crown. Even so, the colonies made headway against British restraints, though they could not again pass legal tender laws. New York was permitted to renew its land bank in 1771. After a long struggle, New Jersey exacted consent for the establishment of a land bank in 1774. Pennsylvania continued to emit currency and in 1773 renewed its land bank. Maryland issued £173,733 to pay war debts and over half a million doilars to finance improvements and to establish a land bank. Virginia's council annulled two land bank acts passed by the lower house, but the province emitted £40,000 for other purposes. North Carolina, closely confined by the British government, issued treasury notes and debenture bills, while South Carolina emitted "public orders" and "tax certificates," which were in effect a non-legal tender currency.

Parliament in 1773 legalized colonial monetary practices as carried on under the restrictive acts of 1751 and 1764. A question had arisen as to how far the prohibition of legal tender applied. To clarify the matter, Parliament passed an explanatory act which declared that the prohibition ruled out only those laws which made currency legal tender in private transactions. The colonies were allowed to make it legal tender in payments to the government. In stating the latitude permitted by existing law, Parliament defined the essential workings of the currency finance system. The act is worth quoting because it verifies the general survey given above:

Whereas the want of gold and silver currency in several of his Majesty's colonies and plantations in America may make it necessary, as well for the publick advantage as in justice to those persons who may have demands upon the publick treasuries in the said colonies for services performed, that such publick creditors should be secured in the payment of their just debts and demands, by certificates, notes, bills, or debentures, to be created and issued by the authority of the general assemblies . . . on the securities of any taxes or duties given and granted to his Majesty—for and towards defraying expenses incurred for publick services; and that such certificates, notes, bills, or debentures, should be made chargeable on the publick treasurers of the said colonies and received and taken by them as a legal tender in discharge of any such duties or taxes, or of any debts whatsoever, due to the publick treasuries . . . be it enacted . . . That . . . any certificates, notes, bills or debentures which shall . . . be voluntarily accepted by the creditors of the publick . . . may be made . . . to be a legal tender for the publick treasurers . . . for the discharge of any duties, taxes, or other debts whatsoever . . .

Had the Revolution not occurred, Britain might have reached a solution of colonial monetary problems. As early as 1754, Richard Jackson and Franklin exchanged plans to form one or more land banks based on capital loaned from the Bank of England or subscribed by private investors. It was expected that land bank notes would provide a circulating medium for the continent. Later, when the Stamp Act was under discussion, Franklin and Thomas Pownall broached a similar scheme, as an alternative way of gaining a revenue from the colonies. They envisaged a continental land bank with a branch office in each province, centrally managed in Britain. The bank was to issue legal tender notes on loan at 5 per cent interest, the principal to be repaid over a period of ten years. The notes would circulate as currency throughout the American colonies. Franklin and Pownall pressed this scheme for three or four years.

By 1767, it appears that the Secretary of Trade concurred in the idea that the restraining act of 1764 should be modified to permit the colonies to establish loan offices which would emit legal tender notes valid for all transactions except payment of sterling debts. A bill for this purpose was being prepared and the ground laid for its introduction into the House of Commons, when the colonial agents learned that the Commons would probably seize the opportunity to declare the income arising from the loan offices subject to the appropriation of the crown. As the colonial agents could not risk this outcome, they gave up the project. Saying he had hoped to make better use of his plan for a continental land bank, Pownall published the details of it in the 1768 edition of his Administration of the Colonies.

Any solution of the money problem under British auspices was forestalled by the Revolution. When it was too late, the British government instructed its peace commissioners of 1778 in a number of schemes which might have borne fruit if attempted earlier.

A view of the evidence suggests that generations of historical scholarship have fostered a mistaken impression of the monetary practices of the colonies. The efforts of the American provinces to create a medium of exchange, erect a system of agricultural credit, and equip their governments with the means of incurring and discharging responsibilities, hardly constitute a "dark and disgraceful" picture; nor, on the whole, is the record one of failure. Most of the colonies handled their currency with discretion and were successful in realizing the purposes associated with its use. Except for New England, where depreciation had given it a bad name, paper money was the "ancient system," which had long served well the needs of trade and the ordinary processes of government. Although mindful of its dangers, men of property accepted it as useful and necessary. In time of war, all the colonies but one were fully prepared to adopt the methods of currency finance as the only way of meeting an emergency. Emissions might then be over-large, as the Revolution was to prove, but the common need precluded any nice regard for the effect on contracts.

FOR FURTHER READING: M. L. Burstein, "Colonial Currency and Contemporary Monetary Theory: A Review Article," *Explorations in Entrepreneurial History*, III (Spring, 1966), pp. 220–233, emphasizes the relevance of colonial monetary problems to twentieth-century experience. Roger Weiss, "The Issue of Paper Money in the American Colonies, 1720–1774," *Journal of Economic History*, XXX (December, 1970), pp. 770–784, surveys the views of various writers on this issue. Arno Press has published a standard work, L. van Horn Brock, *The Currency of the American Colonies, 1700–1764* (New York, 1978).

5

ECONOMIC GROWTH AND THE AMERICAN REVOLUTION

PROBLEM: *Did the economic expansion of the American colonies contribute to the outbreak of the Revolution?*

One of the most controversial issues in American Colonial History revolves about the effects of British mercantilism on the economic development of the colonies. Did British regulations restrict American trade and manufacturing? Thus, the Navigation Act of 1660 allowed the shipment of Colonial goods only in British or American bottoms. It also provided for certain enumerated commodities such as sugar and tobacco, which Americans were allowed to sell only in British markets. Manufacturing regulations such as the Woolens Act of 1699, the Hat Act of 1732, and the Iron Act of 1750 were designed to limit the competition of artisans in the colonies with those of the mother country. At the same time the Currency Act of 1751 prohibited the issuance of paper money by New England legislatures. But, while these acts appeared formidable on the statute books, few were enforced consistently or effectively before 1763. Moreover, many Colonial merchants enjoyed increasing prosperity in the eighteenth century. Nor is the evidence conclusive to indicate that British regulations seriously retarded colonial manufacturing. Since the effects of British mercantile legislation are not clearly discernible it is not surprising that historians have disagreed over the impact of British mercantilism on the colonies, and its influence in fomenting Revolutionary sentiment. Representative of one group is Robert P. Thomas, who argued that British imperial

79

policies did not restrict American economic growth. Applying quantitative methods, Thomas concluded that British mercantile legislation did not affect the colonies negatively, and placed few, if any, injurious burdens on Americans. Such a view challenged the conclusions of historians like Lawrence A. Harper who, in assessing the evidence, believed that British policies did indeed place heavy burdens on the colonists and kindled their sentiments for independence. The arguments presented by these divergent analyses form a brief introduction to one of the major problems concerning public policies in the Colonial era. Was there a mercantilist "system"? How did British imperial legislation retard or promote the American economy? In what ways did British imperial restrictions promote Revolutionary sentiment?

A Quantitative Approach to the Study of the Effects of British Imperial Policy upon Colonial Welfare: Some Preliminary Findings

ROBERT P. THOMAS

Historians have long debated whether the American colonies on balance benefited or were hindered by British imperial regulation. George Bancroft thought the regulations worked a definite hardship on the colonies. George L. Beer believed these regulations nicely balanced and that the colonies shared in the general advantages. Lawrence Harper, in a now classic article, actually attempted to calculate the cost and found that British policies "placed a heavy burden upon the colonies." Oliver Dickerson wrote that "no case can be made . . . that such laws were economically oppressive," while Curtis P. Nettels, writing at the same time to the same point, stated: "British policy as it affected the colonies after 1763 was restrictive, injurious, negative." It is quite evident that a difference of opinion exists among reputable colonial historians over this important historical issue.

In this paper an effort is made to meet this issue head on. I shall attempt to measure, relative to a hypothetical alternative, the extent of the burdens and benefits stemming from imperial regulation of the foreign com-

Reprinted with permission from *The Journal of Economic History*, XXXI (1971), pp. 420–428.

merce of the thirteen colonies. The main instruments of this regulation were the Navigation Acts, and we shall confine our attention to evaluating the effect of these Acts upon colonial welfare. Various other imperial regulations such as the Revenue Acts, enacted after 1764, the modification of naturalization and land regulations, the interference with colonial issues of paper money, and the various regulations discouraging manufactures will not be dealt with in this paper. The assumption is that the direct effects of these regulations upon the economic welfare of the American colonists were insignificant compared to the effects of the Navigation Acts.

The hypothesis of this paper is that membership in the British Empire, after 1763, did not impose a significant hardship upon the American colonies. To test this hypothesis I shall endeavor to bias the estimates against the hypothesis, thus not attempting to state what actually would have happened but only that it would not have amounted to as much as my estimate. The end result will, therefore, err on the side of overstating the real costs of the Navigation Acts to the thirteen colonies.

The traditional tools of economic theory will guide the preparation of these estimates. Two series of estimates will be prepared where possible: one, an annual average for the period 1763–1772, based upon official values; the other, for the single year 1770. The official trade statistics for the year 1770 have been adjusted to make them more accurate.

*   *   *

Is it legitimate for the historian to consider alternative possibilities to events which have happened? . . . To say that a thing happened the way it did is not at all illuminating. We can understand the significance of what did happen only if we contrast it with what might have happened.

MORRIS RAPHAEL COHEN

All attempts at measurement require a standard to which the object being measured is made relative or compared. In the case of this paper, the colonies either on balance benefited or were burdened by British imperialism, relative to how they would have fared under some alternative political situation. The problem is to pick the most probable alternative situation.

The only reasonable alternative in this case is to calculate the burdens or benefits of British regulation relative to how the colonies would have fared outside the British Empire but still within a mercantilist world. Considered within this political environment there is little doubt that prior to February 1763, when the Treaty of Paris was signed, the American colonies on balance benefited from membership in the British Empire. Before that date, the colonies were threatened on two sides by two superior colonial powers. C. M. Andrews has pointed out that, before 1763, in addition to remaining within the protection of Great Britain, the

American colonies had only one other alternative: domination by another European power, probably France or Spain. Clearly, from a colonial point of view, belonging to the British Empire was superior to membership in any other.

The French and Indian War ended the menace of foreign domination through the cession to Great Britain of Canada by the French and of Florida by Spain. Immediately, thereupon, several Englishmen voiced their fears that these spoils of victory, by removing the foreign threat, made inevitable the independence of the American colonies. Even the French Foreign Minister, Choiseul, lent his voice to this speculation when, soon after the Treaty of Paris, he predicted the eventual coming of the American Revolution. In 1764, Choiseul went so far as to send his agents to America to watch developments. Knollenberg has pointed out that English suspicions of a desire for independence on the part of the colonies do not prove that the suspicions were well founded. They do, however, suggest that an independent America was, by 1763, a distinct possibility; and thereafter the American colonists possessed another alternative to membership in a European empire. This alternative was an independent existence outside the British Empire but still within a mercantilist world.

The alternative situation that I shall employ to calculate the economic effects of the Navigation Acts after 1763 is that of a free and independent thirteen colonies outside the British Empire. This new nation would, therefore, be subject to most of the same restrictions hindering foreign nations attempting to carry on commerce with the eighteenth-century British Empire.

*   *   *

Had the wealth and economic potential of the thirteen Atlantic colonies depended solely on farming, their growth history might have paralleled that of many another slowly developing agricultural settlement. However . . . an indigenous commercial economy developed, unique in colonial history and conducive to sustained growth.

GEORGE ROGERS TAYLOR

This "unique" commercial economy developed within the British Empire subject to the rules and regulations of the Navigation Acts. The American colonies in a sense grew up with the empire, which after the successful conclusion of the Seven Years' War in February 1763, was the wealthiest, most populous colonial empire in the world. It included the kingdom of Great Britain and Ireland with the outlying islands of Europe; trading forts on the Gold Coast of Africa; enclaves in India, and some minor islands in Asia; Newfoundland, Hudson Bay, Nova Scotia, Quebec, the thirteen American colonies, East Florida, and West Florida on the continent of North America; the Bahamas, Bermuda, Jamaica, Antigua,

Barbados, and the Leeward and Windward groups of minor islands in the West Indies, as well as the settlement of Belize in Central America.

The American colonies by 1763 formed the foundation of Great Britain's Atlantic empire and had become, as a group, England's most important commercial ally. The basis of this commerce was a vigorous colonial export trade. The total exports in 1770 amounted to £3,165,225. Trade with Great Britain and Ireland accounted for 50 per cent of colonial exports. The West Indies trade constituted another 30 per cent, and commerce with southern Europe and the Wine Islands, another 17 per cent. Trade with Africa and South America accounted for most of the residual.

The colonists, of course, used their exports to purchase imports. They were Great Britain's most important customer and Great Britain their most important supplier. The British Isles shipped to the American colonies in 1768 (a year for which a detailed breakdown is available) £2,157,000 worth of goods, or nearly 75 per cent of all colonial imports, which totaled £2,890,000. Of this, £421,000 were British reexports from northern Europe. The West Indies, the other important source of imports, accounted for 20.5 per cent of the colonial imports; southern Europe and the Wine Islands, 2.9 per cent; and Africa, a little less than 2.0 per cent.

The thirteen American colonies carried on this foreign commerce subject to the constraints of a series of laws designed to alter the trade of the British Empire in the interests of the mother country. This commercial system can be viewed as being made up of four types of laws: (1) laws regulating the nationality, crews, and ownership of the vessels in which goods could be shipped; (2) statutes regulating the destination to which certain goods could be shipped; (3) laws designed to encourage specific primary industries via an elaborate system of rebates, drawbacks, import and export bounties, and export taxes; (4) direct prohibition of colonial industries and practices that tended to compete with English industries or to harm a prominent sector of the British economy or even, occasionally, the economy of a British colony. These laws, it should be stressed, did not regulate the American colonies alone, but with occasional local modifications applied equally to the entire British Empire.

The laws regulating the nationality of vessels were designed to insure a monopoly of the carrying trade of the empire to ships of the empire. In the seventeenth and eighteenth centuries the freight factor on goods traded internationally probably averaged at least 20 per cent, and these laws were designed to insure that this revenue stayed within the empire. The Navigation Acts also insured, to the extent that they were effective, that England would be the entrepôt of the empire and that the distributing trade would be centered in the British Isles.

The commodity clauses of these various regulatory Acts controlled the destination to which certain goods could be shipped. These enumerated commodities generally could be shipped only to England. The original list contained tobacco, sugar, indigo, cotton-wool, ginger, fustic and other dyewoods. Later, naval stores, hemp, rice, molasses, beaver skins, furs, and copper ore were added. The Sugar Act of 1764 added coffee, pimiento, coconuts, whale fins, raw silk, hides and skins, potash and pearl ash to the list. In 1766, the law was amended to prohibit the direct export of any colonial product north of Cape Finisterre.

There were exceptions and compensations to these commodity clauses which benefited the American colonies. Rice, after 1730, could be directly exported south of Cape Finisterre and, after 1764, to South America. Tobacco was given a monopoly in Great Britain, as its local cultivation was prohibited. While the list appears extensive, of the enumerated commodities only tobacco, indigo, copper ore, naval stores, hemp, furs and skins, whale fins, raw silk, and potash and pearl ash were products of the thirteen colonies, and only tobacco, rice, and perhaps indigo and naval stores could be considered major exports of the colonies that later became the United States.

An elaborate series of laws was enacted by the English Parliament to encourage specific industries in the interest of a self-sufficient empire. These included preferential tariffs for certain goods of colonial origin. A distinctive feature of these laws was an elaborate system of rebates and drawbacks to encourage the exports of certain commodities from England and extensive bounties to encourage the production of specific goods for export to Great Britain.

Most enumerated goods benefited from a preferential duty. These goods were thus given a substantial advantage in the markets of the mother country. Goods receiving preferential treatment included cotton-wool, ginger, sugar, molasses, coffee, tobacco, rice, naval stores, pitch, rosin, hemp, masts, whale fins, raw silk, potash and pearl ash, bar and pig iron, and various types of lumber. Certain of these goods also received drawbacks of various amounts upon their reexport from Great Britain. Foreign goods competing in the English market with enumerated colonial commodities were thus subject to a disadvantage from these preferential duties.

A system of bounties was also implemented to encourage the production of specific commodities in the colonies or to allow the British manufacturers to compete with foreign exports in the colonial markets. The production of naval stores, silk, lumber, indigo, and hemp was encouraged in the colonies with bounties. In the mother country the manufacture of linen, gunpowder, silks, and many nonwoolen textiles was encouraged by a bounty to allow these products to compete with similar foreign manufactures in the colonial markets.

Certain of the colonial commodities favored by legislation were given what amounted to a monopoly of the home market of the mother country. The colonial production of tobacco, naval stores, sugar and sugar products was so favored. In the case of tobacco, the major share of total imports was reexported, so the local monopoly proved not a great boon.

In economic terms, the Navigation Acts were designed to insure that the vast bulk of the empire's carrying trade was in ships owned by Englishmen. The design of the commodity clauses was to alter the terms of trade to the disadvantage of the colonists, by making all foreign imports into the colonies, and many colonial exports whose final destination was the Continent, pass through England. The effect was to make colonial imports more expensive and colonial exports less remunerative by increasing the transportation costs of both. Finally, through tariff preferences, bounties, and outright prohibitions, resources were allocated from more efficient uses to less.

I shall approach the problem of assessing the overall effect of the various British regulations of trade by considering their effect on the . . . exports of colonial products. . . . An assessment will then be undertaken of compensating benefits arising from membership in the British Empire. Finally, an attempt will be made to strike a balance on the total impact of British imperial policy upon the colonial economy.

*　　*　　*

The enumeration of key colonial exports in various Acts . . . hit at colonial trade both coming and going. The Acts . . . placed a heavy burden upon the colonies.

LAWRENCE HARPER

In spite of the extravagant language that has been used to condemn the system, the grower of enumerated commodities was not enslaved by the legal provisions of enumeration . . . . Enumeration clearly did not hamper the expansion of the tobacco raising business in America . . . . It has been assumed by many writers that enumeration imposed a serious burden upon rice planters. The ascertainable facts do not support this assumption.

OLIVER DICKERSON

The export trade between the colonies and the mother country was subjected to regulations which significantly altered its value and composition over what it would have been if the colonies had been independent. The total adjusted value of exports from the American colonies to Great Britain in 1770 was £1,458,000, of which £1,107,000, or 76 per cent, were enumerated goods. Such goods were required to be shipped directly to Great Britain. The largest part, 85.4 per cent, of the enumerated goods was subsequently reexported to northern Europe and thus when competing in these markets bore the burden of an artificial, indirect routing through England to the Continent. The costs of this indirect route took the form of an added transhipment, with the consequent port charges and fees, middlemen's commissions, and what import duties were retained upon reexport. The enumerated goods consumed in England benefited from preferential duties relative to goods of foreign production. A few of these enumerated commodities also were favored with import bounties.

The additional transport costs borne by enumerated goods upon their reexport had the effect of lowering the prices received by the colonial producer and depressing the quantity exported. In economic terms, the world market price as shown in Graph 1 would, in the absence of regulation, be P_2 and exports would be Q_2. The effect of the additional cost of shipment through England is to raise the price to the consumer to P_3. Colonial exports, consequently, are reduced to Q_1. Therefore, both consumers and producers suffer from the enumeration of colonial exports whose final destination is not England.

The incidence of this burden depends upon the elasticities of supply and demand for the product. The direct cost to the producer as shown in Graph 1 is the unit burden times the quantity produced ($P_2P_1 \cdot Q_1$). The burden on the reduced output is equal to the return that would be earned on the additional output over what the resources would earn in their next-best alternative. This cost is illustrated by the shaded triangle in Graph 1 and represents the sum of the direct and indirect burdens.

In order to calculate the direct burden borne by the colonial producers of enumerated goods that were reexported from England, we need to know three separate time series. In the case of tobacco, we need to know the world market price in a European port, the price actually received in the colonies, and the actual reexports of tobacco from England—all three of which are readily available.

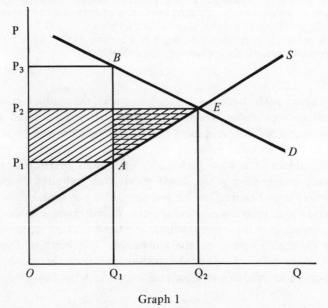

Graph 1

The price that would have existed in the colonies in the absence of enumeration can be estimated, given the above information. It was estimated by dividing the observed Amsterdam price of Virginia tobacco before the Revolution by the ratio of Amsterdam to Philadelphia tobacco prices after the Revolution. The postwar ratio of prices reflects the advantages received by the colonists by shipping directly to northern Europe rather than indirectly through England. This procedure provides us with an estimate of the price of tobacco in the colonies (P_2 on Graph 1) had tobacco not been subject to enumeration. The difference between the estimated price (P_2) and the actual price (P_1) is the unit burden suffered by reexported colonial tobacco.

Calculated in this manner, the price of tobacco in 1770 colonial America, had the colonies been independent, would have been over 49 per cent higher than it actually was. The average price for the decade 1763–1772 would have been 34 per cent higher than was actually recorded. These higher prices indicate that tobacco planters suffered a burden on the tobacco they actually grew in 1770 of £262,000 and, for the decade, an average annual burden of £177,000.

The direct burden is only a portion of the total colonial loss due to enumeration. The hypothetical higher tobacco prices would certainly have stimulated an increase in the supply of tobacco. Assuming that a 1 per cent increase in price would generate a 1 per cent increase in supply, the resulting increase in supply would have been about 39,000,000 pounds in 1770, or an annual average of 29,000,000 pounds for the decade. The loss to the colonies of this foregone output is the calculated value of the shaded triangle in Graph 1, which is £64,000 for 1770, or an average of £30,000 for the decade. Thus, the total burden on tobacco amounts to £326,000 for the year 1770, or an average of £207,000 for the period 1763–1772.

The calculation of the encumbrance suffered by rice proceeded in the same manner as the calculation of the burden on tobacco, except that Charleston prices were used instead of Philadelphia prices since South Carolina was the center of colonial rice production. The burden on the price of rice reexports was calculated to be an appreciable 105 per cent. This amounted to £95,000 in 1770, or £110,000 average for the decade 1763–1772.

The indirect loss attributable to the expected increase in rice exports with the increase in price amounted to £25,000 for 1770, or an average of £29,000 for the longer period. In the case of rice, an elasticity of supply of .5 was assumed, due to the limited area of southern marshlands suitable to the cultivation of rice. The whole burden on rice products totaled £120,000 for 1770, or an average of £139,000 for the period 1763–1772.

Tobacco and rice together accounted for the vast bulk of the enumerated products that were reexported and therefore bore most of the burden. If we apply the weighted average of the tobacco and rice burden to the remainder of enumerated reexports, and adjust for the expected increase in supply, we obtain an estimated additional burden of £53,000 for 1770, or an annual average of £35,000 for the ten-year period.

However, to arrive at the total burden on enumerated exports we must allow for the benefits that colonial exports received from preferential duties or bounties. Most enumerated commodities benefited from one or the other: beaver skins, furs, and copper ore appear to be the only exceptions. Enumerated goods consumed in Great Britain amounted to £161,570 in 1770, or an average of £126,716 for the decade. The average preference amounted to 38 per cent of the price of enumerated products consumed in the mother country. Again, assuming an elasticity of supply of one, we find that in the absence of these preferential duties the first-order effects would result in a decline in the amount of these enumerated commodities consumed in England of about £61,000 for 1770, or an average of £48,000 for the decade. The benefit of preferential duties to the colonists is the gain enjoyed by those exports that would have been sent to England in the absence of preferential duties had the colonies been independent (or £38,000 in 1770 and £30,000 average for the decade) plus the gain on the commodities actually sent that would not have been sent to England had the colonies been free. This amounted to £17,000 in 1770, or £9,000 as the annual average between 1763 and 1772. The benefit accruing to the colonies from preferential duties thus totals £55,000 for 1770, or £39,000 for the decade average.

In addition to preferential duties, the Crown annually spent large sums

TABLE 1

NET BURDEN ON COLONIAL FOREIGN COMMERCE

	1770	1763–1772
Exports		
Tobacco	£ 326,000	£ 207,000
Rice	120,000	139,000
Other	53,000	35,000
Burden	499,000	381,000
Preference	55,000	39,000
Bounty	33,000	35,000
Benefit	88,000	74,000
Imports		
Burden	121,000	144,000
Net burden on foreign commerce	£ 532,000 or $ 2,660,000	£ 451,000 or $ 2,255,000

in the form of bounties to promote certain industries. The recorded bounties for the year 1770, for instance, totaled £47,344. These payments were designed to divert resources from more efficient uses into industries where they were employed less efficiently but where, for political purposes, they were thought better occupied. Thus it was better to obtain naval stores in the American colonies at a higher cost than to rely upon foreign imports. Part of the bounty, therefore, was a payment for the inefficient allocation of colonial resources and was no gain to the colonies.

The calculation of the approximate proportion of these payments that exceeded the amount required to pay the cost of the inefficiency is not difficult. Since in every case Great Britain continued to import substantial amounts of these commodities from foreign as well as colonial sources, the demand for bountied goods from the colonies can reasonably be assumed to have been perfectly elastic. That is, the colonies could have sold as much of these goods in England as they desired without lowering the market price. This is shown in Graph 2 as a horizontal demand schedule (D) and OB is the market price of the commodity.

The effect of a per-unit bounty is to increase the supply of the commodity; this is shown as an increase in the quantity supplied from Q_1 to Q_2. The net benefit to the colonies of the total bounty (shown on Graph 2 as the area $ABCD$) is the shaded portion of that rectangle. The total bounty payment less the cost of an inefficient use of resources (the unshaded area of the rectangle $ABCD$) gives the net benefit, which must be less than the bounty payment. In order to measure the actual benefit derived by the colonies from the bounty payments we need know only the percentage of the market price represented by the bounty and the elasticity of supply of the commodity.

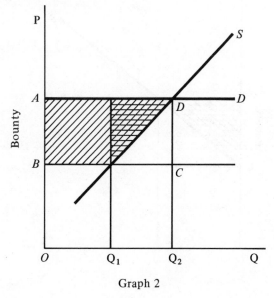

Graph 2

The export of colonial naval stores was stimulated by bounty payments in significant amounts. The average for the decade 1763–1772 totaled £33,000, and for the year 1770 the payment amounted to £29,803. The average bounty amounted to about 28 per cent of the price; therefore, assuming an elasticity of supply of one, the bounty was responsible for roughly 28 per cent of the exports of naval stores to Great Britain. Figured on this basis, the net gain to the colonists from the bounty on naval stores was 86 per cent of the payment. This amounted to an average of £28,000 for the decade, or £26,000 for the single year 1770.

The second largest bounty payments were for the production of indigo; in 1770 this amounted to £8,732 and for the decade an average of £8,065. Evidently, the indigo bounty not only stimulated increased output but was responsible for the entire output, since the production of indigo in the colonies disappeared after independence. Therefore, the net benefits of the indigo bounty are derived by calculating the value of the triangle as shown in Graph 3. In the absence of the bounty, no indigo would have been exported. The effect of the bounty was to stimulate an export equal to Q_1. The net gain to the colonists from the indigo bounty at best is equal to, and is probably something less than, one half the amount of the bounty. We estimated that 50 per cent of the bounty payment for indigo was gain for indigo producers—gain they would not have enjoyed if the colonies had been independent. This totaled £4,400 in 1770, or £4,000 as the annual average for the decade.

The importation of colonial lumber into Great Britain also received a bounty which, according to Beer, totaled £6,557 in 1769. Sufficient data are not available to allow a calculation of the gain to the colonists

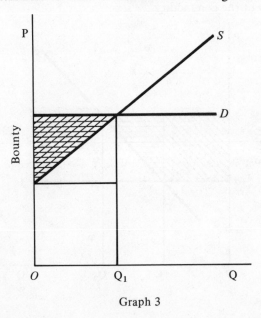

Graph 3

from this payment, but it appears that the bounty was just sufficient to pay the added cost of shipping lumber to England. This payment was necessary to divert lumber from the West Indies, which was the colonies' natural market, and to attract it to England. It appears justifiable to assign the entire payment as the cost of a less efficient use of resources. Nevertheless we shall include 50 per cent as a net gain to the colonists, which amounts to £3,300.

The total net gain to the colonies from the bounties paid for colonial products was, therefore, £33,000 in 1770 and an average of £35,000 for the decade. Our analysis of the effect of the Navigation Acts on colonial exports has included the burden on exports, the benefit of the preferential duties, and the net gain from bounty payments. The sum total of these burdens and benefits is a net burden upon exports of £411,000 for 1770. The average annual burden for the decade 1763–1772 was calculated to be £307,000.

* * *

My findings with reference to the effect of the Navigation Acts upon the economy of the thirteen colonies indicate a net burden of £532,000, or $2,660,000, in 1770. The average burden for the decade 1763–1772, based upon official values, was somewhat lower— £451,000, or $2,255,000. These estimates are near the lowest estimates made by Harper and seem to strengthen his case that exploitation did exist.

Considering for a moment only the value of the losses on colonial exports and imports, the per capita annual cost to the colonist of being an Englishman instead of an American was $1.24 in 1770. The average per capita cost for the decade based upon official values was a somewhat

TABLE 2

SUMMARY OF THE RESULTS

Burdens	1763–1772	1770
Burden on colonial foreign commerce	£ 451,000 or	£ 532,000 or
Burden per capita[a]	$ 2,255,000	$ 2,660,000
Benefits	$ 1.20	$ 1.24
Benefit of British protection	£ 351,000 or	£ 351,000 or
Benefit per capita	$ 1,775,000	$ 1,775,000
Balance[b]	$ .94	$ .82
Estimate 1	$ −.26	$ −.42

[a] Population for the decade average was figured to be 1,881,000, and for 1770 to be 2,148,000.
[b] The balance was obtained by subtracting the per capita benefits from the per capita burden.

lower $1.20. The benefits per capita in 1770 were figured to be 82 cents, and for the decade 94 cents. Subtracting the benefits from the burdens for 1770 shows a per capita loss of 42 cents. The estimate for the decade shows a smaller loss of 26 cents a person. It is unlikely, because of the nature of the estimating procedures employed, that these losses are too low. Conversely it is not at all improbable, and for the same reasons, that the estimated losses are too high.

Suppose that these findings reflect the true magnitude of the cost of the Navigation Acts to the thirteen colonies. The relevant question becomes: How important were these losses? Albert Fishlow ... believed that the average per capita income in the 1780's "could not have been much less than $100." George Rogers Taylor ... hazarded a guess that per capita income did not grow very rapidly, if at all, between 1775 and 1840. Therefore, assuming that average per capita income hovered about $100 between 1763 and 1772, what would it have been had the colonies been independent?

The answer is obvious from Table 2: it would not have been much different. The largest estimated loss on this basis is .54 of 1 per cent of per capita income, or 54 cents on a hundred dollars. Suppose for a moment that my estimates are off by 100 per cent; then, in that case the largest burden would be slightly more than 1 per cent of national income. It is difficult to make a convincing case for exploitation out of these results.

Mercantilism and the American Revolution

LAWRENCE A. HARPER

The cynic who declared that history is the process whereby a complex truth becomes a simplified falsehood may have had in mind interpretations of the American Revolution. Even before the Revolution occurred, Vergennes prophesied that France's loss of Canada would eventually bring it about. The very document which made the severance final attributed the blame to George III, a fashion which has been generally followed. . . . These points are called to attention merely to remind us . . . that there are many interpretations. Our immediate task is to concentrate upon one—the relation of English mercantilism to the American Revolution.

The term "mercantilism" is one of those words which have different meanings for different people. On the one hand, George Louis Beer

Reprinted by permission from Lawrence A. Harper, "Mercantilism and the American Revolution," *Canadian Historical Review*, XXIII, No. 1 (March, 1942), pp. 1–15.

claimed that English mercantilism was a well-balanced system designed for the benefit of the colonies as well as the mother country, and on the other, Sir William Ashley declared that the regulations of English mercantilism were either pious formulas nullified in the actual world of commerce by fraud and evasion, or merely a codification of commercial habits which would have been followed in any case. For reasons which have been explained more fully elsewhere we shall reject Beer's claim that there was no exploitation and accept the statements of the mercantilists themselves that they planned to exploit the colonies for the benefit of the mother country. We shall deny the Ashley view that there was no actual regulation and conclude from more recent studies of the evidence that the English laws did regulate trade and commerce.

These two conclusions provide us with a working definition of English mercantilism in its colonial aspects. It had as its purpose, exploitation, and as its means, regulation. Both phases of the problem, exploitation *and* regulation, are important. To understand the relationship of mercantilism and the Revolution we must not only analyse the extent to which the colonists were exploited but also consider the skill with which they were regulated.

An analysis of how the colonists were exploited is no easy task, as any one knows who has struggled with the many statutory ambiguities involved. The calculations involved in estimating the burdens placed upon the colonial economy are complicated. They call for arithmetical computations involving duties, preferences, or drawbacks of such odd amounts as 1s. 10d. and 15 16/75 of a twentieth of a penny per pound of tobacco. They run afoul of complicated analyses of costs and close decisions about the incidence of taxation. The answer required some thousands of hours of WPA and NYA labour in tabulating the necessary data and hundreds more in analysing and correlating them, the details of which have been compressed in thirty-eight rather dull pages. All that can be attempted here is to state the conclusions and indicate the grounds upon which they are based. We can, however, simplify our analysis of the mercantilist code which exploited the colonies by dividing it into four parts: first, the basic provisions concerning the trans-Atlantic trade; second, the supplementary measures restricting manufactures; third, the subsidiary rules with reference to the American trade; and fourth, the much discussed measures enacted after the French and Indian War.

In examining the first part, we find that the basic provisions concerning the trans-Atlantic trade placed a heavy burden upon the colonies. By means of the Navigation Acts England attempted both to keep foreign vessels out of the colonies and to enable English merchants to share in the more profitable parts of the trans-Atlantic trade. The enumeration of key colonial exports in various Acts from 1660 to 1766 and the Staple Act of 1663 hit at colonial trade both coming and going. The Acts required the colonies to allow English middlemen to distribute such crops as tobacco and rice and stipulated that if the colonies would not buy English manufactures, at least they should purchase their European goods in England. The greatest element in the burden laid upon the colonies was not the taxes assessed. It consisted in the increased costs of shipment, transshipment, and middleman's profits arising out of the requirement that England be used as an *entrepôt*.

The burdens were somewhat lightened by legislation favouring the colonies, but not as much as usually alleged. The suppression of tobacco production in England, for example, was comparatively unimportant to the colonies since the great quantities of colonial tobacco re-exported caused its price to be determined by a world rather than an English market. Moreover, the motive was not goodwill for the colonists but fiscal, since the heavy revenues derived from tobacco could be collected more easily at the waterfront than upon the farm. Likewise, although colonial shipbuilders and shipowners approved the clauses of the Navigation Acts which eliminated Dutch rivals, they did not need such protection. They had managed to carry cargoes and to build ships which could be sold in the world market before the laws were enacted and they continued to do so after the Revolution. The fact is that colonial shipowners suffered, directly, and colonial shipbuilders, indirectly, under the Navigation Acts since other clauses enabled English shipowners (as contrasted with American) to carry eighty per cent of the trade between the British Isles and the Thirteen Colonies whereas they carried only twenty per cent after the Revolution.

Similarly the drawbacks, bounties, and tariff preferences, of which we are so often reminded, did not materially offset the burdens placed upon the trans-Atlantic trade. The drawbacks paid by English customs authorities on foreign products re-exported to the colonies should not be listed as a benefit to the colonies. There would have been no duties to be drawn back except for the requirement that the colonists purchase their European goods in England. The portion of the duties which England retained, while less than it might have been, was obviously greater than nothing at all. Likewise, *bounties paid upon English manufactures* exported to the colonies, were of advantage to the English producer, who received them whether his goods were exported to the colonies or anywhere else, rather than of benefit to the colonial consumer who otherwise would, and often did, buy competitive European goods.

On the other hand, however, the bounties páid upon colonial products were of real advantage to the colonies. They sustained the growth of indigo in South Carolina, did much to foster the development of naval stores in North Carolina, encouraged the lumber industry in New England, and at the end of the colonial period averaged more than £65,000 a year for the Thirteen Colonies alone. Similarly the preferences granted colonial products were beneficial in so far as they operated. Although they had no effect upon such commodities as tobacco and rice and their effect upon other commodities is somewhat uncertain, colonial raw silk, naval stores, and lumber definitely benefited. Yet the total sum represented by such preferences was never great and it is doubtful whether the benefit the Thirteen Colonies thus derived amounted to even one-twentieth of that obtained by the British West Indian planters who in the year 1773 alone, pocketed £446,000, thanks to a preferential rate which enabled their sugar to hold the English market despite a five-shilling-per-hundred-weight differential in price.

The uncertainties underlying many of our calculations do not permit an exact statement, but judging from calculations for the year 1773, it would seem that after all proper allowances have been made for bounties and other preferences, the net burden imposed upon the Thirteen Colonies by the restraints upon the trans-Atlantic trade was between two million and seven million dollars a year. In these days of astronomical budgets such figures do not seem especially impressive, but the annual per capita burden represented by the lower estimate would come close to meeting all the expenses of operating the national government during Washington's administration, and an annual per capita tax based upon the higher estimate would, in addition to paying the current expenses of government, have raised in twelve years (from 1790–1801) a sum sufficient to pay both the domestic and foreign debt incurred by the United States government during the Revolutionary War.

When we turn to the second part of our discussion, the supplementary measures restricting manufacture, we find a difference of opinion concerning the effect of English restrictions upon manufacturing wool, hats, and iron. The earlier tendency was to dismiss the regulations as immaterial, but recently some have swung the pendulum to the other extreme and argue that the restraints were very important. Neither extreme appears to accord with the facts. In the case of hats, proximity to the source of supply of furs and the comparatively simple process of manufacturing had led to the development of an industry which appears to have been injured by the legislation, but the hat industry played only a minor part in the total economy. Woollen manufactures were, of course, much more important, but there is much evidence to indicate that the English prohibitions had little material effect. The colonies found that they were handicapped by an inadequate supply of good wool when they tried to develop homespun goods at the time of the Revolution— and even as late as 1791 Hamilton found that an adequate supply of labour was one of the chief stumbling blocks to his programme for encouraging industry. It required an embargo, a war, and a protective tariff before large-scale woollen manufacturing began to develop, and it did not pass beyond the household stage until many years after being freed of English mercantilism—which, incidentally, had never forbidden the manufacture of homespun for domestic use or local distribution.

In the case of iron manufactures the British legislation encouraged the development of pig and bar iron and tried to discourage the manufacture of more advanced forms, but in both respects the influence of the legislation is doubtful. Because of the proximity of iron ore to forests America had a great advantage in producing crude iron, before coke replaced charcoal, and probably did not need legislative encouragement. With such an advantage in producing crude iron it was only natural that some more advanced iron articles would be produced in the colonies, whatever thorough-going mercantilists might dream about having the crude iron sent over to England and having it returned in the form of pots, pans, and other manufactures.

The various disallowances of colonial laws which were intended to foster colonial manufacturing further illustrate the English intention of discouraging it but, despite that intent, English mercantilism as a whole probably had a greater tendency to promote than to hinder colonial industry. The colonies' most dangerous industrial competitors were in many respects, not the English, but the Dutch, the Germans, and other Europeans—to say nothing of the natives of India—against whose competition the provisoes of the Staple Act of 1663 provided a very useful tariff barrier. Moreover, the large sums which mercantilism withheld from the colonies reduced their available cash, and probably forced many colonists to use homespun or other American products instead of buying British.

The third point of our inquiry into colonial exploitation by England should not detain us long. Until the Molasses Act of 1733 the inter-American trade had been left virtually alone except for the requirement that the English colonies trade in English or colonial ships. Even after 1733, the prohibitive duties on foreign sugar, molasses, and rum were usually evaded. Such evasion required bribery, fraud, or concealment which probably served as a mildly protective tariff in favour of the British sugar islands, but the prices quoted in the Thirteen Colonies for sugar, molasses, and rum do not indicate that the legislation had any radical effect upon the trade.

The fourth part of our inquiry—that relating to the period after 1763 —is a different matter. The researches of Schlesinger and others have demonstrated how the British measures of that period aroused the resentment of the merchants who unleashed an avalanche of agitation which soon went beyond their control. The agitation was not directed toward revolution at first, but agitation by its very nature promotes conditions favourable for revolution—and revolution followed as a natural sequence. Yet, conceding all the irritation thus aroused, we must still face the questions: Were the measures unduly exploitive? Did they fundamentally upset the economic equilibrium? Were they fatal ills which would inevitably lead to the death of the Empire, or merely minor upsets from which the Empire might have recovered—granted otherwise favourable conditions and good luck?

In reviewing the period it does not seem fair to blame British mercantilism for prescribing regulations which were demanded by the circumstances of the time. The British currency and land policies seem to fall under this category. The restrictions upon paper money undoubtedly distressed those who lacked funds, but they merely affirmed a truth which Americans had to learn from sad experience—that in the eighteenth century at least, no political alchemy could transmute paper into gold. Similarly the Proclamation of 1763 and the Quebec Act of 1774 essentially concerned imperial problems and American imitation of the policy after independence was not mere flattery but a tribute to its inherent soundness. The measures disappointed those who had hoped to acquire fortunes from land speculation, but what else could the British have done? Neither they nor the United States government after them could allow private individuals to stir up trouble by moving into Indian territory before the way had been prepared for settlement by negotiations which extinguished the Indians' claims to the area. In view of the British debt it was merely good fiscal policy to charge for the land, and the prices and terms of sale proposed by the British mercantilists seem very reasonable when compared with the prices and terms adopted by the federal government after 1787. And what solution did the Thirteen States themselves find for the conflicting claims to the territory west of the Alleghanies except to create a new governmental unit?

To one who frankly does not profess to be an expert on the point, it is difficult to understand how British mercantilism discriminated materially against the colonists. It is true that in the manœuvering for land grants, British interests sometimes clashed with colonial interests, but we hear fully as much about clashes between different colonial groups. Both the small frontiersmen and the big speculators were charged more for land than they were accustomed to pay, but it was not as much as they were to be charged by the United States government thereafter. In the readjustments which accompanied the establishment of the new policies the fur traders of the Thirteen Colonies suffered somewhat because of the machinations of British opponents but their loss was not great, and in any event by the Revolutionary period trade in furs formed only a negligible fraction of the colonial economy.

The pre-Revolutionary taxation measures, however, are a different matter, and one for which British mercantilism must bear full responsibility. Yet in analysing the figures we find that the average annual revenue raised by the Sugar Acts, the Townshend Acts, and all the other taxes collected in the Thirteen Colonies by the British government amounted to only £31,000. This sum barely exceeded the indirect taxes which were collected on colonial merchandise passing through England. Moreover, both the taxes collected indirectly in England and directly in the colonies failed to equal the bounties which the British government was paying to the colonies—to say nothing of the advantages which they were deriving from preferential duties on their shipments to England. More interesting still, calculated on an annual per capita basis, the taxes collected during the Revolutionary period directly in the colonies and indirectly in England, totalled less than one-seventh of the taxes assessed at the beginning of the century.

Yet even though the amount of taxation was not great, we must consider the possibility that the form of its assessment detrimentally affected colonial interests. The Tea Act, for one, definitely injured the illicit trade in tea by so reducing the price of the legal article that it lessened, if it did not eliminate, the profit from smuggling. However unfair smugglers may have thought such tactics, they can hardly be said to have injured the economy of the country—especially since tea was not a pivotal commodity.

Molasses, the rum which was made from it, and the provision trade which accompanied it, however, were vital factors in colonial economy, and historians have often called attention to their importance in such books as *Rum, Romance, and Rebellion.* The Sugar Act of 1764 served notice that the British government intended to make its regulations effective when it lowered the duty on foreign sugar and molasses and prohibited the importation of foreign rum entirely. The provisions concerning sugar and rum were comparatively immaterial since no great quantities were imported, but the duty of 3d. per gallon on molasses was another matter, since literally millions of gallons came from the foreign West Indies. Many feared that the trade could not bear a tax of 3d. per gallon, and in response to their pleas the duty was reduced in 1766 to 1d. per gallon and the tax was assessed on both British and foreign molasses. The excitement aroused by these taxes leads one to look for evidence of the havoc which they wrought in trade, but an examination of the wholesale prices of molasses does not disclose any noticeable change attributable to the legislation. And if we carry our investigations further we find that the tax which the federal government placed and kept upon imports of molasses after 1790 almost equalled the 3d. per gallon placed upon foreign molasses in 1764 and materially exceeded the 1d. duty retained after 1766. In brief, whatever the connection between rum and romance, the statistics of colonial trade disclose no correlation between rum and rebellion.

In so far as the statistics can be followed, the correlation between wine and rebellion is much closer. The Sugar Act of 1764 had also placed a duty upon wines which gave those imported by way of Britain a preferential rate of £3 per ton. The preference was not sufficient to enable the English to capture the trade in Madeira wine, but it enabled them to gain a flourishing trade in port which previously had been negligible. Yet such an infringement of colonial taste hardly seems to justify a revolt—especially when we note that the quantity involved was not large, and that by the post-Revolutionary period Americans preferred port and other wines to Madeira.

Thus, an analysis of the economic effects of British mercantilism fails to establish its exploitive aspects as the proximate cause of the Revolution. The only measures which afforded a sufficient economic grievance were the *entrepôt* provisions of the Navigation Acts, which governed the trans-Atlantic trade. They helped to create a fundamental economic unbalance, but cannot be connected directly with the Revolution. The colonists had lived under them for more than a century without desiring independence and even in the Revolutionary period with few exceptions the *entrepôt* provisions were accepted as the mother country's due for the protection which she afforded. In fact, the official representatives of the colonies were willing to guarantee the British commercial system provided that the measures of political taxation were withdrawn. If there were any inexorable economic forces which were inevitably drawing the colonies toward revolution, they are hard to detect and the colonists were unaware of them.

Anyone who maintains that the Revolution resulted from the inevitable clash of competing capitalisms must reckon with several points: That burdens upon the trans-Atlantic trade were proportionately greater at the beginning of the eighteenth century than in 1776; that the restraints of the land and currency policies were basically the same as those prescribed by the federal government; and that after 1766 the taxes laid on molasses by Britain were less than those imposed by the United States after 1790. He should also explain why the surplus colonial capital alleged to be bursting its confines did not venture into the manufacturing enterprises which the law did not prohibit; why the colonists did not finance their own middlemen in England; and, finally, why they did not pay their debts. If by a clash of expanding capitalism is meant that colonists with money were irritated because their freedom of action was restrained by outside regulation, one must immediately concede that the charge is justified; but such colonial resentment seems more properly classified as a political rather than an economic factor. It is merely an old point dressed in new garb and was better expressed by John Adams when he declared that the American Revolution began when the first plantation was settled.

When we turn, however, from the economic effects of mercantilism to its regulatory aspects, we are faced with a different story. We can establish a direct correlation between mercantilism and the Revolution. Although earlier English regulations had been reasonably satisfactory the regulatory technique of the British government under George III was pitifully defective. As a mother country, Britain had much to learn. Any modern parents' magazine could have told George III's ministers that the one mistake not to make is to take a stand and then to yield to howls of anguish. It was a mistake which the British government made repeatedly. It placed a duty of 3d. per gallon on molasses, and when it encountered opposition, reduced it to 1d. It provided for a Stamp Act and withdrew it in the face of temper tantrums. It provided for external taxes to meet the colonial objections and then yielded again by removing all except one. When finally it attempted to enforce discipline it was too late. Under the circumstances, no self-respecting child—or colonist— would be willing to yield.

Moreover, British reforming zeal came at a very bad time. The colonists were in a particularly sensitive state due to the post-war deflation and the economic distress which accompanied it. The British also attempted to exert unusual control at a time when the removal of the French from Canada had minimized the colonists' dependence upon Britain. Most important of all, the reforms followed one another too rapidly.

In social reform, irritation often is to be measured not so much by what a regulation attempts to achieve as by the extent to which it changes established habits. The early history of English mercantilism itself offers a good illustration of the point. Bitter complaints came from Virginia and Barbados when tobacco and sugar were first enumerated because those colonies had become accustomed to conditions of comparatively free trade, whereas few or no complaints were heard from Jamaica which had developed under the restrictive system. The mercantilist system was geared for leisurely operation and before George III's reign succeeded by virtue of that fact. Its early restraints led to Bacon's rebellion in Virginia but fortunately for the mother country the pressure against New England was deferred until the next decade when it, too, led to an explosion in the form of revolt against Andros. These uprisings were separated both geographically and chronologically so that neither attained dangerous proportions, and both were followed by a reasonably satisfactory settlement of at least some of the colonial grievances.

During the Revolutionary era, however, the tempo of reform was not leisurely. Doubtless all the colonists were not irritated by any one British reform, but each individual had his own feeling of grievance which enabled him to agree fervently with the complaints of others against British policy and thus add to the heated tempers of the time. The politician who objected to the political implications in taxation reforms found an audience in the land speculators and frontiersmen who complained that the colonists were being deprived of the reward of their blood and suffering by the Proclamation of 1763 and the Quebec Act of 1774. Debtors and inflationists chimed in to tell of the iniquities of the Currency Act; lawyers and printers could not forget the threat to their interests in the Stamp Act. On Sundays the preachers thundered against the dangers of popery in Quebec and voiced their fear that Britain planned to establish an Anglican Church in the colonies. The merchant was always ready to explain not merely how harmful British taxes were to colonial economy, but how irksome were the new administrative rules and regulations. Such chronological and geographical barriers as existed were overcome and a community of antagonisms was maintained by the Committees of Correspondence and other agitators, but such revolutionary forces could not have succeeded if the different elements of the colonies had not recently experienced a mutual sense of grievance.

In short, many of the misunderstandings which have arisen in connection with mercantilism and the American Revolution have grown out of the failure to distinguish between the two phases of mercantilism: exploitation and regulation. The fact that the colonists were exploited by English mercantilism does not necessarily mean that mercantilism caused the American Revolution. Economic forces are not magnets which inexorably move men in predetermined patterns. For better or for worse, men try to regulate their economic as well as their political destiny. A large part of governmental activity consists in attempting to mould economic conduct and to minimize the friction which results from clashes or constraints. English mercantilism was such an attempt. It succeeded rather well in minimizing friction until 1764. For the next decade it bungled badly, and the penalty was the loss of the Thirteen Colonies.

FOR FURTHER READING: Roger Ransom, "British Policy and Colonial Growth: Some Implications of the Burden From the Navigation Acts," *Journal of Economic History*, XXVIII (September, 1968), pp. 427–435. Instructive also is P. D. McClelland, "The Cost to America of British Imperial Policy," *American Economic Review*, LIX (May, 1969), pp. 370–381. The findings of Harper are supported by Gary M. Walton, "The New Economic History and Burdens of the Navigation Acts," *Economic History Review*, Second Series, XXIV, No. 4 (1971), pp. 533–542.

6

ECONOMIC GROWTH AND THE CONSTITUTION

PROBLEM: *Was the Constitution framed mainly to protect moneyed interests?*

Perhaps one of the most famous and most widely read works of American History ever published was Charles A. Beard's *An Economic Interpretation of the Constitution of the United States*. Half a century after its first appearance (1913) historians still debate many of the questions which it raised. Breaking new ground, and diverging from the political approach of previous students of the Constitutional Convention, Beard raised the issue: "Were members of the Constitutional Convention motivated primarily by economic considerations?" Beard himself strongly implied the affirmative. Four groups of men, he wrote, concerned mainly with the protection of their private property had prime influence in the drafting of the Constitution. They represented owners of personal property, real estate, slaves, and government securities. Since three-fourths of all eligible voters in 1787 were disfranchised by property qualifications, and never had an opportunity to express their opposition to the Constitution at the ballot box, these interests were also able to secure its adoption by ratifying conventions. This provocative interpretation has called forth hundreds of rebuttals. Towering above many is Forrest MacDonald's *We, the People*. Following Beard's suggestion that his own hypotheses be further tested, McDonald challenged Beard's underlying premise that mere possession of property was evidence of a desire to protect personal interests. In fact, he concluded that the evidence does not show property interests to have had a decisive voice either in the Philadelphia convention or in the ratifying bodies. Both of these writers raise important queries. Have political institutions in America been established mainly to protect private property? What interest groups were protected by the Constitution? How did the Constitution affect the national economy?

An Economic Interpretation of the Constitution

CHARLES A. BEARD

THE ECONOMIC INTERESTS OF THE MEMBERS
OF THE CONVENTION

A survey of the economic interests of the members of the Convention presents certain conclusions:

A majority of the members were lawyers by profession.

Most of the members came from towns, on or near the coast, that is, from the regions in which personalty was largely concentrated.

Not one member represented in his immediate personal economic interests the small farming or mechanic classes.

The overwhelming majority of members, at least five-sixths, were immediately, directly, and personally interested in the outcome of their labors at Philadelphia, and were to a greater or less extent economic beneficiaries from the adoption of the Constitution.

1. Public security interests were extensively represented in the Convention. Of the fifty-five members who attended no less than forty appear on the Records of the Treasury Department for sums varying from a few dollars up to more than one hundred thousand dollars. Among the minor holders were Bassett, Blount, Brearley, Broom, Butler, Carroll, Few, Hamilton, L. Martin, Mason, Mercer, Mifflin, Read, Spaight, Wilson, and Wythe. Among the larger holders (taking the sum of about $5000 as the criterion) were Baldwin, Blair, Clymer, Dayton, Ellsworth, Fitzsimons, Gilman, Gerry, Gorham, Jenifer, Johnson, King, Langdon, Lansing, Livingston, McClurg, R. Morris, C. C. Pinckney, C. Pinckney, Randolph, Sherman, Strong, Washington, and Williamson.

It is interesting to note that, with the exception of New York, and possibly Delaware, each state had one or more prominent representatives in the Convention who held more than a negligible amount of securities, and who could therefore speak with feeling and authority on the question of providing in the new Constitution for the full discharge of the public debt:

Langdon and Gilman, of New Hampshire.
Gerry, Strong, and King, of Massachusetts.
Ellsworth, Sherman, and Johnson, of Connecticut.
Hamilton, of New York. Although he held no large amount personally, he was the special pleader for the holders of public securities and the maintenance of public faith.
Dayton, of New Jersey.
Robert Morris, Clymer, and Fitzsimons, of Pennsylvania.
Mercer and Carroll, of Maryland.
Blair, McClurg, and Randolph, of Virginia.
Williamson, of North Carolina.
The two Pinckneys, of South Carolina.
Few and Baldwin, of Georgia.

2. Personalty invested in lands for speculation was represented by at least fourteen members: Blount, Dayton, Few, Fitzsimons, Franklin, Gilman, Gerry, Gorham, Hamilton, Mason, R. Morris, Washington, Williamson, and Wilson.

3. Personalty in the form of money loaned at interest was represented by at least twenty-four members: Bassett, Broom, Butler, Carroll, Clymer, Davie, Dickinson, Ellsworth, Few, Fitzsimons, Franklin, Gilman, Ingersoll, Johnson, King, Langdon, Mason, McHenry, C. C. Pinckney, C. Pinckney, Randolph, Read, Washington, and Williamson.

4. Personalty in mercantile, manufacturing, and shipping lines was represented by at least eleven members: Broom, Clymer, Ellsworth, Fitzsimons, Gerry, King, Langdon, McHenry, Mifflin, G. Morris, and R. Morris.

5. Personalty in slaves was represented by at least fifteen members: Butler, Davie, Jenifer, A. Martin, L. Martin, Mason, Mercer, C. C. Pinckney, C. Pinckney, Randolph, Reed, Rutledge, Spaight, Washington, and Wythe.

It cannot be said, therefore, that the members of the Convention were "disinterested." On the contrary, we are forced to accept the profoundly significant conclusion that they knew through their personal experiences in economic affairs the precise results which the new government that they were setting up was designed to attain. As a group of doctrinaires, like the Frankfort assembly of 1848, they would have failed miserably; but as practical men they were able to build the new government upon the only foundations which could be stable: fundamental economic interests.

THE POLITICAL DOCTRINES OF THE MEMBERS
OF THE CONVENTION

It is now interesting to inquire whether the members of the Convention at large entertained substantially identical views as to the political science of the system. There are several difficulties in the way of such an investigation. Not all of the delegates, indeed not all of the most influential, were speech makers or writers or philosophers. As intensely practical men they were concerned with tangible results, not with the manner in which political scientists might view the details of their operations. There is, accordingly, a considerable danger of attempting too much in making generalizations, and to obviate this as far as possible, the method of taking the members in alphabetical order is adopted, and the evidence of the views entertained by each is fully documented.

The leaders in politics and political philosophy in the eighteenth century were not far removed from that frank recognition of class rights which characterized English society, and they were not under the necessity of obscuring—at least to the same extent as modern partisan writers —the essential economic antagonisms featuring in law and constitution making. Their clarity of thought was greatly facilitated by the disfranchisement of the propertyless, which made it unnecessary for political writers to address themselves to the proletariat and to explain dominant group interests in such a manner as to make them appear in the garb of "public policy."

There does not appear, of course, in the writings of American political scientists in the eighteenth century, that sharp recognition of class rights which characterizes the feudal legists, because within the propertied interests politically represented in the government, there were divisions which had to be glossed over; and there were also mutterings of unrest on the part of the disfranchised which later broke out in the storm that swept away the property qualifications on voters and introduced political equalitarianism. Under these circumstances the supporters of the Constitution had to be somewhat circumspect in the expression of their views; but, happily for science, the proceedings at Philadelphia during the drafting of the Constitution were secret, and they were able to discuss with utmost frankness the actual politico-economic results which they desired to reach. Fortunately, also, fragmentary reports of these proceedings have come down to us, and have been put in a definitive form by Professor Farrand.

Abraham Baldwin, of Georgia, did not indulge in any lengthy disquisitions on government in the Convention, and his literary remains are apparently very meagre. However, his view that the Senate of the United States ought to represent property came out in the debate on June 29, over a motion by Ellsworth to the effect that the "rule of suffrage in the second branch be the same as that established by the Articles of Confederation." Baldwin immediately opposed the proposition, saying, "He thought the second branch ought to be the representation of property, and that in forming it therefore some reference ought to be had to the relative wealth of their constituents, and to the principles on which the senate of Massachusetts was constituted." At the time the senate of that commonwealth rested upon special freehold and personalty qualifications, and the members were apportioned among the several districts on the basis of the amount of taxes paid by each. It is thus apparent that Baldwin wished the Senate of the new government to be based frankly upon property.

Gunning Bedford, of Delaware, did not participate extensively in the debates of the Convention, but it seems from the character of the few remarks that he made that he favored a more democratic form than was finally adopted, although he signed the Constitution. This inference is drawn from a brief notice of his objection to the establishment of a council of revision composed of the executive and a certain number of the judiciary to exercise a sort of censorship over the acts of Congress. Madison records as follows:

Mr. Bedford was opposed to every check on the Legislative, even the Council of Revision first proposed. He thought it would be sufficient to mark out in the Constitution the boundaries to the Legislative Authority, which would give all the requisite security to the rights of the other departments. The Representatives of the People were the best judges of what was for their interest, and ought to be under no external controul whatever. The two branches would produce a sufficient controul within the Legislature itself.

Jacob Broom was among those who wished to "lessen the dependence of the general government on the people," to use Jefferson's phrase, by lengthening the terms of public officers. He seconded Read's motion to increase the term of Senators to nine years; he opposed the election of the executive by popular vote, and supported Luther Martin's resolution in favor of election by electors appointed by the legislatures of the several states; he wished to give life tenure to the executive, that is, during good behavior, and he favored the suggestion that Congress should be given a negative over state legislatures. Broom seldom spoke in the Convention, but there is no doubt that he believed in a restricted and well "balanced" democracy.

Pierce Butler, of South Carolina, on more than one occasion urged the desirability of making property at least one of the elements in the distribution of representation. On June 6, when Charles Pinckney moved that the lower house of the national legislature should be chosen by the state legislatures and not by the people, Butler said:

I am against determining the mode of election until the ratio of representation is fixed—if that proceeds on a principle favorable to wealth as well as numbers of free inhabitants, I am content to unite with Delaware (Mr. Read) in abolishing the state legislatures and becoming one nation instead of a confederation of republics.

In connection with a discussion of the Senate, "he urged that the second branch ought to represent the states according to their property." Later in the sessions of the Convention he again "warmly urged the justice and necessity of regarding wealth in the apportionment of representation." He was also particularly solicitous about slave property, and he declared that "the security which the southern states want is that their negroes may not be taken from them."

Daniel Carroll favored the popular election of the executive, but he advocated a three-fourths vote in Congress to overcome the executive veto. Speaking on this point, "He remarked that as a majority was now to be the quorum, seventeen in the larger and eight in the smaller house might carry points. The advantage that might be taken of this seemed to call for greater impediments to improper laws." Carroll did not indulge in any philosophic reflections in the Convention so that his "political science," if he had worked out any definite system, is not apparent in the records.

George Clymer entertained the notions of government which were common to the Federalists of his time. He held that "a representative of the people is appointed to think *for* and not *with* his constituents"; and invariably, during the course of his career, he "showed a total disregard to the opinions of his constituents when opposed to the matured decisions of his own mind." It was on these principles that he "warmly opposed the proposition introducing a clause in the Constitution which conferred upon the people the unalienable right of instructing their representatives."

W. R. Davie, altough he is reputed to have been an accomplished orator and profound student, does not figure extensively in Madison's meagre records. At no point does he expound any philosophy of government. His views were always practical. On the proposition to count slaves in apportioning representation, he threw down the gauntlet to the Convention, and declared that if the rate was not at least three-fifths, North Carolina would not federate. As to the basis of government Davie "seemed to think that wealth or property ought to be represented in the second branch; and numbers in the first branch."

Davie fully understood the significance of the obligation of contract clause which was designed as a check on the propensities of popular legislatures to assault private rights in property, particularly personalty. Speaking in the convention of North Carolina on this clause, he said: "That section is the best in the Constitution. It is founded on the strongest principles of justice. It is a section, in short, which I thought would have

endeared the Constitution to this country." Davie undoubtedly understood and approved the doctrines of balanced classes in the government,
as expounded in Adams' *Defence of American Constitutions.*

At no time does Davie appear to have courted popular favor in his
native state, for a writer speaking of his candidacy for the legislature in
1798 says:

The "true Whigs," as they styled themselves, dined together under the oaks
and toasted Mr. Jefferson. The other party, who were called "aristocrats," ate
and drank in the house on entirely different principles. General Davie dined
in the house with the "aristocrats." The "true Whigs" took offence at this and
resolved to oppose his selection, and it was only with much address that they
were kept quiet. . . . If any person had had the impudence to dispute the election, General Davie would certainly not have been returned. The rabble, which
in all places is the majority, would have voted against him.

John Dickinson, of Delaware, frankly joined that minority which was
outspoken in its belief in a monarchy—an action that comported with his
refusal to sign the Declaration of Independence and his reluctance to
embark upon the stormy sea of Revolution. At the very opening of the
Convention, on June 2, he expressed his preference for a regal government, although he admitted that the existing state of affairs would not
permit its establishment in America. Madison records him as saying:

A limited Monarchy he considered as one of the best Governments in the
world. It was not certain that the same blessings were derivable from any other
form. It was certain that equal blessings had never yet been derived from any
of the republican form. A limited monarchy, however, was out of the question.

Dickinson was also among the members of the Convention who wished
to establish a property qualification for voters because he thought no
other foundation for government would be secure. In the debate on this
subject on August 7, according to Madison's notes:

Mr. Dickinson had a very different idea of the tendency of vesting the right
of suffrage in the freeholders of the Country. He considered them as the best
guardians of liberty; And the restriction of the right to them as a necessary
defence agst. the dangerous influence of those multitudes without property &
without principle, with which our Country like all others, will in time abound.
As to the unpopularity of the innovation it was in his opinion chimerical. The
great mass of our Citizens is composed at this time of freeholders, and will be
pleased with it.

According to King's notes:

Dickinson—It is said yr. restraining by ye Constitution the rights of Election
to Freeholders, is a step towards aristocracy—is this true, No. —we are safe by
trusting the owners of the soil—the Owners of the Country—it will not be

unpopular—because the Freeholders are the most numerous at this Time—The Danger to Free Governments has not been from Freeholders, but those who are not Freeholders—there is no Danger—because our Laws favor the Division of property—The Freehold will be parcelled among all the worthy men in the State—The Merchants & Mechanicks are safe—They may become Freeholders besides they are represented in ye State Legislatures, which elect the Senate of the U.S.

No member of the Convention distrusted anything savoring of "levelling democracy" more than *Oliver Ellsworth*. Later as Chief Justice he denounced from the bench Jefferson and the French party as "the apostles of anarchy, bloodshed, and atheism." In the Convention, he opposed the popular election of the President and favored associating the judges with the executive in the exercise of a veto power over acts of Congress. He believed in the restriction of the suffrage to those who paid taxes. He was a warm advocate of judicial control, in general, and thoroughly understood the political significance of the system.

Thomas Fitzsimons, the wealthy merchant and stockbroker from Pennsylvania, was, after his kind, not a loquacious man, but rather a man of action—a practical man; and the records of the Convention contain no lengthy speech by him. When Gouverneur Morris, on August 7, proposed to restrain the right to vote to freeholders, Fitzsimons seconded the motion, apparently without saying anything on the point. While he thus sympathized with the movement to set the Constitution frankly on a property basis, Fitzsimons was naturally more interested in such matters as protection to manufactures and harbor improvements.

Benjamin Franklin, who at the time of the Convention was so advanced in years as to be of little real weight in the formation of the Constitution, seems to have entertained a more hopeful view of democracy than any other member of that famous group. He favored a single-chambered legislature, opposed an absolute veto in the executive, and resisted the attempt to place property qualifications on the suffrage. He signed the Constitution when it was finished, but he was accounted by his contemporaries among the doubters, and was put forward by the opponents of ratification in Pennsylvania as a candidate for the state convention, but was defeated.

Elbridge Gerry, of Massachusetts, participated extensively in the debates of the Convention, but his general view of government was doubtless stated in his speech on May 31, when he expressed himself as not liking the election of members of the lower house by popular vote. He said on this point:

The evils we experience flow from the excess of democracy. The people do not want virtue; but are the dupes of pretended patriots. In Massts. it has been fully confirmed by experience that they are daily misled into the most baneful measures and opinions by the false reports circulated by designing men, and which no one on the spot can refute. One principal evil arises from the want of due provision for those employed in the administration of Governnt. It would seem to be a maxim of democracy to starve the public servants. He mentioned the popular clamour in Massts. for the reduction of salaries and the attack made on that of the Govr. though secured by the spirit of the Constitution itself. He had, he said, been too republican heretofore: he was still, however, republican, but had been taught by experience the danger of the levelling spirit.

When the proposition that Senators should be elected by the state legislatures was up for consideration,

Mr. Gerry insisted that the commercial and monied interest wd. be more secure in hands of the State Legislatures, than of the people at large. The former have more sense of character, and will be restrained by that from injustice. The people are for paper money when the Legislatures are agst. it. Massts. the County Conventions had declared a wish for a depreciating paper that wd. sink itself. Besides, in some States there are two Branches in the Legislature, one of which is somewhat aristocratic. There wd. therefore be so far a better chance of refinement in the choice.

Nicholas Gilman was by temper and interest a man of affairs, more concerned with the stability of public securities and the development of western land schemes than with political theorizing. From Madison's record he does not appear to have said anything in the Convention.

Nathaniel Gorham was opposed to property qualifications on the suffrage in the federal Constitution and the association of the judiciary with the executive in the exercise of the veto power. Speaking on the latter point, however, he said,

All agree that a check on the legislature is necessary. But there are two objections against admitting the judges to share in it which no observations on the other side seem to obviate. The 1st is that the judges ought to carry into the exposition of the laws no prepossessions with regard to them; 2d that as the judges will outnumber the executive, the revisionary check would be thrown entirely out of the executive hands, and instead of enabling him to defend himself would enable the judges to sacrifice him.

Alexander Hamilton had a profound admiration for the British constitution. "The House of Lords," he said in the Convention, "is a noble institution. Having nothing to hope for by a change and a sufficient interest by means of their property, in being faithful to the national interest, they form a permanent barrier against every pernicious innovation whether attempted on the part of the Crown or of the Commons." Doubtless his maturely considered system of government was summed up in the following words:

All communities divide themselves into the few and the many. The first are the rich and well born, the other the mass of the people. The voice of the people has been said to be the voice of God; and however generally this maxim has been quoted and believed, it is not true in fact. The people are turbulent and changing; they seldom judge or determine right. Give therefore to the first

class a distinct, permanent share in the government. They will check the un-
steadiness of the second, and as they cannot receive any advantage by a change,
they therefore will ever maintain good government. Can a democratic assembly
who annually revolve in the mass of the people, be supposed steadily to pursue
the public good? Nothing but a permanent body can check the imprudence of
democracy. . . . It is admitted that you cannot have a good executive upon a
democratic plan.

In consonance with these principles Hamilton outlined his scheme of
government which included an assembly to consist of persons elected for
three years by popular vote, a senate chosen for life or during good behavior by electors chosen by the voters, and a president also elected for
life or during good behavior by electors chosen by the voters. The Convention failed to adopt his programme, and he entertained a rather uncertain view of the Constitution as it was finally drafted, doubting its
stability and permanency.

William Houstoun, of Georgia, seems to have spoken only once or twice;
but he gave an indication of his political science in a remark which he
made to the effect that the Georgia constitution "was a very bad one, and
he hoped it would be revised and amended." The constitution to which
he alludes was the radical instrument made in 1777, which provided for
a legislature with a single chamber and an unusually wide extension of the
suffrage.

Jared Ingersoll, in spite of his great abilities as a student and lawyer,
seems to have taken no part at all in the debates of the Convention. Such
at least is the view to which Madison's records lead. Something is known,
however, of the political principles which he entertained. Though he became intimately associated with President Reed on his migration to
Philadelphia in 1778, he never accepted the extreme democratic principles embodied in the constitution of that state in 1776. His biographer,
after making an exception of Ingersoll's services in the Convention, says:

I am not aware that he held or sought a position in any popular or representative body whatever. He was what is called conservative in politics; that is to
say, he was not by constitutional temper a rebuilder or reconstructor of anything that had been once reasonably well built; nor was his favorite order of
political architecture, the democratic. After the great subversion in 1801 he
was found as rarely as anybody in Pennsylvania on the side of the majority.
He was known to be inclined to the contrary, so far that with or without his
consent he was selected in that state, in the year 1812, as the opposition or anti-
Madisonian candidate for the office of Vice-President of the United States.

Rufus King correctly understood the idea of a balanced government
independent of "popular whims" and endowed with plenty of strength.
He favored a long term for the President, and speaking on the executive
department in the Convention he

expressed his apprehensions that an extreme caution in favor of liberty might
enervate the government we were forming. He wished the house to recur to

the primitive axiom that the three great departments of governments should
be separate and independent: that the executive and the judiciary should be
so, as well as the legislative: that the executive should be equally so with the
judiciary. . . . He [the executive] ought not to be impeachable unless he hold
his office during good behavior, a tenure which would be most agreeable to
him; provided an independent and effectual forum could be devised; But under
no circumstances ought he to be impeachable by the legislature. This would be
destructive of his independence and of the principles of the constitution. He
relied on the vigor of the executive as a great security for the public liberties.

King also believed in the principle of judicial control—that most effective
check on the popular attacks on property through legislatures.

It was largely on King's initiative that the prohibition against interference with contracts was placed in the Constitution.

William Livingston took a middle ground between the "high-toned"
system of John Adams and the simple democracy of such writers as
"Centinel" of Pennsylvania. *The Defence of the Constitutions* he impatiently characterized as "rubbage"; and a "Humiliating and mortifying
acknowledgement that a man is incapable of governing himself." But for
the opposite party that would set up a simple democratic government
through legislative majorities, Livingston had just as little patience.

The security of the liberties of a people or state depends wholly on a proper
delegation of power. The several component powers of government should be
so distributed that no one man, or body of men, should possess a larger share
thereof than what is absolutely necessary for the administration of government. . . . The people ever have been and ever will be unfit to retain the
exercise of power in their own hands; they must of necessity delegate it somewhere. . . . But it has been found from experience that a government by representation, consisting of a single house of representatives, is in some degree liable
to the same inconveniences which attend a pure democracy; a few leading
men influence the majority to pass laws calculated not for the public good,
but to promote some sinister views of their own. To prevent this, another
representative branch is added: these two separate houses form mutual checks
upon each other; but this expedient has not been found to be altogether effectual. If the legislative power, even tho' vested in two distinct houses is left
without any controul, they will inevitably encroach upon the executive and
judicial; . . . But further, as prejudices always prevail, more or less, in all
popular governments, it is necessary that a check be placed somewhere in the
hands of a power not immediately dependent upon the breath of the people,
in order to stem the torrent, and prevent the mischiefs which blind passions
and rancorous prejudices might otherwise occasion. The executive and judicial
powers should of course then be vested with this check or controul on the
legislature; and that they may be enabled fully to effect this beneficial purpose,
they should be rendered as independent as possible. . . . Tho' it is so short a
time since our governments have been put in motion, yet examples have not
been wanting of the prevalence of this dangerous thirst after more power in
some of our legislatures; a negative therefore lodged in the hands of the executive and judicial powers, is absolutely necessary in order that they may be able
to defend themselves from the encroachments of the legislature.

Livingston thought that there were some grave defects in the Constitution as drafted at Philadelphia and proposed some emendations. He believed that the President should enjoy the appointing power without any control by the Senate; he thought the Chief Justice should hold office during good behavior and be empowered to appoint his colleagues; and he further held that the President, the Chief Justice, and a Superintendent of Finance should be organized into a council of revision to pass upon the acts of Congress.

James McClurg, of Virginia, left the Convention during the early part of August, and was silent on most of the questions before that body. On July 17th, he proposed that the term of the executive should be changed from seven years to "good behavior"; and he was particularly anxious to have the executive independent of the legislature. He said that he·

was not so much afraid of the shadow of monarchy as to be unwilling to approach it; nor so wedded to republican government as not to be sensible of the tyrannies that had been and may be exercised under that form. It was an essential object with him to make the executive independent of the legislature; and the only mode left for effecting it, after the vote destroying his ineligibility the second time, was to appoint him during good behavior.

That McClurg had small respect for legislatures in general is shown by a letter which he wrote to Madison from Virginia on August 7, 1787, in which he said:

The necessity of some independent power to controul the Assembly by a negative, seems now to be admitted by the most zealous Republicans—they only differ about the mode of constituting such a power. B. Randolph seems to think that a magistrate annually elected by the people might exercise such a controul as independently as the King of G. B. I hope that our representative, Marshall, will be a powerful aid to Mason in the next Assembly. He has observ'd the continual depravation of Mens manners, under the corrupting influence of our Legislature; & is convinc'd that nothing but the adoption of some efficient plan from the Convention can prevent Anarchy first, & civil convulsions afterwards.

James McHenry belonged to the conservative party of his state and opposed "radical alterations" in the constitution of that commonwealth as it stood in November, 1791.

Writing in February, 1787, on the property qualifications placed on voters and representatives in Maryland, McHenry explained that "These disabilities, exclusions, and qualifications have for their object an upright legislature, endowed with faculties to judge of the things most proper to promote the public good." He was warmly opposed to the doctrine that the people had a right to instruct their representatives. Democracy was, in his opinion, synonymous with "confusion and licentiousness."

James Madison was the systematic philosopher of the Convention and set forth his views with such cogency and consistency on so many different topics that no short quotations will suffice to state his doctrines. His general scheme of political science was, however, embodied in the tenth number of *The Federalist* which has been discussed above and need not be reconsidered here.

Alexander Martin was among the silent members of the Convention, for Madison records only an occasional and incidental participation by him in the proceedings.

Luther Martin was the champion of the extreme states' rights' view, and entertained rather democratic notions for his time, although, in arguing against the clause prohibiting Congress to issue paper money, he held that, "considering the administration of the government would be principally in the hands of the wealthy," there could be little danger from an abuse of this power. Martin was in fact a champion of paper money in his state, and he opposed that part of the Constitution which prohibited the emission of bills of credit. As a representative of the more radical section of his community, he was against the clauses restricting the states to the use of the gold and silver coin of the United States, and was opposed to the clause forbidding the impairment of the obligation of contract. Speaking on the latter point he said:

There might be times of such great public calamities and distress, and of such extreme scarcity of specie, as should render it the duty of a government for the preservation of even the most valuable part of its citizens in some measure to interfere in their favor, by passing laws totally or partially stopping the courts of justice, or authorizing the debtor to pay by installments, or by delivering up his property to his creditors at a reasonable and honest valuation. The times have been such as to render regulations of this kind necessary in most or all of the states, to prevent the wealthy creditor and the moneyed man from totally destroying the poor, though even industrious debtor. Such times may again arrive. . . . I apprehend, Sir, the principal cause of complaint among the people at large, is the public and private debt with which they are oppressed, and which in the present scarcity of cash threatens them with destruction, unless they can obtain so much indulgence in point of time that by industry and frugality they may extricate themselves.

As might have been expected, a man entertaining such radical notions about the power and duty of a government to interfere with the rights of personality in behalf of the debtor could not have accepted the instrument framed at Philadelphia. In fact, Martin refused to sign the Constitution; he wrote a vehement protest against it to the legislature of his state; he worked assiduously against its ratification; and as a member of the state convention, he voted against its approval by his commonwealth —but in vain.

George Mason thoroughly understood the doctrine of a balanced government. Speaking in the Convention on the function of the upper house, he said:

One important object in constituting the senate was to secure the rights. of property. To give them weight and firmness for this purpose a considerable duration in office was thought necessary. But a longer term than six years would be of no avail in this respect, if needy persons should be appointed. He suggested therefore the propriety of annexing to the office a qualification of property. He thought this would be very practicable; as the rules of taxation would supply a scale for measuring the degree of wealth possessed by every man.

On another occasion, he presented a motion requiring "certain qualifications of landed property, in members of the legislature." Although Mason refused to sign the Constitution, his reasons were based on personal economic interests, not on any objections to its checks on democratic legislatures.

J. F. Mercer, of Maryland, who opposed the Constitution in its final form and became the belligerent anti-federalist leader in that state, does not appear to have been so warmly devoted to the "people's cause," behind the closed doors of the Convention, for he took exceptions to the proposition that the determination of the qualifications of voters should be left to the several states. But his particular objection was "to the mode of election by the people. The people cannot know and judge of the characters of candidates. The worst possible choice will be made."

Thomas Mifflin took no part worthy of mention in the proceedings of the Convention, and expounded no views of government during the debates.

Gouverneur Morris, of Pennsylvania, was the leader of those who wanted to base the new system upon a freehold suffrage qualification; and, on August 7, he made a motion to this effect. In the course of the discussion which followed, Morris said:

He had long learned not to be the dupe of words. The sound of Aristocracy, therefore, had no effect on him. It was the thing, not the name, to which he was opposed, and one of his principal objections to the Constitution as it is now before us, is that it threatens this Country with an Aristocracy. The Aristocracy will grow out of the House of Representatives. Give the votes to people who have no property, and they will sell them to the rich who will be able to buy them. We should not confine our attention to the present moment. The time is not distant when this Country will abound with mechanics & manufacturers who will receive their bread from their employers. Will such men be the secure & faithful Guardians of liberty? Will they be the impregnable barrier agst. aristocracy?—He was as little duped by the association of the words, "taxation & Representation"—The man who does not give his vote freely is not represented. It is the man who dictates the vote. Children do not vote. Why? because they want prudence, because they have no will of their own. The ignorant & the dependent can be as little trusted with the public interest. He did not conceive the difficulty of defining "freeholders" to be insuperable. Still less that the restriction could be unpopular. 9/10 of the people are at present freeholders and these will certainly be pleased with it. As to Merchts. &c. if they have wealth & value the right they can acquire it. If not they don't deserve it.

In all the proceedings of the Convention, Morris took a deep interest and expressed his views freely, always showing his thorough distrust of democratic institutions. As his biographer, Mr. Roosevelt, puts it,

He throughout appears as the *advocatus diaboli;* he puts the lowest interpretation upon every act, and frankly avows his disbelief in all generous and unselfish motives. His continual allusions to the overpowering influence of the baser passions, and to their mastery of the human race at all times, drew from Madison, although the two men generally acted together, a protest against his "forever inculcating the utter political depravity of men, and the necessity of opposing one vice and interest as the only possible check to another vice and interest."

This protest from Madison, however, betrays inconsistency, for on more than one occasion in the Convention he expounded principles substantially identical with those which he reprobated in Morris. Indeed, what appeared to be cynical eccentricity on the part of the latter was nothing more than unusual bluntness in setting forth Federalist doctrines.

Robert Morris, the merchant prince and speculator of Pennsylvania, seems to have broken his rule of absolute silence only two or three times in the Convention, and he apparently made no speech at all. He nominated Washington as president of the assembly, and seconded Read's motion that Senators should hold office during good behavior. There is no doubt that Morris appreciated the relative weight of speeches and private negotiations.

In the proceedings of the Convention, *William Paterson* was chiefly concerned with protecting the rights of small states; but he signed the Constitution, and after its adoption became an ardent Federalist, serving as an associate justice of the Supreme Court. On the bench he was one of the most scholarly and eminent supporters of the doctrine of judicial control over legislation.

William Pierce took little part in the proceedings of the Convention. On the question of states' rights he held a broad view, saying,

state distinctions must be sacrificed so far as the general government shall render it necessary—without, however, destroying them altogether. Although I am here as a representative from a small state, I consider myself as a citizen of the United States, whose general interest I will always support.

On no occasion, apparently, did Pierce indulge in any general reflections on the basis of all government. He did not sign the Constitution, but he explained this fact by saying,

I was absent in New York on a piece of business so necessary that it became unavoidable. I approve of its principles and would have signed it with all my heart had I been present. To say, however, that I consider it as perfect would be to make an acknowledgement immediately opposed to my judgment.

Charles Pinckney was among the members of the Convention who thought that it was desirable to fix the property qualifications of members of the national legislature firmly in the Constitution. Speaking on the subject of property and government he said:

The Committee as he had conceived were instructed to report the proper qualifications of property for the members of the Natl. Legislature; instead of which they have referred the task to the Natl. Legislature itself. Should it be left on this footing, the first Legislature will meet without any particular qualifications of property; and if it should happen to consist of rich men they might fix such qualifications as may be too favorable to the rich; if of poor men, an opposite extreme might be run into. He was opposed to the establishment of an undue aristocratic influence in the Constitution, but he thought it essential that the members of the Legislature, the Executive, and the Judges—should be possessed of competent property to make them independent & respectable. It was prudent when such great powers were to be trusted to connect the tie of property with that of reputation in securing a faithful administration. The Legislature would have the fate of the Nation put into their hands. The President would also have a very great influence on it. The Judges would have not only important causes between Citizen & Citizen but also where foreigners were concerned. They will even be the Umpires between the U. States and individual States as well as between one State & another. Were he to fix the quantum of property which should be required, he should not think of less than one hundred thousand dollars for the President, half of that sum for each of the Judges, and in like proportion for the members of the Natl. Legislature. He would however leave the sum blank. His motion was that the President of the U. S., the Judges, and members of the Legislature should be required to swear that they were respectively possessed of a clear unincumbered Estate to the amount of ——— in the case of the President, &c &c —

Pinckney, in fact, had no confidence in popular government, for on March 28, 1788, he wrote to Madison:

Are you not . . . abundantly impressed that the theoretical nonsense of an election of Congress by the people in the first instance is clearly and practically wrong, that it will in the end be the means of bringing our councils into contempt.

General Charles Cotesworth Pinckney entertained views with regard to the special position that should be enjoyed by property, which were substantially identical with those held by his cousin. He proposed that no salary should be paid to members of the Senate. As this branch, he said, "was meant to represent the wealth of the country, it ought to be composed of persons of wealth; and if no allowance was to be made the wealthy alone would undertake the service." General Pinckney also wished to extend property qualifications not only to members of the legislature, but also to the executive and judicial departments.

Edmund Randolph was not only fully aware of the distress to which property had been put under the Articles of Confederation, but he also understood the elements of a "balanced" government. Speaking on the subject of the structure of the Senate, he said:

If he was to give an opinion as to the number of the second branch, he should say that it ought to be much smaller than that of the first, so small as to be exempt from the passionate proceedings to which numerous assemblies are liable. He observed that the general object was to provide a cure for the evils under which the U. S. Laboured; that in tracing these evils to their origin every man had found it in the turbulence and follies of democracy: that some check therefore was to be sought for agst. this tendency of our governments: and that a good Senate seemed most likely to answer the purpose. . . . Mr. Randolph was for the term of 7 years. The Democratic licentiousness of the State Legislatures proved the necessity of a firm Senate. The object of this 2d. branch is to controul the democratic branch of the Natl. Legislature. If it be not a firm body, the other branch being more numerous, and coming immediately from the people, will overwhelm it. The Senate of Maryland constituted on like principles had been scarcely able to stem the popular torrent. No mischief can be apprehended, as the concurrence of the other branch, and in some measure, of the Executive, will in all cases be necessary. A firmness & independence may be the more necessary also in this branch, as it ought to guard the Constitution agst. encroachments of the Executive who will be apt to form combinations with the demagogues of the popular branch.

George Read was most outspoken in his desire to see the Articles of Confederation completely discarded. He said that

he was against patching up the old federal system: he hoped the idea would be dismissed. It would be like putting new cloth on an old garment. The Confederation was founded on temporary principles. It cannot last; it cannot be amended.

He favored vesting an absolute veto power in the executive; and he proposed that Senators should hold office during good behavior.

John Rutledge held that the apportionment of representatives should be on a basis of wealth and population. He favored a property qualification for the legislative, executive, and judicial departments; and he thought that Senators should not be paid. In fact, he was one of the most ardent champions of the rights of property in government in the Convention. He was strictly opposed to the introduction of sentimental considerations in politics, for, speaking on an aspect of slavery and the Constitution, he said:

Religion & humanity had nothing to do with this question—Interest alone is the governing principle with Nations—The true question at present is whether the Southn. States shall or shall not be parties to the Union. If the Northern States consult their interests they will not oppose the increase of Slaves which will increase the commodities of which they will become the carriers.

Roger Sherman believed in reducing the popular influence in the new government to the minimum. When it was proposed that the members of the first branch of the national legislature should be elected, Sherman said that he was "opposed to the election by the people," insisting that it ought to be by the state legislatures. "The people," he said, "immediately should have as little to do as may be about the government. They want information and are constantly liable to be misled."

Richard Dobbs Spaight does not seem to have made any very lengthy speeches in the Convention, but his occasional motions show that he was not among those who believed in "frequent recurrence to the people." On September 6, he moved that the length of the President's term be increased to seven years, and finding this lost he attempted to substitute six years for four. Spaight was the one member of the Convention, however, who came out clearly and denounced judicial control; but he nevertheless proved a stout champion of the Constitution in North Carolina—defending it warmly against charges to the effect that it was aristocratic in character.

Caleb Strong carried into the Convention the old Massachusetts tradition in favor of frequent elections. He favored a one year term for representatives, voted against a seven year term for President, and also opposed a seven year term for Senators. He supported the Constitution, however, in his native state, and was a member of the convention that ratified it.

George Washington's part in the proceedings of the Convention was almost negligible, and it does not appear that in public document or private letter he ever set forth any coherent theory of government. When he had occasion to dwell upon the nature of the new system he indulged in the general language of the bench rather than that of the penetrating observer. For example, in his Farewell Address, which was written largely by Hamilton, he spoke of the government's being "the offspring of our own choice, uninfluenced and unawed, adopted upon full investigation, and mature deliberation, completely free in its principles, in the distribution of its powers, uniting security with energy." He feared, however, the type of politics represented by the Democratic Societies which sprang up during his administration, and looked upon criticism of the government as akin to sedition. Like Jefferson, he also viewed with apprehension the growth of an urban population, for in a letter to La Fayette at the time of the French Revolution, he said, "The tumultuous populace of large cities are ever to be dreaded. Their indiscriminate violence prostrates for the time all public authority."

Hugh Williamson was against placing property qualifications on voters for members of Congress; and he was opposed to the association of the judges with the executive in the exercise of the veto power. He preferred to insert a provision requiring a two-thirds vote for every "effective act of the legislature." He was, however, an opponent of the paper money party in North Carolina and in the Convention he supported a proposition forbidding the states to pass ex post facto laws, on the ground that "the judges can take hold of it."

James Wilson was among the philosophers of the period who had seriously pondered on politics in its historical and practical aspects. In the Convention he took a democratic view on several matters. He favored the annual election of representatives by the people, he advocated the popular election of United States Senators, and he believed also in the popular election of the President. He furthermore opposed the proposition to place property qualifications on voters. His check on popular legislation was to be found in judicial control, at first in the association of the judges with the executive in its exercise, and later in its simple, direct form. In fact, Wilson shared the apprehensions of his colleagues as to the dangers of democratic legislatures, though he did not frankly advocate direct property checks. He doubtless believed that judicial control would be sufficient.

George Wythe was a representative of the old school of lawyers in Virginia, and he was a profound student of historical jurisprudence, although he apparently made no attempt to apply his learning to any of the general political questions before the Convention. He was a warm advocate of the doctrine of judicial control and gave practical effect to principles while on the bench in Virginia.

The conclusion seems warranted that the authors of *The Federalist* generalized the political doctrines of the members of the Convention with a high degree of precision, in spite of the great diversity of opinion which prevailed on many matters.

Charles A. Beard's Pioneer Interpretation
of the Making of the Constitution

FORREST MCDONALD

The day was Monday, September 17, 1787, the place, Philadelphia. The long and, as tradition has it, steaming hot summer was finally ending. Throughout the city, serenely unaware that historians were one day to know this as the Critical Period of American history, Philadelphians were busy preparing a record wheat crop for export. Inside a crowded room in the State House (later to be rechristened Independence Hall) thirty-odd men penned their signatures to a document they had styled a "Constitution for the United States of America."

Reprinted by permission of the author from *We the People*, by Forrest McDonald. Copyright 1958 by The University of Chicago.

There was no exuberance, no display of enthusiasm, and very little reverential solemnity. Fourteen members of the body had previously walked out for one reason or another, most of them because they had personal business they considered more deserving of attention or because the hot clash of personalities had been too much for them. Even now, at the very end, a half dozen men were wrangling about minor details, and three others flatly refused to sign the instrument. Another group was already worrying about and planning for the strenuous campaign for ratification which lay ahead. Mostly, however, the atmosphere pervading the room was one of exhaustion and a sense of relief that the four-month ordeal was over.

The importance of the event insured that the making of the Constitution of the United States would become the subject of debate, study, and writing for many years to come. In addition the actors in the drama helped to fan the flames of debate and to provoke perhaps even more writing than the subject itself warranted. Almost as if to vex future scholars, the members of the Philadelphia Convention kept their proceedings secret and passed down to historians only the most fragmentary of notes; the Constitution was deliberately couched in ambiguous language; the disputants in the contest over ratification clouded both the contest and the conditions that shaped it by publishing reams of misleading, often fantastic propaganda. Partly because of the nature of the event, partly because of the chaotic record left by the participants, the mountains of historical writings on the subject have often been colored by emotionalism and shrouded in confusion. The men in the Convention have been depicted as a group of demigods, a band of ruthless conspirators, and virtually every intermediate brand of humanity. The document has been characterized at one extreme as scarcely less sacred than the Holy Bible, at the other as the greatest single barrier to the progress of social justice. Interpretation of the ratification has run the gamut from the noblest act of a free people under divine guidance to an unprincipled *coup d'état*.

Early in 1913 there emerged from this historiographical maze a work that was destined to become a classic. In that year Charles A. Beard, then a young professor of politics at Columbia University, published his *An Economic Interpretation of the Constitution of the United States*, a brilliant, challenging, and provocative study that has towered over everything else written on the subject, before or since. No other work on the making or the nature of the Constitution has been so much debated, so widely known, and ultimately so widely accepted.

The central points in the thesis advanced by Professor Beard were these: "Large and important groups of economic interests were adversely affected by the system of government under the Articles of Confederation, namely, those of public securities, shipping and manufacturing, money at interest; in short, capital as opposed to land." After failing to safeguard their rights, "particularly those of the public creditors," through the regular legal channels, these groups called a convention in the hope of obtaining "the adoption of a revolutionary programme." In other words, the movement for the Constitution originated with and was pushed through by "a small and active group of men immediately interested through their personal possessions in the outcome of their labors. . . . The propertyless masses were . . . excluded at the outset from participation (through representatives) in the work of framing the Constitution. The members of the Philadelphia Convention which drafted the Constitution were, with a few exceptions, immediately, directly, and personally interested in, and derived economic advantage from, the establishment of the new system."

In essence, then, the Constitution was "an economic document drawn with superb skill by men whose property interests were immediately at stake; and as such it appealed directly and unerringly to identical interests in the country at large." It was based "upon the concept that the fundamental private rights of property are anterior to government and morally beyond the reach of popular majorities."

The system "consisted of two fundamental parts—one positive, the other negative." The positive part comprised four great powers conferred on the new government: "taxation, war, commercial control, and disposition of western lands." This meant for the manufacturers a protective tariff; for trade and shipping groups, tariffs and other legislation against foreign shipping; for money interests the prevention of "renewed attempts of 'desperate debtors' like Shays"; and for public creditors, ample revenues for the payment of their claims. The negative portion placed restrictions on the states: "Two small clauses embody the chief demands of personalty against agrarianism: the emission of paper money is prohibited and the states are forbidden to impair the obligation of contract."

In the contest over ratification, Beard concluded, only about a fourth of the adult males were eligible—or interested enough—to vote on the question, and the Constitution was ratified by no more than a sixth of the adult males. In five states it was "questionable whether a majority of the voters participating . . . actually approved the ratification." "The leaders who supported the Constitution in the ratifying conventions represented the same economic groups as the members of the Philadelphia Convention; and in a large number of instances they were also directly and personally interested in the outcome of their efforts." Of the voters on ratification, those favoring the Constitution were "centred particularly in the regions in which mercantile, manufacturing, security, and personalty interests generally had their greatest strength." The holders of public securities "formed a very considerable dynamic element, if not the preponderating element, in bringing about the adoption of the new system." The opposition, on the other hand, came almost exclusively from the

agricultural regions and from the areas in which debtors had been formu-
lating paper-money and other depreciatory schemes. In short, "the line of
cleavage for and against the Constitution was between substantial personalty interests on the one hand and the small farming and debtor interests on the other."

*   *   *

Professor Beard interpreted the making of the Constitution as a simple,
clear-cut series of events. When all the groups that became Federalists are
brought together and analyzed, he asserted, and all the anti-Federalists are
brought together and analyzed, the events can be seen as mere manifestations of a fundamentally simple economic conflict. His analysis led him to
formulate three basic propositions, one regarding the Philadelphia Convention and two regarding the contest over ratification. In the light of
the data in the foregoing chapters, we may now focus our attention upon
these three key propositions of Beard's economic interpretation of the
Constitution.

THE PHILADELPHIA CONVENTION

From his analysis of the Philadelphia Convention, Beard concluded that
the Constitution was essentially "an economic document drawn with
superb skill" by a "consolidated economic group . . . whose property
interests were immediately at stake"; that these interests "knew no state
boundaries but were truly national in their scope."

From a thorough reconsideration of the Philadelphia Convention, however, the following facts emerge. Fully a fourth of the delegates in the
convention had voted in their state legislatures for paper-money and/or
debtor-relief laws. These were the very kinds of laws which, according
to Beard's thesis, the delegates had convened to prevent. Another fourth
of the delegates had important economic interests that were adversely
affected, directly and immediately, by the Constitution they helped write.
The most common and by far the most important property holdings of
the delegates were not, as Beard has asserted, mercantile, manufacturing,
and public security investments, but agricultural property. Finally, it is
abundantly evident that the delegates, once inside the Convention, be-
haved as anything but a consolidated economic group.

In the light of these and other facts presented in the foregoing chapters, it is impossible to justify Beard's interpretation of the Constitution
as "an economic document" drawn by a "consolidated economic group
whose property interests were immediately at stake."

THE CONTEST OVER RATIFICATION, FIRST PROPOSITION

Beard asserted that the ultimate test of the validity of an economic interpretation of the Constitution would rest upon a comparative analysis

of the economic interests of all the persons voting for and all the persons voting against ratification. He made an analysis of the economic interests of some of the leaders in the movement for ratification and concluded that "in the ratification, it became manifest that the line of cleavage for and against the Constitution was between substantial personalty interests on the one hand and the small farming and debtor interests on the other."

For the purpose of analyzing this proposition it is necessary to employ Beard's own definitions of interest groups. In the paragraphs that follow, as in the foregoing chapters, the term "men of personalty interests" is used to mean those groups which Beard himself had in mind when he used the term, namely, money, public securities, manufacturing and shipping, and western lands held for speculation.

From a thorough reconsideration of the contests over ratification the following facts emerge.

1. In three states (Delaware, New Jersey, and Georgia) the decisions of the ratifying conventions were unanimous, and it is therefore impossible to compare the interests of contending parties. The following analyses of the conventions in these three states may be made, however.

In Delaware almost 77 per cent of the delegates were farmers, more than two-thirds of them small farmers with incomes ranging from 75 cents to $5.00 a week. Slightly more than 23 per cent of the delegates were professional men—doctors, judges, and lawyers. None of the delegates was a merchant, manufacturer, banker, or speculator in western lands.

In New Jersey 64.1 per cent of the delegates were farmers, 23.1 per cent were professional men (physicians, lawyers, and college presidents), and only 12.8 per cent were men having personalty interests (one merchant, three iron manufacturers, and one capitalist with diversified investments).

In Georgia 50 per cent of the delegates were farmers (38.5 per cent slave-owning planters and 11.5 per cent small farmers), 11.5 per cent were frontiersmen whose economic interests were primarily agrarian, 19.2 per cent were professional men (lawyers, physicians, and professional officeholders), and only 11.5 per cent had personalty interests (all merchants). The interests of 7.7 per cent of the delegates were not ascertained.

Beard assumed that ratification in these states was pushed through by personalty interest groups before agrarian and paper-money groups could organize their forces. The opposite is true. In each of these three states agrarian interests dominated the conventions. In each state there were approximately equal numbers of delegates who had voted earlier for and against paper money.

2. In two states in which the decision was contested (Virginia and North Carolina) the great majority of the delegates on both sides of the question were farmers. In both states the delegates who voted for and the

delegates who voted against ratification had substantially the same amounts of the same kinds of property, most commonly land and slaves. A large number of the delegates in the Virginia convention had voted on the question of repudiation of debts due British merchants, and the majority of the delegates who had favored such repudiation voted for ratification of the Constitution. Large numbers of delegates in both North Carolina conventions were speculating in western lands. In the first convention a great majority of these land speculators opposed the Constitution; in the second a substantial majority of them favored ratification.

Beard assumed that ratification in these states represented the victory of wealthy planters, especially those who were rich in personalty other than slaves, over the small slaveless farmers and debtors. The opposite is true. In both states the wealthy planters—those with personalty interests as well as those without personalty interests—were divided approximately equally on the issue of ratification. In North Carolina small farmers and debtors were likewise equally divided, and in Virginia the great mass of the small farmers and a large majority of the debtors favored ratification.

3. In four states (Connecticut, Maryland, South Carolina, and New Hampshire) agrarian interests were dominant, but large minorities of delegates had personalty interests.

In Connecticut 57.8 per cent of the delegates who favored ratification and 67.5 per cent of those who opposed ratification were farmers. Ratification was approved by 76.2 per cent of all the delegates, by 81.8 per cent of the delegates having personalty interests, and by 73.3 per cent of the farmers in the convention. Here, then, four delegates out of five having substantial personalty interests favored the Constitution. On the other hand, three of every four farmers also favored the Constitution.

In Maryland 85.8 per cent of the delegates who voted for ratification were farmers, almost all of them wealthy slave-owning planters; 27.3 per cent of the opponents of ratification were farmers, all of them substantial slave-owning planters. The opponents of ratification included from three to six times as large a proportion of merchants, lawyers, and investors in shipping, confiscated estates, and manufacturing as did the delegates who favored ratification. It is to be observed, however, that because the vote in the Maryland ratifying convention was almost unanimous (63 to 11), statistics on the attitudes of the various interest groups would show that every major interest group except manufacturers favored the Constitution. A majority of the areas and of the delegates that had advocated paper money also favored the Constitution.

In South Carolina 59 per cent of the delegates who voted for ratification were large slave-owning planters and 10.7 per cent were lesser planters and farmers. Of the delegates who voted against ratification, 41.7 per cent were large slave-owning planters and 34.2 per cent were lesser planters and farmers. Merchants, factors, and mariners favored ratification, 70 per cent to 30 per cent, a margin almost identical to the vote of the entire convention—67 per cent for, 33 per cent against—and manufacturers, artisans, and mechanics were unanimous in support of the Constitution. On the other hand, 35.7 per cent of the delegates who favored ratification were debtors who were in a desperate plight or had borrowed paper money from the state. Only 15.1 per cent of those who voted against ratification were debtors or had borrowed paper money from the state. No fewer than 82 per cent of the debtors and borrowers of paper money in the convention voted for ratification.

As respects New Hampshire, comparisons are difficult because of the lack of adequate information concerning 28.2 per cent of the delegates. Of the delegates whose interests are known, 36.9 per cent of those favoring the Constitution and 25 per cent of those opposing it were farmers; of the known farmers in the convention 68.7 per cent favored ratification. If it is assumed, however, that all the delegates whose interests are not ascertainable were farmers (as in all likelihood most of them were), then 49.1 per cent of the delegates favoring ratification were farmers, 54.3 per cent of those opposing ratification were farmers, and 52.8 per cent of the farmers in the convention voted for ratification. Delegates whose interests were primarily in personalty (merchants, tradesmen, manufacturers, and shipbuilders) voted in favor of ratification, 60.9 per cent to 39.1 per cent. Delegates from the towns which had voted for and against paper money divided almost equally on the question of ratification: 42 per cent of the towns that had voted for paper money and 54 per cent of those that had voted against paper money sent delegates who voted for the Constitution.

Beard assumed that in these states ratification was the outcome of class struggles between commercial and other personalty groups (Federalists) on the one hand and farmers and advocates of paper money (anti-Federalists) on the other. This generalization is groundless. In each of these states a majority of the men having personalty interests favored ratification, but in each of them a similar majority of the farmers also favored ratification. In one of these states there was no great demand for paper money, in another a large majority of the friends of paper money favored ratification, and in the other two the advocates of paper money were divided almost equally on the question of ratification.

4. In four states (Massachusetts, Pennsylvania, New York, and Rhode Island) men having personalty interests were in a majority in the ratifying conventions.

In Massachusetts, in the popular vote (excluding that of Maine) men whose interests were primarily non-agrarian favored the Constitution by about three to two, and men whose interests were primarily agrarian opposed the Constitution by about 55 per cent to 45 per cent. In the ratifying convention 80 per cent of the merchants and shippers engaged in water-borne commerce, 77 per cent of the artisans and mechanics, and

64 per cent of the farmers favored ratification. About 83 per cent of the retail storekeepers, 85 per cent of the manufacturers, and 64 per cent of the miscellaneous capitalists opposed ratification. One-fourth of those favoring and one-sixth of those opposing the Constitution were farmers. Of the personalty groups combined, 57.5 per cent opposed and 42.5 per cent favored ratification. The realty groups combined, including artisans and mechanics, favored ratification by 67 per cent to 33 per cent.

In Pennsylvania only 34.8 per cent of the delegates favoring ratification were farmers, and only 26.1 per cent of the opponents were farmers. Almost three-fourths—72.7 per cent—of the farmers in the convention favored ratification. The great majority of the delegates on both sides, however, 84.7 per cent of those favoring and 91.3 per cent of those opposing the Constitution, had substantial investments in one or more of Professor Beard's four forms of personalty.

New York delegates are difficult to classify as farmers because almost all farmers in the convention were also landlords with tenants. Delegates to the state's convention may be classified as elected Federalists, converts from anti-Federalism, delegates who abstained from voting, and anti-Federalists. Of the delegates about whom there is sufficient data on which to generalize, fewer than 20 per cent of each group consisted of farmers who had no tenants and who owned none of Beard's four forms of personalty.

Rhode Island delegates do not lend themselves to occupational classification because almost everyone in the state normally combined in his own economic activities several kinds of functions. Only 11.8 per cent of the delegates favoring ratification and only one of the delegates opposing ratification were found to have no interests except farming. The early opponents of paper money formed the original core of those favoring ratification, yet in the final vote 62 per cent of the delegates voting for ratification and 63 per cent of those opposing ratification were men who had borrowed paper money from the state.

Beard's thesis—that the line of cleavage as regards the Constitution was between substantial personalty interests on the one hand and small farming and debtor interests on the other—is entirely incompatible with the facts.

THE CONTEST OVER RATIFICATION, SECOND PROPOSITION

Beard was less certain of the foregoing point, however, than he was of this next one:

Inasmuch as so many leaders in the movement for ratification were large security holders, and inasmuch as securities constituted such a large proportion of personalty, this economic interest must have formed a very considerable dynamic element, if not the preponderating element, in bringing about the adoption of the new system. . . . Some holders of public securities are found among the opponents of the Constitution, but they are not numerous.

This proposition may be analyzed in the same manner that Beard's more general personalty-agrarian conclusion was analyzed. To repeat, Beard asserted that public securities were the dynamic element within the dynamic element in the ratification. This assertion is incompatible with the facts. The facts are these:

1. In three states (Delaware, New Jersey, and Georgia) there were no votes against the Constitution in the ratifying conventions, and hence no comparisons can be made. If public securities were the dynamic element in the ratification, however, it would be reasonable to expect that the great majority of the delegates in these states which supported the Constitution so unreservedly should have been security holders. But the fact is that in Delaware only one delegate in six owned securities, in New Jersey 34 per cent of the delegates, and in Georgia only one delegate.

2. In two states (New Hampshire and North Carolina) the numbers of security holders among the delegates were very small. In New Hampshire only 10.5 per cent of those who voted for and only 2.2 per cent of those who voted against ratification held securities. In the first North Carolina convention only 2.4 per cent of the friends and only 1.1 per cent of the opponents of ratification held securities. In the second convention only 2.0 per cent of those favoring and only 3.9 per cent of those opposing the Constitution were security holders. Superficially these facts tend to substantiate Beard's thesis, for these virtually security-less states were slow to ratify the Constitution. It has been shown, however, that actually the reluctance of these states to adopt the Constitution and their vulnerability to raids on their securities by outsiders were both merely surface manifestations of the same underlying conditions—the isolation, the lack of information, and the lethargy of the majority of the inhabitants of North Carolina and New Hampshire.

3. In three states (Rhode Island, Maryland, and Virginia) where there were contests and considerable numbers of security holders, the advocates and the opponents of ratification included approximately the same percentages of security holders: in Rhode Island, 50 per cent of the advocates and 47 per cent of the opponents; in Virginia, 40.5 per cent of the advocates and 34.2 per cent of the opponents; and in Maryland, 17.4 per cent and 27.3 per cent respectively. The facts relative to these three states clearly contradict Beard's thesis.

4. In two states (Massachusetts and Connecticut) the advocates of ratification included a considerably larger percentage of holders of securities than did the opponents. In Massachusetts 31 per cent of the ratificationists and only 10.1 per cent of the anti-ratificationists were security

owners, and in Connecticut 36.7 per cent and 15 per cent respectively. The situations in these two states, and in these two states alone, tend strongly to support Beard's thesis.

5. In three states (Pennsylvania, South Carolina, and New York) a considerably larger percentage of the delegates opposing ratification than of the Federalist delegates held public securities. In Pennsylvania 73.9 per cent of the opponents and 50 per cent of the supporters of ratification were security owners, in South Carolina 71 and 43 per cent respectively, and in New York 63 and 50 per cent respectively. The facts pertaining to these states not only fail to harmonize with Beard's thesis but indicate that there the precise opposite of his thesis is true.

In the light of the foregoing facts it is abundantly evident that there are no more grounds for considering the holding of public securities the dynamic element in the ratification than for considering this economic interest the dynamic element in the opposition. There were, indeed, some holders of public securities among the opponents of the Constitution and, contrary to Beard's assertion, they were as numerous as the security holders among the supporters of the Constitution.

On all counts, then, Beard's thesis is entirely incompatible with the facts. Beard's essential error was in attempting to formulate a single set of generalizations that would apply to all the states. Any such effort is necessarily futile, for the various interest groups operated under different conditions in the several states, and their attitudes toward the Constitution varied with the internal conditions in their states.

FOR FURTHER READING: Old but still provocative is O. G. Libby, *The Geographical Distribution of the Vote of the Thirteen States on the Federal Constitution, 1787–88* (Madison, 1894). Of the critics, see Robert E. Brown *Charles A. Beard and the Constitution: A Critical Analysis of "An Economic Interpretation of the Constitution"* (Princeton, 1956). Elaborating on Beard's position is Merrill Jensen, *The New Nation, A History of the United States During the Confederation, 1781–1789* (New York, 1950).

7

FINANCE IN THE NATIONAL PERIOD

PROBLEM: *What was the impact of Andrew Jackson's bank policies?*

For over a century a dispute raged in the United States between the advocates of a decentralized as opposed to a centralized banking system. The defenders of the former argued that a national bank was dangerous because it concentrated power over loans and currency expansion in a relatively small group of men who would follow their own selfish interests. But a large number of small banks would prevent the concentration of such powers, and the dangers of abuse. On the other hand, the proponents of a centralized bank system stressed its useful functions, especially of providing needed investment capital and credit, and of keeping the amount of currency in circulation flexible. Only a centralized institution could provide such services. Whether a centralized or decentralized banking system was best suited to promote American economic expansion thus became an issue. It came out clearly in Andrew Jackson's struggle against the Second Bank of the United States. Arthur M. Schlesinger, Jr., a brilliant young historian, formerly of Harvard University, found that the menace to representative government by the Second Bank of the United States under its aggressive president, Nicholas Biddle, fully justified its destruction at the hands of Andrew Jackson. Schlesinger believed that directors of the Bank wielded unwarranted political and economic power to the detriment of farmer-debtors and Eastern workingmen. As

130

a monopoly, its political power provided numerous opportunities for abuse and undermined the principle of equality in American society. This view has been challenged in recent decades, particularly as quantitative historians have analyzed the economic characteristics of the Bank War. As one of the ablest of these, Peter Temin, has argued that the influence of the Second Bank of the United States on the American economy has been greatly exaggerated by many historians, including Schlesinger. If Jackson's destruction of the Bank was followed by inflation and depression, Temin believes, these events were not necessarily related. Other economic influences, not directly tied to President Jackson's policies, were at work. These included changes in the money supply in England and America and increasing British demands for American goods. Both authors point to significant issues relating to the dispute over central banking in the Jacksonian era. To what extent did economic conditions shape the political controversies of the decade? Conversely, how did politics affect the economic functions of banking? How did the Second Bank of the United States control and regulate economic activity?

The Bank War

ARTHUR M. SCHLESINGER, JR.

BEGINNINGS OF THE BANK WAR

In 1836 the charter of the Second Bank of the United States was to expire. This institution was not in the later sense a national bank. It was a banking corporation, located in Philadelphia, privately controlled, but possessing unique and profitable relations with the government. To its capital of thirty-five million dollars, the government had subscribed one fifth. It served as repository of the public funds, which it could use for its own banking purposes without payment of interest. It could issue bank notes up to the physical ability of the president and cashier to sign them; after 1827 it evaded this limitation by the invention of "branch drafts," which looked and circulated like notes but were actually bills of exchange. The

Bank was not to be taxed by the states and no similar institution was to be chartered by Congress. In return for these privileges the Bank paid a bonus of one and a half million dollars, transferred public funds and made public payments without charge, and allowed the government to appoint five out of the twenty-five directors. The Secretary of the Treasury could remove the government deposits provided he laid the reasons before Congress.

I

Even advocates of the Bank conceded that this charter bestowed too much power. That staunch conservative Hezekiah Niles, writing in the heat of the fight for renewal, declared he "would not have the present bank re-chartered, with its present power . . . for the reason that the bank has more power than we would grant to any set of men, unless responsible to the people" (though he ultimately supported the Bank). Nathan Appleton, who had tried vainly to modify the charter in 1832, wrote carefully but emphatically in 1841: "A great central power, independent of the general or state governments, is an anomaly in our system. Such a power over the currency is the most tremendous which can be established. Without the assurance that it will be managed by men, free from the common imperfections of human nature, we are safer without it."

There could be no question about the reality of the Bank's power. It enjoyed a virtual monopoly of the currency and practically complete control over credit and the price level. Biddle's own testimony disclosed its extent:

Q. Has the bank at any time oppressed any of the State banks?
A. Never. There are very few banks which might not have been destroyed by an exertion of the powers of the bank. None have ever been injured.

To radical Democrats like Taney, Biddle's tone implied that he thought himself entitled to credit for his forbearance. "It is this power concentrated in the hands of a few individuals," Taney declared, "—exercised in secret and unseen although constantly felt—irresponsible and above the control of the people or the Government for the 20 years of its charter, that is sufficient to awaken any man in the country if the danger is brought distinctly to his view."

There could be no question either about the Bank's pretensions to complete independence of popular control. Biddle brooked no opposition from within, and the government representatives sat through the directors' meetings baffled and indignant. "I never saw such a Board of *directors*," raged Henry D. Gilpin, "—it is a misuse of terms of *directed.* . . . We know absolutely nothing. There is no consultation, no exchanges of sentiments, no production of correspondence, but merely a rapid, superficial, general statement, or a reference to a Committee which will probably never report." He added, "We are perfect cyphers."

Biddle not only suppressed all internal dissent but insisted flatly that the Bank was not accountable to the government or the people. In 1824 the president of the Washington branch had written Biddle, "As . . . there are other interests to be attended to [besides those of the Bank], especially that of the Government, I have deemed it proper to see and consult with the President." Biddle hotly replied, "If . . . you think that there are other interests to be attended to besides those with which you are charged by the administration of the bank, we deem it right to correct what is a total misapprehension. . . . The moment this appointment [of the five government directors] takes place the Executive has completely fulfilled its functions. The entire responsibility is thenceforward in the directors, and no officer of the Government, from the President downwards, has the least right, the least authority, the least pretence, for interference in the concerns of the bank. . . . This invocation of the Government, therefore . . . is totally inconsistent with the temper and spirit which belong to the officers of the bank, who should regard only the rights of the bank and the instructions of those who govern it, and who should be at all times prepared to execute the orders of the board, in direct opposition, if need be, to the personal interests and wishes of the President and every officer of the Government."

In Biddle's eyes the Bank was thus an independent corporation, on a level with the state, and not responsible to it except as the narrowest interpretation of the charter compelled. Biddle tried to strengthen this position by flourishing a theory that the Bank was beyond political good or evil, but Alexander Hamilton had written with far more candor that "such a bank is not a mere matter of private property, but a political machine of the greatest importance to the State." The Second Bank of the United States was, in fact, as Hamilton had intended such a bank should be, the keystone in the alliance between the government and the business community.

II

Though conservative Jeffersonians, led by Madison and Gallatin, had come to accept Hamilton's Bank as necessary, John Taylor's dialectics and Randolph's invective kept anti-Bank feeling alive, and men in the old radical tradition remained profoundly convinced of the evil of paper money. Jackson's hard-money views prompted his opposition to the Tennessee relief system in 1820. "Every one that knows me," as he told Polk in 1833, "does know, that I have been always opposed to the U. States Bank, nay all Banks." Benton, from talks with Macon and Randolph and his observations of the collapse of the paper system in 1819, similarly concluded that the only safeguard against future disaster lay in restricting the system; and that, to this end, the government should deal only in gold and silver, thus withdrawing support from the issues of privately owned banks. Van Buren, Cambreleng, Taney and Polk more or less shared these views.

The ordinary follower of Jackson in the West also regarded the Bank with strong latent antagonism, but for very different reasons. Its policy in 1819 of recalling specie and checking the note issue of state banks had gained it few friends in any class, and, in Kentucky especially, the Relief War kept resentments alive. But this anti-Bank feeling owed little to reasoned distrust of paper money or to a Jeffersonian desire for specie. As a debtor section the West naturally preferred cheap money; and Kentucky, for example, which most vociferously opposed the United States Bank, also resorted most ardently to wildcat banking of its own. The crux of the Kentucky fight against the Bank was not the paper system, but outside control: the Bank's sin lay not in circulating paper money itself, but in restraining its circulation by Kentucky banks. Almost nowhere, apart from doctrinaires like Jackson and Benton, did Westerners object to state banks under local control.

Indeed, during the eighteen-twenties, even the Philadelphia Bank to a considerable degree overcame the Western prejudices against it. In Tennessee, for example, until 1829 "both [Governor William] Carroll and the legislature favored federal as well as state banks, nor does anything in the history of the state indicate that there was any general feeling against such institutions before Jackson became President." Caleb Atwater, a lusty Jackson man from Ohio and something of a professional Westerner, expressed a widespread feeling when he wrote in 1831, "Refuse to recharter the bank, and Pittsburgh, Cincinnati, Louisville, St. Louis, Nashville, and New Orleans, will be crushed at one blow." Even Frank Blair's first large-scale blast against the Bank in the *Argus of Western America* after Jackson's election did not come until December 23, 1829, many months after Eastern groups had begun to agitate the question. This editorial—actually prefaced by an anti-Bank quote from a Van Buren paper in New York—appealed to the Kentucky fear of Eastern control; and all through 1830 the *Argus* continued to focus on the power and privileges of the Bank and the consequent peril to the Commonwealth Bank of Kentucky, never on the general implications of the paper system.

Some writers have talked of frontier life as if it bred traits of "individualism" and equality which made Westerners mystically opposed to banks. Actually, like all other groups in the population, Westerners favored banks when they thought they could profit by them and fought them when they thought others were profiting at their expense. The Western enthusiasm for an assault on the Bank came, not from an intuitive democratic *Weltschmerz* born in the American forest, nor from a Jeffersonian dislike of banks, but from a farmer-debtor desire to throw off restraints on the local issue of paper money.

Similar objections to control from Philadelphia ranged many Easterners against the Bank. State institutions hoped, by falling heir to the government deposits, to enlarge their banking capital, at no expense to themselves. Special grievances multiplied the motives. The state banks of New York, for example, envied the United States Bank because its loan operations were not restricted by Van Buren's safety-fund system. New York City had long resented the choice of Philadelphia as the nation's financial capital. Thus in a fight against the Bank Jackson could expect the backing of a decent minority of the local banking interests.

But there was still another and more reliable source of support. In March, 1829, after the grim depression winter, a group of Philadelphia workingmen, under the very shadow of the Bank, called a meeting "opposed to the chartering of any more new banks." The hard times were blamed upon the "too great extension of paper credit," and the gathering concluded by appointing a committee, "without confining ourselves to the working classes," to draw up a report on the banking system. The committee, which was dominated by intellectuals, included two leading economists, William M. Gouge, editor of the *Philadelphia Gazette*, and Condy Raguet, editor of the *Free Trade Advocate*, as well as William Duane, the famous old Jeffersonian journalist, his son William J. Duane, a lawyer, Roberts Vaux, the philanthropist, Reuben M. Whitney, a disgruntled businessman and former director of the Bank, and William English and James Ronaldson, two trade-union leaders. A week later the committee pronounced its verdict on the paper system:

That banks are useful as offices of deposit and transfer, we readily admit; but we cannot see that the benefits they confer in this way are so great as to compensate for the evils they produce, in . . . laying the foundation of *artificial* inequality of wealth, and, thereby, of *artificial* inequality of power. . . . If the present system of banking and paper money be extended and perpetuated, the great body of the working people must give over all hopes of ever acquiring any property.

This view was spreading rapidly through the Middle and Northern states of the East in the late eighteen-twenties. The working class was no more affected by an instinctive antipathy toward banking than the backwoodsmen beyond the Alleghenies; but they never enjoyed the Western opportunity of having banks under their own control. Their opposition, instead of remaining fitful and capricious, began slowly to harden into formal anti-banking principle. Their bitter collective experience with paper money brought them to the same doctrines which Jackson and Benton gained from the Jeffersonian inheritance.

III

The war against the Bank thus enlisted the enthusiastic support of two basically antagonistic groups: on the one hand, debtor interests of the West and local banking interests of the East; on the other, Eastern workingmen and champions of the radical Jeffersonian tradition. The essential incompatibility between cheap money and hard could be somewhat concealed in the clamor of the crusade. Yet that incompatibility remained, and it came to represent increasingly a difference between the Western and Eastern wings of the party, as the state banking group gradually abandoned the Jackson ranks. It was, indeed, a new form of the distinction between Western and Eastern readings of "equality." The West, in its quest for political democracy and home rule, did not object to paper money under local control, while the submerged classes of the East, seeking economic democracy, fought the whole banking swindle, as it seemed to them, root and branch.

The administration took care not to offend its cheap-money adherents by openly avowing hard-money ideas. Yet, the drift was unmistakable, and it rendered ineffective some of Jackson's Western followers for whom the battle was being pressed on lines they could not understand. Richard M. Johnson, for example, a staunch relief man and ancient foe of the Bank, served on the House committee which investigated the Bank in 1832; but he could take no real part in a hearing dominated by Cambreleng's hard-money views, and, though he signed Cambreleng's report, he confessed later that he had not asked a question or looked at a Bank book. In general, the Western politicians, torn between the hard-money leanings of the White House and the cheap-money preferences of the folks back home, tended to pursue an erratic course.

Only the intellectuals, who did not have to think about re-election, effected a quick adjustment. Amos Kendall, who had been originally a hard-money man, perhaps from his Eastern upbringing, found no difficulty in reverting to his earlier opinions. Frank Blair also rapidly shifted his ground after coming to Washington. These were not basic reversals of position. Their allegiance, after all, had been primarily to a social class, not to a set of financial theories. The experience of the Kentucky relief system taught that salvation was not to be bought so cheaply: however much inflation might temporarily benefit a frontier state with a large debtor element, it was at best a risky expedient, imposed by political necessity; it never could serve as the basis of a national economic policy. Kendall and Blair, liberated from their local obligations, naturally turned to hard-money ideas as affording the only permanent solutions for the financial problems in favor of the non-business classes.

Thomas Hart Benton had long awaited the opportunity to fight for this solution. In the eighteen-twenties, when he fumed about the paper system, Nathaniel Macon would remark that it was useless to attempt reform unless the administration was with you. Now, at last, the administration seemed to be with him. Jackson's first message had expressed grave doubts about the constitutionality and expediency of the Bank. In 1830 the President continued to make ominous allusions to the subject of recharter. But the administration position was still not clear. Jackson's views were widely regarded as the expressions of private prejudice, not of party policy. Few people interpreted the Maysville veto as opening a campaign which might end by involving the Bank. Even now, the Bank was confidently conducting backstairs negotiations with Secretary McLane to work out a formula for recharter, and it had inspired an effective press campaign to counteract Jackson's pronouncements. Benton, watching impatiently, concluded that someone (who else but Benton?) would have to set forth the hard-money case.

He tried several times to get the floor in the Senate, but the friends of the Bank succeeded always in silencing him by parliamentary technicalities. Finally, on February 2, 1831, he outmaneuvered the opposition and launched his comprehensive indictment:

First: Mr. President, I object to the renewal of the charter . . . because I look upon the bank as an institution too great and powerful to be tolerated in a Government of free and equal laws. . . .
Secondly, I object . . . because its tendencies are dangerous and pernicious to the Government and the people. . . . It tends to aggravate the inequality of fortunes; to make the rich richer, and the poor poorer; to multiply nabobs and paupers. . . .
Thirdly, I object . . . on account of the exclusive privileges, and anti-republican monopoly, which it gives to the stockholders.

And his own policy? "Gold and silver is the best currency for a republic," he thundered; "it suits the men of middle property and the working people best; and if I was going to establish a working man's party, it should be on the basis of hard money; a hard money party against a paper party." The words reverberated through the hall—"a hard money party against a paper party"—as Mr. Webster of Massachusetts hastily rose to call for a vote which defeated Benton's resolution against recharter.

But the words also reverberated through the country. The *Globe* speedily reprinted the speech, the party press took it up, and pamphlets carried it through the land, to be read excitedly by oil lamp and candlelight, talked over heatedly in taverns and around fireplaces, on steamboats and stagecoaches, along the crooked ways of Boston and the busy streets of New York and on isolated farms in New Hampshire, Missouri, Iowa, Michigan, Arkansas. Nathaniel Macon read it with deep pleasure in North Carolina. "You deserve the thanks of every man, who lives by the sweat of his face," he told Benton, adding with sturdy candor, ". . . I observe some bad grammar,—you must pardon my freedom."

*   *   *

IV

. . . In their nature as corporations, banks gave rise to one set of objections, springing from their monopoly of financial prerogative through special charter. Indeed, they provided so much the most flagrant instances of abuse of corporate privilege that they were mainly responsible for fixing national attention on the problem.

Their power over the currency was viewed as an especially grave encroachment on the domain of government. The regulation of the currency, in the words of Benton, was "one of the highest and most delicate acts of sovereign power . . . precisely equivalent to the power to create currency"; and he considered it "too great a power to be trusted to any banking company whatever, or to any authority but the highest and most responsible which was known to our form of Government." Commercial credit was another matter, "an affair of trade," as Cambreleng put it, "and not of government"; and the logic of this position pointed to the abolition of banks of note issue, on the one hand, and the establishment of free competition among banks of discount and deposit, on the other. The crucial error of the federal government, according to the hard-money advocates, lay in accepting bank notes in the payment of federal dues, by which it thus extended and virtually underwrote the credit of the banks. The remedy was to exclude bank notes from government payments.

The behavior of banks in practice, moreover, violated the national faith in popular rule. The most powerful argument against Biddle's Bank was always its calm assumption of independence. "The Bank of the United States," Jackson charged, "is in itself a Government which has gradually increased in strength from the day of its establishment. The question between it and the people has become one of power." Biddle's conduct, in 1834, in refusing to allow a House committee to investigate the Bank records or examine the Bank officers, was simply the climax of his oft-expressed theory of the Bank's independence. "This powerful corporation, and those who defend it," as Taney said, without much exaggeration, "seem to regard it as an independent sovereignty, and to have forgotten that it owes any duties to the People, or is bound by any laws but its own will."

But Biddle was simply exhibiting on a larger scale habits long established in banking experience. William Graham Sumner concisely summed up the pretensions of the banks:

The bankers had methods of doing things which were customary and conventional, but . . . contrary both to ordinary morality and to law as applied to similar matters outside of banks. . . . The banks also disregarded law so habitually that it became a commonplace that law could not bind them. . . . We search almost in vain through the law reports for any decisions on the rights or authority of the State over banks or the duties of banks to the State.

It may be said that no attempts were made to test or enforce the right of the State against banks, and that, as a matter of practice, it had none. The banks were almost irresponsible. Such decisions as bear at all on the authority of the State over banks proceed from the attempts of the banks to resist the exercise of any authority whatever.

Such a situation obviously could not be long borne. As Theophilus Fisk put it, "Either the State is sovereign, or the Banks are."

V

The social argument—the battle against domination by "the rich and powerful"—represented the culmination of the hard-money doctrine. The economic and political arguments, though capable of standing by themselves, were ultimately directed at conditions preliminary to the question: who shall rule in the state? The recurrent economic crises were evil, not only in themselves, but because they facilitated a redistribution of wealth that built up the moneyed aristocracy. The irresponsible political sovereignties were evil, not only in themselves, but because they provided the aristocracy with instruments of power and places of refuge.

The Bank War compelled people to speculate once again about the conflict of class. "There are but two parties," exclaimed Thomas Hart Benton, giving the period its keynote; "there never has been but two parties . . . founded in the radical question, whether PEOPLE, or PROPERTY, shall govern? Democracy implies a government by the people. . . . Aristocracy implies a government of the rich . . . and in these words are contained the sum of party distinction."

The paper banking system was considered to play a leading role in this everlasting struggle. Men living by the issue and circulation of paper money produced nothing; they added nothing to the national income; yet, they flourished and grew wealthy. Their prosperity, it was argued, must be stolen from the proceeds of productive labor—in other words, from the honest but defenseless "humble members of society"; and Gouge extensively annotated the modes of plunder.

The system was further important in the strategy of the warfare. Taney described the big Bank as "the centre, and the citadel of the moneyed power." "A national bank," declared the Massachusetts Democratic convention of 1837, "is the bulwark of the aristocracy; its outpost, and its rallying point. It is the bond of union for those who hold that Government should rest on property." To a lesser degree all banks acted as strongholds of conservatism. They provided the funds and often the initiative for combat. Their lawyers, lobbyists and newspapers were eternally active. Politicians would gather in their board rooms and consult their presidents and accept gifts of stock. More than any other kind of corporate enterprise, banks boldly intervened in politics when they felt their interests menaced.

The hard-money policy attacked both the techniques of plunder and the general strategy of warfare. By doing away with paper money, it proposed to restrict the steady transfer of wealth from the farmer and laborer to the business community. By limiting banks to commercial credit and denying them control over the currency, it proposed to lessen their influence and power. By reducing the proportion of paper money, it proposed to moderate the business cycle, and order the economy to the advantage of the worker rather than the speculator. It was a coherent policy, based on the best economic thought of the day, and formulated on a higher intellectual level than the alternative of the opposition.

By origin and interest, it was a policy which appealed mainly to the submerged classes of the East and to the farmers of the South rather than to the frontier. Historians have too long been misled by the tableau of Jackson, the wild backwoodsman, erupting into the White House. In fact, the hard-money doctrine, which was not at all a frontier doctrine, was the controlling policy of the administration from the winter of 1833 on; and for some time it had been the secret goal of a small group, led by Jackson, Taney, Benton and Kendall, and passively encouraged by Van Buren. From the removal of the deposits to the end of Van Buren's presidency in 1840 this clique of radical Democrats sought to carry out the policy in its full implications. As soon as the hard-money program was divorced from the glamour of the Hero of New Orleans and had to rest on its inherent appeal, it did very badly in the West.

Andrew Jackson ably summed up its broad aims. "The planter, the farmer, the mechanic, and the laborer," he wrote, "all know that their success depends upon their own industry and economy, and that they must not expect to become suddenly rich by the fruits of their toil." These classes "form the great body of the people of the United States; they are the bone and sinew of the country." Yet "they are in constant danger of losing their fair influence in the Government." Why? "The mischief springs from the power which the money interest derives from a paper currency, which they are able to control, from the multitude of corporations with exclusive privileges which they have succeeded in obtaining in the different States." His warning to his people was solemn. "Unless you become more watchful . . . you will in the end find that the most important powers of Government have been given or bartered away, and the control over your dearest interests has passed into the hands of these corporations."

VI

Taney and Benton worked out the details of the immediate hard-money measures. They proposed to increase the metallic basis of the currency in two directions: by the restoration of gold to circulation, and by the suppression of small notes. The first measure had been for many years close to Benton's heart. Gold had long been undervalued, at the ratio of 15 to 1, with the result that no gold eagles and only a scattering of other gold coins had been minted since 1805, and most of these rapidly left the country. Benton argued that, if the gold were not thus expelled, the amount of specie derivable from foreign commerce, added to the amount obtained from American mines, could supply all financial needs without recourse to small notes or "shinplasters." In June, 1834, his bill to revise the valuation to 16 to 1 passed Congress. As an expression of the strictly economic intentions of the hard-money policy, it made a broad appeal to all men of good will, winning the support of John Quincy Adams, Webster and Calhoun. Only diehards like Clay and Horace Binney opposed it.

The Economic Consequences of the Bank War

PETER TEMIN

The 1830's are fascinating and important years in American history. They witnessed both the emergence of the complex phenomenon known as Jacksonian democracy and the rise and collapse of one of the fastest inflationary movements of the nineteenth century. These two events generally are thought to have been causally connected, since one of the defining acts of Jacksonian democracy was the veto and destruction of the Second Bank of the United States: the celebrated Bank War. The demise of this bank is thought to have removed the only effective constraint on the state banks, leading to credit expansion and inflation.

The purpose of this essay is to take issue with this view and also with the views of several recent, unorthodox investigators. I will suggest instead that the inflation of the 1830's was the result of a fortuitous combination of events, none of which could have produced the price rise by itself, and most of which were not connected with the political acts of President Jackson. Together they maintained a tenuous balance for a few years, but the rapid dissipation of this balance placed intolerable strains upon the existing monetary arrangements and led to the well-known panics of the late 1830's.

The paper is divided into four parts. In the first, the events to be explained are outlined and the inadequacies of previous explanations exposed.

Reprinted from *Journal of Political Economy*, LXXVI (1968), pp. 257–271, by Peter Temin, by permission of The University of Chicago Press. Copyright © 1968 by The University of Chicago. Table and footnotes omitted.

In the second and third, a new explanation is advanced, and empirical evidence is mustered to document the theory. . . .

I

The Second Bank of the United States was chartered in 1816. It was the only bank chartered by the federal government, and it had two special functions in addition to its normal banking activities. It was the fiscal agent of the federal treasury, acquiring as a result the responsibility for a large volume of interregional transactions, and it was supposed to encourage the establishment of a uniform national currency to replace the chaotic issues of state-chartered banks. The latter task was accomplished in two ways. The Second Bank issued its own notes, and it promptly returned the notes of state banks which it received in payment for government obligations (or any other obligations) to the issuing banks for redemption in specie, that is, in silver or gold. In the eyes of several historians, the Second Bank, by taking responsibility to aid the economy in times of crisis, became a fledgling central bank, and its president, Nicholas Biddle, a pioneer central banker.

For reasons that continue to be debated, President Jackson vetoed the bill renewing the Second Bank's twenty-year charter in 1832. This was probably the decisive engagement of the Bank War, but the transfer of the government's deposits in 1833–34 from the Second Bank to state banks had more immediate impact. Biddle's reaction to the loss of these deposits was to restrict credit and accumulate reserves, a policy that lasted from the fall of 1833 into the summer of 1834. This policy led, in turn, to great stringency in the money market and to a recession of unknown magnitude; but to the extent that the Bank's policy was designed to convince the government of the Bank's value, it was a failure.

In March, 1834, Biddle wrote to a colleague that "the Executive, by removing the public revenues has relieved the Bank from all responsibility for the currency." Inflation, or so the traditional story goes, was the consequence.

The precise extent and duration of the inflation depends on the measure used. I will use Smith and Cole's price index, which employs weights designed to show "the tone of business in the northeastern section of the country." This index drifted downward through the 1820's (with a small upward deviation from trend in 1825) to a trough in the summer of 1830. It then rose about 20 per cent in the next three years, peaking in the fourth quarter of 1833. As a result of Biddle's contraction, prices fell to a new trough in the second quarter of 1834 at a level only about 5 per cent above the trough in 1830. Prices rose rapidly from this new trough and reached a peak level 50 per cent above it during the first quarter of 1837. The fall from this peak was irregular: prices fell in 1837, rose in 1838, and fell in

1839 and succeeding years to a trough in the first quarter of 1843, about 20 per cent below the low point in either 1830 or 1834.

One can view these data either as describing an inflation lasting from 1830 to 1837 with a temporary interruption in 1834 or as describing a combination of a mild inflation before 1833 followed by an independent, sharper price rise from 1834 to 1837. The latter view is more common, but I shall tend toward the former in this essay—albeit with emphasis on the speed of the price rise after 1834.

The presumed link between the Bank War and the price rise can be seen in this representative quotation: "The decease of the Bank of the United States with its wholesome if unpopular habit of presenting notes of local banks for payment, released the last brake [on speculation]." This statement rests on the implicit assumption that the state banks were anxious to expand their liabilities without increasing their reserves but were prevented from doing so by the restraining actions of the Second Bank. This constraint being removed, the banks indulged their desires, increasing their liabilities at the cost of lower reserve ratios. The resultant increase in the stock of money then led to the observed rise in prices.

The stock of money did rise with prices, as this theory requires. However, the aggregate reserve ratio of the banking system did not fall between the opening of the Bank War and the start of 1837, as it also requires. The aggregate reserve ratio reached its low point for the period 1820–44 at the end of 1831, when it stood at 15 per cent; and it was between 16 and 18 per cent at the end of each year between 1832 and 1836, except for 1834 when it was higher. A decline in the reserve ratio—that is, an increase in the stock of money due to unsupported bank expansion—cannot be used as an explanation for the price rise of the 1830's.

An alternative view of the inflation was presented by George Macesich in 1960. He argued that an exogenously determined capital inflow led to an excess supply of foreign exchange, a fall in the exchange rate to the specie point, a resultant specie inflow, and an increase in the stock of money. This argument, like the traditional one, fails because of problems with an intermediate step. There was an inflow of both capital and specie during the 1830's, but the connection between them was not as Macesich described. In only one year during the inflation, 1834, did the exchange rate reach the specie point, and most of the specie inflow cannot be seen as a balancing item in the international accounts. . . .

II

I would like to argue that the price movements of the 1830's may be seen as the result of two independent developments. On the one hand, there was the interaction of a slowly rising demand for real balances with a very rapid—and temporary—increase in the supply of nominal balances. On the other hand, there was a temporary rise in the British demand for American securities and cotton that permitted (and even helped to induce) prices in the United States to rise relative to those of its trading partners.

The demand for real balances may be seen as a function of interest rates, price changes, wealth, real income, and tastes. The absence of data on tastes does not pose an insurmountable problem to the estimation of this function; we may assume that people did not change the total amount of money they wished to hold at given levels of the other variables, although the form in which they wished to hold this money may have been changed by the financial vicissitudes of the 1830's. The absence of data on wealth and income, on the other hand, is more serious. As there is a reasonable consensus that the path of income was not smooth in the 1830's and early 1840's, it would be foolhardy to estimate the demand for money on interest rates, price changes, and a time trend (serving as a proxy for wealth and income) alone.

A more indirect approach is indicated. The variables affecting the demand for money may be partitioned into secular and temporary influences. A regression of the real money stock on a time trend will show its dependence on long-run demand influences, and the errors from this regression will show the effects of transitory factors. We do not have enough data to perform a multiple correlation analysis, but a discussion of the errors from this simple regression will provide a reasonable, albeit imprecise, substitute.

A simple time trend rising at 4 per cent per annum explains 82 per cent of the variance of the real money stock from 1830 through 1844. The stock of real balances was above its trend from late 1835 to late 1837, reaching a peak deviation of 14 per cent in late 1835. It was below its trend from late 1838 to late 1842, reaching a peak deviation of 11 per cent in late 1841. The influence of other factors appears clearly, even though the Durbin-Watson statistic of 1.12 does not reject (at a 5 per cent confidence level) the hypothesis of no autocorrelation in the residuals.

Monetary theory predicts that the demand for money should fall when interest rates rise, and rise when they fall, but there is no evidence that interest rates were lower in the mid-1830's than in the early 1840's. Nor is there any evidence of a negative relationship between these two variables in shorter intervals. Our theory also predicts that *if* price changes affect the demand for money, they will act to lower the demand in times of inflation. The rise in the demand for money during the inflationary years of the 1830's implies that this effect may be neglected. Transitory changes in real wealth probably were not large enough to be important, leaving income to be considered. The traditional story assumes that real income rose above its trend in the mid-1830's and fell below it in the early 1840's, behaving much as the deviations of the demand for real balances from its trend. In the absence of further information, we may attribute the observed deviations of the demand for real balances from its trend to income movements, remembering that the deviations were small compared to the changes in the supply of money.

The comparative smallness of the inferred income movement should not be surprising. There was a construction boom in the 1830's, which rivaled the inflation as a topic for contemporary discussion, but the effect of this boom on national income was small. Investment was only about 10 per cent of GNP in the 1830's, and canal and railroad construction was only part of this. There were few unemployed resources at the start of the boom, and the rise in construction could not produce a rise in income—and therefore a rise in the demand for real balances—of appreciable magnitude. (The boom may have benefited from the increasing supply of money, but the stability of interest rates in the 1830's suggests that it owed more to the success of the Erie Canal and the excitement of the cotton boom for its origin.) Similarly, the trade deficit of the mid-1830's—to be discussed shortly—increased the demand for real balances only slightly. The deficit moved with income, but it was not large enough to affect the conclusions drawn from consideration of income movements alone.

This comparatively stable demand for real balances was faced with an extraordinary increase in the supply of money produced by the impact of international specie flows on the American banking system. The slow outward flow of specie that the United States had experienced in the 1820's was replaced about 1830 by a short-lived but rapid inflow. The major cause of this reversal was a rise in the difference between the silver imported from Mexico and the silver exported to the Orient, but the inflow was swelled by specie balancing the capital inflow during the recession of 1834 and specie received in payment of a French indemnity in 1836. None of these flows can be viewed as the result of the price rise in the United States or of internal developments other than the Bank War, and the specie imports attributable to the Bank War amounted to only $8 million out of total imports of $40 million between 1830 and 1836.

Friedman and Schwartz have introduced a decomposition of the stock of money, showing that it can be viewed as a function of the stock of specie (or high-powered money), the reserve ratios of banks, and the proportion of money that is held by the public in the form of specie (as opposed to bank notes or deposits). If the two ratios stay constant, the stock of money is strictly proportional to the stock of specie, and the marginal effect of an added dollar of specie is given by the ratio of the existing stock of money to the existing stock of specie. As a result of the confidence in the banking system that developed during the 1820's, the ratio of money to specie in the United States had risen to a level in the early 1830's that allowed specie flows to have powerful effects on the supply of money. The rise in the stock of money in the 1830's consequently followed directly from the specie imports of that decade.

The combination of a relatively stable demand for real balances and a rapidly rising supply of money led to a rise in prices. This rise in prices in turn led to a balance-of-payments deficit on current account. (The rapid rise in income in the 1830's, of course, acted in the same direction.) In the absence of compensating capital movements, foreign exchange would have become scarce, and its price would have risen. When it rose enough to offset the cost of shipping specie, specie would have been shipped abroad to cover the deficit, limiting the inflation that the specie inflow could cause.

This limit was not effective in the 1830's due to a large rise in the capital exports from Great Britain to the United States in these years. The British exported capital in the 1820's to South America, but the countries of that region soon defaulted on their bonds, and the British turned toward North America. There was a lull in all British foreign lending in the late 1820's, and when British capital exports rose thereafter, capital imports to the United States rose with them. Measuring from 1827—a year of no British capital exports—to 1837, the capital imports to the United States amounted to about three-fifths of all capital exports from Britain.

The shift in the direction of British capital exports could have come about either because of a change on the supply side—a shift in the behavior of British lenders—or because of an increase in the American demand. It seems likely that changes took place on both sides of the market. In the United States, there was a demand for capital to build canals in imitation of the fabulously successful Erie Canal and, during the mid-1830's, to finance the import surplus resulting from the high internal prices. In Britain, there was an exportable surplus, a disillusionment with the direction capital exports had taken in the 1820's, and admiration for the repayment of the U.S. government debt. In addition, the British investors were willing to supply capital to the cotton-growing states at the same time that their willingness to pay high prices for raw cotton reduced the impact of American price rises on the American balance of trade.

The interest-rate differential between British consols and Massachusetts or Boston bonds was approximately half a percentage point higher in the 1830's than in the 1820's, but this was the result of a long-term downward drift of British interest rates that continued irrespective of the flow of capital to the United States. In the absence of greater-than-usual price incentives for capital to flow to the United States, the causes of the large flow must have lain partly in England—in the availability of capital and in sanguine British expectations about the American future. For present purposes, it is sufficient to establish that there was an increase in the supply of capital available to the United States large enough to obviate a specie outflow in payment for the import surplus of the 1830's. And, as mentioned above, the high British demand for American cotton reduced the import surplus to be expected at any given price level and so induced an even greater inflation than might have resulted from the capital and specie flows alone. It therefore contributed to the speed of the inflation after 1834.

This increased supply of capital could not have produced the American inflation by itself, however. Had the United States imported capital without also retaining more of its Mexican silver imports, either its income would have had to rise or specie would have had to be imported from Europe to effect the necessary transfer of resources. In the former case, there would have been no inflation; in the latter, specie would have flowed from England to the United States. The inflation came to an end in 1837 when the Bank of England took measures to restrain its loss of specie. Had the Bank of England lost specie earlier to the United States, it undoubtedly would have taken restrictive measures earlier, terminating the American inflation and importation of capital. Consequently, it was the *combination* of an increased supply of specie and an increased supply of foreign capital that produced the rapid American inflation of the 1830's.

III

Not all parts of the preceding argument lend themselves to extensive documentation. The demand for real balances and the supply of foreign capital in particular are known only approximately, and the evidence pertaining to these functions has been presented in the course of the exposition. For the supply of money, on the other hand, the case is altogether different. It is possible to describe in detail the forces increasing this supply in the 1830's, showing that the increase in the supply of money was a cause, not a result, of the price rise in the United States. This demonstration supports the interpretation presented here at the same time that it documents the refutation of earlier hypotheses.

Data on the money stock in the United States are presented in the first column of Table 1. This series differs from previous ones in definition and in the dating used. Most investigators have followed the treasury in reporting the monetary stock as of January 1 of each year. As the treasury reports were submitted in the first week of January each year, however, it is obvious that the data refer to the stock near the end of the previous year, and they are labeled as such in Table 1. The data on the stock of specie come from a different and less reliable source than the banking data. In all probability they are too low, since the implied proportion of money held in the form of specie by the public (the last column of Table 1) seems unrealistically low in the early 1830's. On the other hand, the changes in this stock—as opposed to its level—agree tolerably well with the international flow of specie, and an adjustment of the level would leave the discussion essentially unchanged.

TABLE 1

THE MONEY STOCK AND ITS DECOMPOSITION

End of Year	Money ($ million)	Specie ($ million)	Reserve Ratio (%)	Proportion of Money Held as Specie (%)
1830	114	32	23	6
1831	155	30	15	5
1832	150	31	16	5
1833	168	41	18	8
1834	172	51	27	4
1835	246	65	18	10
1836	276	73	16	13
1837	232	88	20	23
1838	240	87	23	18
1839	215	83	20	23
1840	186	80	25	24
1841	174	80	23	30
1842	158	90	33	35
1843	194	100	35	26
1844	214	96	27	24

The money stock at the start of the 1830's was no larger than it had been during the 1820's; in fact, it was lower than it had been in the years just before 1830. It rose to a peak at the end of 1836, coincident with the peak in prices and just before the suspension of specie payments in May, 1837. The new trough in 1842 was at a higher level than the 1830 level, but the larger demand for real balances in the later year resulting from the intervening expansion of the economy caused prices to be lower.

The remaining columns of Table 1 shows the three quantities isolated by Friedman and Schwartz as determinants of the money stock (shown as simple functions of the magnitudes Friedman and Schwartz used). The stock of specie, the reserve ratio, and the proportion of money held as specie all had fallen during the 1820's. The export of specie is too small to be analyzed with confidence, but we can infer that the two ratios fell because of increased confidence in the banking system supervised by the Second Bank. As discounts on bank notes of distant banks fell, people were willing to hold proportionately more bank notes and deposits, while banks were enabled to reduce their reserves. The effects of these changes were to leave the size of the money stock essentially unchanged but to decrease the amount of specie contained in it. By the start of the 1830's, therefore, a rise in the stock of specie by one dollar, *ceteris paribus*, would increase the stock of money by four or five dollars. (Of course, if the stock of specie has been underestimated, this multiplier has been overestimated.)

Starting at the end of 1831, a new set of influences on the money stock appeared. The reserve ratio and the proportion of money held as specie stopped declining, remaining stationary or rising in the course of the inflation.

With the exception of 1834, the reserve ratio fluctuated within narrow limits from 1831 through 1836. The deviation of the 1834 data from this pattern can be related to the Bank War; but while it is easy to see why banks would have increased their reserve ratios during the contraction enforced upon them by the Second Bank, it is hard to see why the public should have been willing to hold such a large proportion of their monetary assets as liabilities of these same beleaguered banks. It is likely that the reserve ratio shown for 1834 is too high and the proportion of money held as specie too low. In any case, the lack of a downward trend in the reserve ratio after 1831 shows that the Bank War did not produce the inflation by allowing banks to expand the money supply without attention to reserves.

The upward trend in the proportion of money held as specie began before the crisis of 1837. After that date, the rise in this ratio—as well as the rise in the reserve ratio—can be understood as a reaction to the crisis, but the rise before then is problematical. Contemporary comments propose the hypothesis that it was due to a change in the price of gold in the United States. The United States was on a bimetallic standard, the price of gold being fifteen times the price of silver before 1834. As the world (that is, London) price of gold was higher than this relative to silver, the United States was on an effective silver standard. A law of 1834 decreased the amount of gold in a dollar, leaving the amount of silver unchanged, thus changing the price of gold from fifteen to sixteen times the price of silver. This was slightly higher than the London price ratio, and the intent of the change was to attract gold to the United States and to encourage the use of metallic—as opposed to paper—currency. Even if the assumption that people preferred gold to silver were sound, the presumption that the increased public holdings of specie in the 1830's were composed of gold would be incorrect. Since gold was undervalued before 1834, there was little or no gold in the country at that time, and the imports of gold in the 1830's were not enough to have supplied the public with their increased holdings of specie.

Silver (as well as gold) was flowing into the country after 1834—despite its presumed undervaluation—and it is to the total inflow of specie that we must look. . . . The stock of specie in late 1836 was about $40 million higher than it had been in 1831, a rise that easily explains the rise in the stock of money by about $120 million in the same time. Although changes in all three determinants affected year-to-year changes in the money stock, the changes in the stock of specie were the only ones that consistently and strongly acted to increase the stock of money: the reserve ratio in 1836 was at its 1831–32 level, and the proportion of money held as specie was higher—decreasing the money supply for a given stock of specie. . . .

To discover if any of the specie imports from Europe were balancing items, it is necessary to discover what the equilibrium exchange rate was. The relevant exchange rate is between pounds and dollars, specie being considered as a balancing item primarily in Anglo-American trade. As the price of silver was not officially fixed in England, par usually is assumed to have been determined by the gold content of the pound and the dollar. But gold was undervalued in America relative to Britain before 1834, and gold was not shipped to the United States. Consequently, par as determined by the price of gold was not an equilibrium level.

There was a market for silver in London, and gold was worth about 15.7 times as much as silver on this market in the early 1830's. Gold was worth only fifteen times as much as silver in the United States, and the price of silver in terms of gold was about 5 per cent less in England than in the United States. Americans would import silver at an exchange rate 5 per cent above the rate at which they would ship gold because they could buy silver more cheaply than gold in England, and the exchange rate was prevented from falling to "gold par" by these shipments. The cost of shipping specie was about 2 or 3 per cent of its value, and the shipment of silver was profitable when the exchange rate fell to about 2 or 3 per cent *above* gold par.

The act of 1834 raised the price of gold on August 1, 1834, to sixteen times the price of silver, making silver worth about 2 per cent more in England than in America relative to gold. This was not enough incentive to create an export of silver from the United States in return for an import of gold, but it destroyed the incentive to import silver rather than gold when there was a choice. Gold par became relevant to discussions of American specie imports at this time, and the change in the equilibrium exchange rate (2 per cent) was far less than the change in the bimetallic ratio (7 per cent).

We do not have data on exchange rates; they have to be derived from the price of bills of exchange. Bills of exchange were credit instruments as well as a means of exchanging currency, and the price of a bill on London understates the exchange rate by the interest charge for the duration of the bill. Nevertheless, this price stayed above 2 per cent above gold par before 1834 and above 2 per cent below gold par during the remainder of the 1830's with the sole exception of 1834. The low price of foreign exchange in 1834 encouraged the importation of specie, and we may attribute the $8 million imported from Europe in this year to this profitable opportunity. Biddle's contraction, by decreasing the demand for imports and causing specie to be imported to balance the inflow of capital, had the paradoxical result of aiding the inflation temporarily halted by the contraction.

The inflow of European gold in 1836 was not the result of an excess supply of foreign exchange. Most of this import was in payment of a

French indemnity for damage done to Americans during the Napoleonic Wars under a treaty signed July 4, 1831. The delay in payment resulted from the failure of the French legislature to appropriate the necessary money and caused some bitterness between the Second Bank (which was to collect the indemnity) and the Jackson administration; the timing of this inflow clearly was independent of the American inflation.

But while gold was imported during the inflation as a balancing item in 1834 and as payment for an indemnity in 1836, the major imports of specie were in silver. It can be seen from Table 2 that almost all the silver imports came from Mexico and that they were partially offset by a small but persistent flow of silver to Asia, primarily to China. In the 1820's the outflow of silver to Asia balanced the inflow of silver from Mexico, nullifying any inflationary effects of the imports. This balance was destroyed in the 1830's by a small rise in imports from Mexico and a larger fall in the exports to China.

Silver was a commodity export for Mexico, and the increase in its quantity during the mid-1830's was probably due to an increase in supply. The price of silver was fixed in terms of American currency, and the inflation reduced the quantity of goods bought by a unit of silver. Consequently, the added imports from Mexico were not produced by offers of higher prices for them.

The decline in exports of silver to China and Asia was large enough to make the annual amount of silver retained from the Mexican imports rise from zero in the late 1820's to about $4 million in the 1830's, contributing about $20 million of silver to the American stock of specie between 1831 and 1836. The Chinese were increasing their consumption of opium in the 1830's, and they abandoned their traditional desire for silver in favor of a demand for bills on London to buy opium from British India. The Second Bank facilitated this change by introducing long-dated bills of exchange (the China or India bills), especially for the Eastern trade. It would not be too misleading to say that the Opium War was more closely connected to the American inflation than the Bank War between Jackson and Biddle.

IV

It has been natural to see the events of the years following the Bank War as a test of Jackson's policies toward the Second Bank of the United States. Although commendation of Jackson for his actions would be inappropriate here, it nevertheless must be admitted that the test is not quite fair. There were economic vicissitudes after the destruction of the Second Bank, but do we want to say, "*Post hoc, ergo propter hoc*"? Historians have not been noteworthy for their attempts to reconstruct the causal connection between the Bank War and the inflation, relying explicitly or implicitly on the presumed effects of the former on the money supply. When the determinants of this supply are examined, however, a completely different picture emerges.

The money supply rose for a variety of reasons, and most of them were not connected with Jackson. The introduction of opium into China, the payment of the French indemnity, and the increase in the output of Mexican mines all helped to increase the supply of money independently of Jackson. In addition, the responsiveness of the supply of money to specie imports derived from the high ratio of money to specie permitted by the banking system established before Jackson's election. Only the specie inflow in 1834 caused by the recession of that year can be connected unambiguously to Jacksonian politics.

This rise in the supply of money led to a rise in prices because it was faced with a comparatively stable demand for real balances and a rise in the supply of foreign capital available to the United States. The British willingness to lend in the United States in the 1830's was substantially independent of American politics, although, to the extent it was a reaction to the retirement of the public debt, it owed something to the American tariff policies. Similarly, the stable demand for real balances is hard to link with politics. Taking everything into consideration, Jackson must be given a small part in creating the inflation of the 1830's.

It is a separate question, of course, whether Jackson's new policies in 1836 brought this inflation to its spectacular close. But the inflation was produced by the conjunction of several forces, and it is doubtful whether they could have been kept in balance by any institutional framework available in the 1830's. To the extent that the crisis of 1837 and the subsequent deflation resulted from the disharmony of forces only tenuously and briefly connected, they too cannot be used as impartial tests of Jacksonian policies.

FOR FURTHER READING: Biddle's policies are questioned in Jacob P. Meerman, "The Climax of the Bank War: Biddle's Contraction, 1833–1834," *Journal of Political Economy*, LXXI (August, 1963), pp. 378–388. Harry N. Scheiber, "The Pet Banks in Jacksonian Politics and Finance, 1833–1841," *Journal of Economic History*, XXIII (June, 1963), pp. 198–214, analyzes U.S. Treasury policy in its political as well as its economic context. Robert V. Remini, *Andrew Jackson and the Bank War* (New York, 1967) views the struggle as a political conflict between Jackson and Biddle. Peter Temin's views are elaborated more fully in *The Jacksonian Economy* (New York, 1969).

8

THE ECONOMY OF THE ANTE-BELLUM SOUTH

PROBLEM: *Was slavery profitable?*

For over a century historians, not unlike former plantation owners and abolitionists, have disagreed whether or not slavery as a labor system was profitable for the master class. One group, for whom Ulrich B. Phillips, a leading historian of the South, was a spokesman has contended that it was essentially unremunerative, that it contained within itself the seeds of its own destruction. Phillips noted that the overcapitalization of slaves due to rising prices, the expense of maintaining the ill and aged, and the inefficiency of forced labor made slavery unprofitable. But this viewpoint has been challenged vigorously by others who find that slavery was indeed profitable for the owners. Perhaps the most sophisticated expression of this stand was taken by two young economists, Alfred Conrad and John Meyer of Harvard University, who dealt with the issue by utilizing economic theories. Analyzing slavery from the perspective of modern capital investment theory they concluded that the annual returns from human property were not less than those from other forms of investment. Most likely this controversy has not yet ended, but the following selections contain arguments frequently used on both sides of the issue. What factors need to be considered in assessing the profitability of slavery, or any labor system? How did noneconomic factors affect the profitability of slavery? Have moral considerations affected the views of writers about the economics of slavery?

The Economic Cost of Slaveholding
in the Cotton Belt

ULRICH B. PHILLIPS

Apart from mere surface politics, the ante-bellum South is largely an un-known country to American historians. The conditions, the life, the spirit of its people were so different from those which prevailed and still prevail in the North that it is difficult for northern investigators to interpret correctly the facts which they are able to find. From the South itself they have received little assistance; for before the war Southerners were content, as a rule, to transmit traditions without writing books, and since the war they have been too seriously engrossed in adapting themselves to new conditions to feel any strong impulse towards a scientific recon-struction of the former environment. When the South shall have been interpreted to the world by its own writers, it will be highly useful for students of other sections and other countries to criticize and correct, utilize and supplement the southern historical literature. At the present time, however, the great need seems to be that of interpretation of devel-opments in the South by men who have inherited Southern traditions. This consideration will perhaps justify the following incomplete study.

Whether negro slavery was an advantage in the early colonies and whether it became a burden in the later period, and, if so, how the change occurred, and why the people did not relieve themselves of the incubus—these are a few of the fundamental problems to which the student must address himself. The present essay, based on a study of slave prices, deals with the general economic conditions of slaveholding, and shows the great transformation caused by the opening of the cotton belt and the closing of the African slave trade.

As regards the labor supply, the conditions at the outset in the new world of America were unlike those of modern Europe, but similar to those of Asia and Europe in primitive times. The ancient labor problem rose afresh in the plantation colonies, for land was plentiful and free, and men would not work as voluntary wage-earners in other men's employ when they might as readily work for themselves in independence. There was a great demand for labor upon the colonial estates, and when it be-came clear that freemen would not come and work for hire, a demand developed for servile labor. At first, recourse was had to white men and women who bound themselves to serve three or four years to pay for their transportation across the sea, and to English criminals who were sent to the colonies and bound to labor for longer terms, frequently for five

Reprinted from the *Political Science Quarterly*, XX (June, 1905), pp. 257–275.

or seven years. Indian slaves were tried, but proved useless. Finally the negroes were discovered to be cheap and useful laborers for domestic service and plantation work.

For above half a century after the first negroes were brought to Virginia in 1620, this labor was considered a doubtful experiment; and their numbers increased very slowly until after the beginning of the golden age of the colony toward the end of the reign of Charles II. But the planters learned at length that the negroes could be employed to very good advantage in the plantation system; and after about 1680 the import of slaves grew steadily larger.

In the West Indies the system of plantations worked by slaves had been borrowed by the English settlers from the Spaniards; and when the South Carolina coast was colonized, some of the West India planters immigrated and brought this system with them. In view of the climate and the crops on the Carolina coast, negro slave labor was thought to be a *sine qua non* of successful colonizing. The use of the slaves was confined always to the lowlands, until after Whitney invented the cotton gin; but in the early years of the nineteenth century the rapid opening of the great inland cotton belt created a new and very strong demand for labor. The white farming population already in the uplands was by far too small to do the work; the lowland planters began to move thither with their slaves; the northern and European laboring classes were not attracted by the prospect of working alongside the negroes; and accordingly the demand for labor in the cotton belt was translated into an unprecedented demand for negro slave labor.

Negro slavery was established in the South, as elsewhere, because the white people were seeking their own welfare and comfort. It was maintained for the same economic reason, and also because it was thought to be essential for safety. As soon as the negroes were on hand in large numbers, the problem was to keep their savage instincts from breaking forth, and to utilize them in civilized industry. The plantation system solved the problem of organization, while the discipline and control obtained through the institution of slavery were considered necessary to preserve the peace and to secure the welfare of both races. Private gain and public safety were secured for the time being; but in the long run, as we shall see, these ends were attained at the expense of private and public wealth and of progress.

This peculiar labor system failed to gain strength in the North, because there was no work which negro slaves could perform with notable profit to their masters. In certain parts of the South the system flourished because the work required was simple, the returns were large, and the shortcomings of negro slave labor were partially offset by the ease with which it could be organized.

Once developed, the system was of course maintained so long as it appeared profitable to any important part of the community. Wherever the immediate profits from slave labor were found to be large, the number of slaves tended to increase, not only through the birth of children, but by importations. Thus the staple-producing areas became "black belts," where most of the labor was done by slaves. With large amounts of capital invested in slaves, the system would be maintained even in times of depression, when the plantations were running at something of a loss; for, just as in a factory, the capital was fixed, and operations could not be stopped without a still greater loss. When property in slaves had become important, the conservative element in politics became devoted, as a rule, to the preservation of this vested interest. The very force of inertia tended to maintain the established system, and a convulsion or crisis of some sort was necessary for its disestablishment in any region.

As a matter of fact, it was only in special industries, and only in times of special prosperity, that negro slave labor was of such decided profit as to escape condemnation for its inherent disadvantages. But at certain periods in Virginia and in the lower South, the conditions were unusual: all labor was profitable; hired labor was not to be had so long as land was free; indentured white servants were in various ways unsatisfactory, and negro slaves were therefore found to be of decided profit to their masters. The price of Africans in colonial times was so low that, when crops and prices were good, the labor of those imported repaid their original cost in a few years, and the planters felt a constant temptation to increase their holdings of land and of slaves in the hope of still greater profits.

Thus in Virginia there was a vicious circle: planters bought fresh lands and more slaves to make more tobacco, and with the profits from tobacco they bought more land and slaves to make more tobacco with which to buy yet more land and slaves. The situation in the lower South was similar to that in Virginia, with rice and indigo, or sugar, or in latter times cotton, substituted for tobacco. In either case the process involved a heavy export of wealth in the acquisition of every new laborer. The Yankee skipper had a corresponding circle of his own: he carried rum to Guinea to exchange for slaves, slaves to the plantation colonies to exchange for molasses, molasses to New England to exchange for more rum, and this rum again to Guinea to exchange for more slaves. The difference was that the Yankee made a genuine profit on every exchange and thriftily laid up his savings, while the Southern planter, as a rule, invested all his profit in a fictitious form of wealth and never accumulated a surplus for any other sort of investment.

From an economic point of view the American system of slavery was a system of firmly controlling the unintelligent negro laborers, and of capitalizing the prospective value of the labor of each workman for the whole of his life. An essential feature of that system was the practice of buying and selling the control over the slave's labor, and one of the indexes to the economic situation at any time may be found in the quotations of slave prices.

The slave trade had no particular local home or "exchange," but it extended throughout all the slaveholding districts of America. Though the number and frequency of slave sales was relatively small, the traffic when once developed had many of the features of modern stock or produce markets. It cannot be forgotten, of course, that the slave trade involved questions of humanity and social organization, as well as the mere money problem; but from the financial point of view the slave traffic constituted simply an extensive commodity market, where the article dealt in was lifetime labor. As in any other market, the operations in the slave trade were controlled by economic laws or tendencies. There were bull influences and bear influences, and occasional speculative campaigns. And when at times the supply was subjected to monopoly control, the prices tended to go wild and disturb the general system of finance in the whole region.

In the general slave market there was constant competition among those wishing to sell, and among those wishing to buy. The volume of the colonial slave trade and the rate of slave prices tended to fluctuate to some extent with the tides of prosperity in the respective staple-producing areas; but during the colonial period the plantations in the different regions were of such varied interests, producing tobacco, rice, indigo, cotton, sugar, and coffee, that depression in one of these industries was usually offset, so far as concerned the slave-trader, by high profits in another. Barbados was the information station. The slave ships touched there and gathered news of where their "ebony" was to be sold the highest. The Royal African Company had the best system of intelligence, and about 1770 and 1780 it sold its cargoes at a fairly uniform price of £18 to £22 per head, while the independent traders appear to have obtained from £15 to £25, according to the chances of the market. American-born slaves, when sold, brought higher prices than fresh Africans, because their training in plantation labor and domestic service rendered them more valuable. The prices of the home-raised slaves varied considerably, but so long as the African trade was kept open the price of field hands of all sorts was kept reasonably near to the price of the savage African imports.

In the very early period the sellers in the slave markets were more eager than the buyers, and the prices ranged nearly as low as the cost of purchasing slaves in Africa and transporting them to America; but great prosperity in all the different groups of plantations at the same period soon greatly increased the demand, and the ships in the traffic proving too few, prices rapidly advanced. After this, however, there came a decline in tobacco profits; then the war of revolt from Great Britain depressed all the staple industries simultaneously, and following that the

American production of indigo was ruined by foreign competition. Thus in 1790–95 slave prices reached the bottom of a twenty years' decline.

The developments following Whitney's invention of the cotton gin revolutionized the situation. Slave prices entered upon a steady advance, which was quickened by the prohibition of the African trade in 1808. They were then held stationary by the restrictions upon commerce, and were thrown backward by the outbreak of war in 1812. But with the peace of Ghent the results of the new cotton industry and of the cessation of African imports became strikingly manifest. The inland fields of the lower South proved to be peculiarly adapted for the production of cotton. The simplicity of the work and the even distribution of the tasks through the seasons made negro slave labor peculiarly available. With the increasing demand of the world for cotton, there was built up in the South perhaps the greatest staple monopoly the world had ever seen. The result was an enormous demand for slaves in the cotton belt. American ports, however, were now closed to the foreign slave trade. The number of slaves available in America was now fixed, the rate of increase was limited, and the old "tobacco South" had a monopoly of the only supply which could meet the demand of the new "cotton South."

Till 1815 "colonial" conditions prevailed and the market for slave labor was relatively quiet and steady. In 1815 began the "ante-bellum" régime, in which the whole economy of the South was governed by the apparently capricious play of the compound monopoly of cotton and slave labor. The price of cotton was governed by the American output and its relation to the European demand. And the price of slaves was governed by the profits in cotton and the relation of the labor demand to the monopolized labor supply.

For an understanding of slaveholding economics, a careful study of the history of slave prices is essential. Prior to the middle of the eighteenth century, the scarcity of data, the changing value of gold, the multiplicity of coinage systems and the use of paper money with irregular depreciations unfortunately present so many obstacles that any effort to determine the fluctuation of slave prices would be of very doubtful success. For the following periods the study is feasible, although under the best of existing circumstances slave prices are hard to collect and hard to compare. The proportion of the slave population on the market at any time was very much smaller than the student could wish for the purpose of his study; and many of the sales which were made are not to be found in the records. The market classification of the slaves was flexible and irregular; and, except in Louisiana, most of the documents in the public archives do not indicate the classification. To make thoroughly accurate comparison of slave prices at different times and places, we should need to know, among other things, the sex, age, strength and nativity of the slaves; the purity or mixture of blood of the negroes, mulattoes, quadroons, mestizos, etc.; and their special training or lack of it. For such statistical purposes, however, the records have many shortcomings. In many cases they state simply that the slave Matt or Congo or Martha, belonging to the estate of William Jones, deceased, was sold on the date given to Thomas Smith, for, say, $300, on twelve months' credit. Such an item indicates the sex and states the price, but gives little else. In other instances the slaves are classed as infants, boys, men (or fellows) and old men; girls, wenches and old women. Whole families were often sold as a lot, with no individual quotations given. Women were hardly ever sold separate from their young children. In the dearth of separate sale quotations, any study of the prices of female slaves would have to be based chiefly upon appraisal values, which of course were much less accurate than actual market prices.

The sales made by the professional slave traders were generally recorded each in a bill of sale; but in most of the localities these were not transcribed into the formal books of record, and the originals have mostly disappeared. The majority of the sales of which records are to be found were those of the slaves in the estates of deceased persons. These sales were at auction; and except in abnormal cases, which may often be distinguished, they may be taken as fairly representative of slave prices for the time and place.

There was always a great difference between the values of individual slaves. When the average price of negroes ranged about $500, prime field hands brought, say, $1,000, and skilled artisans still more. At that rate, an infant would be valued at about $100, a boy of twelve years and a man of fifty at about $500 each, and a prime wench for field work at $800 or $900.

The most feasible comparison of prices is that of prime field hands, who may be defined as well-grown, able-bodied fellows, with average training and between eighteen and thirty years of age. To find the current price of prime field hands in lists where no classification is given, we take the average of the highest ordinary prices. We ignore any scattering extreme quotations, as applying probably to specially valuable artisans, overseers of domestic servants, and not to field hands. Where ages are given, we take the average of the prices paid for grown fellows too young to have received special training. We leave aside, on the other hand, the exceptionally low quotations as being due to infirmities which exclude the slave from the prime grade. The professional slave traders in the domestic traffic dealt mostly in "likely young fellows and wenches." In the quotations of the sales of these traders, when no details are recorded, we may assume that the average, except for children, will range just a little below the current rate for prime field hands.

In view of all the hindrances, the production of a perfectly accurate table of prices cannot be hoped for, even from the exercise of the utmost

care and discrimination. The table which follows is simply an approximation of averages made in a careful study of several thousand quotations in
the state of Georgia.[1]

The parallel quotations of cotton prices[2] afford a basis for the study of
slave-labor capitalization. In examining these quotations it will be noticed
that during many brief periods the prices of slaves and cotton rose and
fell somewhat in harmony; but that in the whole period under review the
price of cotton underwent a heavy net decline, while slave prices had an
extremely strong upward movement. The change which took place in the
relative slave and cotton prices was really astonishing. In 1800 a prime
field hand was worth in the market about 1500 pounds of ginned cotton;
in 1809, about 3000 pounds; in 1818, about 3500; in 1826, about 5400; in
1837, about 10,000; in 1845, about 12,000; in 1860, 15,000 to 18,000. In his
capacity for work, a prime negro in 1800 was worth nearly or quite as
much as a similar slave in 1860; and a pound of cotton in 1860 was not
essentially different from a pound of cotton in 1800. But our table shows
that within that epoch of three-score years there was an advance of some
1000 or 1200 per cent in the price of slaves as measured in cotton.

The decline in the price of cotton was due in some measure to a lessen-
ing of cost, through improvements in cultivating, ginning and marketing.
The advance in slave prices was due in part to the increasing intelligence
and ability of the negroes and to improvements in the system of directing
their work on the plantations, and also in part to the decline in the value
of money. But the ten-fold or twelve-fold multiplication of the price of
slaves, when quoted in terms of the product of their labor, was too great
to be explained except by references to the severe competition of the
planters in selling cotton and in buying slaves. Their system of capitalized
labor was out of place in the modern competitive world; and burdened
with that system all the competition of the cotton planters was bound to
be of a cut-throat nature. In other words, when capital and labor were
combined, as in the American slaveholding system, there was an irresistible tendency to overvalue and overcapitalize slave labor, and to carry it to
the point where the financial equilibrium was unsafe, and any crisis
threatened complete bankruptcy.

Aside from the expense of food, clothing, and shelter, the cost of slave
labor for any given period of time was made up of several elements:

[1] The sources used for this tabulation are the documents in the Georgia state archives
and the records of Baldwin, Oglethorpe, Clarke, and Troup counties, all lying in the
Georgia cotton belt, together with bills of sale in private hands, travelers' accounts,
and articles in the newspapers of the period. Instances of sudden rise or fall in slave
prices and sales of large and noted estates were often reported in the local press with
comments. There is no printed collection of any large number of slave-price quotations.
[2] The cotton price averages are made from the tables given by E. J. Donnell in his
Chronological and Statistical History of Cotton, New York, 1872, with the aid of the
summaries published by G. L. Watkins, *Production and Price of Cotton for One Hundred Years*, U.S. Department of Agriculture, Washington, 1895.

SLAVE AND COTTON PRICES IN GEORGIA

Year	Average Price of Prime Field Hands	Economic Situation and the Chief Determinant Factors	Average N.Y. Price of Upland Cotton	Years
1755......	£55			
1773......	60			
1776–1783.	......	War and depression in industry and commerce.		
1784......	70	Peace and returning prosperity.		
1792......	$300	Depression due to Great Britain's attitude toward American commerce.		
1793......	......	Cotton gin invented.		
1800......	450	....	30 cents.	1795–1805
1808.......	......	African slave trade prohibited.		
1809......	600	Embargo moderates rise in prices..................	19 cents.	1805–1810
1813......	450	War with Great Britain....	12 cents.	1813
1818......	1000	Inflation.	29 cents.	1816–1818
1819......	......	Financial crisis............	16 cents.	1819
1821......	700	Recovery from panic......	14 cents.	1821
1826......	800	Moderate prosperity.......	15 cents.	1824–1827
1827......	......	Depression.		
1828......	700	....	10 cents.	1827–1828
1835......	900	Flush times...............	17½ cents.	1835
1837......	1300	Inflation—crash............	13½ cents.	1837
1839......	1000	Cotton crisis.............	13½ cents.	1839
1840......	700	Cotton crisis; acute distress.	9 cents.	1840
1844......	600	Depression................	7½ cents.	1844
1845......	......	Severe depression.........	5½ cents.	1845
1848......	900	Recovery in cotton prices. Texas demand for slaves.	9½ cents.	1847–1848
1851......	1050	Prosperity	12 cents.	1851
1853......	1200	Expansion of cotton industry and simultaneous rise in tobacco prices..........	11 cents.	1850–1860
1859......	1650			
1860......	1800			

(1) Interest upon the capital invested in the slave.

(2) Economic insurange against (a) his death, (b) his illness or accidental injury, and (c) his flight from service.[3] Of course insurance poli-

[3] Physicians' and attorneys' fees should perhaps be included under the head of insurance. It may be noted that doctors' charges were generally the same for slaves as for white persons. To illustrate how expensive this charge often was, we may cite an instance given in the records of Troup county, Georgia, where Dr. Ware collected from Col. Truitt's estate $130.50 for medicine and daily visits to a negro child, from November 29, 1858, to January 5, 1859.

cies were seldom taken out to cover these risks, but the cost of insurance against them must be reckoned in the cost of slave labor for any given period.

(3) The diminishing value of every mature slave by reason of increasing age. Because of the "wear and tear" of his years and his diminishing prospect of life and usefulness, the average slave of fifty-five years of age would be worth only half as much as one of twenty-five years, and after fifty-five the valuation decreased still more rapidly. In computing the cost of any group of slaves it will be necessary to set over against this depreciation the value of the children born; but, on the other hand, the cost by groups would be increased by the need of supporting the disabled negroes who were not in the working gangs.

(4) Taxation assessed upon the capitalized value of the slaves. In the slaveholding region as a whole, in the later ante-bellum period, the total assessed value of slave property was at least as great as that of all the other sorts of property combined.

The rate of slave hire would furnish a good index of the current price of slave labor year by year, if sufficient quotations on a stable basis could be obtained. But on account of the special needs or wishes of the parties to the individual bargains, there were such opportunities for higgling the rate in individual cases that the current rate is very elusive. The following averages, computed from a limited number of quotations for the hire of men slaves in middle Georgia, are illustrative: In 1800, $100 per year; in 1816, $110; in 1818, $140; in 1833, $140; in 1836, $155; in 1841, $140; in 1860, $150. These were in most cases the years of maximum quotations in the respective periods. The local fluctuations in short periods were often very pronounced; but in the long run the rate followed a gradual upward movement.

The relation between the price of slaves and the rate of their hire should theoretically have borne, in quiet periods, a definite relation to the rate of interest upon capital; but the truth is that in the matter of slave prices there was, through the whole period after the closing of the African trade, a tendency to "frenzied finance" in the cotton belt. Slave prices were largely controlled by speculation, while slave hire was regulated more largely by the current rate of wages for labor in general. The whole subject of these relations is one for which authentic data are perhaps too scanty to permit of thorough analysis.

Negro slave labor was expensive, not so much because it was unwilling as because it was overcapitalized and inelastic. The negro of himself, by reason of his inherited inaptitude, was inefficient as a self-directing laborer in civilized industry. The whole system of civilized life was novel and artificial to him; and to make him play a valuable part in it, strict guidance and supervision were essential. Without the plantation system, the mass of the negroes would have been an unbearable burden in America; and except in slavery they could never have been utilized, in the beginning, for plantation work. The negro had no love of work for work's sake; and he had little appreciation of future goods when set over against present exemption from toil. That is to say, he lacked the economic motive without which voluntary civilized industry is impossible. It is a mistake to apply the general philosophy of slavery to the American situation without very serious modification.[4] A slave among the Greeks or Romans was generally a relatively civilized person, whose voluntary labor would have been far more productive than his labor under compulsion. But the negro slave was a negro first, last, and always, and a slave incidentally. Mr. Cairnes and others make a great mistake when they attribute his inefficiency and expensiveness altogether to the one incident of regulation. Regulation actually remedied in large degree the disadvantages of using negro labor, though it failed to make it as cheap, in most employments, as free white labor would have been. The cotton planter found the negro already a part of the situation. To render him useful, firm regulation was necessary. The forcible control of the negro was in the beginning a necessity, and was not of itself a burden at any time.[5]

In American slaveholding, however, the capitalization of labor-value and the sale and purchase of labor-control were permanent features; and when the supply was "cornered" it was unavoidable that the price should be bid up to the point of overvaluation. And this brings us to the main economic disadvantage of the system.

In employing free labor, wages are paid from time to time as the work is done, and the employer can count upon receiving from the products of that labor an income which will enable him to continue to pay its wages in the future, while his working capital is left free for other uses. He may invest a portion of his capital in lands and buildings, and use most of the remainder as circulating capital for special purposes, retaining only a small percentage as a reserve fund. But to secure a working force of slaves, the ante-bellum planter had to invest all the capital that he owned or could borrow in the purchase of slaves and lands; for the larger his plantation was, within certain limits, the more economies he could introduce. The temptation was very strong for him to trim down to the lowest possible limit the fund for supplies and reserve. The slaveholding system thus absorbed the planter's earnings; and for such absorption it had unlimited capacity, for the greater the profits of the planters the more slaves

[4] Palgrave's *Dictionary of Political Economy* contains an excellent article upon slavery, in which it is indicated that harshness and compulsion were not always essential in slave labor; that the motive force was often a sort of feudal devotion to the master; and, further, the negro slave labor was practically essential for developing the resources of the hot malarial swamp regions.

[5] The current rate of hire today for negro workmen in agriculture in Georgia is from $8 to $12 per month; but for the year 1904, the state of Georgia leased out its able-bodied convicts at an average rate of $225 per year. When under strict discipline, the average negro even today, it appears, is worth twice as much as when left to his own devices.

they wanted and the higher the slave prices mounted. Individual profits, as fast as made, went into the purchase of labor, and not into modern implements or land improvements. Circulating capital was at once converted into fixed capital; while for their annual supplies of food, implements and luxuries the planters continued to rely upon their credit with the local merchants, and the local merchants to rely upon their credit with northern merchants and bankers.

Thus there was a never-ending private loss through the continual payment of interest and the enhancement of prices; and, further, there was a continuous public loss by the draining of wealth out of the cotton belt by the slave trade. With the stopping of the African slave trade, the drain of wealth from the lower South was not checked at all, but merely diverted from England and New England to the upper tier of the Southern states; and there it did little but demoralize industry and postpone to a later generation the agricultural revival.

The capitalization of labor lessened its elasticity and its versatility; it tended to fix labor rigidly in one line of employment. There was little or no floating labor in the plantation districts, and the planter was obliged to plan in detail a whole year's work before the year began. If he should plant a larger acreage than his "force" could cultivate and harvest, a part of the crop would have to be abandoned, unless by chance some free negro or stray Irishman could be found for the odd job. As an illustration of the financial hardships which might befall the slaveholder, it may be noted that in 1839 William Lowndes Yancey happened to lose his whole force of slaves through poisoning in the midst of the working season. The disaster involved his absolute ruin as a planter, and forced him to seek some other opening which did not require the possession of capital.

In the operation of cotton production, where fluctuating and highly uncertain returns demanded the greatest flexibility. the slaveholding system was rigid. When by overproduction the price of cotton was depressed, it could be raised again only by curtailing the output in the American cotton belt, which had the monopoly. But the planter, owning cotton lands and slaves trained in the cotton field alone, found it hard to devote his fields with success to other crops or to sell or lease his negroes to anyone else, for no one else wanted them for any other purpose than cotton production. In fact, the proportion of the Southern resources devoted to cotton production tended always to increase. To diminish the cotton output required the most heroic efforts. As a rule, the chances of heavy gains from cotton planting outweighed those of loss, in the popular estimation; and the strong and constant tendency was to spoil the market by over-supply.

There were uncertain returns in cotton-raising, and great risks in slave-owning. The crop might be heavy or light in any year, according to the acreage and the weather, and prices might be away up or away down.

A prime slave might be killed by a rattlesnake or crippled in a log-rolling or hanged for murder or spirited away by the underground railroad. All these uncertainties fostered extravagance and speculation.

In the cotton belt, inflation and depression followed each other in rapid succession; but the times of prosperity brought less real advantage and periods of depression caused greater hardship in the slaveholding South than in any normally organized community. For by the capitalizing of labor, profits were generally absorbed through the purchasing of additional slaves at higher prices, while in time of need the cotton-planter found it impossible to realize upon his investment because his neighbors were involved in the same difficulties which embarrassed him and when he would sell they could not buy.

When after the peace in 1815 the system of industry and finance of the ante-bellum South had fully developed itself, the South and its leaders were seized in the grip of social and economic forces which were rendered irresistible by the imperious laws of monopoly. The cotton-planters controlled the South, and for some decades they dominated the policy of the federal government; but the cotton-planters themselves were hurried hither and thither by their two inanimate but arbitrary masters, cotton and slavery.

Cotton and slavery were peculiar to the South, and their requirements were often in conflict with the interests and ideas prevailing in the other parts of the United States. As that conflict of interests and sentiments was accentuated, it became apparent that the South was in a congressional minority, likely to be overridden at any time by a northern majority. Ruin was threatening the vested interests and the social order in the South, and the force of circumstances drove the southern politicians into the policy of resistance. To the leaders in the South, with their ever-present view of the possibility of negro uprisings, the regulations of slavery seemed essential for safety and prosperity. And when they found themselves about to become powerless to check any legislation hostile to the established order in the South, they adopted the policy of secession-seeking, as they saw it, the lesser of the evils confronting them.

Because they were blinded by the abolition agitation in the North and other historical developments which we cannot here discuss, most of the later generation of ante-bellum planters could not see that slaveholding was essentially burdensome. But that which was partly hidden from their vision is clear to us to-day. In the great system of southern industry and commerce, working with seeming smoothness, the negro laborers were inefficient in spite of discipline, and slavery was an obstacle to all progress. The system may be likened to an engine, with slavery as its great fly-wheel—a fly-wheel indispensable for safe running at first, perhaps, but later rendered less useful by improvements in the machinery, and finally becoming a burden instead of a benefit. Yet it was retained, because it was still considered essential in securing the adjustment and regular working of the complex mechanism. This great rigid wheel of slavery was so awkward and burdensome that it absorbed the momentum and retarded the movement of the whole machine without rendering any service of great value. The capitalization of labor and the export of earnings in exchange for more workmen, always of a low degree of efficiency, together with the extreme lack of versatility, deprived the South of the natural advantage which the cotton monopoly should have given. To be rid of the capitalization of labor as a part of the slaveholding system was a great requisite for the material progress of the South.

The Economics of Slavery
in the Ante-Bellum South

ALFRED H. CONRAD AND JOHN R. MEYER

OBJECTIVES AND METHODS

The outstanding economic characteristics of southern agriculture before the Civil War were a high degree of specialization and virtually exclusive reliance on a slave labor force. The large-scale, commercial dependence upon slave labor was to distinguish the ante bellum South not only from other regions in its own time but from all regions at all other times in American agricultural history. Because of this unique historical status, ante bellum southern agriculture has been a subject for special historical attention. Above all else, attention has been focused upon the proposition that, even without external intervention, slavery would have toppled of its own weight. This allegation has its source in the assertions of slave inefficiency to be found in the writings of men who lived with slavery: American or English liberals like G. M. Weston, H. R. Helper, or J. E. Cairnes and southern slaveowners who, in a religious, self-righteous age, could find every motive for the protection of the slave system except that it was personally profitable. The argument is to be found most strongly stated in the work of later southern historians, especially C. W. Ramsdell and U. B. Phillips, who take the position that the Civil War, far from being an irrepressible conflict, was an unnecessary blood bath. They argue that slavery had reached its natural limits and that it was cumbersome and inefficient and, probably within less than a generation, would have destroyed itself. To the question why emancipa-

Reprinted from *The Journal of Political Economy*, LXVI, No. 2 (April, 1958), pp. 95–122, 440–443, by permission of John R. Meyer.

tion was not resorted to, they reply that slavery was for the southerners an important (and evidently expensive) duty, part of their "unending task of race discipline." On the other side, Lewis Gray and Kenneth Stampp have strongly contested this view, contending that southern plantation agriculture was at least as remunerative an economic activity as most other business enterprises in the young republic.

The evidence employed in this debate has been provided by the few, usually fragmentary, accounting records that have come down to us from early plantation activities. The opposing parties have arranged and re-arranged the data in accordance with various standard and sometimes imaginary accounting conventions. Indeed, the debate over the value of the different constituent pieces of information reconstructs in embryo much of the historical development of American accounting practices. For example, virtually all the accounting valuation problems have been discussed with relation to the slave question, including the role and meaning of depreciation, the nature and accountability of interest charges, and the validity of distinctions between profits and payments of managerial wages. But, despite the fact that the problem is ostensibly one in economic history, no attempt has ever been made to measure the profitability of slavery according to the economic (as opposed to accounting) concept of profitability. This paper is an attempt to fill this void.

Thus this paper is devoted to establishing methodological as well as historical points. Specifically, we shall attempt to measure the profitability of southern slave operations in terms of modern capital theory. In doing so, we shall illustrate the ways in which economic theory might be used in ordering and organizing historical facts. An additional methodological point is also made evident by this exercise, namely, how the very simple statistical concepts of range and central tendency as applied to frequency distributions of data can be employed in interpreting or moderating inferences from historical facts.

In executing these tasks, we must ask first what it is we are talking about and, second, whether we can say anything that can be proved or disproved. For example, we must ask what the slave economy was. Was it cotton culture? Was it cotton and sugar and tobacco? Was it all of ante bellum southern agriculture? In answering, we shall define slavery in terms of two production functions. One function relates inputs of Negro slaves (and the materials required to maintain the slaves) to the production of the southern staple crops, particularly cotton. The second function describes the production of the intermediate good, slave labor—slave-breeding, to use an emotionally charged term which has colored, even determined, most of the conclusions about this problem.

What do we mean by "efficiency"? Essentially, we shall mean a comparison of the return from the use of this form of capital—Negro slaves—with the returns being earned on other capital assets at the time. Thus we mean to consider whether the slave system was being dragged down of its own weight; whether the allocation of resources was impaired by the rigidity of capitalized labor supply; whether southern capital was misused or indeed drawn away to the North; and, finally, whether slavery must inevitably have declined from an inability of the slave force to reproduce itself.

The hypothesis that slavery was an efficient, maintainable form of economic organization is not a new one, of course. Nor are we, by one hundred years, at least, among the first to conclude that Negro slavery was profitable in the ante bellum South. What we do feel to be novel, however, is our approach. Postulating that American Negro slavery was characterized by two production functions, we argue that an efficient system developed in which those regions best suited to the production of cotton (and the other important staples) specialized in agricultural production, while the less productive land continued to produce slaves, exporting the increase to the staple-crop areas. It is this structure that we are examining.

We propose to test the hypothesis by putting appropriate values on the variables in the production functions and computing the rate of return over cost, the stream of income over the lifetime of the slave. This rate of return, the marginal efficiency of slave capital, must, in turn, be shown to be at least equal to the rate of interest currently available in the American capital markets. It is further necessary to show that appropriate markets existed to make this regional specialization possible and that slavery did not necessarily imply the disappearance or misallocation of capital. Evidence on the ability of the slave force to maintain itself numerically will be had as a corollary result. For these purposes it is necessary to obtain data on slave prices and cotton prices, the average output of male field hands and field wenches, the life-expectancy of Negroes born in slavery, the cost of maintaining slaves during infancy and other nonproductive periods, and, finally, the net reproduction rate and the demographic composition of the slave population in the breeding and using areas.

Looked upon simply as a staple-commodity agriculture, the southern system must appear to have been burdened—possibly even to have been on the verge of collapse—under the weight of areas of inefficient, unprofitable farming. We submit that this view is in error and that the error arises from the failure to recognize that an agricultural system dependent upon slavery can be defined operationally only in terms of the production function for both the final good—in our case, cotton—and the production function for the intermediate good—Negro slaves. Considered operationally, in terms of a neoclassical two-region, two-commodity trade system, it must be seen that a slave system produces labor as an intermediate good. The profitability of the system cannot be decided without considering the system's ability to produce chattel labor efficiently.

They're saying the system of production produced ①COTTON ②) slaves. (2 commodity system)

There are also non-historical reasons for taking up once again the economics of ante bellum southern slavery. A detailed re-evaluation of the profits of plantation slavery in the American South might help us evaluate the possibilities, first, that the near-slavery existing today in many highly agricultural, underindustrialized lands is an institution that can be expected to disappear automatically or, second, that dislodging it will require substantial governmental pressure or interference. These are, of course, often key policy questions in former colonial countries that are just beginning to develop modern industrial economics.

The possible relevance of the American experience in this connection increases, moreover, as the underlying economic motivations of a slave system are analyzed and established. This happens primarily because, once these motives are recognized, it becomes possible better to understand and predict the political structures that will accompany slavery. In other words, the interrelationships between certain economic and political goals of slavery can be better understood once the underlying economic factors are understood. . . .

REPRODUCTION, ALLOCATION, AND

SLAVE MARKETS

It thus remains to be determined whether an efficient supply mechanism —efficient in both its generative and its allocative functions—existed in the ante bellum South. That the slave force might reproduce itself was not sufficient; there must also have been a capital market capable of getting the labor to the areas where production was expanding if slavery was to be profitable. It will be useful to introduce the secondary propositions by stating several arguments which together form the orthodox opposition to the present hypothesis. The arguments follow, in every case accompanied by a citation as a talisman against any possible charge that we are setting up straw men: (i) slaves are notoriously inefficient and unwilling workers; (ii) slave property, unlike wage labor, must be supported in the years before and after the slave is economically productive; (iii) slaveholding absorbed plantation earnings; (iv) slave economies are constantly threatened by decline because they cannot in general maintain the number of slaves; and (v) capitalization of the labor force inhibits the efficient allocation of labor.

The first and second of these arguments are implicitly tested in the computation of the rate of return on slave capital. We are not concerned with efficiency per se, however that might be measured, or with the efficiency of slaves as opposed to free white laborers. The more sophisticated version of this efficiency argument—that slave ineptness forced the planters to use a particularly wasteful form of agriculture—is probably untestable because of the difficulties of identification where impetus or motives are being considered. It might be suggested as a partial answer, however, that extensive farming was not peculiarly a characteristic of slave agriculture or even of plantation cotton culture. It was common to all North American colonial agriculture and, as late as the end of the nineteenth century, was reputed to be characteristic of farming in the Northwest wheat lands. It is, generally, a salient feature of agriculture where labor is scarce relative to land. But, insofar as slaves were inefficient, the inefficiency must be reflected in the returns computed in our model. Similarly, the costs of maintaining slaves in infancy and dotage are accounted for in our cost of production.

The third argument—that the South lost from the payment of interest and the constant enhancement of prices (and, therefore, overcapitalization of the labor force)—rests in part upon two misapprehensions, attributable to U. B. Phillips: (1) that capitalization involves a net loss through the payment of interest and (2) that slaves were, somehow, a fictitious form of wealth. We have already shown that slave capital earned returns at least equal to those earned by other contemporary forms of capital. For the overcapitalization part of the argument, it remains to be shown that slave prices did not run away from cotton values.

The last two of the assertions state the negative of our principal secondary hypothesis, which is that an efficient market system existed for the supply of slaves to the rapidly growing cotton industry of the Southwest from the exhausted land of the Old South. It will be shown below that the slave population, in all but the Louisiana sugar area, more than reproduced itself. It will be further shown that the border states were not being depleted to provide for western needs but that only the natural increase was being exported. Finally, avoiding the emotion-wracked testimony of the time, we will attempt to demonstrate the existence of regional specialization and an efficient market by comparing the demographic composition of the cotton and border states and by examining the price behavior in the market for Negro slaves.

A. THE REPRODUCTION OF THE SLAVE LABOR FORCE

The history of slavery is full of examples of slave economies which could not reproduce their population and collapsed because of a failure of supply. Frequently, as in the Roman case, the supply was dependent upon a steady flow of military prisoners. The Augustan peace and the stabilization of the borders of the empire are credited with the decline of Roman slavery for this reason. Similarly, the labor supply in the Caribbean sugar islands could be maintained only by importation. It is generally argued that slavery disappeared from Jamaica because of the inability of the slave population to reproduce itself once the slave trade had been closed and not because of abolition in 1834.

By contrast, the ante bellum cotton-slave economy of the southern states managed to maintain and allocate its labor supply by a system of regional specialization which produced slaves on the worn-out land of the Old South and the border states for export to the high-yield cotton land of the Mississippi and Red River valleys. For the whole nation the Negro rate of increase in the six decades before the Civil War was only slightly below the rate for the white population; for most of the period, the slave rate was very much above that for free Negroes. In the South the disparity between Negro and white rates of increase is in favor of the

TABLE 12

PERCENTAGE DECENNIAL INCREASE IN WHITE AND NEGRO POPULATION, 1790–1860

INCREASE DURING PRECEDING TEN YEARS

CENSUS YEAR	Total	White	Negro		
			Total	Slave	Free
1800....	35.1	35.8	32.3	28.1	82.2
1810....	36.4	36.1	37.5	33.1	71.9
1820....	33.1	34.2	28.6	29.1	25.3
1830....	33.5	33.9	31.4	30.6	36.8
1840....	32.7	34.7	23.4	23.8	20.9
1850....	35.9	37.7	26.6	28.8	12.5
1860....	35.6	37.7	22.1	23.4	12.3

Source: Bureau of the Census, *Negro Population in the United States, 1790–1915* (Washington, D.C., 1918), Tables 2 (chap. ii) and 1 (chap. v) and pp. 25 and 53. The sharp declines in the rate of increase for slaves in the decades ending in 1840 and 1860 probably reflect the generation cycle following the increase in importations, mostly of mature Negroes, in the years just prior to 1808.

Negro rate; considering the relative rates of immigration of whites and Negroes after the first decade of the nineteenth century, the discrepancy in natural increase is even more striking. The evidence in Table 12 does not admit of any doubt that the slave population was capable of producing a steady supply of labor for the plantation economy.

B. SLAVE MARKETS AND ALLOCATION

The more important issue, however, is whether or not the slave force could be allocated efficiently. The natural rate of increase was more than sufficient in the Old South to meet the needs of agriculture in the region, but in the West it was less than sufficient to meet the demands for increased cotton production. By direct export and by the migration of planters with their work forces, the eastern areas supplied the needs of the Southwest. In every decade before the Civil War, the increase of slaves in the cotton states was much above and in the Atlantic and border states much below the rate of increase for the whole slave population. Indeed, in the decades ending in 1840 and 1860, the net rate of population increase in the Old South was only slightly above the level sufficient to maintain the population at a constant level, 4.5 per cent and 7.1 per cent (see Table 13). From 1790 to 1850 the increase of slaves in the Atlantic states was just 2 per cent per annum, while in the Gulf states (including Florida), Arkansas, and Tennessee the rate was 18 per cent per annum. A rough but probably conservative estimate of the export from the selling states between 1820 and 1860 is given by W. H. Collins. Taking the difference between the average natural increase and the actual rate in the selling states, Collins arrived at the following estimates:

1820–30	124,000
1830–40	265,000
1840–50	146,000
1850–60	207,000

Collins estimated that at least three-fifths of the removals from the border states were due to emigration to the Southwest rather than to export. While this has little bearing upon the issue of allocative efficiency, it does have significance for the corollary assertion that the slaveowners of the border states, consciously or unconsciously, were engaged in a specialized breeding operation, producing chattel labor for the growing Southwest. In 1836 the *Virginia Times* estimated that, "of the number of slaves exported [from Virginia], not more than one-third have been sold, the others being carried by their masters, who have removed." Ruffin supposed that the annual sales in 1859 "already exceed in number all the increase in slaves in Virginia by procreation." Bancroft goes beyond these estimates and states that "in the 'fifties, when the extreme prejudice against the interstate traders had abated and their inadequate supplies were eagerly purchased, fully 70 per cent of the slaves removed from the Atlantic and the border slave states to the Southwest were taken after purchase or with a view to sale, that is, were the objects of slave-trading." Whatever the accuracy of these several estimates, which range from two-fifths to four-fifths of total exports of slaves from the border and the Atlantic states, it is clear that sales of slaves provided an important capital gain for the exporting states. There is ample documentary evidence that planters in the Old South were aware of this, that some welcomed it and depended upon it, and that others were fearful of its effect upon the agriculture of the area and upon the tenability of slavery. Some spoke frankly about Virginia as a "breeding state," though the reply to such allegations was generally an indignant denial. Whether systematically bred or

TABLE 13

PERCENTAGE RATE OF POPULATION INCREASE, BY RACE, IN THE COTTON AND BORDER STATES, 1790–1860

DECADE ENDING	COTTON STATES*		BORDER STATES†	
	White	Negro	White	Negro
1800....	42.9	47.4	27.9	24.4
1810....	37.5	61.3	23.5	23.4
1820....	38.8	48.0	19.5	15.5
1830....	40.0	46.8	19.0	14.0
1840....	31.3	37.6	21.1	4.5
1850....	34.1	35.6	34.5	11.0
1860....	27.6	29.0	39.2	7.1

Source: Ernst von Halle, *Baumwollproduktion und Pflanzungswirtschaft in den Nordamerikanischen Sudstaaten* (Leipzig, 1897), p. 132. His sources were Tucker, *Progress of the United States* (to 1840), *Census of Population* (1850 and after), and H. Gannett, *Statistics of the Negroes in the United States.*

* North Carolina, South Carolina, Georgia, Florida, Alabama, Mississippi, Louisiana, Texas, Arkansas, and Tennessee.

† Delaware, Maryland, District of Columbia, Virginia, West Virginia, Kentucky, and Missouri.

not, the natural increase of the slave force was an important, probably the most important, product of the more exhausted soil of the Old South.

The existence of such specialization is evident in the demographic composition of the cotton and breeding areas and in the price behavior in the markets for slaves. Table 14 demonstrates that the selling states

TABLE 14

SLAVE POPULATION BY AGE
(Per Cent)

AGE (YEARS)		1860			1850	
	TOTAL	Selling States*	Buying States†	TOTAL	Selling States*	Buying States†
Under 15	44.8	45.6	43.8	44.9	45.6	44.3
15–19	11.4	11.5	11.4	11.1	11.3	11.0
20–29	17.6	16.5	18.9	18.0	17.0	18.9
30–39	11.7	10.7	11.8	11.3	10.5	12.1
20–49	36.4	34.4	38.1	36.4	34.6	38.1
50 and over	7.5	8.5	6.7	7.5	8.5	6.6

Source: J. C. G. Kennedy, *Population of the United States in 1860* (Washington, D.C., 1864), "Classified Population," Tables No. 1, by state; J. D. B. DeBow, *Statistical View of the United States, . . . Being a Compendium of the Seventh Census* (Washington, D.C., 1854), Part II, Table LXXXII, pp. 89–90.

* Virginia, Maryland, Delaware, South Carolina, Missouri, Kentucky, District of Columbia.

† Georgia, Alabama, Mississippi, Florida, Texas, Louisiana.

contained, in 1850 and 1860, a greater proportion of children under fifteen years and a substantially greater proportion of slaves above the age of fifty than did the buying states. While the disproportions are not great enough to characterize the selling states as a great nursery, the age composition is in the direction which our hypothesis would lead one to expect. The relationship between the prices of men and women in the slave market, when compared with the ratio of hiring rates for male and female field hands, gives an even stronger indication that the superior usefulness of females of breeding age was economically recognized. The relative hiring rates for men and women in 1860, shown in Table 15, can be taken as a measure of their relative values in the field.

TABLE 15

ANNUAL HIRING RATES FOR MALE AND FEMALE SLAVES (INCLUDING RATIONS AND CLOTHING), BY STATES, 1860

State	Men	Women	Ratio (Men : Women)
Virginia	$105	$ 46	2.28
North Carolina	110	49	2.25
South Carolina	103	55	1.87
Georgia	124	75	1.65
Florida	139	80	1.74
Alabama	138	89	1.55
Mississippi	166	100	1.66
Louisiana	171	120	1.43
Texas	166	109	1.52
Arkansas	170	108	1.57
Tennessee	121	63	1.92

To compare to these rates, we have purchase prices of male and female slaves, in the same markets, in 1859 and 1860. The purchase prices should reflect the relative usefulness of the sexes for field work. More than this, however, if there is any additional value to slave women—for breeding purposes, presumably—there should be a premium in the form of a narrower price differential than is found in the hiring rates. The prices shown in Table 16 are taken from Table A in the Appendix. Whenever possible, 1860 is used; wherever necessary, 1859. Table 16 includes age designations and, when available, a description of the grade or class represented in the average price. This evidence is a striking confirmation of the validity of the model. In every case but one, the purchase-price differential is narrower than the hiring-rate differential. The price structure clearly reflects the added value of females due to their ability to generate capital gains. It is especially interesting in this regard to note that the price ratios in Virginia and South Carolina, the two breeding states represented in the list, show practically no differential. This evidence

TABLE 16

SELECTED PRICES OF MALE AND FEMALE SLAVES, 1859 AND 1860

State (Year)	Age	Condition	Male Price	Female Price	Ratio
Virginia (1859)	17–20	Best	$1,350–$1,425	$1,275–$1,325	1.07
South Carolina	....	Prime	$1,325	....	
	....	Wench	......	$1,283	} 1.03
South Carolina (1859)	....	Field hand	$1,555	......	
	....	Girl	......	$1,705	} .91
Georgia	21	Best field hand	$1,900	......	
	17	(9 mo. inf.)	......	[$2,150]	} .88
Georgia (1859)	....	Prime, young	$1,300	......	
		Cotton hand			1.04
	....	houseservant	......	$1,250	
Alabama (1859)	19	....	$1,635	......	
	18, 18, 8	....	......	$1,193	} 1.37
Mississippi	....	No. 1 field hand	$1,625	$1,450	1.12
Texas	21, 15	....	$2,015	$1,635	1.23
Texas (1859)	17, 14	....	$1,527	$1,403	1.09

clearly shows that the Old South recognized in the market the value of its function as the slave-breeding area for the cotton-raising West.

C. THE "OVERCAPITALIZATION" OF THE LABOR FORCE

The aspect of slave economics that causes the most confusion and outright error is that which relates to the capitalization, and, in the ante bellum southern case, the presumed overcapitalization, of slave labor. Phillips speaks of an "irresistible tendency to overvalue and overcapitalize" and argues that slaveholding had an unlimited capacity for absorbing the planters' earnings through the continual payment of interest and the enhancement of prices. For the Cotton Belt this was presumably aggregated into a continuous public drain of wealth, first, to England and New England and, later, to the upper South. Moreover, a series of writers from Max Weber down to the most recent theorists of economic growth have argued that capitalization tends to rigidify the pattern of employment. "Free labor is necessary to make free transfers of labor possible. A production organization cannot be very flexible if it has to engage in the purchase or sale of slaves every time it changes its output." But this is really a question of how good the market is; no one, after all, claims that manufacturing is made suicidally inflexible by the fact that expanding sectors must buy the capitalized future earnings of machinery. There are three issues to be distinguished in this argument: first, the alleged tendency toward overcapitalization; second, the inflexibility of chattel labor and the difficulty of allocating it, geographically and industrially; and, third, the loss of wealth.

First, was the southerner his own victim in an endless speculative inflation of slave prices? The assertion of an irresistible tendency to overvalue and overcapitalize must mean that he was so trapped, if it means anything. Phillips answered the question by comparing the price of cotton with the price of prime field hands, year by year. He found, or believed he found, a permanent movement toward overcapitalization inherent in American slaveholding. But speculative overexpansion is capable of reversal: from the inflation of 1837 to the bottom of the depression in 1845, slave prices fell as sharply as cotton prices. If the rise from that lower turning point is a demonstration of speculative mania, it was a mania solidly based on the increase in the value of the crop per hand, owing to the concentration of production in more fertile areas, the greater efficiency of the American-born slaves, lowered transportation costs, and the development of new high-yield varieties of cotton from the fourth decade of the century on. Finally, the choice of the initial period in Phillips' analysis exaggerates the decline in cotton prices relative to the price of slaves: at the turn of the century the demand for cotton was increasing rapidly, supporting remarkably high prices, while the unrestricted African slave trade kept domestic slave prices well below the level that might be expected in view of the level of profits. Table 17 clearly demonstrates the relationship among slave prices, cotton prices, and the value of cotton output per slave (of field work age, ten to fifty-four). Several things become clear in this comparison. To begin, the relationship between slave and cotton prices is significant for Phillips' purposes only if there is no increase in productivity. While he is struck by the fact that slave prices rise more rapidly than cotton prices in the long upswing starting in the early 1840's, it is equally striking to observe that (New Orleans) slave prices rose about one and one-half times between the low point in 1843–45 to 1860, while values of cotton production per hand rose more than three times from the low in 1842. This was recognized in the *New Orleans Daily Crescent* in 1860, as follows:

> Nor do we agree with our contemporaries who argue that a speculative demand is the unsubstantial basis of the advance in the price of slaves. . . . It is our impression that the great demand for slaves in the Southwest will keep up the prices as it caused their advance in the first place, and that the rates are not a cent above the real value of the laborer who is to be engaged in tilling the fertile lands of a section of the country which yields the planter nearly double the crop that the fields of the Atlantic States do.

Furthermore, it would appear that slave prices fluctuate less than do cotton prices. This and the less clear-cut lag of the slave prices make it difficult to accept the image of unwary planters helplessly exposing themselves in a market dominated by speculators. It would make more sense to argue simply that the rising trend of slave prices coupled with a growing slave population is in and of itself strong evidence of the profitability of slavery.

D. THE EFFICIENCY OF ALLOCATION

The second point relates to geographic allocation and, to a lesser extent, to the mobility of the slave labor force among crops. The slave prices in all regions move very closely with cotton prices and products per hand. It is clear, too, that the eastern prices move directly with the cotton-area slave prices, although in the last two decades the rate of increase of prices fell behind in the breeding area. If the market were extremely imperfect and the transfer between the breeding and consuming states inefficient, in contradiction to our hypothesis, then there should be much less evidence of regional arbitrage than is found here. In response to the western demand, Virginia and the other eastern states shipped their natural increase to the cotton areas. Indeed, it is frequently argued that the transfer was too efficient and that the Old South was being continuously depressed by the high price of labor occasioned by western demand. Edmund Ruffin, particularly, took this position and argued that slave trade could not bring profits to Virginia but could result only in the paralysis of her industry. If true, this argument would be supported empirically by increasing real estate values on the western lands and decreasing values in the Atlantic and border states. That is, the chain of high cotton profits–high slave prices–increased cost of farming in the Old South should have depressed land prices in that area. Emigration, by reducing demand, should have meant more downward pressure. The only influence which operated in the direction of maintaining the value of land in the older states was the profit to be had from the increase and sale of slaves. Indeed, in 1850 and 1860, the value per acre of farm land and buildings in the border states was $7.18 and $12.33, and, in the Lower South for the same two census years, $4.99 and $8.54. Undoubtedly, the western cotton land earned a considerable rent in farming over the older land. It was this rent which maintained the flow of migration to the Cotton Belt. But that migration depended upon and supported the prosperity of the breeding states. It is not clear that slavery was able to continue only by skinning the topsoil and moving on, leaving exhausted land and low slave and land value in its wake. Quite the contrary, the evidence can plausibly be interpreted as indicating a unified, specialized economy in which the settlers on the naturally superior western lands (superior even before the deterioration of the older regions by single-crop cultivation of tobacco and cotton) were able to bid slave labor

TABLE 17

VALUE OF COTTON PRODUCTION AND
SLAVE POPULATION, 1802–60, NEW ORLEANS PRICES

Year	Crop (Thousands of Pounds)	Average Price (Cents per Pound)	Value (Thousands)	No. of Slaves Aged 10-54 Years*	Crop Value per Slave	Price of Prime Field Hand	Crop Value per Hand per Dollar Slave Price
1802....	55,000	0.147	$ 8,085	550,708	$ 14.68	$ 600	.02
1803....	60,000	.150	9,000	568,932	15.82	600	.03
1804....	65,000	.196	12,740	587,157	21.70	600	.04
1805....	70,000	.233	16,310	605,381	26.94	600	.05
1806....	80,000	.218	17,440	623,606	27.97	600	.05
1807....	80,000	.164	13,120	641,831	20.44	600	.03
1808....	75,000	.136	10,200	660,055	15.45	640	.02
1809....	82,000	.136	11,152	678,280	16.44	780	.02
1810....	85,000	.147	12,495	696,505	17.94	900	.02
1811....	80,000	.089	7,120	717,376	9.93	860	.01
1813....	75,000	.155	11,625	759,118	15.31	600	.03
1814....	70,000	.169	11,830	779,989	15.17	650	.02
1815....	100,000	.273	27,300	800,860	34.09	765	.05
1816....	124,000	.254	31,496	821,731	38.33	880	.04
1817....	130,000	.298	38,740	842,602	45.98	1,000	.05
1818....	125,000	.215	26,875	863,473	31.12	1,050	.03
1819....	167,000	.143	23,881	884,344	27.00	1,100	.03
1820....	160,000	.152	24,320	905,215	26.88	970	.03
1821....	180,000	.174	31,320	933,517	33.55	810	.04
1822....	210,000	.115	24,150	961,818	25.11	700	.04
1823....	185,000	.145	26,825	990,120	27.04	670	.04
1824....	215,000	.179	38,485	1,018,421	37.99	700	.05
1825....	255,000	.119	30,345	1,046,723	28.99	800	.04
1826....	350,000	.093	32,550	1,075,024	30.28	840	.04
1827....	316,900	.097	30,739	1,103,326	27.86	770	.04
1828....	241,399	.098	23,657	1,131,627	20.91	770	.03
1829....	296,812	.089	26,416	1,159,929	22.77	770	.03
1830....	331,150	.084	27,817	1,208,034	23.03	810	.03
1831....	354,247	.090	31,882	1,247,489	25.56	860	.03
1832....	355,492	.100	35,549	1,275,061	27.88	900	.03
1833....	374,653	.112	41,961	1,302,633	32.21	960	.03
1834....	437,558	.155	67,821	1,330,206	50.99	1,000	.05
1835....	460,338	.152	69,971	1,357,778	51.53	1,150	.05
1836....	507,550	.133	67,504	1,385,350	46.79	1,250	.04
1837....	539,669	.090	48,510	1,412,923	34.38	1,300	.03
1838....	682,767	.124	84,663	1,440,495	58.77	1,220	.05
1839....	501,708	.079	39,635	1,468,067	27.00	1,240	.02
1840....	834,111	.091	75,904	1,507,779	50.34	1,020	.05
1841....	644,172	.078	50,245	1,568,022	32.04	870	.04
1842....	668,379	.057	38,098	1,611,269	23.65	750	.03
1843....	972,960	.075	72,972	1,654,516	44.11	700	.06
1844....	836,529	.055	46,009	1,697,762	27.10	700	.04
1845....	993,719	.068	67,573	1,741,009	38.81	700	.06
1846....	863,321	.099	85,469	1,784,256	47.90	750	.06

TABLE 17

1847....	766,599	.070	53,662	1,827,503	29.36	850	.04
1848....	1,017,391	.058	59,009	1,870,750	31.54	950	.03
1849....	1,249,985	.108	134,998	1,913,996	70.53	1,030	.07
1850....	1,001,165	.117	117,136	1,979,059	59.19	1,100	.05
1851....	1,021,048	.074	75,558	2,034,482	37.14	1,150	.03
1852....	1,338,061	.091	121,764	2,080,554	58.53	1,200	.05
1853....	1,496,302	.088	131,675	2,126,626	61.92	1,250	.05
1854....	1,322,241	.084	111,068	2,172,698	51.12	1,310	.04
1855....	1,294,463	.091	117,796	2,218,770	53.09	1,350	.04
1856....	1,535,334	.124	190,381	2,264,843	84.06	1,420	.06
1857....	1,373,619	.112	153,845	2,310,915	66.57	1,490	.05
1858....	1,439,744	.115	165,571	2,356,988	70.25	1,580	.04
1859....	1,796,455	.108	194,017	2,403,060	80.74	1,690	.05
1860....	2,241,056	0.111	$248,757	2,460,648	$101.09	$1,800	.06

Source: *Crops:* Computed from the data on number of bales and average weight of bales in James L. Watkins, *Production and Price of Cotton* for One Hundred Years (U.S. Department of Agriculture, Miscellaneous Series, Bull. 9, Washington, D.C., 1895). *Price:* Gray, op. cit., Table 41 "Weighted Yearly Averages and Monthly Prices in Cents per Pound of Short-Staple Cotton at New Orleans for the Crop Years 1802–1860." *Slaves:* Bureau of Census, Negro Population in the United States, 1790–1915, "Slave and Free Colored Population at Each Census by Sections and Southern Divisions: 1790–1860," p. 55, and "Negro Population in Years Specified Classified by Sex and Age Periods; 1830–1910," p. 166. *Slave Prices:* Estimated visually from the chart "Approximate Prices of Prime Field Hands in Hundreds of Dollars per Head: . . . at New Orleans. . . ," in V. B. Phillips, *Life and Labor in the Old South* (Boston, 1935), p. 177.
To estimate the slave population in the intercensal years, the increase over each decade was divided into equal parts and assigned to each year in the decade. The proportion of Negroes in the field-work age brackets (between the ages of ten and fifty-four) was .641 in 1863, .635 in 1850, .621 in 1840 and .610 in 1830. The census-year proportions at the beginning and end of each decade were averaged for use in intervening years. For the years before 1830, an estimate of .60 was used. There is no implication that we have measured the number of field hands, but it should be noted that the range .60–.65 brackets several contemporary estimates of the slave population employed in cotton agriculture (see, e.g., P. A. Morse, Southern Slavery and the Cotton Trade," *De Bow's Review,* XXIII [1857], 475–82.)

away from general farming and to make wholesale removal unnecessary, if indeed there had ever been such a necessity.

E. SLAVERY AND SOUTHERN ECONOMIC GROWTH

Finally, there are two economic arguments about slavery and potential southern growth to be considered. The assertion that slavery per se was inimical to economic growth rests in part upon the alleged inefficiency of slave labor in industrial pursuits and in part upon the loss of capital that might otherwise have gone into industrialization and diversification.

The inefficiency argument is not supported very securely. There were slaves employed in cotton factories throughout the South. Slaves were used in the coal mines and in the North Carolina lumbering operations. In the ironworks at Richmond and on the Cumberland River, slaves comprised a majority of the labor force. Southern railroads were largely built by southern slaves. Crop diversification, or the failure to achieve diversi-

fication, appears to have been a problem of entrepreneurship rather than
of the difficulties of training slaves. In the face of the demand for cotton
and the profits to be had from specializing in this single crop, it is hardly
difficult to explain the single-minded concentration of the planter.

In what ways was slavery allegedly responsible for the drain of capital
from the South? The lack of diversification, to the extent of a failure even
to provide basic supplies, made necessary the import of much food and
virtually all manufactured articles from the North. But half of this assertion, the argument that laid the responsibility for the single-crop culture
upon slavery, has been found questionable already.

The major avenues by which wealth is said to have been drained from
the cotton states were the excessive use of credit (through dependence
upon factors' services) and the "absorption" of capital in slaves. The
dependence upon advances was, in effect, a dependence upon the New
York or London money market and was, therefore, an impediment to
the accumulation of capital in the South. Good crop years bring the
temptation to expand production; bad years do not bring any release from
the factors. But resort to factoring is characteristic of speculative, commercial agriculture, whether or not the labor force is organized in
slavery. It is also frequently argued that slavery gave southern planters
a taste for extravagant, wasteful display, causing the notorious lack of
thrift and the relative lack of economic development, compared to that
experienced in the North and West. This is a doubtful inference, at best.
Slavery did not make the Cavalier any more than slavery invented speculation in cotton. However, insofar as successful slave management required military posture and discipline, the southerner's expensive image
of himself as a *grand seigneur* was encouraged. It is beyond the scope
of this paper to offer hypotheses about the reasons for the relative degrees
of entrepreneurship in Charleston and Boston; in this context it is sufficient to state that slavery per se does not seem to have been responsible
for the excessive reliance upon factoring and external sources of credit.

There remains only the absorption of capital in slaves to set the responsibility for lack of growth in the South upon the peculiar institution.
Earnings that might have gone out of the South to bring in investment
goods were fixed in the form of chattel labor. For the early years, during
the external slave trade, there is some plausibility to this argument, though
it is difficult to see how the capitalization of an income stream, excellent
by contemporary standards, can be said to count as a loss of wealth. In
the later years there was, except to the extent that northern or English
bankers drew off the interest, a redistribution of wealth only within the
slave states: from the cotton lands back to the less profitable field agriculture of the older section. And, to the extent that the old planting
aristocracy used the profits to maintain the real or fancied magnificence
of the preceding century, capital was absorbed. Slavery made this possible,
so long as the natural increase could be shipped off. But, as Russel pointed

out, slavery also made the profits in the cotton fields and the resultant demand for eastern hands. We are left with the conclusion that, except insofar as it made speculation in cotton possible on a grander scale than would otherwise have been the case and thereby weakened whatever pressure there might have been for diversification, capitalization of the labor force did not of itself operate against southern development.

IV. CONCLUSION

In sum, it seems doubtful that the South was forced by bad statesmanship into an unnecessary war to protect a system which must soon have disappeared because it was economically unsound. This is a romantic hypothesis which will not stand against the facts.

On the basis of the computation of the returns to capital in our model of the ante bellum southern economy and the demonstration of the efficiency of the regional specialization, the following conclusions are offered:

1. Slavery was profitable to the whole South, the continuing demand for labor in the Cotton Belt insuring returns to the breeding operation on the less productive land in the seaboard and border states. The breeding returns were necessary, however, to make the plantation operations on the poorer lands as profitable as alternative contemporary economic activities in the United States. The failure of southern agriculture on these poorer lands in the post bellum period is probably attributable, in the main, to the loss of these capital gains on breeding and not, as is so often suggested, to either the relative inefficiency of the tenant system that replaced the plantations or the soil damage resulting from war operations. These factors were unquestionably contributing elements to the difficulties of post bellum southern agriculture, but they were of relatively small quantitative importance compared with the elimination of slave-breeding returns.

2. There was nothing necessarily self-destructive about the profits of the slave economy. Neither the overcapitalization argument nor the assertion that slavery must have collapsed because the slaves would not reproduce themselves is tenable. Slave prices did not outpace productivity, and the regional slave price structure would imply a workable transfer mechanism rather than the contrary.

3. Continued expansion of slave territory was both possible and, to some extent, necessary. The maintenance of profits in the Old South depended upon the expansion, extensive or intensive, of slave agriculture into the Southwest. This is sufficient to explain the interest of the Old South in secession and does away with the necessity to fall back upon arguments of statesmanship or quixotism to explain the willingness to fight for the peculiar institution.

4. The available productive surplus from slavery might have been used

What about the artificial market price of Cotton based on slave labour costing?

for economic development or, as in totalitarian regimes in this century, for militarism. In spite of this good omen for development, southern investment and industrialization lagged. It is hard to explain this except on the social ground that entrepreneurship could not take root in the South or on the economic ground that the South did not really own the system but merely operated it. Furthermore, the American experience clearly suggests that slavery is not, from the strict economic standpoint, a deterrent to industrial development and that its elimination may take more than the workings of "inexorable economic forces." Although profitability cannot be offered as a sufficient guaranty of the continuity of southern slavery, the converse argument that slavery must have destroyed itself can no longer rest upon allegations of unprofitability or upon assumptions about the impossibility of maintaining and allocating a slave labor force. To the extent, moreover, that profitability is a necessary condition for the continuation of a private business institution in a free-enterprise society, slavery was not untenable in the ante bellum American South. Indeed, economic forces often may work toward the continuation of a slave system, so that the elimination of slavery may depend upon the adoption of harsh political measures. Certainly that was the American experience.

FOR FURTHER READING: For a negative estimate see Thomas P. Govan, "Was Plantation Slavery Profitable?" *Journal of Southern History*, VIII (November, 1942), pp. 513–535. A contrary view is expressed by Kenneth Stampp in *The Peculiar Institution* (New York, 1956). A vast literature on this issue has developed during the past two decades. A fine appraisal of the problem is by Harold D. Woodman, "The Profitability of Slavery: A Historical Perennial," *Journal of Southern History*, XXIX (August, 1963), pp. 303–325. A succinct evaluation of studies before 1967 is by Stanley L. Engerman, "The Effects of Slavery Upon the Southern Economy: A Review of the Recent Debate," *Explorations in Entrepreneurial History*, IV (Winter, 1967), pp. 71–97. J. D. Foust and D. Swan, "Productivity and Profitability of Antebellum Slave Labor: A Micro Approach," *Agricultural History*, XLIV (January, 1970), pp. 39–62, support Conrad and Meyer. Much discussion has revolved around Robert W. Fogel and Stanley L. Engerman, *Time on the Cross: The Economics of American Negro Slavery* (Boston, 1974), and a sharp rejoinder by Herbert Gutman, *Slavery and the Numbers Game: A Critique of Time on the Cross* (Urbana, 1975). Eugene Genovese considers the issue in *Roll, Jordan, Roll* (New York, 1974).

9

TECHNOLOGY AND ECONOMIC CHANGE IN NINETEENTH CENTURY AMERICA

PROBLEM: *What influences promoted the spread of technology in nineteenth century America?*

One of the most significant economic characteristics of the United States during the first half of the nineteenth century was the increased application of technology to industry and farming. In undertaking the mechanization of countless processes in manufacturing as well as agriculture, Americans wrought what contemporaries and later observers considered as an Industrial Revolution and an Agricultural Revolution. Although the nature of this economic transformation has often been described by economic historians, they have disagreed about the reasons for these far-reaching changes and the timing of them. Many of the problems surrounding this issue are reflected in the adoption of the reaper between 1830 and 1860, one of the more important inventions of the period. Professor Paul David, an economist, concluded that the acceptance of this labor-saving machine by American farmers before the 1850's was largely due to their preference for innovation and their orientation to the production of marketable crops. Only then was the reaper more profitable than hand labor. This contention was challenged by Robert Ankli, another economist, who held that not the price, but the quality of reapers became a prime consideration for many farmers during this period when they considered the reaper as a substitution for hand labor. Both writers raise broad issues

183

concerning the influences that stimulated technological progress in America. How did the availability of labor relate to
technological change? How did environmental conditions
affect the spread of mechanization? To what extent did market forces influence the diffusion of technological adaptation?

The Mechanization of Reaping
in the Anti-Bellum Midwest

PAUL A. DAVID

The widespread adoption of reaping machines by Midwestern farmers
during the years immediately preceding the Civil War provides a striking
instance of the way that the United States' nineteenth-century industrial
development was bound up with *concurrent* transformations occurring in
the country's agricultural sector. On the record of historical experience,
as Alexander Gerschenkron has cogently observed, "the hope that industry
in a very backward country can unfold from its agriculture is hardly realistic." Indeed, even when one considers countries that are not very backward it is unusual for agricultural activities to escape an uncomplimentary
evaluation of their efficacy in creating inducements for the growth and
continuing proliferation of industrial pursuits. As Albert Hirschman puts
it, "agriculture certainly stands convicted on the count of its lack of direct
stimulus to the setting up of new activities through linkage effects: the
superiority of manufacturing in this respect is crushing." But having conceded that much regarding the general state of the world, the student of
economic development in nineteenth century America is compelled to
stress the anomalous character of his subject, to insist that in a resource-
abundant setting, highly market-oriented, vigorously expanding, and tech-
nologically innovative agriculture did provide crucial support for the
process of industrialization.

Such support in the form of sufficiently large demands for manufactures and supplies of raw material suitable for industrial processing would,
undoubtedly, have been less readily forthcoming from a small, or economically backward agrarian community. It is precisely in this regard that

United States industrialization may be seen as having diverged most markedly from the historical experience of continental European countries, where backward agriculture militated against gradual industrial growth, and the successful pattern of modernization of the economy tended to be characterized by an initial disengagement of manufacturing from the agrarian environment.

However, to treat the generation of demand for manufactures during the process of industrialization as taking place within a framework of static, pre-existing intersectoral relations, summarized by a set of input-output coefficients, does not prove to be an entirely satisfactory way of looking at the connections between the character of agriculture and the growth of industrial activities in the United States. Adherence to such an approach leads one, *inter alia*, to gloss over the problems of accounting for alterations in the structure of intersectoral dependences, although those alterations often constitute a vital aspect of the process of industrialization. It is not wholly surprising that pursuit of a static "linkage" approach has tended to promote the misleading notion that the expansion and modernization of the agrarian sector constituted a temporal pre-condition for rapid industrial development in the United States, whereas in many crucial respects it is far more useful to regard the two processes as having gone hand in hand. As a small contribution to the study of the interrelationship between agricultural development and industrialization in the American setting, this essay ventures to inquire into the way that—with the adoption of mechanized reaping—an important element was added to the set of linkages joining these two sectors of the mid-nineteenth century economy.

*   *   *

The spread of manufacturing from the eastern seaboard into the transmontane region of the United States during the 1850's derived significant impetus from the rise of a new demand for farm equipment in the states of the Old Northwest Territory. That impetus was at least partially reflected by the important position which activities supplying agricultural investment goods came to occupy in the early structure of Midwestern industry. In the still predominantly agrarian American economy of the time it is not unexpected that a substantial segment of the total income generated by industrial activities was directly attributable to the manufacture of durable producers' goods specifically identified with the farmer's needs—leaving aside the lumber and related building materials flowing into construction of farm dwellings, barns, sheds, and fences. If, in addition to value added in the production of agricultural implements and machinery in 1859/60, one were also to include half the value added by the manufacture of wagons and carts, saddles and harnesses, and the variety of items turned out by blacksmiths' shops, the resulting aggregate would represent over 4 per cent of the value added by the nation's entire industrial sector.

That is, rather more than the proportion contributed by the manufacture of machine shop and foundry products, which at the date in question ranked as the country's seventh largest industry in terms of current value added. However, on the eve of the Civil War the production of agricultural implements and machinery *alone* generated just as large a proportion of total industrial value added in the preponderantly agrarian Western states; in Illinois, this single branch of manufacturing accounted for fully 8 per cent of the total value added by the state's industries in 1859/60.

To appreciate the importance of the position that the agricultural implements and machinery industry assumed in the structure of Illinois' early manufacturing sector, it must be realized that at the time there was no single branch of industry which in the nation as a whole contributed so large a portion of aggregate value added in manufacturing. Cotton goods production, America's largest industry in 1859/60, accounted for only 6.6 per cent of the national aggregate.

When one looks at a rapidly developing center of industrial activity in the Midwest such as was Chicago during the 1850's, the manufacture of agricultural implements and machinery is found to have had still greater relative importance as a generator of income. The growth of agricultural commodity-processing industries, especially meat-packing in Chicago during the latter half of the century suggests that the Garden City's meteoric rise to the status of second manufacturing center in the nation by 1890 might be taken as a demonstration of the strength of *forward* linkages from commercial agriculture. It is not an object of the present essay to assess the validity of that impression. Nevertheless, it should be remarked that during Chicago's first major spurt of industrial development, a movement which saw manufacturing employment in the city rise from less than 2000 in 1850 to approximately 10,600 by 1856, the forward-linked processing industries were less significant to the industrial life of the city than was an activity based on *backward* linkage from agriculture. The branch of manufacturing in question was the farm implements and machinery industry: in 1856 it accounted for 10.8 per cent of total value added by Chicago's industrial sector, compared with 6.3 per cent contributed by the principal processing industries, meat-packing, flour- and grist-milling, and distilling, combined.

Among the salient characteristics of the agricultural scene in the antebellum Midwest, two appear as having been crucial to the emergence during the 1850's of a substantial regional manufacturing sector bound by demand-links reaching backward from commercial agriculture. First, the settlement of the region and the extension of its agricultural capacity during that decade proceeded with great rapidity, encouraged by favorable terms of trade and improvements in transportation facilities providing interior farmers with access to distant markets in the deficit foodstuff areas to the east. Between the Seventh and Eighth Censuses of Agriculture over a quarter of a million farming units came into existence, and about 19 million acres of improved farm land were added in Illinois, Indiana, Michigan, Iowa and Wisconsin. This represented a rate of increase in the number of farms of 7 per cent per annum, and a 9 per cent annual rate of expansion in improved acreage.

Secondly, agricultural practise in this region of recent settlement was not the static crystallization of long experience typical of stable agrarian societies. Far from being a closed issue, choices among alternative production techniques were rapidly being altered and Western farming was thereby being carried in the direction of greater capital-intensity and higher labor productivity. On the eve of the Civil War this burgeoning farm community was in the midst of a hectic process of transition from hand methods to machine methods of production, from the use of rudimentary implements to reliance on increasingly sophisticated machinery. Among the items of farm equipment being introduced on a large scale in the Midwest during the 1850's were steel breakers and plows, seed drills and seed boxes, reapers and mowers, threshers and grain separators. An editorial pronouncement appearing in the *Scientific American* during 1857 suggests the extremes to which the mechanization of farming had proceeded:

> every farmer who has a hundred acres of land should have at least the following: a combined reaper and mower, a horse rake, a seed planter, and mower; a thresher and grain cleaner, a portable grist mill, a corn-sheller, a horse power, three harrows, a roller, two cultivators and three plows.

The importance that the newly introduced reaping and mowing machines (especially the former) had assumed among the products of the agricultural implements and machinery industry of the Midwest by the end of the 1850's provides some indication of the direct impact of the shift to more capital-intensive farming techniques upon the expansion of an agrarian market for industrial products. According to the Census of 1860, reapers and mowers accounted for 42 per cent of the gross value of output of all agricultural implements and machinery in Illinois and for 78 per cent of the gross value of output of the corresponding industrial group in Chicago. A few years earlier, in 1856, when the Midwestern boom was still in full swing, reaper and mower production in Chicago had dominated that center's farm equipment output-mix to an even greater degree.

Despite the fact that the history of commercial production of mechanical reaping machines in the United States stretched back without interruption to the early 1830's, this industry was one that only began to flourish in the 1850's. From 1833, the date of the first sale of Obed Hussey's reaping machine, to the closing year of that decade, a total of 45

such machines had been purchased by American farmers. At the end of
the 1846 harvest season Cyrus H. McCormick determined to abandon his
efforts of the previous six years at manufacturing his reaping machine on
the family farm in Rockbridge County, Virginia, and set about transferring the center of his activities to a more promising location, Chicago.
The known previous sales of all reaping machines at that time aggregated
to a mere 793, but by 1850 some 3,373 reapers in all had been produced
and marketed in the United States since 1833. A scant eight years later
it was reckoned that roughly 73,200 reapers had been sold since 1845,
fully 69,700 of them since 1850. And most of that increase had resulted
from the burst of production enjoyed by the industry during the five years
following 1853!

The major portion of this production had taken place in the interior
of the country, and it is apparent that in the absence of farmers' readiness
to substitute machinery for labor during the 1850's, an equally rapid pace
of agricultural expansion—had such in fact been feasible—would have
provided a considerably weaker set of demand stimuli for concurrent industrial development in the region. The latter facet of the late ante-bellum
agrarian scene must, therefore, be the prime focus of our interest; it cannot
be taken as a given, but must be explained. That should not, however,
be regarded as a dismissal of the first-mentioned aspect of Midwestern
agricultural development in this period. As shall be seen when we come to
grips with the problem of explaining the movement of mechanization, the
speed of agricultural expansion and the substitution of machines for farm
labor were intimately connected developments between which causal influences flowed in both directions.

*   *   *

In view of the consequences for agricultural and industrial development
that followed from the mechanization of reaping during the 1850's, it
might be supposed that this episode in the modernization of American
farming and the formation of backward linkages between the enterprises
of field and factory would have been thoroughly explored by economic
historians. To be sure, virtually all the standard accounts of the development of agriculture in the United States up to 1860 mention the introduction of the machines that Obed Hussey and Cyrus H. McCormick had
invented in the 1830's. Yet, the literature remains surprisingly vague about
the specific technical and economic considerations touching the adoption
of these devices by American farmers. We have called attention to the
fact that although the twenty years prior to 1853 had witnessed a slow,
limited diffusion of the new technique, the first major wave of popular
acceptance of the reaper was concentrated in the mid-1850's. Thus, the
intriguing question to which an answer must be given is: why only at
that time were large numbers of farmers suddenly led to abandon an old,

labor-intensive method of cutting their grain, and to switch to the use of a machine that had been available since its invention two decades earlier?

In this inquiry, the impact of the mechanization of small grain harvesting upon U.S. agriculture is not the prime subject of concern. Nevertheless, it would hardly be possible to account for the upsurge of demand for reaping machinery without considering the economic implications of the new harvesting technology and the specific circumstances surrounding it.

*   *   *

Although the questions considered in the preceding pages are very specific, we have arrived at answers with rather broader implications. Historians of United States agriculture have maintained that during the nineteenth century the transfer of grain farming to new regions lying beyond the Appalachian barrier played a significant part in raising labor productivity in agriculture for the country as a whole. The connection between the spatial redistribution of grain production and the progress of farm mechanization figures prominently among the reasons that have been advanced to support this contention. Some writers suggest that inasmuch as heavier reliance was placed on the use of farm machinery in the states of the Old Northwest before the Civil War, and, similarly, in the Great Plains and Pacific Coast states during the last quarter of the century, the geographical transfer of agriculture into these areas was tantamount to a progressive shift of grain farming towards the relatively capital-intensive region of the technological spectrum. But, the mechanism of this putative interaction between spatial and technological change has not been fully clarified, and as a result, important aspects of the interrelationship between the historical course of industrialization and the settlement of new regions in the United States remain only imperfectly perceived.

To make some headway in this direction it is necessary to distinguish two possible modes of interaction between spatial and technological changes in United States agriculture: one involves adjustments of production methods in response to alterations of relative prices that were associated, either causally or consequentially, with the geographical relocation of farming; the other turns on purely technological considerations through which regional location influenced choices among available alternative techniques. Now, the general statement that the conditions under which farmers located in the country's interior carried on grain production especially favored the spread of mechanization is sufficiently imprecise to embrace both interaction mechanisms, the influences of market conditions as well as those of technological factors peculiar to farming in the different regions. One may well ask whether such ambiguity is justified. Without establishing the dominance of purely technical considerations it would be unwarranted to suggest that shifts of small grain farming away from the Eastern seaboard automatically, in and of themselves, accounted for increases in the extent to which that branch of United States agriculture became mechanized.

In the case of reaping operations, it is certainly true that there were technical features of Midwestern farming which in contrast with those characteristic of the Eastern grain regions proved inherently more congenial to the general introduction of ante-bellum reaping machines. On the comparatively level, stone-free terrain of the Midwest, the cumbersome early models of the reaper were less difficult for a team to pull, less subject to malalignment and actual breakage; because the fields were unridged and crops typically were not so heavy as those on Eastern farms, the reapers cut the grain close to the ground more satisfactorily, and the knives of the simple cutting mechanism were not so given to repeated clogging.

Yet, despite the relatively favorable technical environment (and larger average small grain acreages on farms) in the Midwest, we have seen that the prevailing factor and product market conditions during the 1840's and early 1850's militated against extensive adoption of mechanical reaping equipment even in that region. Against such a background the fact that a large-scale transfer of small grain production to the Old Northwest Territory took place during the 1850's does not appear so crucial a consideration in explaining the sudden rise in the proportion of the total American wheat crop cut by horse power between 1850 and 1860. Instead, it seems appropriate to emphasize that during the Midwestern development boom that marked the decade of the 1850's the price of labor—as well as the prices of small grains—rose relative to the price of reaping machines, and that the pressure on the region's labor supply reflected not only the expanded demand for farm workers, but also the demand for labor to build railroads and urban centers throughout the region—undertakings ultimately predicated on the current wave of new farm settlement and the expected growth of the Midwest's agricultural capacity. If one is to argue the case for the existence of an important causal relationship between the relocation of grain production and the widespread acceptance of mechanical reaping during the 1850's, the altered market environment, especially the new labor market conditions created directly and indirectly by the quickening growth of Midwestern agriculture, must be accorded greater recognition, and the purely technical considerations be given rather less weight than they usually receive in this connection.

There is, however, a sense in which the decline in the cost of reaping machines relative to the farm labor wage rate may be held to have reflected the interaction of the technical factors favoring adoption of the early reapers in the Midwest with that region's emergence as the nation's granary during the 1850's. The rising share of the United States wheat crop being grown in the interior did mean that, *ceteris paribus*, a larger proportion of the national crop could be harvested by horse power without requiring the building of machines designed to function as well under the terrain and crop conditions of the older grain regions as the early reapers did on the prairies. For the country as a whole, as well as for the Midwest, this afforded economies of scale in the production of a simpler, more standardized line of reaping machines. It thereby contributed to maintaining a situation in which the long run aggregate supply schedule for harvesting machinery was more elastic than the farm labor supply. Thus it may be said, somewhat paradoxically, that the movement towards regional specialization in small grain farming directly made possible greater efficiency in manufacturing and thereby promoted the simultaneous advance of mechanized agriculture and industrial development in the ante-bellum Midwest. . . .

The Coming of the Reaper

ROBERT E. ANKLI

Recent work in economic history, focusing on technological change and on the diffusion of various innovations, has contributed much to our reconstruction of the past. One of the more intriguing problems in this subject has been that of the diffusion of the reaper. Although patents were independently granted to McCormick and Hussey in the early 1830s, it was not until the 1850s that sales grew rapidly. In a celebrated article, Paul David explained the delay in adoption as a function of the price of a reaper relative to that of the labor it would replace. This paper questions the robustness of his explanation. It makes two points. The reaper manufacturer could not hope to make large sales until the farmer could "afford" to buy a reaper. Illinois wheat output serves to illustrate the importance of this point. Second, a farmer would not buy a reaper until he was confident that the machine could perform when he needed it. The manufacturer needed a "sound" product.

I

Economists argue that a firm will adopt an innovation if it believes that the expected profit when using the device in the optimal fashion will ex-

Reprinted from *Papers Presented at the Twenty-Second Annual Meeting of the Business History Conference, 12–13 March 1976* (Urbana, Illinois, 1976), pp. 1–14. Paul Uselding, editor.

ceed profit from continuing production using the existing but older technology also in its optimal fashion.   Symbolically,

$$(1) \quad \pi_R{}^* = (O_R{}^*P^*)C_R, \qquad \pi_R{}^* = (O_R{}^*P^*) - C_R$$

expected profits using a reaper equal expected gross revenue $(O_R{}^*P^*)$ less the cost of the reaper (C_R). Also,

$$(2) \quad \pi^* = (O_H{}^*P^*) - C_H$$

expected profits using hand harvest techniques equal gross revenue $(C_H{}^*P^*)$ less costs of hand harvesting (C_H). Diffusion of the reaper is then a function of $\pi_R{}^* - \pi_H{}^*$ with a positive first derivative if the function is continuous and differentiable over the relevant range. So,

$$(3) \quad \text{Sale of reapers} = f[P^*(O_R{}^* - O_H{}^*) - (C_R - C_H)].$$

This is our basic equation which is pictured graphically in the chart.

Profits will be maximized at the point where a tangent to the cost of harvesting is parallel to the total revenue line. With the original total revenue, profit is maximized at H using hand harvest techniques and R using a reaper. If total revenue increases, the profit-maximizing positions will move out to H' and R' respectively. There is a point R (the threshold) where the two harvesting techniques cost the same. As the chart is drawn, it would clearly pay the farmer to expand his output from H to R be-

Threshold Farm size, total revenue, and sales of reapers

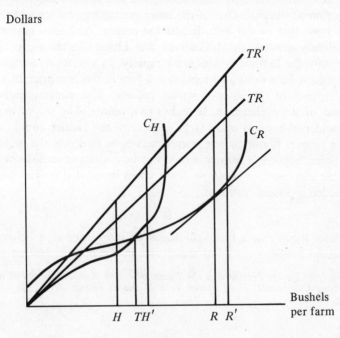

cause the cost functions are nonlinear, yet he might not do so because other costs, of land breaking and fencing, for example, which are not included in the costs shown on the chart, might lower his expected profit below that at H. In addition it would take some time to expand acreage if land breaking and fencing were required. In order to determine when a farmer might decide to buy a reaper, it is necessary to look at revenue and costs in detail.

II

Total revenue is the product of the price of wheat times the yield times the number of acres sown to wheat. Let us consider each of these variables in turn. The average of the July-August spring wheat price at Chicago for the years 1850 to 1853 was only 55 cents per bushel, whereas the average for the following four years was $1.09 per bushel. This observation has led many agricultural historians such as Paul Gates to argue that "Illinois, Wisconsin, Iowa, and Minnesota farmers enjoyed real prosperity and were in a position to buy and pay for reapers." Another test would be to compare the relative price of corn with that of wheat. If the relative price of wheat rose, there would be substitution toward wheat. There was a tendency for this ratio to fall during the middle 1850s, perhaps inducing at least a relative shift from corn to wheat production.

The prices we have been considering are Chicago prices, which would be higher than actual farm prices; but the 1850s were years of rapid railway expansion, so interior prices would have been rising relative to Chicago prices. This means the percentage increase of the farm price of spring wheat would be even greater than the Chicago price shows.

Equally important in understanding the diffusion of the reaper are possible changes in expected output ($O_R{}^* - O_H{}^*$). There are several related points. An increase in expected output per acre would increase total revenue and cause a more rapid diffusion of the reaper. In terms of the chart, TR moves to TR' because of an increase in yield instead of an increase in the price per bushel of wheat. The optimal move, using hand harvest techniques, would be from H to H' but because the cost functions are nonlinear and because the threshold point has been passed, it is cheaper to adopt a reaper and to expand to R'. This may be an important factor in explaining the specific way in which reaper sales increased.

There is some evidence that grain often went unharvested because of lack of help. This was a problem because the farmer did not know how many harvest hands would be available when he sowed his grain. Another major problem the farmer faced was the marketing of grain. Unless he lived close to a waterway, the distance he could profitably wagon-haul a load of wheat was fairly limited. The 1850s marked the coming of the railroad to Illinois. The spreading of this network tended to have two effects. First, the farmer might expect it to raise the price he received for

his grain by reducing his transport costs and thus encourage him to prepare to ship more to market, but, equally as important, it meant that farmers could ship a much greater amount of grain to market. In 1848 Illinois
had 55 miles of railroad. By 1860 it had 2,760 with most of the increase
coming between 1853 and 1856.

Some writers have suggested that the decision to purchase a reaper depended upon crop prospects. Thus William T. Hutchinson wrote

The number of sales depended upon the weather more than on other businesses,
and a late spring, excessive rain or drought, or any other of the abnormal and
uncontrollable circumstances to which the farmer was subjected, spelled a bad
season for agent and manufacturer alike. Most grain-growers had no surplus in
the bank and could not buy machinery unless there were prospects of a good
crop and a fair market for grain. Nor would a salesman wish to press a machine
upon a farmer who did not seem able to pay. A crop outlook that was discouraging late in April frequently became favorable within a month and under
such circumstances more orders for reapers would be rushed to the factory
than could be filled. Late shipments on slow canal-boats often arrived at their
destination too late and Eastern agents in particular complained of tardy de-
liveries.

There is evidence that in some years McCormick did not supply all he
could have sold. Output and yield per acre are ex post measures and, as
such, are only a proxy for prospective crop conditions. Nevertheless, they
are informative. . . .

Finally, the decision to buy a reaper and to expand acreage might have
been one and the same decision. Improved farm land for the state of Illinois increased from 66.1 to 91.4 acres per farm between the 1850 and 1860
censuses. For the northern part of the state improved land increased from
58.1 to 98.9 acres per farm.

*   *   *

III

Costs were the next determining factor in the adoption of the reaper.
The two main costs were the wages of harvest labor and the cost of a
reaper. Paul David developed a "threshold model (the point T in the
chart) in order to explain the adoption of the reaper. He compared the
periods 1849–53 and 1854–57. He assumed that output was independent of
the method of harvesting, so that only costs would determine the harvesting method. He found that the price of labor rose relative to the price of
a reaper during this period, so that the threshold (measured in acres) fell.
Following his choice of data, the threshold declined from 46.5 acres for
the first period to 35.1 acres for the second period. Though his argument
is suggestive, it is not persuasive. My studies have shown that the threshold is fairly sensitive to the values chosen for the parameters. The

threshold concept suffers from two shortcomings. First, output and revenue do not enter into the calculations. David does not even provide yearly data on sales of the reaper for the two periods. In fact, there is a strong correlation between reaper sales and time itself, that is, sales simply grow over time. This is because his first period was one of very poor wheat years in Illinois, whereas the second period was one of very good years. . . .

Second, labor costs are defined very narrowly in David's paper. It might be thought that the availability of labor would be reflected in the price of labor. Certainly if the supply of labor can be represented as a continuous function, this would be so, but there are references in the literature that indicate this may not be an appropriate assumption. David Schob reports from a farm diary in 1845, "Becker in tribulation about his crop! hands very scarce—worth $1.50 in cash at what Mr. Schillaber gives and he monopolizes them." Another Illinois farmer reported that he swung the cradle for 27 consecutive days, because he could not find help and he decided to give up farming. Such a situation was exacerbated because farmers often planted more than they could harvest and hoped they could later find the help. This shortage was to be even more severe in years such as 1855 when the harvest was very heavy.

There were often complaints about the quality of farm labor, and James Campell, who became a state senator in New Jersey said, "The only object I had in view at first was to aid agriculture and place the farmer beyond the power of a set of drinking harvest hands with which we have been greatly annoyed." In such a case a backward bending supply curve of labor is conceivable. However, it is equally true that farm laborers as well as farmers themselves lacked mechanical aptitudes. In spite of this there still might be reasons to prefer a reaper. If this appears to be irrational prejudice for machinery, keep in mind that cradling was demanding physical labor, performed during the hottest months of the year. The combination of heat and humidity particularly affected those persons who were subject to fevers and ague. Schob reports that a "mutiny" occurred on the Indiana farm of Calvin Fletcher in 1839 because of the excessive heat. Fletcher also had problems in 1850 and 1853. This is the type of situation the farmer could not plan for and, of course, his own illness or that of his farm hands might spell disaster. Such a probability would not be reflected in the price ratio or in a threshold, but it would provide a positive inducement to replace hand labor.

IV

Central to my argument is the belief that the farmer was willing to purchase a reaper once a reliable one become available. The last section showed that output prospects became increasingly more favorable as the

1850s progressed, but this does not explain why farmers did not purchase reapers in greater numbers before 1850. It is argued that a reliable reaper was not really available before that date. We may consider this from the inventor-manufacturers' side as well as the farmers'.

The problems these early inventors faced should not be minimized. The farmer wanted an all-purpose machine that would cut grass as well as the small grains he might sow. However,

some grasses are tall and large and easy to cut, others are short and wiry, and hard. Timothy grain stands well; clover is usually prostrate and tangles. The taller grasses sway in the wind, and incline away from the advancing machinery. Grainfields are weedy and sometimes difficult grasses are encountered in them. Rye is tall and wheat comparatively short. Both become tangled, lodged (lodging is the rule with heavy oats) and strawbroken at times. Overripe grain becomes so "fluffy" that good work cannot be done in harvesting it. Fractious teams and ignorant labor can also be added to the unfavorable conditions confronting inventors.

The manufacturers' problem was that there were annoying defects to be worked out of the machines and new ideas could be given field tests only during the short harvest season.

The story of the invention of the raker's seat illustrates the obstacles to be surmounted when changes in the construction of the reaper were necessary or a new appliance had to be added to its carefully balanced framework. The general form of seat desired and the most advantageous position for the riding rakeman could be readily determined, but a year of study was required with experimental construction work in the shops of Walnut Grove and Cincinnati, and trials in the grain of four states, before Cyrus McCormick finally discovered how this device could be utilized in the most convenient location without sacrificing the efficient operation of the other elements of the reaper.

McCormick's slow pace in the early years resulted from these sorts of problems. Although he sold two machines in 1840, they did not come up to expectations. He spent the next year experimenting and consequently sold none. Six machines were sold in 1842. "Early in the year he expected to make more for this harvest, but he finally 'concluded to wait another year's experience, and additional testimony from different parts of the state, before hazarding a great deal.' "

A second problem, which David mentions, is that McCormick began his work in the East. But the hilly countryside of the East also caused more problems for the successful operation of a machine than did the more level Midwest. McCormick did not go West until 1844.

Equally as important, McCormick did not manufacture his own machines until 1848 but rather licensed others, who were not always as careful as he would have been and consequently were giving his product a bad name. Careless production proved disastrous to other manufacturers.

For example, J. S. Wright received so many orders for the 1857 harvest that he used green lumber in the machines with the result that the hot sun warped and twisted them. The Panic of 1857 did the rest. C. W. Marsh also reported that he and his brother foolishly began producing harvesters in 1860 by having parts produced at various locations, only to find the machines poorly constructed and unsalable. He goes on to report a disastrous field trial,

At the request of our customers we gave a public trial in a field of barley on the eve of the 4th of July and the machine failed to satisfy. It was our first experience in cutting and binding barley. The grain was thick and short; we could not get the machine low enough, binding was difficult and something broke. The trial was a failure and our customers "went back" on our orders.

All this suggests dating the beginning of the reaper industry from 1848 when McCormick moved to Chicago and took control of his production.

The farmer needed a machine that would work. This meant that McCormick would have to teach farmers how to use this "complicated" machine, since farmers were not used to such machinery. If he decided to purchase a reaper but did not also hire the normal quota of harvest hands, he might lose a large part of his crop if his machine broke down. An improving machine would gradually convince farmers that the purchase of a reaper would be profitable. . . . McCormick supplied his agents and each reaper with spare parts. In 1853 when a gear worked poorly, McCormick sent free replacements. The point is that people were learning to trust McCormick and his machines. Success likewise breeds success. McCormick's reaper won the highest award at the London Fair of 1851. This served as effective advertising. The spread of agents (sometimes even one of the McCormick brothers stopped to chat with farmers) also helped. The problems such a manufacturer faced may be compared with the problems foreign auto manufacturers have when they attempt to break into the American market—lack of spare parts on hand and lack of an effective marketing organization.

VI

In summary, this paper has looked at the many problems surrounding the adoption of the reaper. Particular attention was paid to various revenue factors and cost factors that are not easily quantifiable. It is suggested that the farmer was willing to buy a reaper as soon as a reliable machine became available and that this did not occur until after McCormick moved to Chicago in 1848. Various nonwage considerations also increased the demand for reapers, most important, the extreme heat and humidity in Illinois. Finally, the demand for reapers in an individual year depended upon the prospects for the coming crop and it was not until the middle 1850s that Illinois wheat output turned favorable.

FOR FURTHER READING: Two excellent general works provide an understanding of technological changes in American agriculture. Clarence Danhof, *Change in Agriculture: the Northern United States, 1820–1870* (Cambridge, 1969) relates farm labor costs to differing environmental conditions while Paul W. Gates, *The Farmer's Age, 1815–1860* (New York, 1968), places the transformation in proper historical perspective. On the reaper, William T. Hutchinson, *Cyrus Hall McCormick* (2 vols., New York, 1930, 1935), and Alan T. Olmstead, "The Mechanization of Reaping and Mowing in American Agriculture, 1833–1870," *Journal of Economic History*, XXXV (June, 1975), pp. 327–352 are informative. An excellent broad work on the impact of technology during this period is H. J. Habakkuk, *American and British Technology in the Nineteenth Century* (Cambridge, England, 1962).

10

ECONOMIC
EFFECTS
OF THE
CIVIL WAR $(1861 - 65)$

PROBLEM: *Did the Civil War promote industrial expansion?*

The assumption that the Civil War was a prime factor in stimulating industrialization after 1865 has been widely held by economists as well as by historians, but rarely subjected to the test of historical or statistical evidence. Not until 1961 did a leading economic historian, Thomas C. Cochran, openly take issue with this view. Utilizing statistics and stressing long-term trends he sought to demonstrate that instead of promoting economic development, the war actually may have retarded it. Nevertheless, production trends are only one indicator of economic growth, critic Stephen Salsbury points out in assessing Professor Cochran's thesis. Salsbury questions Cochran's selection of 1840 as the year signifying the beginning of industrial expansion. If, instead, the decade prior to the Civil War is compared with the one immediately following, great increases in selected areas of industrial production are noticeable. Moreover, Salsbury also underscores important political and social effects of the conflict which may have hastened industrialization, although their impact has not as yet been assessed precisely. If neither author presents conclusive proof concerning the effect of the war upon American economic development, both point to important elements that need to be considered in the appraisal of the problem, and raise questions. Why did the war have little influence on production trends in some important basic industries? What other

factors need to be considered in determining the influence of
the war on the economy? What forms of military organization
and techniques were adaptable to private business after the
war?

Did the Civil War Retard Industrialization?

THOMAS C. COCHRAN

In most textbook and interpretative histories of the United States the
Civil War has been assigned a major role in bringing about the American
Industrial Revolution. Colorful business developments in the North—
adoption of new machines, the quick spread of war contracting, the
boost given to profits by inflation, and the creation of a group of war
millionaires—make the war years seem not only a period of rapid economic change but also one that created important forces for future
growth. The superficial qualitative evidence is so persuasive that apparently few writers have examined the available long-run statistical series
before adding their endorsement to the conventional interpretation. The
following quotations taken from the books of two generations of leading
scholars illustrate the popular view.

"The so-called Civil War," wrote Charles A. and Mary R. Beard in
1927, ". . . was a social war . . . making *vast changes* in the arrangement
of classes, in the accumulation and distribution of wealth, *in the course of
industrial development.*" Midway between 1927 and the present, Arthur
M. Schlesinger, Sr., wrote: "On these tender industrial growths the Civil
War *had the effect of a hothouse.* For reasons already clear . . . nearly
every branch of industry grew lustily." Harold U. Faulkner, whose textbook sales have ranked near or at the top, said in 1954: "In the economic
history of the United States the Civil War was extremely important. . . .
In the North *it speeded the Industrial Revolution* and the development of
capitalism by the prosperity which it brought to industry." The leading
new text of 1957, by Richard Hofstadter, William Miller, and Daniel
Aaron, showed no weakening of this interpretation: "The growing demand for farm machinery as well as for the 'sinews of war' led to American industrial expansion. . . . Of necessity, *iron, coal, and copper* production boomed during the war years." A sophisticated but still essentially
misleading view is presented by Gilbert C. Fite and Jim E. Reese in a

Reprinted by permission from *The Mississippi Valley Historical Review*, XLVIII
(September, 1961), pp. 197–210.

text of 1959: "The Civil War proved to be a boon to Northern economic development. . . . Industry, for example, was not created by the war, but wartime demands *greatly stimulated and encouraged industrial development* which already had a good start." In a reappraisal of the Civil War, in *Harper's Magazine* for April, 1960, Denis W. Brogan, a specialist in American institutions, wrote: "It may have been only a catalyst but the War *precipitated the entry* of the United States *into the modern industrial world*, made 'the take-off' (to use Professor W. W. Rostow's brilliant metaphor) come sooner."

In all of these reiterations of the effect of the Civil War on industrialism, statistical series seem to have been largely neglected. None of the authors cited reinforce their interpretations by setting the war period in the context of important long-run indexes of industrial growth. Since 1949, series for the period 1840 to 1890 that would cast doubt on the conventional generalizations have been available in *Historical Statistics of the United States, 1789–1945*. In 1960 a new edition of *Historical Statistics* and the report of the Conference on Research in Income and Wealth on *Trends in the American Economy in the Nineteenth Century* have provided additional material to support the argument that the Civil War retarded American industrial development. These volumes give data for many growth curves for the two decades before and after the war decade—in other words, the long-run trends before and after the event in question. The pattern of these trends is a mixed one which shows no uniform type of change during the Civil War decade, but on balance for the more important series the trend is toward retardation in *rates* of growth rather than toward acceleration. This fact is evident in many series which economists would regard as basic to economic growth, but in order to keep the discussion within reasonable limits only a few can be considered here.

Robert E. Gallman has compiled new and more accurate series for both "total commodity output," including agriculture, and "value added by manufacture," the two most general measures of economic growth available for this period. He writes: "Between 1839 and 1899 total commodity output increased elevenfold, or at an average decade rate of slightly less than 50 per cent. . . . Actual rates varied fairly widely, high rates appearing during the decades ending with 1854 and 1884, and a very low rate during the decade ending with 1869." From the over-all standpoint this statement indicates the immediately retarding effect of the Civil War on American economic growth, but since most of the misleading statements are made in regard to industrial growth, or particular elements in industrial growth, it is necessary to look in more detail at "value added by manufacture" and some special series. Gallman's series for value added in constant dollars of the purchasing power of 1879 shows a rise of 157 per cent from 1839 to 1849; 76 per cent from 1849 to 1859; and only 25 per cent from 1859 to 1869.[1] By the 1870's the more favorable prewar rates were resumed, with an increase of 82 per cent for 1869–1879, and 112 per cent for 1879–1889. Thus two decades of very rapid advance, the 1840's and the 1880's, are separated by thirty years of slower growth which falls to the lowest level in the decade that embraces the Civil War.

Pig-iron production in tons, perhaps the most significant commodity index of nineteenth-century American industrial growth, is available year-by-year from 1854 on. Taking total production for five-year periods, output increased 9 per cent between the block of years from 1856 to 1860 and the block from 1861 to 1865. That even this slight increase might not have been registered except for the fact that 1857 to 1860 were years of intermittent depression is indicated by an 81 per cent increase over the war years in the block of years from 1866 to 1870. If annual production is taken at five-year intervals, starting in 1850, the increase is 24 per cent from 1850 to 1855; 17 per cent from 1855 to 1860; 1 per cent from 1860 to 1865; and 100 per cent from 1865 to 1870. While there is no figure available for 1845, the period from 1840 to 1850 shows 97 per cent increase in shipments, while for the period 1870 to 1880 the increase was 130 per cent. To sum up, depression and war appear to have retarded a curve of production that was tending to rise at a high rate.

Bituminous coal production may be regarded as the next most essential commodity series. After a gain of 199 per cent from 1840 to 1850 this series shows a rather steady pattern of increase at rates varying from 119 to 148 per cent each decade from 1850 to 1890. The war does not appear to have markedly affected the rate of growth.

In the mid-nineteenth century copper production was not a basic series for recording American growth, but since three distinguished authors have singled it out as one of the indexes of the effect of the war on industry it is best to cite the statistics. Before 1845 production of domestic copper was negligible. By 1850 the "annual recoverable content" of copper from United States mines was 728 tons, by 1860 it was 8,064 tons, by 1865 it was 9,520 tons, and by 1870 it was 14,112 tons. In this series of very small quantities, therefore, the increase from 1850 to 1860 was just over 1,000 per cent, from 1860 to 1865 it was 18 per cent, and from 1865 to 1870 it was 48 per cent.

[1] Historical Statistics (1960 ed.), 402. "Constant" or "real" means dollars adjusted to eliminate price changes. It should be remembered that all series expressed in current dollars need to be corrected for rather violent price movements during these fifty years. Precise adjustments would vary with every series, and would involve many problems, but the movement of wholesale prices in general (Warren-Pearson Index) may be roughly summarized as follows. In 1850 prices were 12 per cent lower than in 1840, but by 1860 they were 11 per cent higher than in 1850. From 1860 to 1865 prices rose 99 per cent, but by 1870 the increase for the decade was only 46 per cent. By 1880 the decline for the decade was 26 per cent, and for the decade ending in 1890 it was 18 per cent. Ibid., 115. In other words, current dollars are a very unreliable indicator, particularly as applied to wholesale prices.

Railroad track, particularly in the United States, was an essential for industrialization. Here both the depression and the war retarded the rate of growth. From 1851 through 1855 a total of 11,627 miles of new track was laid, from 1856 through 1860, only 8,721 miles, and from 1861 through 1865, only 4,076 miles. After the war the rate of growth of the early 1850's was resumed, with 16,174 miles constructed from 1866 through 1870. Looked at by decades, a rate of over 200 per cent increase per decade in the twenty years before the war was slowed to 70 per cent for the period from 1860 to 1870, with only a 15 per cent increase during the war years. In the next two decades the rate averaged about 75 per cent.

Next to food, cotton textiles may be taken as the most representative consumer-goods industry in the nineteenth century. Interference with the flow of southern cotton had a depressing effect. The number of bales of cotton consumed in United States manufacturing rose 143 per cent from 1840 to 1850 and 47 per cent from 1850 to 1860, but *fell* by 6 per cent from 1860 to 1870. From then on consumption increased at a little higher rate than in the 1850's.

While woolen textile production is not an important series in the over-all picture of industrial growth, it should be noted that, helped by protection and military needs, consumption of wool for manufacturing more than doubled during the war, and then *fell* somewhat from 1865 to 1870. But Arthur H. Cole, the historian of the woolen industry, characterizes the years from 1830 to 1870 as a period of growth "not so striking as in the decades before or afterwards."

Immigration to a nation essentially short of labor was unquestionably a stimulant to economic growth. Another country had paid for the immigrant's unproductive youthful years, and he came to the United States ready to contribute his labor at a low cost. The pattern of the curve for annual immigration shows the retarding effect of both depression and war. In the first five years of the 1850's an average of 349,685 immigrants a year came to the United States. From 1856 through 1860 the annual average fell to 169,958, and for the war years of 1861 to 1865 it fell further to 160,345. In the first five postwar years the average rose to 302,620, but not until the first half of the 1870's did the rate equal that of the early 1850's. Had there been a return to prosperity instead of war in 1861, it seems reasonable to suppose that several hundred thousand additional immigrants would have arrived before 1865. . . .

Much American business expansion was financed by short-term bank loans continuously renewed. Thus major increases in business activity should be mirrored in increases in bank loans, both for financing short-term transactions and for additions to plant and working capital that would, in fact, be paid off gradually. If there was a really great Civil War boom in business activity it should be indicated in the series "total loans" of all banks. But it is not. In constant dollars, bank loans fell slightly between 1840 and 1850, and rose nearly 50 per cent by 1860. It should be noted that none of these three decadal years were periods of high prosperity. During the war Confederate banking statistics were not reported by the comptroller of the currency, but by 1866 there is a comparable figure for the nation as a whole, and in constant dollars it is some 35 per cent below that of 1860. Even by 1870 the constant dollar value of all loans was more than 15 per cent lower than just before the war. If instead of examining loans one looks at total assets of all banks the decline in constant dollars from 1860 to 1870 is reduced to 10 per cent, the difference arising from a larger cash position and more investment in government bonds.[2]

Net capital formation would be a more proper index of economic growth than bank loans or assets. Unfortunately, neither the teams of the National Bureau of Economic Research nor those of the Census Bureau have been able to carry any reliable series back of 1868. From colonial times to 1960, however, the chief single form of American capital formation has undoubtedly been building construction. Farm houses, city homes, public buildings, stores, warehouses, and factories have year-by-year constituted, in monetary value, the leading type of capital growth. Gallman has drawn up series for such construction based on estimating the flow of construction materials and adding what appear to be appropriate mark-ups. Admittedly the process is inexact, but because of the importance of construction in reflecting general trends in capital formation it is interesting to see the results. The rate of change for the ten-year period ending in 1854 is about 140 per cent; for the one ending in 1859 it is 90 per cent; for 1869 it is 40 per cent; and for 1879 it is 46 per cent. Taking a long view, from 1839 to 1859 the average decennial rate of increase was about 70 per cent, and from 1869 to 1899 it was about 40 per cent.[3] The *rate* of advance in construction was declining and the war decade added a further dip to the decline.

Since the decline in rate is for the decade, the exact effect of the war years can only be estimated, but the logic of the situation, reinforced by the record of sharp cut-backs in railroad building, seems inescapable: the Civil War, like all modern wars, checked civilian construction. The first year of war was a period of depression and tight credit in the Middle West, which checked residential and farm construction in the area that grew most rapidly before and after the war. In both the East and the West the last two years of the war were a period of rapid inflation which was regarded by businessmen as a temporary wartime phenomenon. The logical result would be to postpone construction for long-term use until

[2] The reader is again warned that deflation of current dollar values for this early period is an inexact process.
[3] Gallman has two alternate series which I have averaged. For the purposes of this paper either series leads to the same conclusions.

after the anticipated deflation. The decline in private railroad construction to a small fraction of the normal rate exemplifies the situation.

Lavish expenditure and speculation by a small group of war contractors and market operators gambling on the inflation seem to have created a legend of high prosperity during the war years. But the general series on fluctuations in the volume of business do not bear this out. Leonard P. Ayres's estimates of business activity place the average for 1861 through 1865 below normal, and Norman J. Silberling's business index is below its normal line for all years of the war. Silberling also has an intermediate trend line for business, which smooths out annual fluctuations. This line falls steadily from 1860 to 1869. Much of Silberling's discussion in his chapter "Business Activity, Prices, and Wars" is in answer to his question: "Why does it seem to be true that despite a temporary stimulating effect of war upon some industries, wars are generally associated with a long-term retarding of business growth . . . ?" He puts the Civil War in this general category.

Collectively these statistical estimates support a conclusion that the Civil War retarded American industrial growth. Presentation of this view has been the chief purpose of this article. To try to judge the non-measurable or indirect effects of the war is extremely difficult. But since further discussion of the conventional qualitative factors may help to explain the prevailing evaluation in American texts, it seems appropriate to add some conjectural obiter dicta.

Experience with the apparently stimulating effects of twentieth-century wars on production makes the conclusion that victorious war may retard the growth of an industrial state seem paradoxical, and no doubt accounts in part for the use of detached bits of quantitative data to emphasize the Civil War's industrial importance.[4] The resolution of the paradox may be found in contemporary conditions in the United States and in the nature of the wartime demand. The essential wastefulness of war from the standpoint of economic growth was obscured by the accident that both of the great European wars of the twentieth century began when the United States had a high level of unemployment. The immediate effect of each, therefore, was to put men to work, to increase the national product, and to create an aura of prosperity. Presumably, the United States of the mid-nineteenth century tended to operate close enough to full employment in average years that any wasteful labor-consuming activities were a burden rather than a stimulant.

By modern standards the Civil War was still unmechanized. It was fought with rifles, bayonets, and sabers by men on foot or horseback. Artillery was more used than in previous wars, but was still a relatively

---

[4] Ayres, Silberling, and some other students of economic activity such as Herbert Hoover, however, blame the breakdown of the 1930's on the dislocations caused by World War I. *Ibid.*, 65–66. See also *The Memoirs of Herbert Hoover: The Great Depression, 1929–1941* (New York, 1952), 105.

minor consumer of iron and steel. The railroad was also brought into use, but the building of military lines offset only a small percentage of the over-all drop from the prewar level of civilian railroad construction. Had all of these things not been true, the Confederacy with its small industrial development could never have fought through four years of increasingly effective blockade.

In spite of the failure of direct quantitative evidence to show accelerating effects of the war on rates of economic growth, there could be long-run effects of a qualitative type that would gradually foster a more rapid rate of economic growth. The most obvious place to look for such indirect effects would be in the results of freeing the slaves. Marxists contended that elimination of slavery was a necessary precursor of the bourgeois industrialism which would lead to the socialist revolution. The creation of a free Negro labor force was, of course, of great long-run importance. In the twentieth century it has led to readjustment of Negro population between the deep South and the northern industrial areas, and to changes in the use of southern land.

But economically the effects of war and emancipation over the period 1840 to 1880 were negative. Richard A. Easterlin writes: "In every southern state, the 1880 level of per capita income originating in commodity production and distribution was below, or at best only slightly above that of 1840. . . . [This] attests strikingly to the impact of that war and the subsequent disruption on the southern economy." In general the Negroes became sharecroppers or wage laborers, often cultivating the same land and the same crops as before the war. In qualification of the argument that free Negro labor led to more rapid industrialization it should be noted that the South did not keep up with the national pace in the growth of nonagricultural wealth until after 1900. . . .

To sum up this part of the obiter dictum, those who write of the war creating a national market tied together by railroads underestimate both the achievements of the two decades before the war and the ongoing trends of the economy. The nation's business in 1855 was nearly as intersectional as in 1870. Regional animosities did not interfere with trade, nor did these feelings diminish after the war. By the late 1850's the United States was a rapidly maturing industrial state with its major cities connected by rail, its major industries selling in a national market, and blessed or cursed with financiers, security flotations, stock markets, and all the other appurtenances of industrial capitalism.

But when all specific factors of change attributable to the war have been deflated, there is still the possibility that northern victory had enhanced the capitalist spirit, that as a consequence the atmosphere of government in Washington among members of both parties was more friendly to industrial enterprise and to northern-based national business operations than had formerly been the rule. It can be argued that in spite of Greenbackers and discontented farmers legislation presumably favorable to industry could be more readily enacted. The Fourteenth Amendment, for example, had as a by-product greater security for interstate business against state regulation, although it was to be almost two decades before the Supreme Court would give force to this protection. By 1876, a year of deep depression, the two major parties were trying to outdo each other in promises of stimulating economic growth. This highly generalized type of argument is difficult to evaluate, but in qualification of any theory of a sharp change in attitude we should remember that industrialism was growing rapidly from general causes and that by the 1870's it was to be expected that major-party politics would be conforming to this change in American life.

Massive changes in physical environment such as those accompanying the rise of trade at the close of the Middle Ages or the gradual growth of industrialism from the seventeenth century on do not lend themselves readily to exact or brief periodization. If factory industry and mechanized transportation be taken as the chief indexes of early industrialism, its spread in the United States was continuous and rapid during the entire nineteenth century, but in general, advance was greater during periods of prosperity than in depressions. The first long period without a major depression, after railroads, canals, and steamboats had opened a national market, was from 1843 to 1857. Many economic historians interested in quantitative calculations would regard these years as marking the appearance of an integrated industrial society. Walter W. Rostow, incidentally, starts his "take-off" period in the 1840's and calls it completed by 1860. Others might prefer to avoid any narrow span of years. Few, however, would see a major stimulation to economic growth in the events of the Civil War.

Finally, one may speculate as to why this exaggerated conception of the role of the Civil War in industrialization gained so firm a place in American historiography. The idea fits, of course, into the Marxian frame of revolutionary changes, but it seems initially to have gained acceptance quite independently of Marxian influences. More concentrated study of the war years than of any other four-year span in the nineteenth century called attention to technological and business events usually overlooked. Isolated facts were seized upon without comparing them with similar data for other decades. The desire of teachers for neat periodization was probably a strong factor in quickly placing the interpretation in textbooks; thus, up to 1860 the nation was agricultural, after 1865 it was industrial. Recent study of American cultural themes suggests still another reason. From most standpoints the Civil War was a national disaster, but Americans like to see their history in terms of optimism and progress. Perhaps the war was put in a perspective suited to the culture by seeing it as good because in addition to achieving freedom for the Negro it brought about industrial progress.

The Effect of the Civil War on American Industrial Development

STEPHEN SALSBURY

Much has been written about the Civil War. Until quite recently, however, historians were concerned mainly with its cause and they largely ignored the economic effects of the War. In the nineteenth century most northerners simply blamed the War on slavery. In the same period southerners merely accused politicians of being irresponsible and claimed that fanatical abolitionists ignited the conflict. But to Charles A. Beard, writing in the 1920's, these old statements seemed unconvincing.

Beard viewed America's history as a great movement away from Jefferson's agrarian type of society to the capitalistic, industrial, mechanized, and urban society that we have now. In his view, the forces that moved people were economic ones and not idealistic concerns over states' rights or over the immorality of slavery. Beard's pre-Civil War America consisted of a northern, capitalistic, industrial economy with, opposing it, the southern agricultural system. He saw the economic interest and political power of the South, in the Electoral College, the Senate, House of Representatives, and Supreme Court, as frustrating the economic needs of the rapidly growing industrial north.

Professor Louis Hacker stated the Beard thesis in its most extreme and naked form in his book, *The Triumph of American Capitalism.* "By 1860," he summarized,

a critical situation had arisen in American affairs. Because the southern planter capitalists were in control of the instrumentalities of the national state and, as a result, were thwarting the advance of the (too slowly) growing northern industrial capitalism, their claims to power had to be challenged. This the newly formed Republican party did. The partial success of the Republican party at the polls in 1860 drove the southern leaders—pushed on by extremists in their midst who were under heavy economic pressures—into secession. The Civil War broke out. The Union government, after the departure of the southern legislators, was now wholly possessed by the Republican party.

In Beard's words, the Civil War was the "social cataclysm in which the capitalists, laborers, and farmers of the North and West drove from power in the national government the planting aristocracy of the South. Viewed under the light of universal history, the fighting was a fleeting incident; the social revolution was the essential portentous outcome."

Reprinted by permission from Stephen Salsbury, "The Effect of the Civil War on American Industrial Development," in Ralph Andreano (ed.), *The Economic Impact of the American Civil War*, pp. 161–168 (Schenkman Publishing Co.: Cambridge, Mass., 1962).

This explanation of the causes of the Civil War led Beard and Hacker to the conclusion that the conflict spurred economic growth in the United States:

The Second American Revolution (Civil War), while destroying the economic foundation of the slave-owning aristocracy, assured the triumph of business enterprise. As if to add irony to defeat, the very war which the planters precipitated in an effort to avoid their doom augmented the fortunes of the capitalist class from whose jurisdiction they had tried to escape. Through financing the federal government and furnishing supplies to its armies, northern leaders in banking and industry reaped profits far greater than they had ever yet gathered during four years of peace. When the long military struggle came to an end they had accumulated huge masses of capital and were ready to march resolutely forward to the conquest of the continent —to the exploitation of the most marvelous natural endowment ever bestowed by fortune on any nation.

But Beard made no systematic use of statistical evidence in trying to analyze the War's effect.

Prior to 1860 southern planters successfully used their power in the national government to oppose measures such as the tariff, the Homestead Bill, national banking, etc., favored by the northern industrialists and western farmers. Beard, however, made no attempt truly to evaluate the importance of such measures in economic terms and merely assumed that because northern capitalists could not get their way, their plans for expansion and profits were hindered and that economic growth was thus retarded. Starting with this assumption, Beard saw the War as aiding industrialism. He argued that the transference of power from the Democratic to the Republican party (a condition which lasted, with two short exceptions, from the 1860's until 1932) enabled businessmen to shape government policies in ways that were most helpful to their plans for profit and expansion.

Beard cited the policies and legislation which, he claimed, specifically aided economic growth. He considered as most important the direct federal aid to the vast transcontinental railroad projects; it started with the subsidy and land grant to the Union Pacific and Central Pacific railroads in 1862 and included federal land grants in the following years to the Northern Pacific, Kansas Pacific, Santa Fe (Atlantic and Pacific), and Southern Pacific routes. The protective tariff was named as specifically aiding economic growth. He named also the acts designed to make easy the removal of land (whether farmland, timberland, or mineral land) from the public domain to private hands, the Immigration Act of 1864 which gave federal blessing to the importation of workingmen under contracts "analogous to the indentured servitude of colonial times," and the national banking laws and many others.

But more important than any specific legislative act, according to

Beard's interpretation, was the ascendancy of the Republican party in Washington; this created a climate that tolerated no interference with the private capitalists. Gone were the Jacksonian ideas that opposed the concentration of economic power in the hands of large corporations. After 1860, Leland Stanford, Collis P. Huntington, John D. Rockefeller, John M. Forbes, Jay Gould, and Mark Hanna had almost unlimited freedom to do as they pleased. And when men such as these ran into trouble with labor, their control of the government assured them that federal power would be used to smash opposition.

Charles Beard's main effort was to explain why the United States in the period between 1860 and 1910 became the world's most productive and powerful industrial nation. In giving his explanation, he made only a random use of statistics. But while he was perfectly content to make almost totally undocumented assertions, such as that which attributed the post-Civil War boom to "huge masses of capital made available by war profits far greater than . . . [capitalists] had ever yet gathered," Louis Hacker attempted to support this argument by statistical evidence. He used, for instance, an analysis of the census data to substantiate the thesis that "industrial capitalism (more particularly, *heavy* industry) benefited from the Civil War and it continued to make great forward strides (despite a severe depression) after the political victory was firmly secured."

Lately, the role of the Civil War in positively contributing to the American Industrial Revolution has been questioned. Among the most recent and able of these questioning re-evaluations is Thomas C. Cochran's *"Did the Civil War Retard Industrialization?"* In "reiterations of the effect of the Civil War on industrialism," he writes, giving examples, "statistical series seem to have been largely neglected." Cochran's conclusion, after an examination of statistics (available mainly in the 1949 and 1960 editions of *Historical Statistics of the United States* and in the report of the Conference of Research on Income and Wealth in *Trends in the American Economy in the Nineteenth Century*), strongly suggests that the Civil War slowed industrial growth.

Cochran observes that generally during the two decades preceding the Civil War (1840–1860) and the two decades (1870–1890) following the ten-year census period in which the war occurred, the rate of growth exceeded that of the "war decade" (1860–1870). In short, he points to rapid expansion between 1840 and 1860, then actual stagnation in some areas, and but slight increases in most others during the war period (1861–1865), which caused a slower growth rate for the decade 1860–1870, and finally a resumption of rapid growth in the decades between 1870 and 1890.

Behind Cochran's conclusion that the Civil War retarded industrial growth lies the very unstatistical and also partly unsubstantiated assumption that by 1840 all the ingredients favorable to fast industrial growth were overwhelmingly present in the American society. This implies that by the end of the Van Buren administration, the ground was laid for an almost continuous and uninterrupted expansion. This expansion, however, did not occur and the assumption is made that disruptive effects of the Civil War removed vital capital building goods and services from the economy between 1861 and 1865, making the growth after 1865 less rapid than it otherwise would have been.

Now, available statistics do indicate certain American economic reverses during the War. Cotton production almost ended, cotton textile manufacturing in the North fell sharply, and so did the construction of new railroad tracks. Yet, despite this, other segments such as bituminous coal, Pennsylvania anthracite, pig iron, and railroad rails continued to expand, although some at a slightly reduced rate. From this point of view, statistics show that the economy grew less rapidly during the five Civil War years than at other times. We might fairly conclude that war disruption was partially, at least, responsible for this.

Yet the conclusions of Beard, Hacker, and the other historians who claim that the Civil War speeded the Industrial Revolution do not stand or fall on an analysis of the short run, immediate effects which the War had upon the economy. Rather, these conclusions, which see the War as assuring the "triumph of capitalism," and as producing a long term surge of industrial production, rest on longer range analyses.

Professor Cochran's arguments may be met by comparing the post-Civil War growth rate with prewar activity. If one does this, some surprising results present themselves. Let us, for example, instead of comparing the three decades 1850–1860, 1860–1870, 1870–1880, as Cochran does, compare the decade preceding the Civil War (1850–1860), with that immediately following it (1865–1875). Pig iron production in tons, which he considers as "the most significant commodity index of nineteenth century American industrial growth," increased about 50 per cent between 1850 and 1860, but more than doubled between 1865 and 1873 before it fell, due to the depression which started in 1873. Bituminous coal, "the second most essential commodity series," tells a similar story: here production increased slightly less than 100 per cent during the decade of 1850–1860, while during the years 1865–1875 it increased by about 145 per cent. Railroad track construction, which he deems "essential for industrialization," tell an even more striking story: during the period 1850–1860 about 20,000 miles of track were laid down, compared to roughly 40,000 during the decade 1865–1875. Clearly then, in these three areas which Cochran considers the most important indicators of nineteenth century economic growth, the postwar decade evidences a substantial boom with growth rates much above those of the pre-Civil War era.

Although this kind of analysis tends to cast doubt on the argument and could be used to support Hacker's assertion that "industrial capitalism (more particularly, heavy industry) benefited from the Civil War," such a conclusion would have the weakness which plagues any attempt to assess the economic effects of the Civil War by reference to growth rates, and industrial or agricultural output. Such statistics tell us only how much was produced, or how much the growth rate declined or increased, but they do not tell us why. This returns us to the nonstatistical explanation of Beard which conflicts dramatically with Cochran's underlying assumption that all the ingredients for rapid economic growth dominated the American society by the beginning of William Harrison's administration.

Professor Cochran recognizes that what he calls "indirect effects" may have had some influence upon post-Civil War economic development. For purposes of analysis we can put these "indirect effects" into two categories. First, there were the changes in the political and social system which the War produced; and second there were the stimulants, such as inflation and the creation of a substantial federal debt, which resulted directly from the War itself. Relative to the second category, Cochran admits that "sharp wartime inflation had the usual effect of transferring income from wage, salary, and interest receivers to those making profits, . . . (which) meant concentration of savings in the hands of entrepreneurs who would invest in new activities." He also points out that inflation "eased the burdens of those railroads which had excessive mortgage debts." But Cochran seems willing to dismiss these effects of the War with the casual statement that "a great deal of new research would be needed to establish causal connections between the inflationary reallocation of wealth, 1863 to 1865, and the high rate of industrial progress in the late 1870's and 1880's." With this sentiment one can only agree. We add that until such attempts are made one must be careful about characterizing the Civil War as a retarder of industrialization.

Cochran's analysis is similar in his statements about the effect of expanded and superior credit resulting from the establishment of national banks and the increase of the national debt from $64,000,000 in 1860 to over $2,700,000,000 in 1866. He gives no statistics which would indicate the impact of the new banking system and the enormous federal debt, but merely states that "since 1800 a multiplication of banks had made credit relatively easy to obtain in the United States, and in the North this continued to be the situation." Further, he observes that the War destroyed southern banking, and that by 1875 some 40 per cent of the banks were still outside the national banking system. With these statements there can be little disagreement, yet it is difficult to see how they prove or disprove the thesis that the War retarded economic growth. In precise terms, how easy was credit to obtain before 1860? Was there ample credit for large scale ventures? Was there any change in this picture after 1865? If there was, did it result from the War? These questions still remain to be answered. And the fact that some "40 per cent of the banks" in 1875 were outside the national banking system seems almost irrelevant without a great deal of additional analysis which is not supplied.

Finally, Cochran recognizes that he must meet the argument which asserts that the Civil War changed the social structure of the nation. He agrees that there is a "possibility that the northern victory had enhanced the capitalist spirit"; but he maintains that this "highly generalized argument is difficult to evaluate." This is undoubtedly true (and the same statement could be made about most attempts to explain human behavior). But the Beard thesis is not so vague but what it is subject to some trenchant criticism. It is possible to analyze in detail the measures which the Republican Party enacted, and to determine how they affected economic growth. It has already been suggested that it may be feasible to measure the amount of investment capital made available by the creation of the national banking system, and the large national debt. There might also be a thorough quantitative study of government aid to internal improvements. While it is true that "federal and state administrations preceding the Civil War could . . . be regarded as friendly to business," it might be well to compare, as Professor Cochran suggests, federal and state aid during and after the Civil War with that in other periods. This should include an attempt to determine the precise amount in constant dollars made available to transportation enterprises by the various state and local governments and the national Congress. We do have readily available information on federal land granted for such purposes. Some idea of the new Republican attitude can be gained from the fact that, in the single year 1865, the national government granted more land for internal improvements than in all years prior to 1861.

There can be no doubt that the exodus from Washington of southern congressmen speeded by ten years or more the building of our entire transcontinental railroad network. Mr. Cochran suggests that such ventures were "built for speculative purposes uneconomically ahead of demand . . ." and thus concludes without supplying any evidence that they may "for a decade or even two have consumed more capital than their transportation services were then worth to the economy." Although this judgment is not necessarily wrong, it will take much research to prove it one way or the other. Certain it is that the building of our vast transcontinental railway systems, which is partially reflected in 40,000 miles of track laid down between 1865 and 1875, had enormous economic effects both from the point of view of consuming (thus stimulating) the products of heavy industry, and of opening up agricultural land in California, Kansas, Nebraska, Wyoming, Colorado, Utah, Idaho, Montana, Washington, Oregon, Arizona, Nevada, and New Mexico. Here it must be noted that since the first transcontinental road was not finished until May, 1869, the statistical impact of these roads on agriculture would not be seen until the decade 1870–1880.

Professor Cochran's assertion that the Union Pacific, during its first decade, was a drain on the economy has been sharply challenged by Robert Fogel. Fogel not only analyzes the rate of return on the Union Pacific's cash expenditures; he also presents estimates of the line's "social return," that is, the increased national income due to the railroad but not reflected in the company's earnings. In both respects Professor Fogel finds the Union Pacific a success, returning an average of 11.6 per cent on its cash expenditures for the first decade of its operation, and an average social return of 29.9 per cent for the same period. While it must be conceded that the social return statistics as yet mean little since we have few comparable figures for other railroads or other kinds of investments, it is only by this type of investigation that we will finally be able, through the aid of numbers, to shed light upon the question of the economic effect of the Civil War on the railroads.

Finally, however, we must face the inherent limits of statistics. Cochran's argument that the Civil War's contribution to the "spirit of capitalism" is difficult to measure is all too correct. Such actions as those of the Republican-appointed Supreme Court, which interpreted the Fourteenth Amendment to the Constitution to insure the sanctity of corporate property and to protect it from attacks by hostile state legislatures, are not subject to statistical measurement. Yet they vitally affected industrial development, at least the industrialism which characterized nineteenth century America.

In summary, historians must not discard or avoid statistics; they can prove invaluable in drawing a clear picture of what happened. Numbers may even answer questions such as, was the Union Pacific a stimulant to economic growth? and if so how? and in what areas of the economy? Yet the broader question—did the Civil War accelerate industrialism by placing in undisputed power men of business?—is only partially susceptible to statistical analysis. We can gain insight into the impact of some measures (tariffs, aid to railroads, land distributed under the Homestead Act, etc.) through numerical data, yet historians must never fail to integrate such information with interpretations based upon nonstatistical social, political, and psychological analysis.

FOR FURTHER READING: W. M. Persons, "Business and Financial Conditions Following the Civil War," *Review of Economics and Statistics* (1920), II, Supplement; Louis Hacker, *The Triumph of American Capitalism* (New York, 1940); and Ralph Andreano (ed.), *The Economic Impact of the American Civil War* (Cambridge, 1962) present views about the effects of the war upon the national economy. David T. Gilchrist and W. D. Lewis (eds.), *Economic Change in the Civil War Era* (Greenville, Delaware, 1965) have collected essays that bear on the various dimensions of the issue. A sophisticated appraisal of the complexities of this problem is by Stanley L. Engerman, "The Economic Impact of the Civil War," *Explorations in Entrepreneurial History*, III (Spring, 1966), pp. 176–199.

11

AGRICULTURE IN THE LATER NINETEENTH CENTURY

PROBLEM: *What were the causes of agricultural unrest between 1865 and 1900?*

One of the most heated public issues during the later nineteenth century was the dispute over the causes of agricultural unrest. Farm groups like the Grangers, a farm organization especially strong in the Middle West during the 1870's, placed the blame on alleged exploitations of middlemen such as railroads, money lenders, and mortgage companies. The Greenbackers of the 1880's, who advocated the issuance of paper money by the federal government to overcome depression, made a similar analysis. During the hard times of the 1890's another farmers' movement, the Populists, also found the exactions of middlemen to be a prime cause of agricultural depression. The complaints of farm leaders found a sympathetic ear among later historians, of whom Robert Higgs is representative. Higgs indicated that high railroad rates as well as other charges by middlemen were indeed responsible for the farmers' plight. On the other hand, historians like Allan Bogue have doubted whether excessive charges by middlemen contributed to farm crisis. As an example, Bogue examined the detailed history of a Kansas mortgage company and found that its charges generally were not excessive. Whether high interest rates were a cause of the farmer's woes, therefore, is open to question. Both these selections, however, pave the way for further examination of agricultural unrest during the later nineteenth century. What were the most important reasons for agricultural depression? Why

216

did the farmer's relative share of the national income decline? Were the reform programs of the Grangers, Greenbackers, and Populists well adapted to meet existing agricultural problems?

Railroad Rates and the Populist Uprising

ROBERT HIGGS

A prominent Populist complaint concerned "high" railroad freight rates. During the past two decades, however, economic historians have generally dismissed this complaint as inconsistent with the facts. The historians are apparently unanimous in believing that railroad freight rates fell steeply and steadily throughout the Gilded Age. The purpose of the present paper is to show that this belief, insofar as it concerns farmers, is probably false. The evidence upon which it rests is certainly inadequate, consisting almost exclusively of nominal rates. While these were typically falling, so were prices generally until the late 1890s, when secular deflation finally gave way to secular inflation. Since only the *relative* price of transportation is meaningful, nominal transport rates must be compared with a relevant price index.

When this comparison is made, periods of increase as well as periods of decline in *real* freight rates are evident. For the whole period 1867–96 the trend is approximately horizontal; in brief, farmers were not benefiting from lower transportation charges during the three decades before 1897.

The amounts of cotton, corn, or wheat exchanged for a ton-mile of railroad transportation were substantially unchanged throughout the Gilded Age. This finding makes the Populist complaint about "high" railroad freight rates a good deal more comprehensible.

Some years ago Theodore Saloutos argued: "Historians have repeatedly attributed the plight of the farmers, at least in part, to high freight rates, yet available figures show conclusively that the rates dropped drastically during the last half of the nineteenth century." This was apparently convincing, for one is hard pressed to find any historian of the past two decades maintaining the position that Saloutos considered common before he wrote. Saloutos's conclusion rests upon a reference to the U.S. Industrial Commission's *Report*, Vol. 10, which contains a few scattered comments about the decline of nominal rates between the 1850s or 1860s and

Reprinted by permission from *Agricultural History*, XLIV (July, 1970), pp. 291–297.

the late 1890s. The fourth volume of the commission's report summarized the testimony before it as showing that "freight rates in the United States have decreased steadily and with considerable rapidity during the past 30 years." Again the conclusion rests exclusively on the decline of nominal rates. Recently, Robert Fogel has relied on nominal rates, commenting that "the average cost of commodity transportation by railroad dropped more than 50 percent during the Gilded Age—from 1.925 cents per ton-mile in 1867 to 0.839 cents in 1895."

Of course, if all money prices change in the same proportion, all relative prices are preserved. A few writers have recognized that the decline in nominal freight rates must be compared with the decline in the price level: Edward Kirkland notes that "one explanation of these declines in rates was, of course, the general deflationary character of the decades"; and Douglass North says that, although the eastern rates fell most rapidly, "the dip in rates even west of Chicago [was] far greater than the general decline in the level of prices; as a result, the farmer was surely receiving additional benefits." Neither Kirkland nor North presents a series of nominal freight rates deflated by a price index to support his statement.

North also argues that the increasing ratio of the average wheat price received by farmers in the West North Central states to the average U.S. wheat price implies that transport rates were declining during this period. This is an incorrect deduction. In effect, the U.S. price is a weighted average of state prices. If (as was actually the case) the proportion of output originating in the West North Central states were increasing, the observed ratio would increase simply because the West North Central prices —which were always lower than the U.S. average for locational reasons— had more weight in determining the national average. Notably, between 1871–75 and 1891–95 the West North Central region increased its share of national wheat production from 26 to 41 per cent.

Probably the most sophisticated treatment of the issue is H. T. Newcomb's, presented in 1898. Newcomb shows, for the years 1867–96, index numbers of the freight rate per ton-mile along with index numbers of nine different farm product prices. There is some question about these farm product prices, since no source is given for them; but even if their quality were not contested, the conclusion drawn from them should be. Newcomb says:

The substantial regularity of the decline in railway rates is especially notable, as is also the fact that for any series of years after the earliest, which may be selected, it is greater than the decline in the price of any crop. Including 1896, the reduction in the price of only one crop, and that of minor importance, is seen to have been greater than that in freight rates, while the decline in the latter has been 23 per cent greater than in the price of wheat and 12 per cent greater than in that of hay.

The evidence presented, however, will not support these statements. In his comparisons of 1896 with the base period 1867–72 Newcomb falls victim to what statisticians call the regression fallacy: namely, the selection of particular points to draw a conclusion unwarranted by the data considered as a whole. One who wishes to draw an opposing conclusion might note that in 1894 the price of wheat in relation to its price during 1867–72 was lower than an index of railroad rates relative to the same base, and therefore that wheat prices fell faster than railroad rates before 1894; but this conclusion is no more warranted than is Newcomb's. The issue here concerns the direction of a *trend* movement, and *all* the data must be taken into account in determining this trend. This can be done, for example, by fitting a least-squares regression line to the time series.

The figures used here to represent changes in nominal freight rates are taken from Newcomb's compilation for the early years, from the Interstate Commerce Commission after 1889. The series (represented below by the symbol t) is constructed by dividing total freight revenue by total ton-miles carried; it is an overall index, covering all kinds of goods, movements in all directions, and both short and long hauls. Newcomb correctly comments,

[this] is an especially desirable measure of changes in freight charges from period to period, because, unlike published schedules of rates, which in earlier years were deviated from so frequently as to render them in many instances of but the slightest value as showing the actual charges, the rate per ton per mile takes account of all concessions from published charges except in those instances, it is impossible to say how frequent, in which rebates were charged as operating expenses.

The data are increasingly comprehensive over time. They are representative in 1867 of 23 percent of total U.S. railroad mileage; after 1872 of more than 50 percent; and after 1888, with the Interstate Commerce Commission in operation, of virtually all. The sample is sufficiently large to allay much doubt that it is representative, except possibly during the very early years when less than half the national mileage is included. For the conclusions drawn here this slight inadequacy is of no consequence. The freight rate index, which Newcomb expressed in terms of gold prices, has been adjusted to reflect the currency premium on gold before 1879.

To determine changes in the position of farmers vis-à-vis the railroads, the prices *received by farmers* for three important crops (wheat, corn, and cotton, each typically shipped substantial distances by railroad) have been examined. These data were collected by field correspondents of the U.S. Department of Agriculture. It is important that prices received by farmers rather than prices at a secondary market be used, and, because errors of this sort are frequently encountered, it may be useful, as a digression, to show just what is involved. For example, if the Warren-Pearson index of farm prices were used a misleading impression would be created because that index apparently relies heavily upon the Aldrich Report, which contains prices for farm products only at New York, Cincinnati, and Chicago. A few symbols will help to clarify the problem. If Pf is the average price received by farmers, Pn the average price at New York, Cincinnati, and Chicago, α the average tonnage shipped to these markets, β the average distance of a shipment to these markets in miles, and t the transport rate per ton-mile, the Warren-Pearson data allow the calculation of an index of Pn/t, where $Pn/t = (Pf + \alpha\beta t)/t$. What is required is an index of Pf/t. The equation defining Pn/t can also be written $Pn/t = Pf/t + \alpha\beta$. Since $\alpha\beta$ was rising during the 1867–96 period, Pn/t is biased upward as an indication of Pf/t. In plain English, one cannot infer from a rise in the Warren-Pearson index of farm prices relative to an index of railroad rates that farmers were improving their terms of trade with the railroads.

Figure 1 shows the movement over time of wheat prices, corn prices, and cotton prices deflated by the index of railroad freight rates for the 1867–1915 period: that is, indexes of Pf/t for each of the three products. Given the descriptions of recent historians, one would expect that despite year-to-year fluctuations the trends of the curves would move steadily upward. It is evident that they do not. In fact, three aspects of the series stand out: first, they are extremely variable from year to year;[1] second, before 1897 the trend is approximately horizontal;[2] and third, real improvement in the farmers' position begins in the late 1890s. Growers of all three crops were put at a particular disadvantage by the depression of the mid-1890s. Wheat growers in 1894 were at their worst position of the entire period, with the exception of the three years 1869, 1870, and 1874. Corn growers in 1896 had not faced such unfavorable terms of trade since 1878. For cotton, where reliable data are unavailable before 1876, the low mark for the entire period was reached in 1894. It must be emphasized, however, that more is involved here than farmers' suffering from the depression of the 1890s. Even if only the years before 1893 are considered, the data still fail to show any substantial (statistically significant) improvement in the farmers' position.

---

[1] It is a mistake to suppose that this variability can be explained solely by the well-known instability of farm prices. Substantial fluctuations in transport rates, fluctuations not associated with movements of prices generally, did occur.

[2] To test the hypothesis that the trend line is horizontal during the period 1867–96, linear trend equations have been calculated by the least-squares regression method. Where Pf/t is the product price deflated by the freight rate index and T is time in years, the equations are:

For wheat,	$Pf/t = 115.8 + 0.984\ T\ (25.6)$,
For corn,	$Pf/t = 438.7 + 11.286\ T\ (143.7)$,
For cotton,	$Pf/t = 140.0 + 0.750\ T\ (19.0)$.

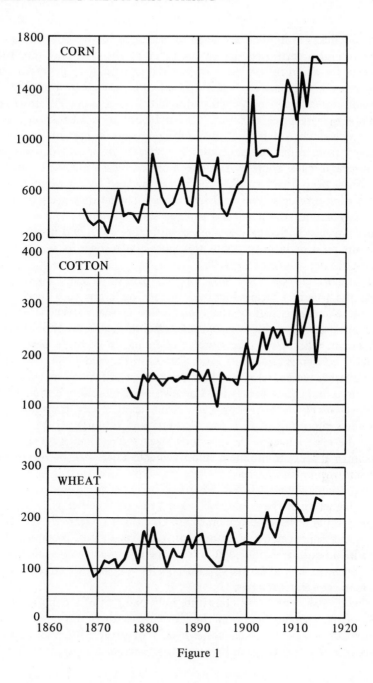

Figure 1

The indexes in figure 1 are open to criticism. Ideally one would deflate the price of a farm product by an index of the transport rate paid by farmers for shipment of *that product* rather than by a general transport rate index. Unfortunately, since data on total revenue and total ton-miles are not available for individual commodities, it is impossible to construct the appropriate price deflators. One is forced to fall back on published rates with all their defects. Newcomb's compilation presents average rates derived from published schedules for wheat, corn, and cotton shipped over several major routes.[3] As a check on the results obtained above, these rates have been used to deflate the prices received by farmers for the corresponding products. The resulting series, for what they are worth, unanimously corroborate the general patterns shown in figure 1. The trends are approximately horizontal for the period before 1897, and in almost every case the ratio of farm prices to transport rate reaches its minimum point during the depression of 1893–96.

Transport charges were an important part of farmers' costs. In some areas the freight charges incurred in moving crops to a market might absorb as much as half of the crops' value at that market. Under these circumstances the failure of transport rates to decline by more than 10 to 15 percent while farm prices were collapsing by 30 to 50 percent was a genuine economic source of farm distress in the mid-1890s. When transport charges were a relatively high proportion of farm costs (e.g., Kansas, Nebraska, and the Dakotas) the Populists were most active and successful, while relatively little protest came from areas where transport charges were less important (e.g., Iowa, Missouri, and Illinois). And most important, the experience of the previous twenty-five years gave farmers no reason to expect an imminent improvement. There can be no doubt that farmers themselves perceived their problems as springing *in part* from "high" freight rates. It is difficult to say whether they objected that rates were higher than they "should" have been or whether they considered their position to have been worsening. One thing is clear: they recognized no recent improvement with respect to railroad rates. Notably, the two decades preceding World War I, for which the data show such substantial improvement in the farmers' position (fig. 1), also witnessed the disappearance of agrarian unrest.

The data analyzed here constitute only one part of a complete explanation of the agrarian unrest of the late nineteenth century. A good many other forces were involved, some clearly of greater importance than the level of railroad rates. John Bowman has concluded from his study of land

---

[3] Newcomb, *Changes in the Rates of Charge*, 45–48. For wheat and corn the routes are: from Atchison, St. Joseph, Kansas City, and Leavenworth to Chicago and to St. Louis; from St. Paul to Chicago and St. Louis; from St. Louis to St. Paul. For cotton: from New Orleans to Boston, to New York, to Philadelphia, and to Baltimore; from Memphis to New York and to Boston; there are seventeen routes in total.

values, for example, that the distressed farmers of Kansas and Nebraska "should have blamed nature and their own inexperience in farming semi-arid land at least as much as they blamed the gold standard and monopolies."[4] It might simply be added that, contrary to existing opinion, changes in real freight rates did not consistently relieve the hardship imposed by nature and inexperience; in fact, rate increases often exacerbated these natural hardships. In sum, the data are consistent with an economic explanation bearing some resemblance to the complaints of the Populists themselves, and this explanation has been unjustifiably dismissed by recent economic historians.

The Land Mortgage Company in the Early Plains States

ALLAN G. BOGUE

"The whole trouble with Western Mortgages comes from the loan agents. . . . These fellows are the vampires that has brot [sic] all the discredit on Kansas." So wrote the Speaker of the Kansas House of Representatives in 1891. Twenty-three years later a New Englander remarked before a meeting of farm mortgage brokers, "Of course, in New England, we have a great deal of conservatism. New England is very skeptical about Western investments, because twenty-five or thirty years ago . . . (New Englanders) were severely swindled. . . ." Damned by both chagrined investors and indignant agrarians, the promoters of the western farm mortgage business in the late nineteenth century have been allowed by historians to stand guilty as charged.

The business of lending money on farms in the States beyond the Missouri River was as old as the settlers' title to the land. Settlers found that their private resources must be supplemented by borrowed capital as they labored to obtain title to their farms and then to equip and stock them. In the twenty-five years which followed the conclusion of the Civil War, the business of purveying mortgages to investors situated in the Eastern States and abroad became an increasingly important one. Fed

---

[4] J. D. Bowman, "An Economic Analysis of Midwestern Farm Land Values and Farm Land Income, 1860 to 1900," *Yale Economic Essays* 5 (Fall 1965): 350.

Reprinted by permission from *Agricultural History*, XXV (January, 1951), pp. 20–33.

by the rapid rush of settlement into the Plains States, and by the accumulation of capital in the hands of eager investors throughout northeastern America and in Europe, the mortgage business reached a peak of activity in the 1870s and 1880s when land mortgage companies were organized.

To estimate the number of these companies exactly is an unrewarding if not impossible task. More than 150 of them came under the surveillance of the fiscal officials of Connecticut, Massachusetts, New York, and Vermont during the years between 1888 and 1895. Most of the companies were organized in the States lying west of the Mississippi River, but some were incorporated in the central and northern States of the eastern seaboard and a few found their genesis abroad. When drought and low prices combined to spread acute depression over the Plains States after 1887, the mortgage companies fared badly. For the most part they acquired imperial domains through foreclosure and then slipped into receivership. Only a handful survived.

At the University of Kansas there are preserved today many of the business records of the J. B. Watkins Land Mortgage Company. Although not entirely complete the collection allows the student to reconstruct the history of one land mortgage company. This article is devoted to a brief summary of the company's history and to a more detailed consideration of the experience and policy of its officials in those aspects of the mortgage business which were most bitterly criticized by the farmer radicals of the Plains States.

THE J. B. WATKINS LAND MORTGAGE COMPANY

After teaching school in Virginia, Pennsylvania, Illinois, and Wisconsin, and graduating from the law department of the University of Michigan, Jabez Watkins established himself at Champaign, Illinois, in 1870. In his efforts to work up a lucrative legal practice Watkins acted as local agent for several firms and individuals lending money to farmers in central Illinois. As he gained experience in money lending he made direct contacts with investors and began building up an organization of local agents for himself.

In August 1873, Watkins transferred his base of operations to Lawrence, Kansas. Although he became a member of the Kansas bar his legal business was subordinated to money lending. In Kansas he found the competition among lending agencies to be less severe than in Illinois; money brought a higher rate of interest; and the lender had a larger number of applicants from which to choose. Watkins began a vigorous advertising campaign in the eastern press to solicit funds. At frequent intervals he visited the New England and central seaboard States to back up his advertising with personal appeals. His efforts were so well rewarded that in 1876 he established an eastern office in New York. Two years later he entered the European field and set up an agency in London, England. Especially fortuitous was his contact with the Quakers. . . .

J. B. Watkins incorporated his loan business under the laws of Colorado with a capitalization of $750,000. For the stock representing this sum he traded 52,000 acres of land, which he had acquired in his northern lending field through foreclosure, deeding, or purchase, along with complete control of the business and its assets at offices located in Lawrence, Dallas, New York, and London. His business, Watkins claimed, was returning a net income of over $77,000 annually. He quoted Jay Gould and James Gordon Bennett to prove that the value of a business with such an income should not be less than $770,000. After its organization the new company still had no liquid working capital, but Watkins placed $100,000 at its disposal. Since he did not endeavor to unload large blocks of stock on the eastern market, he was evidently not interested in promoters' profits. Watkins maintained that he would never sell more than a third of the stock and actually did not sell more than a tenth. He never broke away completely from his original method of selling mortgages, but early in 1887 his company began to sell debenture bonds backed by mortgage paper deposited with the Farmers' Loan and Trust Company of New York as trustee.

In Kansas Watkins at first confined his lending activities to the eastern portion of the State, entering the adjacent counties of Missouri as well. By the mid-seventies he was lending funds on farms in western Iowa. During 1880 and 1881 business was extended into Nebraska and the Territory of Dakota. In the fall of 1881 a branch office was established at Dallas, Texas. Henceforth most of the lending business done by Watkins, and later by the J. B. Watkins Land Mortgage Company, was carried on in Kansas and Texas. During the late 1880s mortgage paper was also obtained in Louisiana, drawn in part on farm and plantation land, but mainly on the unimproved lands which Watkins himself owned.

By 1893 J. B. Watkins had supervised the sale of obligations totaling over $18,000,000. It is impossible to apportion this sum exactly, but some two-thirds of the total was loaned in Kansas and Texas. The greater portion of the remainder was lent in Missouri and Louisiana, while relatively smaller sums were advanced on the security of farm land in Iowa, Nebraska, and the Territory of Dakota. Over $5,000,000 of the total was represented by debenture bonds supported by various types of mortgage paper. During the period of the company's greatest activity some twenty-five full-time employees administered its affairs. The local western agents who, at one time or another, represented Watkins or the company undoubtedly totaled several hundred. By no means the largest of the western mortgage companies, the volume of its business entitled the J. B. Watkins Land Mortgage Company to rank well up among the major corporations of its kind.

Until 1891 the company returned an annual dividend of 10 per cent and by 1893 a surplus of over $500,000 had been set aside. But there were elements of weakness in the business. Profits and surplus were derived in part by constantly revising the value of the company's land upward to parallel the highly speculative rise in land values which was general in the Plains States during the 1880s. Much of the company's operating capital was derived from bank loans. Withdrawal of support by the banks in a period of depression could be painful. In the years after 1887 over 250,000 acres of land were taken by foreclosure as the western "boom" came to an end. Utter collapse in the real estate market made it impossible to realize on the funds tied up in this land. Other companies, faced with the same problem, began to fail as early as 1888. Panicky investors withdrew their funds, thereby reducing the income from commissions. Watkins had borrowed large amounts on his unimproved land in Louisiana and fed the obligations into the paper behind the company's debenture bonds in the expectation that migration into the southwest would soon allow him to sell the land at a profit. Such hope proved chimerical. In the meantime, Watkins, the debtor, was paying large amounts of interest to his company, which stood as the agent of eastern and English investors. The recession of 1891 found Watkins' financial lines dangerously extended. Renewed depression in 1893 forced him to place the mortgage company in receivership in April 1894. Most of its rivals had already preceded it into the same unhappy situation.

By 1893 Watkins was a man of many business interests. In Kansas he owned a newspaper and controlled a canning factory and a national bank, in addition to the J. B. Watkins Land Mortgage Company. In Louisiana he owned, controlled, or managed several development companies, a railroad, and a private banking house. Since Watkins linked his enterprises in Louisiana closely to the business of the mortgage company, it is fair to question whether or not the company can be considered a representative example of the incorporated western loan agency. If we are to believe the Massachusetts Commissioner of Foreign Mortgage Corporations, many of the western mortgage promoters dabbled in other fields. Certainly the operating problems of the J. B. Watkins Land Mortgage Company with which we are primarily concerned in this article were the same as those faced by its rivals.

The Agrarian Indictment of Money Lenders. It is easy to reconstruct the case which the agrarian radicals of the late nineteenth century made against the money lender by consulting a few files of Midwestern newspapers and periodicals.

The Populist and his predecessors considered the mortgage to be a sign of distress. There were few among them who dared suggest that a mortgage might fulfill a useful or productive function for the debtor. But if the mortgage indicated that the borrower was in distress, it represented profit to the money lender. A memorial of the National Farmers' Alliance, printed in the Alliance of Lincoln, Nebraska, in June 1889, pictured the growing indebtedness of the citizens of the country while in the meantime, ". . . there are two classes of men who seem above the reach of adverse financial fortune; money lenders and railroad owners. Of these the former are reaping a harvest of wealth unprecedented in the history of the world."

Agrarian writers devoted much of their energy to proving that the interest rate was high. Occasionally correspondents described rates of interest as high as 36 per cent. Generally they confined themselves to arguing that the use of money was bought too dearly. In extreme cases they asked why the security which was good for a loan at 10 or 12 per cent was not equally good for a loan bearing 5 or 6 per cent.

The money lenders were able to maintain high rates of interest because a highly organized money power had risen in the United States after the termination of the Civil War. The way in which this money power was organized and the tactics which its members followed made it virtually "a conspiracy against the people." The association which the farmers regarded as most synonymous with the organized money power was the American Bankers' Association. In hazy fashion the agrarians believed that the money power was composed of eastern capitalists who employed western agents as their tools. Occasionally a real estate agent or lawyer was admitted to be his own master, but the western bankers and money lenders were regarded alike as proven agents of the money power. The price which the farmer paid for his borrowed money was a monopoly price.

When the representatives of an aroused people attempted to check the onslaught of the money power its agents rallied to corrupt the legislatures. The will of the majority was perverted by the lobbying activities of the few. The editor of the *Kansas Farmer* wrote in 1889: "What was settled by the last legislature was that the combined forces of a corrupt lobby in the interests of money lenders were able to override the representatives of the people and defeat the execution of the popular will." Writing three years later the correspondent of a Nebraska newspaper, the Farmers' Alliance, described the money lenders' lobby as "the largest, best organized, and most shrewdly managed lobby that infested the capital the past session."

As in many lands and at many times the money lender was painted as an unlovely figure. He was a "hyena-faced Shylock" with a singularly unattractive personality. He inveigled the innocent into borrowing money when they really had no need for funds. In the process of making a loan the mortgage agent carried out an investigation of the farmer's personal life and business standing that was little short of a personal insult. Once the loan was made, the money lender busied himself in plotting the downfall of the debtor. In this he was merciless. As one editor put it, "A money lender assuming the role of a philanthropist in his business transactions is about equal to a rum seller preaching temperance."

Shylock was eager to assume ownership of the security if at all possible since he obtained the land for a mere fraction of its value. He was, therefore, little better than a thief. But not content with obtaining debtors' farms at figures well below their true value, Shylock often took a personal judgment against the unfortunates whom he had dispossessed. The borrower might eventually lose much more than his farm.

Operating Practices of the Watkins Company. The history of the J. B. Watkins Land Mortgage Company contributes to a fuller understanding of the catalog of grievances which the agrarian radicals presented. It is often pointed out that Kansas among the Plains States was most severely burdened with debt. The remainder of this article applies specifically to that State unless otherwise noted, but it has obvious application to the other Plains States as well.

It is difficult to arrive at the price which the western farmer paid for borrowed capital. The county records generally show the rate of interest which was specified in the note and mortgage. But in addition to the interest paid to the mortgagee both the mortgage company and the local agent received a commission. Sometimes these commissions were included in the interest rate; at other times they were paid by the mortgagor in cash or possibly by a second note and mortgage. At times the mortgage company paid the local agent his commission; more often the local agent obtained his fee from the borrower. It became customary also to offer the borrower a choice between a high rate of interest and a small commission and a low rate of interest and a large commission. In addition to commission and interest the western farmer paid recording fees and was expected to provide an abstract of title, but such charges were minor ones. If one goes no farther than to the county records it is often impossible to determine which of two farmers was actually paying the most for his borrowed funds.

At no time during twenty years of business in Kansas did J. B. Watkins and his associates charge a uniform rate of interest throughout the lending field. In general the rates rose from east to west as the money lender progressed into areas but newly opened to settlement. The size of the loan, the quality of the security, and the character of the borrower all entered into the determination of lending rates.

In 1874 borrowers were paying a maximum fee of 16 or 17 per cent annually on funds borrowed from Watkins. This payment was made up of the 12 per cent interest allowed under the usury law of Kansas and service charges or commission amounting to another 4 or 5 per cent. Until 1879 Watkins usually reimbursed the local agent, a practise which he never completely abandoned. For a time in the mid 1870s he shared a portion of the commission with some of his eastern investors and until the late eighties paid a commission on the investment funds which eastern agents procured for him.

In October 1881, farmers borrowing from J. B. Watkins and Company in Kingman County, Kansas, on the ninety-eighth meridian, were paying total charges amounting to slightly over 11 per cent annually. These charges were made up of an interest rate of 8 per cent and service charges of 10 per cent. Since the mortgages ran from 3 to 5 years, it was standard procedure to calculate 1 per cent of annual interest as equivalent to a commission of 3 per cent.

Stevens County, Kansas, is located on the Oklahoma border in the second tier of counties east of the Colorado boundary. Here the agent of the J. B. Watkins Land Mortgage Company was attempting to lend money at 11 per cent in March 1887. If he was content with a commission of 3 per cent for his services, borrowers were obtaining money from him for about 12 per cent interest. Two tiers to the east in Kiowa County the equivalent rate was 10 per cent. Rates were dropping swiftly in southwestern Kansas during the spring and early summer of 1887, but they rallied and began to climb as the season proved to be one of drought. The total charges on the type of security desired by Watkins stood at 11 or 12 per cent in the extreme southwestern corner of Kansas as the year ended. By April 1888, officials of the company had decided that the future of agriculture in western Kansas was highly uncertain. Further business in the region was confined to servicing the loans already made.

There was a drop of 4 or 5 per cent in the maximum charges which borrowers paid to Watkins between 1874 and 1881. In 1887 the maximum rate was approximately the same as in 1881, but it had been held up by lending on lands which were less well improved and more recently settled than had been the case in the 1870s and early 1880s. Some companies had made other concessions as well. Borrowers were allowed to pay off the principal in installments or even to pay off the loan completely if notice was given a few months in advance. Such maximum rates were of course obtained on only a portion of the loans made by Watkins' agency. In the central third of Kansas, where Populism was to develop its greatest strength, the farmer with good security could obtain funds in 1886 and 1887 at 6 or 7 per cent, which with commission amounted to 8 or 9 per cent annually.

Certainly the charges which borrowers in Kansas paid to Watkins' company in the 1880s appear high by present-day standards. But we must remember that the loans were usually small. More than $500 was seldom loaned on quarter sections west of the hundredth meridian. The service charge was usually included by the Populist orator as part of the rate. The same procedure has been followed in this article, but it is not customary to do so when giving interest rates. When comparing modern rates with the rates cited by the agrarians, one should remember that the service charge has not yet completely disappeared from the field of farm financing.

Nor can the factor of risk be overlooked. The population in newly settled areas was notoriously fiddlefooted. The possibility that the lender might become an unwilling landowner was ever present. Without doubt many an investor who acquired title to land in the western third of Kansas during the 1880s and '90s remained unconvinced that the rate of interest had been commensurate with the risk involved in his loans.

Finally we distort the perspective of history if we consider the lending rates of the 1880s by themselves. In the territorial period money was lent on landed security in Kansas and Nebraska at rates that were in excess of 36 per cent per annum. By the mid-seventies the borrower in Kansas with good security was paying between 12 and 16 per cent. By 1891 mortgage companies were hard put to find a safe market for funds in Kansas at 8 or 9 percent. Undoubtedly the interest rate lagged behind the falling price level, but this was a normal economic phenomenon. . . .

What of the influence which the mortgage brokers exerted upon the elected representatives of the people in the Plains States? Unquestionably the mortgage men did attempt to influence the legislators. In 1886, one of Watkins' investors inquired nervously whether the legislature of Kansas might not levy a tax upon mortgages held by eastern investors. The attorney of the mortgage company, W. J. Patterson, soothed the easterner by pointing out that there was a large and influential element engaged in the mortgage business throughout the State, whose influence would be thrown solidly against any bill levying on the investments of non-residents.

As the legislative session of 1889 opened in Kansas, numerous members of the House of Representatives announced that they would introduce bills dealing with the credit question. Stirred into action, the representatives of the loan companies met at Kansas City and organized. T. B. Sweet was given authority to take any steps which he thought necessary to check or amend legislation on farm credit. According to Patterson the representatives of the loan agencies generally believed that it would be easy to defeat any adverse legislation in the Senate. Only a Republican-sponsored amendment to the interest law was passed during the session.

Nor was such activity among the mortgage companies confined to Kansas. The files of the Dallas office of the Watkins Company reveal the situation in Texas. In December 1890, Samuel Kerr, of the British and American Mortgage Company, wrote to Watkins' manager in Dallas:

. . . the usual number of harassing measures aimed at money lenders will it appears be introduced at the coming session of the legislature. We were able by employing parties in the swim to defeat or shelve many of those brought forward in previous legislatures.

My own Company . . . have agreed to give their usual subscription of $100 (or more if needed) to secure the services of a good man—or men—to watch the interests at stake and keep us advised. My friends representing other companies have asked me to take charge of any funds subscribed as in former years and to write you asking you to aid the cause. The money will be judiciously expended and an account rendered at the close of the session showing what has been done with it. I hope you will send me your cheque payable to me as treasurer of this fund, for such sum as you may think fit . . .

Although there was an organized effort on the part of the mortgage agencies to influence the course of legislation, there is little evidence to show that this influence was exerted on a major scale. The contribution of the companies in Texas could hardly have amounted to more than $3,000 in 1891. A little entertaining or discreet pressure on key figures is obviously all that could be expected from such a sum. Nor is lobbying in itself prima facie proof of dishonesty or predatory intentions. Some of the money lenders, at least, believed that capital was necessary to develop the Plains States and that a revision of the credit laws would cause investors to withdraw their funds. The mortgage companies were attempting to maintain the status quo; they were not lobbying for severer credit laws.

The mortgage companies were charged with enticing farmers into borrowing money. The activities of J. B. Watkins and his subordinates shed some light upon this charge. During the 1870s when Watkins was endeavoring to build a business, he had examined the assessment rolls of the counties lying in the eastern third of Kansas. From the rolls were taken the names of all farmers whose property appeared sufficient security for a loan. Such farmers soon received circulars advertising the money-lending service of J. B. Watkins and Company. As Watkins' business expanded he discontinued this type of advertising. But only farmers who showed a reasonable chance of repaying their loans had been contacted. Nor were applications for loans ever accepted indiscriminately. At times the number of applications rejected by the Lawrence agency fell little short of half of the total submitted. As the eighties wore on it became less easy to exercise discrimination, but there was still a definite effort to obtain adequate security.

Does the policy of Watkins bear out the charge that the money lender was a "heartless grasping Shylock" ever eager to take his debtor's land? Possibly in the first years of his business at Lawrence, Watkins was not averse to acquiring some real estate by foreclosure. But in the early 1880s his firm wrestled for the first time with the problems posed by foreclosure on a large scale. Drought along the ninety-eighth meridian in 1879 and 1880 forced Watkins to assume title to some 45,000 acres of land between 1881 and 1883. Experience proved that land could be a detriment as well as a source of profit. It was not readily saleable in times of depression and taxes were an ever-present cost. The farms were scattered and therefore difficult to supervise. Since Watkins had pledged himself to assume delinquent loans the interest and principal on loans in foreclosure must be sent to the investors despite the default. Watkins' lieutenants expressed grave concern as the number of foreclosures mounted, and Watkins urged them to take great care that such a situation might not occur again. To the small local lender, exemplified by Hamlin Garland's Jim Butler, foreclosure may well have provided a cheap means of acquiring real estate; to the mortgage agency a large number of foreclosures brought grave problems of financial policy. . . .

The Mortgage Business in Perspective. Important aspects of the western mortgage business have received too little attention as yet.

In the first instance it becomes necessary to make a distinction among money lenders. Few of the land mortgage companies centered their interest on the chattel mortgage business. The chattel mortgage was often used to guarantee the payment of rents on farms owned by the mortgage companies or to furnish additional security when extensions were given to hard-pressed borrowers, but such use was incidental to the main business of lending on real estate security. The chattel mortgage business was carried on mainly by banks or individuals and bore a bad reputation even among the brokers who lent eastern funds on western farms. In 1886 a mortgage broker from New Haven, Connecticut, wrote to his son who was establishing a law office at Topeka: "I do not advise having . . . any Chattel Mortgage man in with you. It would prejudice people against you, that business as done in Topeka is too malodorous." Defending himself against the charge that he was a money lender in the "offensive political sense," L. D. Richards, the defeated Republican candidate for the governorship of Nebraska and president of a loan company, maintained in 1890: "I have never been engaged in the chattel mortgage business and have no mortgages of any kind of my own, but am doing a legitimate loaning business for which no apologies need be made."

The borrower who dealt with the chattel mortgage man was often in dire financial straits and therefore in a weaker bargaining position than was the borrower who dealt with the land mortgage companies. Sometimes of course the chattel mortgage represented an effort to meet the interest on long-term obligations. In some cases the local agents of the mortgage companies dabbled in the field of short-term credit in addition to their work in the long-term field. To their extreme annoyance staff members of the J. B. Watkins Land Mortgage Company discovered that some of the local agents were managing to delay the passage of company funds through their hands sufficiently to use them in the chattel mortgage business. It is unfair to lump the land mortgage companies with the short-term credit agencies when evaluating the credit system of the Plains

States. Sometimes contemporary critics did make the necessary distinction, but all too often money lenders were indicted as one.

The key position of the local agent in the mortgage business should not be overlooked. The agent who transacted the local business of the mortgage companies was frequently a jack-of-all-trades. He might constitute any combination of lawyer, real estate dealer, banker, and loan agent. The towns of the Plains States overflowed with gentlemen of this type, endeavoring to secure a foothold and to grow up with the country. Such was the pressure of competition among them that they were frequently very hungry indeed. Originally Watkins attempted to keep their appetites in check by paying their commissions himself, but as competition among the companies for agents became keener he was forced to let them collect their own fees. Suspicion was strong in the minds of the officials of Watkins' company that the charges levied by the local agents were at times exorbitant. The secretary of the company summed up his opinion of local agents when he wrote: ". . . a commission will warp the integrity and judgement of the best of them."

Significant from the standpoint of the mortgage companies' financial welfare was the danger that the local agents in an effort to work up a large volume of business would negotiate loans on inadequate security. Despite the use of traveling inspectors it was impossible to check all of the loans, and in some cases the damage was done before mortgage company officials became aware of the situation. D. M. Sprankle, the secretary of the J. B. Watkins Land Mortgage Company, claimed that control of the business in western Kansas during 1886 and 1887 was completely out of the hands of the mortgage companies. All of the lending agencies had large amounts of funds on hand for investment and were forced to give their local agents full leeway lest they should switch their services to a rival company. Between them the local agents and the borrowers set the terms. It was during these years that the loans were made which resulted in the large volume of foreclosures in the Plains States between 1888 and 1892. When officials of Watkins' agency considered the possibility of expanding business in Kansas in July 1891, they agreed that henceforth all loans must be closed by a full-time employee of the company. While the overburdened debtor blamed eastern capitalists for his plight, the real villain of the piece was often in residence at the local county seat.

One must also examine the motivation of the western settler. Inherent in agrarian philosophy was the tenet that the settler went to the frontier in a sincere attempt to establish a home which would belong to his family from generation to generation. Agricultural distress resulted when selfish interests strove to wrest this American birthright away from the common man. But did the settler actually look forward to long years of happy residence on a western farm? No doubt foreign settlers, who regarded the land from the standpoint of the European peasant, did hope to establish a farm which would remain in their family for generations. But many settlers of American origin had very different motives.

In 1855 the editor of the Atchison Squatter Sovereign gave one of the texts for land settlement in Kansas when he wrote:

We have never known it to fail that when a claim was taken, and a cabin erected that the pre-emptor could at any time sell his rights for a handsome sum, —more than enough to pay him for his own labor. So there is a speculation to be made in lands here by those with a limited capital.

Nor did petty speculation die out with the coming of the homestead law. It is a recurrent theme in the western press.

It is impossible of course to segregate the genuine settler from the settler speculator. No doubt where circumstances altered cases the one was merged into the other, but undoubtedly the settler speculator was common in pioneer areas. Some years ago Professor James C. Malin used detailed census data in an attempt to turn the spotlight of quantitative research on the behavior of farm operators in selected Kansas townships. Had the settlers been dominated solely by their desire to establish a home for themselves, the exodus of farm operators from pioneer townships should have been greatest in periods of economic depression. He found, however, little difference in the rate of turnover between periods of relative prosperity and periods of economic distress. In good times the settlers were evidently seizing the opportunity to turn their bit of the national heritage into cash and to realize a profit from the rising value of land. . . .

FOR FURTHER READING: The validity of agricultural complaints is stressed by Solon J. Buck, *The Granger Movement* (Cambridge, 1913), W. A. Anderson, "The Granger Movement in the Middle West," *Iowa Journal of History and Politics*, XXII (1924), pp. 3–51, and Herebert S. Schell, "The Grange and Credit Problems in North Dakota," *Agricultural History*, X (April, 1936), pp. 59–83. More skeptical are George W. Miller, "Origins of the Iowa Granger Law," *Mississippi Valley Historical Review*, XL (March, 1954), pp. 657–680, Gerald D. Nash, "The Reformer Reformed: John H. Reagan and Railroad Regulation," *Business History Review*, XXIX (June, 1955), pp. 189–195, and Robert F. Severson, Jr., "The Source of Mortgage Credit for Champaign County, 1865–1880," *Agricultural History*, XXXVI (July, 1962), pp. 150–155. Norman Pollack, *The Populist Response to Industrial America* (Cambridge, 1962) buttresses the farmers' complaints. Anne Mayhew, "A Reappraisal of the Causes of Farm Protest in the United States, 1870–1900," *Journal of Economic History*, XXXII (June, 1972), pp. 464–475.

12

THE RISE OF
BIG BUSINESS

PROBLEM: *Were John D. Rockefeller's contributions to the petroleum industry constructive or destructive?*

Few captains of industry in the later nineteenth century
aroused as much admiration as well as hostility as the undisputed lord of petroleum, John D. Rockefeller. More than
most of his colleagues, he became a symbol embodying the
virtues and the vices of the Big Business leader of his era.
Viewed by contemporaries as having qualities of either saint
or sinner, it was not surprising that later historians also differed in their appraisals of his career. Was he a pioneer
builder of a great new enterprise, or was he a destroyer of
free and healthy competition? In a critical estimate of Rockefeller, journalist Matthew Josephson judged him harshly for
his destructive influence. Without denying his contributions
to the growth of the oil industry, Josephson points to his
ruthlessness in suppressing competition, his use of espionage
and violence to gain competitive advantages, his establishment of monopoly, and his general neglect of the public interest. Josephson wrote during the great depression of the
Thirties, but in more recent years historians have appraised
Rockefeller more favorably. A representative view is presented by Professors Ralph and Muriel Hidy of the Harvard
Business School—leading exponents of the relatively new field
of business history—who stress the oil magnate's positive and
constructive achievements. The Hidys describe Rockefeller's
extraordinary mind, his capacity for detail, his decisiveness,

and his foresight and vision. They also point to his ability to select outstanding subordinates such as Henry Flagler, or the useful William Rockefeller. But, above all, they dwell on his achievement in creating a large, integrated industrial corporation, on standardization of products and methods, and on the development of new business procedures. The ultimate achievement was to create order in the hitherto chaotic petroleum industry. Whether one agrees with Josephson or the Hidys, both provide arguments that can form a basis for evaluating the work of Rockefeller and Big Business leaders in the later nineteenth century. What were some major reasons for Rockefeller's success? Do Rockefeller's constructive accomplishments outweigh his destructive impulses? What are the underlying assumptions of the authors?

The Robber Barons

MATTHEW JOSEPHSON

John Rockefeller, who grew up in western New York and later near Cleveland, as one of a struggling family of five children, recalls with satisfaction the excellent practical training he had received and how quickly he put it to use. His childhood seemed to have been darkened by the misdeeds of his father, a wandering vendor of quack medicines who rarely supported his family, and was sometimes a fugitive from the law; yet the son invariably spoke of his parent's instructions with gratitude. He said:

. . . He himself trained me in practical ways. He was engaged in different enterprises; he used to tell me about these things . . . and he taught me the principles and methods of business. . . . I knew what a cord of good solid beech and maple wood was. My father told me to select only solid wood . . . and not to put any limbs in it or any punky wood. That was a good training for me.

But the elder Rockefeller went further than this in his sage instructions, according to John T. Flynn, who attributes to him the statement:

I cheat my boys every chance I get, I want to make 'em sharp. I trade with the boys and skin 'em and I just beat 'em every time I can. I want to make 'em sharp.

If at times the young Rockefeller absorbed a certain shiftiness and trading sharpness from his restless father, it was also true that his father was absent so often and so long as to cast shame and poverty upon his home. Thus he must have been subject far more often to the stern supervision of his mother, whom he has recalled in several stories. His mother would punish him, as he related, with a birch switch to "uphold the standard of the family when it showed a tendency to deteriorate." Once when she found out that she was punishing him for a misdeed at school of which he was innocent, she said, "Never mind, we have started in on this whipping and it will do for the next time." The normal outcome of such disciplinary cruelty would be deception and stealthiness in the boy, as a defense.

But his mother, who reared her children with the rigid piety of an Evangelist, also started him in his first business enterprise. When he was seven years old she encouraged him to raise turkeys, and gave him for this purpose the family's surplus milk curds. There are legends of Rockefeller as a boy, stalking a turkey with the most patient stealth in order to seize her eggs.

This harshly disciplined boy, quiet, shy, reserved, serious, received but a few years' poor schooling, and worked for neighboring farmers in all his spare time. His whole youth suggests only abstinence, prudence and the growth of parsimony in his soul. The pennies he earned he would save steadily in a blue bowl that stood on a chest in his room, and accumulated until there was a small heap of gold coins. He would work, by his own account, hoeing potatoes for a neighboring farmer from morning to night for 37 cents a day. At a time when he was still very young he had fifty dollars saved, which upon invitation he one day loaned to the farmer who employed him.

"And as I was saving those little sums," he relates, "I soon learned that I could get as much interest for $50 loaned at seven per cent—then the legal rate of interest—as I could earn by digging potatoes for ten days." Thereafter, he tells us, he resolved that it was better "to let the money be my slave than to be the slave of money."

In Cleveland whither the family removed in 1854, Rockefeller went to the Central High School and studied bookkeeping for a year. This delighted him. Most of the conquering types in the coming order were to be men trained early in life in the calculations of the bookkeeper, Cooke, Huntington, Gould, Henry Frick and especially Rockefeller of whom it was said afterward: "He had the soul of a bookkeeper."

In his first position as bookkeeper to a produce merchant at the Cleveland docks, when he was sixteen, he distinguished himself by his composed orderly habits. Very carefully he examined each item on each bill before he approved it for payment. Out of a salary which began at $15 a month and advanced ultimately to $50 a month, he saved $800 in three years, the lion's share of his total earnings! This was fantastic parsimony.

He spent little money for clothing, though he was always neat; he never went to the theater, had no amusements, and few friends. But he attended his Baptist Church in Cleveland as devoutly as he attended his accounts. And to the cause of the church alone, to its parish fund and mission funds, he demonstrated his only generosity by gifts that were large for him then—first of ten cents, then later of twenty-five cents at a time.

In the young Rockefeller the traits which his mother had bred in him, of piety and the economic virtue—worship of the "lean goddess of Abstinence"— were of one cloth. The pale, bony, small-eyed young Baptist served the Lord and pursued his own business unremittingly. His composed manner, which had a certain languor, hid a feverish calculation, a sleepy strength, cruel, intense, terribly alert.

As a schoolboy John Rockefeller had once announced to a companion, as they walked by a rich man's ample house along their way: "When I grow up I want to be worth $100,000. And I'm going to be too." In almost the same words, Rockefeller in Cleveland, Cooke in Philadelphia, Carnegie in Pittsburgh, or a James Hill in the Northwestern frontier could be found voicing the same hope. And Rockefeller, the bookkeeper, "not slothful in business . . . serving the Lord," as John T. Flynn describes him, watched his chances closely, learned every detail of the produce business which engaged him, until finally in 1858 he made bold to open a business of his own in partnership with a young Englishman named Clark (who was destined to be left far behind). Rockefeller's grimly accumulated savings of $800, in addition to a loan from his father at the usurious rate of 10 per cent, yielded the capital which launched him, and he was soon "gathering gear" quietly. He knew the art of using loan credit to expand his operations. His first bank loan against warehouse receipts gave him a thrill of pleasure. He now bought grain and produce of all kinds in carload lots rather than in small consignments. Prosperous, he said nothing, but began to dress his part, wearing a high silk hat, frock coat and striped trousers like other merchants of the time. His head was handsome, his eyes small, birdlike; on his pale bony cheeks were the proverbial side-whiskers, reddish in color.

At night, in his room, he read the Bible, and retiring had the queer habit of talking to his pillow about his business adventures. In his autobiography he says that "these intimate conversations with myself had a great influence upon my life." He told himself "not to get puffed up with any foolish notions" and never to be deceived about actual conditions. "Look out or you will lose your head—go steady."

He was given to secrecy; he loathed all display. When he married, a few years afterward, he lost not a day from his business. His wife, Laura Spelman, proved an excellent mate. She encouraged his furtiveness, he relates, advising him always to be silent, to say as little as possible. His composure, his self-possession was excessive. Those Clevelanders to whom Miss Ida Tarbell addressed herself in her investigations of Rockefeller, told her that he was a hard man to best in a trade, that he rarely smiled, and almost never laughed, save when he struck a good bargain. Then he might clap his hands with delight, or he might even, if the occasion warranted, throw up his hat, kick his heels and hug his informer. One time he was so overjoyed at a favorable piece of news that he burst out: "I'm bound to be rich! *Bound to be rich!*" . . .

In the life of every conquering soul there is a "turning point," a moment when a deep understanding of the self coincides with an equally deep sense of one's immediate mission in the tangible world. For Rockefeller, brooding, secretive, uneasily scenting his fortune, this moment came but a few years after his entrance into the oil trade, and at the age of thirty. He had looked upon the disorganized conditions of the Pennsylvania oil fields, the only source then known, and found them not good: the guerilla fighting of drillers, of refining firms, of rival railroad lines, the mercurial changes in supply and market value—very alarming in 1870— offended his orderly and methodical spirit. But one could see that petroleum was to be the light of the world. From the source, from the chaotic oil fields where thousands of drillers toiled, the grimy stream of the precious commodity, petroleum, flowed along many diverse channels to narrow into the hands of several hundred refineries, then to issue once more in a continuous stream to consumers throughout the world. Owner with Flagler and Harkness of the largest refining company in the country, Rockefeller had a strongly entrenched position at the narrows of this stream. Now what if the Standard Oil Company should by further steps of organization possess itself wholly of the narrows? In this period of anarchic individual competition, the idea of such a movement of rationalization must have come to Rockefeller forcibly, as it had recently come to others.

Even as early as 1868 the first plan of industrial combination in the shape of the pool had been originated in the Michigan Salt Association. Desiring to correct chaotic market conditions, declaring that "in union there is strength," the salt-producers of Saginaw Bay had banded together to control the output and sale of nearly all the salt in their region, a large part of the vital national supply. Secret agreements had been executed for each year, allotting the sales and fixing the price at almost twice what it had been immediately prior to the appearance of the pool. And though the inevitable greed and self-seeking of the individual salt-producers had tended to weaken the pool, the new economic invention was launched in its infantile form. Rockefeller's partners, Flagler and Harkness, had themselves participated in the historic Michigan Salt Association.

This grand idea of industrial rationalization owed its swift, ruthless, methodical execution no doubt to the firmness of character we sense in Rockefeller, who had the temper of a great, unconscionable military captain, combining audacity with thoroughness and shrewd judgment. His plan seemed to take account of no one's feelings in the matter. Indeed there was something revolutionary in it; it seemed to fly in the face of human liberties and deep-rooted custom and common law. The notorious "South Improvement Company," with its strange charter, ingeniously instrumenting the scheme of combination, was to be unraveled amid profound secrecy. By conspiring with the railroads (which also hungered for economic order), it would be terribly armed with the power of the freight rebate which garrotted all opposition systematically. This plan of combination, this unifying conception Rockefeller took as his ruling idea; he breathed life into it, clung to it grimly in the face of the most menacing attacks of legislatures, courts, rival captains, and, at moments, even of rebellious mobs. His view of men and events justified him, and despite many official and innocent denials, he is believed to have said once in confidence, as Flynn relates:

I had our plan clearly in mind. It was right. I knew it as a matter of conscience. It was right between me and my God. If I had to do it tomorrow I would do it again in the same way—do it a hundred times.

The broad purpose was to control and direct the flow of crude petroleum into the hands of a narrowed group of refiners. The refiners would be supported by the combined railroad trunk lines which shipped the oil; while the producers' phase of the stream would be left unorganized— *but with power over their outlet to market* henceforth to be concentrated into the few hands of the refiners. . . .

In John D. Rockefeller, economists and historians have often seen the classic example of the modern monopolist of industry. It is true that he worked with an indomitable will, and a faith in his star à la Napoleon, to organize his industry under his own dictatorship. He was moreover a great innovator. Though not the first to attempt the plan of the pool— there were pools even in the time of Cicero—his South Improvement Company was the most impressive instance in history of such an organism. But when others had reached the stage of the pool, he was building the solid framework of a monopoly.

Rockefeller's problems were far more difficult than those for instance of Carnegie, who quickly won special economies through constructing a very costly, well-integrated, technically superior plant upon a favored site. In the oil-refining business, a small still could be thrown up in the '70's for manufacturing kerosene or lubricating oil at a tenth the cost of the Edgar Thomson steel works. The petroleum market was mercurial compared to iron, steel and even coal; there were thousands of petty capitalists competing for advantage in it. Hence the tactics of Rockefeller, the bold architecture of the industrial edifice he reared, have always aroused the liveliest interest, and he himself appeals to us for many reasons as the greatest of the American industrialists. In no small degree this interest is owing to the legend of "Machiavellian" guile and relentlessness which has always clung to this prince of oil.

After the dissolution of the South Improvement Company, Rockefeller and Flagler had come to a conference of the irate diggers of petroleum with mild proposals of peaceful cooperation, under the heading of the "Pittsburgh Plan." The two elements in the trade, those who produced the raw material from the earth and those who refined it, were to combine forces harmoniously. "You misunderstand us," Rockefeller and Flagler said. "Let us see what combination will do."

There was much suspicion. One of Titusville's independent refiners (one of those whom Standard Oil tried to erase from the scene) made a rather warlike speech against the plan, and he recalls that Rockefeller, who had been softly swinging back and forth in a rocking chair, his hands over his face, through the conference, suddenly stopped rocking, lowered his hands and looked straight at his enemy. His glance was fairly terrifying.

> You never saw such eyes. He took me all in, saw just how much fight he could expect from me, and then up went his hands and back and forth went his chair. . . .

Where a "deal" across the table could not be effected, Rockefeller might try a variety of methods of expropriation. With his measured spirit, with his organized might, he tested men and things. There were men and women of all sorts who passed under his implacable rod, and their tale, gathered together reverently by Miss Tarbell, has contributed to the legend of the "white devil" who came to rule over American industry.

A certain widow, a Mrs. Backus of Cleveland, who had inherited an oil-refinery, had appealed to Mr. Rockefeller to preserve her, "the mother of fatherless children." And he had promised "with tears in his eyes that he would stand by her." But in the end he offered her only $79,000 for a property which had cost $200,000. The whole story of the defenseless widow and her orphans, the stern command, the confiscation of two-thirds of her property, when it came out made a deep stir and moved many hearts.

In another instance a manufacturer of improved lubricating oils set himself up innocently in Cleveland, and became a client of the Standard Oil for his whole supply of residuum oils. The Rockefeller company encouraged him at first, and sold him 85 barrels a day according to a contract. He prospered for three years, then suddenly when the monopoly was well launched in 1874, his supply was cut down to 12 barrels a day, the price was increased on some pretense, and the shipping cost over the railroads similarly increased. It became impossible to supply his trade. He offered to buy of Rockefeller 5,000 barrels and store it so that he might assure himself of a future supply. This was refused.

"I saw readily what that meant," the man Morehouse related to the Hepburn Committee in 1879. *"That meant squeeze you out—Buy out your works. . . .* They paid $15,000 for what cost me $41,000. He [Rockefeller] said that he had facilities for freighting and that the coal-oil business belonged to them; and any concern that would start in that business, they had sufficient money to lay aside a fund and wipe them out—these are the words."

In the field of retail distribution, Rockefeller sought to create a great marketing machine delivering directly from the Standard Oil's tank wagons to stores in towns and villages throughout the United States. But in the laudable endeavor to wipe out wasteful wholesalers or middlemen, he would meet with resistance again, as in the producing fields. Where unexpectedly stout resistance from competing marketing agencies was met, the Standard Oil would simply apply harsher weapons. To cut off the supplies of the rebel dealer, the secret aid of the railroads and the espionage of their freight agents would be invoked again and again. A message such as the following would pass between Standard Oil officials:

We are glad to know you are on such good terms with the railroad people that Mr. Clem [handling *independent* oil] gains nothing by marking his shipments by numbers instead of by names.

Or again:

Wilkerson and Company received car of oil Monday 13th—70 barrels which we suspect slipped through at the usual fifth class rate—in fact we might say we know it did—paying only $41.50 freight from here. Charges $57.40. Please turn another screw.

The process of "Turning the Screw" has been well described by Henry D. Lloyd. One example is that of a merchant in Nashville, Tennessee, who refused to come to terms and buy from Standard Oil; he first found that all his shipments were reported secretly to the enemy; then by a mysterious coincidence his freight rates on shipments of all kinds were raised 50 per cent, then doubled, even tripled, and he felt himself under fire from all parts of the field. He attempted to move his merchandise by a great roundabout route, using the Baltimore & Ohio and several other connecting roads, but was soon "tracked down," his shipments lost, spoiled. The documents show that the independent oil-dealers' clients were menaced in every way by the Standard Oil marketing agency; it threatened to open competing grocery stores, to sell oats, meat, sugar, coffee at lower prices. "If you do not buy our oil we will start a grocery store and sell goods at cost and put you out of business."

By this means, opponents in the country at large were soon "mopped up"; small refiners and small wholesalers who attempted to exploit a given district were routed at the appearance of the familiar red-and-green tank wagons, which were equal to charging drastically reduced rates for oil in one town, and twice as much in an adjacent town where the nuisance of competition no longer existed. There were, to be sure, embittered protests from the victims, but the marketing methods of Standard Oil were magnificently efficient and centralized; waste and delay were overcome; immense savings were brought directly to the refining monopoly.

But where the Standard Oil could not carry on its expansion by peaceful means, it was ready with violence; its faithful servants knew even how to apply the modern weapon of dynamite.

In Buffalo, the Vacuum Oil Company, one of the "dummy" creatures of the Standard Oil system, became disturbed one day by the advent of a vigorous competitor who built a sizable refinery and located it favorably upon the water front. The offices of Vacuum conducted at first a furtive campaign of intimidation. Then emboldened or more desperate, they approached the chief mechanic of the enemy refinery, holding whispered conferences with him in a rowboat on Lake Erie. He was asked to "do something." He was urged to "go back to Buffalo and construct the machinery so it would bust up . . . or smash up," to fix the pipes and stills "so they cannot make a good oil. . . . And then if you would give them a little scare, they not knowing anything about the business. You know how. . . ." In return the foreman would have a life annuity which he might enjoy in another part of the country.

So in due time a small explosion took place in the independent plant, as Lloyd and Miss Tarbell tell the tale, from the records of the trial held several years later, in 1887. The mechanic, though on the payrolls of the Vacuum Oil Company, led a cursed existence, forever wandering without home or country, until in complete hysteria he returned to make a clean breast of the whole affair. The criminal suit against high officials of the Standard Oil monopoly included Henry Rogers and John Archbold, but the evil was laid by them to the "overenthusiasm" of underlings. Evidence of conspiracy was not found by the court, but heavy damages were awarded to the plaintiff, who thereafter plainly dreaded to reenter the dangerous business.

These and many other anecdotes, multiplied, varied or even distorted, spread through the Oil Regions of Pennsylvania and elsewhere through the country (as ogre-tales are fed to children), and were accumulated to make a strange picture of Mr. Rockefeller, the baron of oil. Miss Tarbell in her "History," written in her "muckraking" days, has dwelt upon them with love. She has recorded them in rending tones with a heart bleeding for the petty capitalists for whom alone "life ran swift and ruddy and joyous" before the "great villain" arrived, and with his "big hand reached out from nobody knew where to steal their conquest and throttle their future."

But if truth must be told, the smaller capitalists, in the producing field especially, were themselves not lacking in predatory or greedy qualities; as Miss Tarbell herself admits, they were capable of hurrying away from church on Sundays to tap enemy tanks or set fire to their stores of oil. What they lacked was the discipline to maintain a producers' combination equal in strength to that of the refiners. The other factors in the industry engaged in individualistic marketing or refining ventures were very possibly "mossbacks," as one of the Standard Oil chieftains growled, "left in the lurch by progress." . . .

Up to 1881 the forty-odd companies controlled by Rockefeller and his partners formed a kind of *entente cordiale* bound by interchange of stock. This form of union being found inadequate or impermanent, the counsel of the Standard Oil Company, Samuel C. T. Dodd, came forward with his idea of the Trust. By a secret agreement of 1882, all the existing thirty-seven stockholders in the divers enterprises of refining, piping, buying or selling oil conveyed their shares "in trust" to nine Trustees: John and William Rockefeller, O. H. Payne, Charles Pratt, Henry Flagler, John Archbold, W. G. Warden, Jabez Bostwick and Benjamin Brewster. The various stockholders then received "trust certificates" in denominations of $100 in return for the shares they had deposited; while the Trustees, controlling two-thirds of all the shares, became the direct stockholders of all the companies in the system, empowered to serve as directors thereof, holding in their hands final control of all the properties. The Trustees could dissolve any corporations within the system and organize new ones in each state, such as the Standard Oil of New Jersey, or the Standard Oil of New York. Nor could any outsiders or newly arrived stockholders have any voice in the affairs of the various companies. The Trustees formed a kind of supreme council giving a centralized direction to their industry. Such was the first great Trust; thus was evolved the harmonious management of huge aggregations of capital, and the technique for large-scale industry.

Dodd, the resourceful philosopher of monopoly, defended his beautiful legal structure of the "Standard Oil Trust" both in a pamphlet of 1888 and in an argument before a Congressional committee of that year. It was but the outcome of a crying need for centralized control of the oil business, he argued. Out of disastrous conditions had come "cooperation and association among the refiners, resulting eventually in the Standard Oil Trust [which] enabled the refiners so cooperating to reduce the price of petroleum products, and thus benefit the public to a very marked degree." In these arguments, learned economists of the time, such as Professor Hadley, supported Dodd. The Trust, as perfected monopoly, pointed the way to the future organization of all industry, and abolished "ruinous competition."

From their headquarters in the small old-fashioned building at 140 Pearl Street the supreme council of an economic empire sat together in conference like princes of the Roman Church. Here in utmost privacy confidential news brought by agents or informers throughout the world was discussed, and business policies determined. The management and responsibility was skillfully divided among committees: there was a committee on Crude Oil, a committee on Marketing, on Transportation, and numerous other departments. By these new processes markets or developments everywhere in everybody's business were followed or acted upon.

Every day the astute leaders rounded together by Rockefeller lunched together in Pearl Street, and later in a large and famous office building known as 26 Broadway. No one questioned the preeminence of John D. Rockefeller, though Charles Pratt usually sat at the head of the table. The aggressive Archbold was closest to John D. Rockefeller. His brother, William Rockefeller, an amiable mediocrity, but immensely rich as well, and long trained in the use of money, depended most upon Henry H. Rogers. Rogers took a more dominant place in the management with the passing years. He is described by Thomas Lawson as "one of the most distinguished-looking men of the time, a great actor, a great fighter, an intriguer, an implacable foe."

These, together with Brewster, Barstow, J. H. Alexander and Bostwick, were the leaders who carried on their industrial operations throughout the world like a band of conspiratorial revolutionists. But "there was not a lazy bone nor a stupid head" in the whole organization, as Miss Tarbell has said. Behind them were the active captains, lieutenants, followers and workers, all laboring with the pride, the loyalty, the discipline and the enthusiasm born of the knowledge that "they can do no better for themselves" anywhere than under the "collar" of the Standard Oil. Freed of all moral scruples, curiously informed of everything, they were prompted by a sense of the world's realities which differed strangely from that of the man in the street. They were a major staff engaged in an eternal fight; now they scrapped unprofitable plants, acquiring and locating others; or now they gathered themselves for tremendous mobilizing feats during emergencies in trade. They found ways of effecting enormous economies; and always their profits mounted to grotesque figures: in 1879, on an invested capital of $3,500,000, dividends of $3,150,000 were paid; the value of the congeries of oil companies was then estimated at $55,000,000. Profits were overwhelmingly reinvested in new "capital goods" and with the formation of the Trust capitalization was set at $70,000,000. By 1886 net earnings had risen to $15,000,000 per annum.

"Hide the profits and say nothing!" was the slogan here. To the public, prices had been reduced, it was claimed. But after 1875, and more notably after 1881, despite the fluctuations of crude oil a firm tendency set in for the markets of refined oil products. Upon the charts of prices the rugged hills and valleys of oil markets turn into a nearly level plain between 1881 and 1891. Though raw materials declined greatly in value, and volume increased, the margin of profit was consistently controlled by the monopoly; for the services of gathering and transporting oil, the price was not lowered in twenty years, despite the superb technology possessed by the Standard Oil. Questioned on this, that "frank pirate" Rogers replied, laughing: *"We are not in business for our health, but are out for the dollar."*

While the policy of the monopoly, as economists have shown, might be for many reasons to avoid *maximum* price levels—such as invited the entrance of competition in the field—it was clearly directed toward keeping the profit margin stable during a rising trend in consumption and falling "curve" in production cost. Similarly in perfecting its technology the Trust was guided by purely pecuniary motives, as Veblen points out, and it remains always a matter of doubt if the mightier industrial combinations improved their service to society at large in the highest possible degree. As often as not it happened that technical improvements were actually long delayed until, after a decade or more, as in the case of Van Syckel's pipe line of 1865, their commercial value was proved beyond a doubt. It was only after rivals, in desperation, contrived the pumping of oil in a two-hundred-mile-long pipe line that Rockefeller followed suit. So it was with the development of various by-products, the introduction of tank cars, etc.

The end in sight was always, as Veblen said, increase of ownership, and of course pecuniary gain rather than technical progress in the shape of improved workmanship or increased service to the community. These latter effects were also obtained. But to a surprising degree they seem accidental by-products of the long-drawn-out struggles, the revolutionary upheavals whence the great industrial coalitions sprang.

The greatest service of the industrial baron to business enterprise seemed to lie elsewhere, as Veblen contended. "The heroic role of the captain of industry is that of a deliverer from an excess of business management." It is a "sweeping retirement of business men as a class from service . . . a casting out of business men by the chief of business men."

John D. Rockefeller said that he wanted in his organization "only the big ones, those who have already proved they can do a big business. As for the others, unfortunately they will have to die."

Pioneering in Big Business

RALPH HIDY AND MURIEL HIDY

During the years from 1882 to 1911 the leaders of the Standard Oil group of companies, including the Standard Oil Company (New Jersey), carried out an extraordinary experiment in the management of a business. John D. Rockefeller and his associates successfully created and applied a

From *Pioneering in Big Business, 1882–1911*, pp. 3–5, 24–39, by Ralph W. Hidy and Muriel E. Hidy. Copyright © 1955 by the Business History Foundation, Inc. Reprinted with the permission of Harper and Row, Publishers, Incorporated.

system for operating a large, integrated industrial enterprise which was one of the earliest representatives of Big Business, to use the phrase popular in the United States. As executives of the large combination those men contributed greatly to the rapid development of the American petroleum industry and through it to the growth of the economy as a whole. Being innovators, however, they also made numerous mistakes and learned only slowly that large size and concentrated economic power in a democratic society required conduct conforming to new rules set by popular demand.

The early life of the Standard Oil Company (New Jersey), generally referred to as Jersey Standard, was marked by rapid growth from infancy to early parenthood. Organized as one of the units of the Standard Oil Trust in August, 1882, for its first ten years the corporation existed primarily as the owner of a refinery and other manufacturing establishments at Bayonne; late in the decade the company acquired a few wholesaling facilities in the same northern New Jersey area. As a consequence of a court decision in Ohio in 1892, Standard Oil executives reorganized their enterprise under twenty corporations of which Jersey Standard was one of the three largest; top managers vested this company with direct ownership of extensive additional manufacturing and marketing properties and also made it one of the holding companies within the group of sister corporations. The Jersey Company continued to perform operating functions after it had become the parent of the entire combination in 1899.

As the apex of a pyramid of companies dominating the American petroleum industry, Jersey Standard naturally became the symbol of the much-distrusted Standard Oil "monopoly" in the public mind. In 1911 the Supreme Court of the United States, affirming that general conviction, broke up the combination by divesting the Standard Oil Company (New Jersey) of thirty-three affiliates, thus bringing to a close one eventful and significant phase of the corporation's history. . . .

By 1881 the Standard Oil alliance had brought into its fold a large segment of the American petroleum industry. Within that industry, previously characterized by excessive competition and harassed by depressed conditions, Rockefeller and his associates had created a giant combination. Beginning in 1872–1873 they had proceeded simultaneously to enhance their shareholdings in firms owning gathering lines, refineries, and domestic marketing facilities. Standard Oil had dominance in gathering and refining petroleum, but the influence of the alliance in marketing was distinctly limited, in producing was relatively slight, and in trunk pipelines was only beginning. This general situation of the Standard Oil group of companies on the eve of the birth of Jersey Standard was the result, by and large, of the policies pursued by the team of men who had formed the combination.

As an early corporate product of the Standard Oil combination, Jersey Standard fell heir to the policies and practices of the men who created the alliance. In the course of working together before 1882, this group of executives had set precedents for the management of the Standard Oil family of firms which were to influence vitally the life of the new company.

The Standard Oil alliance in 1881 was the creation of a team of men. As one man paraphrased John D. Rockefeller's own statement, the "secret of the success of the Standard Oil Company was that there had come together a body of men who from beginning to end worked in single-minded co-operation, who all believed in each other and had perfect confidence in the integrity of each other, who reached all their decisions after fair consideration with magnanimity toward each other" in order to assure "absolute harmony."

As an instrument for carrying out the ideas of those men, the combination necessarily took its character from those who made it and managed it. When they chose to create a new corporation, such as Jersey Standard, it became part of the mechanism for pursuing their policies. Extremely significant, therefore, for understanding the history of the company is acquaintance with the individuals who created and directed both the Standard Oil family of companies and the Jersey Company itself. Scores of men made material contributions to the early development of the combination but only a relatively few ranked as outstanding.

John D. Rockefeller (1839–1937) was captain of the team. By all odds the largest holder of shares, he probably would have been chosen the head for that reason alone. Although not the only person to have the conviction in the 1870's that the petroleum industry should be stabilized, he first formulated the idea that the only satisfactory means was to organize a commonly owned unit on a national scale. Allan Nevins has characterized Rockefeller as careful, patient, cautious, methodical, quick to observe and to learn, grave, pious, aloof, secretive, reticent, inscrutable, and taciturn. Rockefeller considered work a duty, loved simplicity, believed in discipline, and possessed little social warmth except with his family and intimate friends. He had a mind of extraordinary force, great power of concentration, and almost infinite capacity for detail. Although he was willing to make decisions and to act forcefully, he possessed not only remarkable foresight, broad vision, and cool judgment, but also willingness to consider the ideas of others.

In the early 1870's Rockefeller began to delegate most details of management to subordinates and thereafter devoted himself primarily to formulation of broad policy. His greatest contribution, beyond the concept of the Standard Oil combination itself, was the persuasion of strong men to join the alliance and to work together effectively in its management. The remarkable fact was that Rockefeller, while still in his thirties, impressed a group of men, almost all older than himself, with his qualities of leadership. His most arduous task later was to preside over meetings of strongly individualistic, positive executives, while they discussed and determined, usually unanimously, strategy and tactics for the combination as a whole.

During the 1860's and 1870's the closest and strongest associate of John D. Rockefeller was Henry M. Flagler (1830–1913). Of average height, slight build, erect figure, unobtrusive and dignified manner, Flagler was an ambitious, patient, and shrewd man of business. It is difficult to determine where the ideas of Rockefeller stop and those of Flagler begin. They were warm personal friends; they talked over their business before, during, and after office hours. Flagler liked to build new things and possessed a faculty for reducing complex problems to their simplest components. His constructive imagination was as broad and as vivid as Rockefeller's. It was caught by a desire to develop Florida, and into its hotels, railroads, and other enterprises he put some $50,000,000, and more of his energy than into Standard Oil, during the 1880's and later. Yet he left his mark on the combination. Having an aptitude for legal affairs, he was a master in drawing up clear, concise contracts. The incorporation of Ohio Standard appears to have been his brain child, and he helped in the later organization of the Trust. Flagler also participated in many negotiations leading to entry of other firms into the Standard Oil family. His special function was the handling of all affairs concerning transportation of both raw materials and finished products, and he drove hard bargains with railroad managers. Gifted with a keen sense of humor and a feeling of personal responsibility to employees, he won the warm respect and loyal support of most subordinates. Not the least important of Flagler's executive positions was the presidency of Jersey Standard during eight of its first seventeen years.

William Rockefeller (1841–1922) was an organizer, a financier, and a marketer. Some of his selling was done in domestic trade east of Ohio, but after 1865 he was the expert in sales for export. Since these accounted later for more than half of the kerosene sales of the combination, they played a dramatic role in its growth, particularly in that of such specialists in manufacturing for export as Jersey Standard. William Rockefeller was also instrumental in persuading Charles Pratt, H. H. Rogers, and other New Yorkers to join the Standard Oil family. From the middle seventies he was the chief representative of the group in all dealings with New York banks and helped to acquire the short-term capital needed during the early days of the combination's development. As significant as any other of William's efforts was his creation of an efficient administrative staff in New York prior to 1882. At that date he became president of the Standard Oil Company of New York, whose central position in the development of the combination will be discussed later. Unwilling to

limit his interests to Standard Oil, William collaborated with James Still-
man of the National City Bank and H. H. Rogers in promotional and
speculative activities in copper, railroads, and gas companies. Less pious
than his older brother, more lavish in his living and less in his giving,
William also amassed a smaller fortune and has been somewhat over-
shadowed by John. It is certain that William was an able organizer, that
his joviality and good humor made him both an excellent marketer and
warmly liked by his fellow workers, and that the history of Standard
Oil would have been vastly different without his activities. . . .

Policies and practices pursued by Standard Oil executives during the
years prior to 1882 emerged in a variety of ways. Some policies were
evidenced by votes of directors of components of the alliance and gradually won more general acceptance among its members. In other instances
precedents and practices developed into policies over time; no formalized
statement ever indicated the direction in which the leaders were traveling, but in a succession of separate steps they evolved a significant behavior pattern.

Many of the concepts and procedures adopted by executives of the
alliance stemmed from their early experience as small businessmen. Probably at no other time during the nineteenth century was economic activity more freely competitive than in the period from 1840 to 1865. The
customs and mores of the small individual enterpriser became the accepted pattern for almost all men. Naturally enough, therefore, Rockefeller and his associates learned in their youth to believe in freedom of
entry into any occupation, in the sanctity of private property, in the
obligation of the owner to manage his own operations, and in the right
to keep his business affairs secret, a concept dating from time immemorial.
As a corollary of that idea, in courts or legislative investigative chambers
a businessman testified to the legal truth, and no more, a practice still
honored by general observance in spite of critical charges of evasiveness
and ambiguity. Since most markets were local, every businessman could
observe his competitors with relative ease, and did. His habit was to use
any competitive device not clearly prohibited by law. Bargaining in the
market place was almost universal, whether for products or for such
services as the transportation of freight. Posted prices were a point of departure for haggling, and price reductions were the most widely utilized
of competitive techniques.

In response to the chaotic and depressed years of the 1870's, however,
Standard Oil men drastically modified some of their socially inherited
concepts about competition. They apparently desired at first to bring all
gatherers of crude oil and refiners of light petroleum fractions into one
commonly owned unit—to create a monopoly. Late in the decade they
added lubricating oil specialists and trunk pipelines to their list of components to be unified. By means of common ownership in an association

of specializing firms, Rockefeller and his associates created a great horizontal and vertical combination, which, on the eve of the birth of Jersey Standard, maintained overwhelming dominance in gathering, storing, and processing petroleum and its derivatives.

Either by design or through pressure of circumstances, the Standard Oil group of executives had not achieved monopoly in any function by 1881. Strong minority interests in many domestic marketing companies within the alliance, and limited coverage of the market by them, set definite limits to the influence of top managers in that field of operations. In almost all sales for export foreign merchants bought oil from companies in the Standard Oil family and carried on marketing in foreign lands. The combination owned few producing properties. United Pipe Lines men failed to keep pace with expansion in Bradford production, and competing gathering and storing facilities kept appearing. Tide-Water Pipe had thrown the first trunk pipeline over the mountains toward the sea and remained a belligerent competitor. Under the agreement with the producers in 1880 the price of crude oil was set on the oil exchanges, not by Standard Oil. In manufacturing, the area of initial intent for monopoly, the top managers of the alliance had stopped short of their goal. They had refused to pay the prices asked by owners of some plants. Others had sprung up in response to inducements offered by the Pennsylvania Railroad, and in 1882 the editor of *Mineral Resources* noted that the combination had "for some reason" not renewed leases on a number of refineries, several of which were doing "a good trade" and "assuming considerable importance." Thus, by that year some of the firms classified by H. H. Rogers in 1879 as being "in harmony" with Standard Oil had gone their independent ways.

Standard Oil executives employed a variety of tactics in carrying out the expansionist program during the 1870's. After the consolidation in Cleveland and the disastrous South Improvement episode, Rockefeller and his associates first won the confidence of competitors through comprehensive voluntary association. They then brought into the alliance the strongest men and firms in specific areas or functions, a policy pursued, with some exceptions, until 1911. Exchange of stock in the different companies by individuals and guarantee of equality in management provided the final assurance needed to convince such strong individualists as Lockhart, Warden, Pratt, and Rogers that combination was to their advantage. All then co-operated eagerly in trying to unify the remaining firms in refining by bringing them into The Central Association, by buying plants whenever feasible, and by leasing other works. If a seller personally chose not to enter the combination, he usually signed an agreement not to engage in the petroleum business for a period of years. In any case, evidence in extant records substantiates the point that Standard Oil men completely and carefully inventoried all properties and paid "good," though not high, prices for them, including compensation for patents, trade-marks, brands, good-will, and volume of business. In many instances prices for properties reflected the desire of Standard Oil officials to enlist the inventive capacities or administrative abilities of the owners in the service of the alliance. The preponderance of the evidence indicates that Rockefeller and his fellow executives preferred to buy out rather than fight out competitors.

At the same time, when Standard Oil men felt it necessary to apply pressure as a means of persuading a rival to lease or sell his plant, they showed no hesitancy in utilizing the usual sharp competitive practices prevailing in the oil industry during the 1870's. On one occasion or another they pre-empted all available staves and barrels, restricted as completely as possible the available tank cars to their own business, and indulged in local price cutting. They meticulously watched and checked on competitive shipments and sales, sometimes in co-operation with railroad men, and diligently negotiated advantageous freight rates on railways, even to the point of receiving rebates or drawbacks on rivals' shipments. All acts were kept secret as long as possible. The size and resources of the alliance gave it overwhelming power, which was sometimes used ruthlessly, though it is worthy of note that numerous oilmen successfully resisted the pressure.

Within the alliance itself executives also retained many of their competitive habits. Although price competition almost completely disappeared within the combination, men and firms raced with each other in reducing costs, devising new techniques, developing products, improving their quality, and showing profits. Top managers believed in competition but not in the undisciplined variety.

In building the alliance the leaders of Standard Oil adopted a long-range view with emphasis on planning, even before they had achieved an organization to carry such an approach into successful operation. They showed a profound faith in the permanence of the industry, a belief not generally held in years when the petroleum business was characterized by instability, rapid exhaustion of producing fields, and doubts about the appearance of new ones. They wanted to plan and to have reasonable assurance that they were taking no more than calculated risks in pushing toward their objectives. A necessary requirement of planning was centralized policy formulation.

That responsibility devolved not upon one man but on a group of executives. The evolution of Standard Oil's committee system, the hallmark of its administrative methods, started early in the seventies. The original bylaws of Ohio Standard provided for an Executive Committee. Its first membership of two, John D. Rockefeller and Flagler, was increased to three during the consecutive terms of Samuel Andrews and O. H. Payne. Archbold replaced the latter in 1879. William Rockefeller, Pratt, Warden, and Bostwick had joined the three Cleveland members the previous year. At that time the Executive Committee absorbed the "Advisory Committee," which had been established as early as 1873 to act in the New York area. William Rockefeller and Bostwick, its first members, had been joined by Pratt and Warden soon after they entered the alliance. The enlarged Executive Committee of 1878 held many of its almost daily meetings at 140 Pearl Street, New York, and two years later made four a quorum because of the geographic split in membership between Cleveland and New York. Members of other committees . . . started consultations before 1882. If the making of decisions as a synthesis of opinion of a group after discussion is a characteristic of modern business, as a recent commentator has implied, then Standard Oil was modern in the 1870's.

In order to have easily available the best data and advice for making decisions, the Rockefellers and their associates built up staffs in Cleveland, New York, and other points. For the use of executives they collected, evaluated, and digested information on crude oil supplies, costs of manufacture, and markets all over the world. The practice of watching and reporting on marketing by competitors everywhere in the United States, not merely locally, was already inaugurated, though not yet systematized. S. C. T. Dodd was engaged as legal navigator; Standard Oil officials desired to operate within the law. A beginning was made in standardizing accounting procedures.

As the emergence of the Executive Committee and the formation of staffs indicated, the creation of the combination permitted a division of labor or specialization within the organization. As Archbold expressed the development in 1888, the grouping of talents within the alliance permitted "various individuals to take up the different features of the business as a specialty and accomplish greater efficiency than can possibly be accomplished by an individual who attempts to cover all in a business."

In the matter of finance, as in other aspects of operations, Ohio Standard set precedents on reporting and central review. In 1877 the directors of that company resolved that all persons responsible for different aspects of the business should make quarterly reports in writing to the board. Two years later, its members unanimously agreed that annual financial statements should be presented. In 1875 the directors had voted that expenditures for new construction in manufacturing exceeding $2,500 should be undertaken only with written consent of seven members of the board, but that resolution was repealed five years later and the company's Executive Committee was given full charge of all matters relating to repairs and new construction.

Since the goal of the members of the alliance was to maximize profits in the long run, they adopted practices to that end. Emphasis was placed on reducing costs, improving and standardizing the quality of products, and striving for new methods of refining, including the engaging of specialists. Stories about John D. Rockefeller's penchant for eliminating waste and effecting economies have been told and retold. As president of the Acme Oil Company in the Oil Regions, Archbold achieved substantial savings through buying supplies in quantity and by making annual contracts regarding the repairing of boilers and barrels for all plants under his jurisdiction. When he purchased a lubricating oil patent in 1879, Archbold guaranteed the owner, Eli E. Hendrick, a salary of $10,000 per year for ten years in return for the devotion of his inventive talents to Acme. Duplicating pipelines were removed, inefficient plants dismantled, strategically located refineries enlarged, and auxiliary manufacturing units developed, all in the name of economy and reduction of costs. By consistently stressing that practice in every function Standard Oil men moved gradually but inevitably toward mass manufacturing and, more slowly, toward mass marketing.

Gathering information, consultation, planning, and experimentation did not always lead to quick action, but the leaders of Standard Oil early indicated flexibility in adopting new methods and thoroughness in carrying them out. Critics voiced the opinion in the late 1870's that Standard Oil, having invested so much in refineries in the Oil Regions, could not take advantage of the pipeline revolution to establish large manufacturing units at the coast. Almost as soon as others had demonstrated the feasibility of building long trunk pipelines the Standard Oil group took action in 1879. It already possessed a system of gathering lines through the United Pipe Lines. After its organization in 1881, the National Transit Company pushed trunk pipeline building vigorously. By the next year it owned 1,062 miles of trunk lines, only 48 of which had been bought from firms outside the alliance. Its policies, enlarged upon in later chapters, illustrate the fact that Standard Oil was not always the earliest to initiate an innovation, but, once launched on a policy, the combination pushed it with a vigor and fervor made possible by efficient organization and ample financial resources.

Standard Oil's financial policy itself was an important element in the successful life of the combination and its components. Not only were the risks spread by the breadth of the alliance's activities, but profits made in one company or phase of the business flowed into development of another when desired. Early in the history of Standard Oil units short-term loans were often obtained from commercial banks, and temporary aid had to be obtained when the properties of The Empire Transportation Company were purchased. A conservative ratio of dividends to net income, however, was soon to permit the accumulation of funds for self-financing.

Ohio Standard furnished an example for the companies in the alliance on the matter of insurance against fire. On the assumption that loss by fire was a normal expense of the petroleum industry and could be carried by a large unit, the directors of the Ohio Company agreed in January,

1877, to insure property in any one place only on the excess of its valuation above $100,000.

As directors of The Standard Oil Company (Ohio), executives of the alliance also set a precedent regarding the ownership of producing properties. In April, 1878, apparently as a result of a suit by H. L. Taylor & Company against John D. Rockefeller and others for breach of contract in a joint producing operation, the directors unanimously voted not to invest any more money in the purchase of crude oil lands. Six months later they resolved to discontinue all activity in producing petroleum and instructed the Executive Committee to dispose of its properties. This point of view had an influence upon the Standard Oil alliance for a decade.

Quite the contrary was the action adopted in regard to pipelines. By 1881 the Standard Oil group was definitely launched on a program for large-scale expansion of its pipeline facilities and soon exercised a greater measure of control over the function. The combination poured an increasing quantity of capital into building lines; the profits from them provided a cushion for all operations of the alliance. The speculatively minded can ask whether the development of the oil industry would have been more rapid or socially beneficial had parallel pipelines competed with each other during the formative years of the industry, and whether the development would have been as efficient, or more so, had the railroad systems controlled competing lines, as had seemed possible in the 1870's. The point remains that the top managers of Standard Oil determined to keep this function in their own hands to the extent possible . . .

The roots of Standard Oil's policies went deep into the personalities and early experiences of Rockefeller and his associates. Though few of their practices had been satisfactorily systematized by 1881, precedents had been established for many later policies of Jersey Standard and other members of the combination.

By the end of 1881 the general public was hard put to make an accurate estimate of Standard Oil's behavior. Legislative investigations and several legal cases had already elicited an enormous amount of conflicting testimony as to the relations of the combination with both railroads and competitors. Rockefeller and his associates had heightened uncertainty and speculation about their activities by their secrecy in building the alliance and by their evasive, often ambiguous, consistently legally accurate testimony on the witness stand. The very newness, size, dominance, and efficiency of the combination, not to mention its absorption of small competitors in adversity and its avid search for the lowest possible railroad rates, all tended to arouse antagonism. In 1882 S. H. Stowell closed his comments on Standard Oil in *Mineral Resources* with an unbiased observer's puzzlement: "There seems to be little doubt that the company

has done a great work, and that through its instrumentality oil refining
has been reduced to a business, and transportation has been greatly
simplified; but as to how much evil has been mixed with this good, it is
not practicable to make a definite statement." It was certain that through
combination managers of Standard Oil had brought a measure of order
to a formerly confused industry, though they thought that the administration of the alliance itself needed further systematization.

FOR FURTHER READING: Matthew Josephson in *The Robber Barons*
(New York, 1934), further develops his criticism of Rockefeller,
and similar to Josephson in their outlook are Henry Demarest
Lloyd, *Wealth Against Commonwealth* (New York, 1922), Ida
Tarbell, *History of the Standard Oil Company* (2 vols., New
York, 1904), and John T. Flynn, *God's Gold* (New York, 1932).
Allan Nevins' *John D. Rockefeller* (Rev. ed., 2 vols., New York,
1953) is a generally favorable judgment. Studies concentrating
primarily on the constructive achievements of the Standard Oil
Company include Ralph and Muriel Hidy, *Pioneering in Big
Business, A History of the Standard Oil Company of New Jersey,
1882–1911* (New York, 1955), Paul H. Giddens, *Standard Oil
Company (Indiana), Oil Pioneer of the Middle West* (New
York, 1955), and Gerald T. White, *Formative Years in the Far
West: A History of Standard Oil of California and Predecessors
through 1919* (New York, 1962). Informative on the broader topic
of business leadership in this period is John Tipple, "The Anatomy
of Prejudice: Origins of the Robber Baron Legend," *Business History Review*, XXXIII (Winter, 1959), pp. 510–522. Indispensable
is Alfred D. Chandler, "The Beginnings of 'Big Business' in American Industry," *Business History Review*, XXXIII (Spring, 1959),
pp. 2–31.

13

IMMIGRANT LABOR IN THE PROGRESSIVE ERA

PROBLEM: *Was immigrant labor exploited in early twentieth century America?*

The years between 1890 and 1914 witnessed a massive migration of peoples to America, from Europe as well as from other regions. These immigrants provided a significant portion of the labor force needed by rapidly expanding industries in the United States. They actively contributed to the rapid expansion of manufacturing during this period. Once they stepped on American soil, many of the newcomers experienced problems not only with the English language but also with finding a niche in the economy of their adopted land. Consequently, many contemporaries as well as later historians assumed that employers often exploited immigrants by paying them wages that were much lower than those earned by native born Americans. The selection by Oscar Handlin, a student of American immigration, reflects this widely held view. In recent years this assumption has been challenged, however. Economist Robert Higgs, after making statistical comparisons, concluded that skilled immigrant craftsmen, after an initial period of acculturation, secured wages equal to those of similarly skilled craftsmen who were native born Americans. If differentials between foreign and non-foreign workers existed, Higgs argues, these were not necessarily related to the foreign birth of workers. Both authors arouse the reader's curiosity concerning the broader dimensions of this issue. Did immigrants depress American wage levels? What impact did immigrant workers have on prevailing American wage structures? What was the relation between ethnicity and wage rates?

The Uprooted

OSCAR HANDLIN

All those who could not immediately move into the interior, purchase at once a farm, and settle down as agriculturists without delay, spent some period as residents of one of the great cities. Here they worked in preparation for the moment when they might leave. Working as they did in a new fashion and in a strange place, it took time to find a way around, to begin to learn the operations of the productive system of which they had become a part.

The difficulty was that a man could live years in an American city without coming to understand the mainsprings of its economy. In the period before the Civil War, before this very tide of immigration began to condition the development of these places, they served a distinctive and narrow function. The cousin, friend, or acquaintance who wished to enlighten the newcomer would have to explain that Boston and New York, that Philadelphia, Baltimore, and New Orleans, were commercial points of exchange. These were valves situated along the coast through which was pumped the flow of goods between the Old World and the New. Here, and at the internal market towns—at Albany, Buffalo, Cleveland, and Chicago, at Pittsburgh, Cincinnati, and St. Louis—commodities were exchanged, were repacked, and were transshipped from one conveyance to another. This was the function of the American city in the early nineteenth century; whoever sought employment there had to find it within this trading structure.

The old resident, leading the immigrant about, could readily show visible evidence of the town's role. The important places were the piers and markets; the critical buildings were the exchange and the shops and countinghouses of the merchants. The weightiest people were those engaged in buying and selling.

What could the peasant do here? He could not trade or do much to help the traders. There was some room for petty shopkeepers; he lacked the training and the capital. Some handicraftsmen supplied clothes and furniture and a variety of other products to the townsfolk; he lacked the skill and tools. Back on the docks at which he had landed were a number of casual jobs with the stevedores. Here and there in the warehouses and stores were calls for the services of porters. But there was a limit to the amount of lifting and carrying to be done. Wandering about in the first days of their arrival, these immigrants learned that beyond these few opportunities there was, at first, no demand for their capacities.

As time went by, they became restless seekers after employment. Yet many remained unsuccessful in the quest or, drifting about, picked up odd jobs that tided them over from week to week. They joined a growing army of the anxious for work, for they could certainly not remain long without income. Perpetually on the verge of destitution, and therefore of starvation, eager to be hired at any rate, these redundant hands accumulated in a fund of available but unused labor.

*　　*　　*

No wonder that the newcomer was somewhat incredulous when he finally learned that outside the city there were jobs, that his power to toil, here so little valued, elsewhere was urgently needed. Yet advertisements in the newspapers, chalked-up notices in the streets, told him it was indeed so. Was he then likely to quibble over terms, inquire closely as to conditions? At the intelligence bureaus, the employment offices whence all these benefits flowed, he was signed on, gathered up into a gang with others like him, and hurried along to his appointed task.

The jovial fellow who humored the men into agreement and who sealed the contract with a dram of the best was agent of a remarkable construction system that kept pace with the unparalleled expansion of the country through the nineteenth century. With no machines, with only pick, shovel, and sledge for tools, the boss and his gang contrived the numerous links that held the nation whole in these years. Out of their labors came first the chain of canals, and then an intricately meshed network of railroads— by 1910, more than 350,000 miles of them. And these tasks were hardly completed before bicycle riders and motorists began to call for and to get a paved highway system; 200,000 miles were already laid in 1910.

Engineers' estimates reckoned up the immense quantities of unskilled labor these projects would take; surveyors' reports revealed that the lines would run through unsettled or partly settled agricultural regions, places where no supply of such labor was available. To get the jobs done meant bringing in from outside the hands for the doing.

Thus the earliest immigrants find their calling. Desperate in the absence of alternative they leave behind wife and child and go to live the hard life of the construction camp. Exposed to the pitiless assaults of sun and snow and dusty winds, they work long hours, are paid low wages; in the lonely distances, away from all other beings, there is no arguing with a contractor who suddenly, arbitrarily lowers his rates. They may not complain of the degrading quarters—broken-down old freight cars or dilapidated shanties quickly thrown together. They can have nothing to say of the compulsion to buy food and supplies from the company's swindling store. To whom can they turn? It is not the railroad or canal that employs them; an intermediary, responsible to no one, battens off their misery.

In any case, until the laborers paid off the price of bringing them there and until they accumulated the fare to return, they were bound to submit to the unscrupulous exploitation of the boss. In many states, the money advanced to get the worker to the job was considered a debt, and the law condemned the unwitting immigrant to serve out his time for the contractor until the debt was cleared. Not until 1907 did the Federal government intervene to halt this practice as peonage.

Those who sampled the life of the construction gang were, therefore, not likely to wish to repeat the experience. For such men, it was a relief to discover, as time went on, that analogous opportunities were gradually opening up within the city itself. The increase of urban population strained existing housing and created a persistent demand for new construction that kept the building trades prosperous. Everywhere streets pushed out into the suburbs where farms had once been; men's muscles had to grade the way, carry and fit the paving blocks. Each seaport dredged and improved its harbor, built imposing piers to accommodate the larger vessels of nineteenth-century commerce. Intricate systems of aqueducts, of gas pipes, of electric wires, of trolley tracks, supplied water and light and transportation for the new city millions.

Every one of these activities, which occupied the attention of a whole century, depended for its execution upon an ample fund of unskilled labor. The immigrants supplied that fund; and in doing so made for themselves a role that could have been occupied by no other element in American society—no other was so thoroughly deprived of the opportunity for choice. In sad succession, from 1830 to 1930, the Irish, the Bohemians, the Slovaks, the Hungarians, the Italians, and many other peoples less numerous took up for a period the service of the pick and shovel.

It was not likely that any among them, at the time, took much pride in their contribution to the nation. Nor was it likely that many individuals among them would long think such employment a satisfactory solution to the problem of finding a job. These tasks were, in their nature, intermittent and transitory; each project, once completed, left the laborers back where they started, face to face with the necessity of looking for another. Wages hung close to the cost of subsistence, never rose to a point that

permitted a man to accumulate the stakes of a fresh start. At the end of a
stint the worker was weaker and older, otherwise no different from what
he was before. Meanwhile, from day to day he ran the risk of total calam-
ity from illness or disabling injury. . . .

To tell the truth, few immigrant laborers knew just how much they
earned. Pay was uncertain in amount; it came at irregular intervals; and
no man could look ahead and predict with security what his next year's
income would be. For that matter, few men could look back and reckon
with exactitude what the past year's income had been. They only knew,
and this was clear enough without computation, that the average earnings
of the unskilled were simply not large enough to support a family. Allowing for the inevitable periods of idleness between jobs, even a moderately
skilled worker found it difficult to provide for a wife and children.

Only by calling upon the earnings of more than one of its members
could the immigrant household make ends meet. Not unless it utilized the
efforts of wife and child, as well as those of the husband, could the family
be certain that there would always be someone working and that the income of the whole would be large enough, secure enough, to withstand
the recurrent shocks of American economic life.

It was not the mere fact that wife and child must exert themselves that
was hurtful. These were no strangers to toil in the Old World, or in the
New. The degradation lay in the *kind* of work. The boys drifted into
street occupations, blacked boots or hawked newspapers, missed thus the
opportunity to acquire a trade and fell into all sorts of outlandish ways.
Or they, and girls too for that matter, entered the shops, where they did
men's work at child's wages. For the women, there was "domestic service"—maid's work in strangers' homes or back-breaking laundering in
their own; or, more often as time went on, service to industry in the
factory or by homework. If it was characteristic of these families that
they somehow found the room for a boarder, that was only another
method of adding to their ranks another breadwinner.

But in America bread never came without complications. The peasant,
new to the means of earning his livelihood, was also new to the means of
spending it. To his misfortune he discovered that he himself added to the
difficulties in making ends meet through inability to use efficiently whatever money came to his hands. In his old life, he had thought of objects
in their individuality and uniqueness; the chair, the hat, the cow. Here
he had to learn to think of them as commodities, subject to a common
quantitative standard of price. Without a clear conception of the relationship of money to things, every transaction involved a set of totally
new conditions.

What good wife, at home, was so lacking in housewifely skills as to buy food? Only the improvident were incapable of nurturing their families out of their own farms and gardens. But in America every crumb was paid for. The unfamiliar processes of shopping, of purchasing goods from impersonal strangers in stores, led to countless losses and often induced the immigrant, whatever the cost, to deal with peddlers, as in the Old World. Furthermore, lack of funds made it inevitable that these people transact their affairs in a most wasteful manner. There was no margin for stock. They bought bread and potatoes by the pound, rather than by loaf or peck, coal by the basket rather than by ton. (And where would they have put more had they the money to invest in quantity?) Purchasers in such small lots could not choose of whom they should buy, or at what terms. They marketed where they could and were at the mercy of those willing to trouble with their trifling custom.

Frequently, the shortage of cash drove the immigrants into the trap of an expensive credit system. In the bitter intervals between earnings they were compelled to turn to the generosity of the local shopkeeper, who would tide them over to the limit of his own slim resources. (What else could the merchant do when all his customers were in the same miserable condition?) As debts mounted up in the grocer's book, the immigrants lost the freedom to shop and paid, in the price of their food, the interest and more.

For one cause and another, the laborer got pitifully little from his labor. The dollars that seemed large enough from the perspective of Europe shrank with disheartening rapidity under the conditions of America. What was left, every waking hour, was the tormenting need to provide, the nagging need to restrict expenditures. Occasional windfalls, not enough to alter his situation, might be spent in bursts of indulgence—a gold watch, a glittering pin. What difference did that make? Day-to-day existence was still close to the bone.

Race, Skills, and Earnings:
American Immigrants in 1909

ROBERT HIGGS

On December 5, 1910, the Immigration Commission presented its voluminous report to the Congress. Though the report covered a multitude of

Reprinted by permission from *The Journal of Economic History*, XXXI (1971), pp. 420–428.

topics, a central theme was that the "new" immigrants from southern and eastern Europe were earning less than the "old" immigrants from north-western Europe because the newcomers were willing to accept a lower standard of living. "They were," the commission concluded, "content to accept wages and conditions which the native American and immigrants of the older class had come to regard as unsatisfactory." The discovery of such "unfair competition," along with its other findings, led the com-mission to recommend legislation restricting the admission of the "new" immigrant groups, and subsequently the immigration laws of 1917, 1921, and 1924 implemented this recommendation.

Only a year after the publication of the commission's report Isaac Hourwich, in a penetrating critique of the report, raised the obvious question: "[W]hy should the employer grant the demand of the immi-grant of long residence for a higher wage when there is said to be an 'oversupply' of recent immigrants willing to accept 'almost any wage above that affording a mere subsistence'?" Hourwich believed that the commission's interpretation confused cause and effect: the lower standard of living of the "new" groups was actually the result, not the cause, of their low earnings. His own explanation maintained that earnings differ-entials reflected skill differentials. "[T]he rapid pace of industrial ex-pansion," he argued, "has increased the number of skilled and supervisory positions so fast that practically all the English-speaking employees have had the opportunity to rise on the scale of occupations." Hourwich's hy-pothesis is clearly a more plausible explanation, but the evidence he pre-sented was limited and, by modern standards, not systematically examined. Moreover, he had a few axes of his own to grind, and his conclusions were sometimes stronger than his evidence would warrant.

In the historical literature a third explanation seems to prevail, main-taining that immigrant workers were somehow "exploited." According to this interpretation ethnic prejudice like that displayed by the members of the Immigration Commission resulted in the recently arrived groups re-ceiving lower earnings than the older groups or the native-born workers. As the new arrivals became "assimilated" and "Americanized" the preju-dice subsided, they became indistinguishable from other Americans, and their earnings increased to a par with those of other workers.

The object of the present paper is first to reformulate precisely and then to test statistically the hypothesis of skill differentials advanced by Hourwich. These tests also shed some light on the hypothesis of ethnic discrimination. Our findings reveal that skill differentials do provide an adequate explanation for earnings differentials among immigrant groups in mining and manufacturing early in the present century and that the evidence does not support the hypothesis of ethnic discrimination. Finally, these findings help to explain the well-known pattern in which each new immigrant group "came in at the bottom" and subsequently "worked its way up."

I

The complete report of the Immigration Commission fills forty-two volumes, the first two being a rather lengthy abstract of the rest, and covers an extensive range of subjects. In their principal study the commission's investigators secured detailed information from 507,256 wage earners, of whom 293,541 were foreign-born, in mining and manufacturing occupations. Although some information was obtained in late 1908, almost 95 per cent of the schedules were secured during the spring and early summer of 1909. The investigators concluded that the depression of 1907–1908 had little influence upon their data, which they judged representative of "normal" times. The geographical scope of the study embraced mainly twenty-three states between the Rocky Mountains and the eastern seaboard; thirty-six industries received special emphasis. Although the samples were not random, the investigators considered them representative of the national situation, and there is little basis for challenging this belief. It is rare indeed that the economic historian is presented with such an enormous, carefully collected and compiled body of data.

As Hourwich recognized, the main deficiency of the commission's report was its propensity to draw unjustified conclusions from the data its investigators had collected. The data themselves present relatively few problems, their shortcomings being errors of omission for the most part. The principal problems with the data shown in Table 1 arise from the ambiguity of the questions put to the employees. One question asked: "What do you earn per week?" Whether the respondent took into account typical unemployment in answering the question is uncertain; and although the investigators were instructed to note "normal" earnings if they differed from actual earnings, we have no way of knowing how diligently they obeyed this instruction. In addition, the precise meanings of "literacy" and "ability to speak English" are quite elusive. The criterion for the latter simply required that the "employee can carry on a conversation in English," which obviously embraces a wide variety of competence in the language. "Literacy," of course, is almost inevitably a crude concept, since it attempts to measure discretely (yes or no) a variable that is necessarily continuous. Despite these problems, however, the information is sufficient to answer the broad questions posed in the present paper. By comparison with the evidence typically available to the economic historian, these data are remarkably free of obvious biases.

In many respects the report is a racist document. The fifth volume is called *Dictionary of Races or Peoples*, and distinctions among various ethnic groups figure prominently throughout the report. The commission identified some rather curious "races": French Canadians and Other Canadians; Russian Hebrews and Other Hebrews; North Italians and South Italians; as well as more familiar "races" like Cubans, Herzegovinians, and Ruthenians. Perhaps because of these racist overtones and the well-known ethnic prejudices of the commission members, scholars have done little to analyze the data contained in the report. Whatever we may think of the "racial" classifications, however, they do provide the basis for testing some interesting and important hypotheses. As long as all the data were collected consistently according to these classifications, we can properly employ a cross section of such groups in our analysis. Information on earnings, ability to speak English, literacy, and duration of American residence for employees in mining and manufacturing appears in Table 1 classified according to ethnic group.

II

Hourwich believed that "race" had nothing to do with earnings; "tables showing variations in weekly earnings by race," he asserted, "are therefore meaningless." Wage differentials among immigrants existed because "the immigrant of long residence has advanced on the scale of occupations and is paid a higher wage for a higher grade of labor."

That earnings were unaffected by "race" seems quite plausible. If we assume a world of wealth-maximizing employers and competitive labor markets, there is no reason to expect that a Swede would consistently have earned more than an equally skilled Macedonian. Under these conditions earning differentials are attributable to differences in marginal productivity, that is, to differences in useful skills. Conveniently for its own purposes, the Immigration Commission neglected to publish information on the earnings of different "races" in the same occupation; in fact, the published occupational classifications are so broad that they are useless for analytical purposes. For example, all employees "in manufacturing and mechanical pursuits" were lumped together. Hourwich erred, however, when he discarded the tabulation of earnings by ethnic group as worthless information. Provided that information can be obtained on the average skill level of each group, we can test the hypothesis that the greater the average skill level of an ethnic group, the higher were its average earnings.

Skills are always difficult to measure, and working with data devoid of occupational classifications only heightens the difficulty; but the task is not insuperable. The literature on immigrant laborers refers repeatedly to a crucial skill, the ability to speak English, about which our information is ample. Lacking the language of the country, the immigrant was virtually certain to remain tied to unskilled, and therefore relatively low-paid, employment. A knowledge of English opened up the possibility of rising into supervisory positions, of gaining new technical skills, of applying old skills that were unusable until combined with the ability to

TABLE 1

CHARACTERISTICS OF ADULT, MALE, FOREIGN-BORN
WORKERS IN MINING AND MANUFACTURING
OCCUPATIONS, 1909

Group	Number Reporting Earnings	Ave. Weekly Earnings in Dollars	Percentage Speaking English	Percentage Literate[a]	Percentage Residing in U.S. 5 Years or More
Armenian	594	9.73	54.9	92.1	54.6
Bohemian and Moravian	1,353	13.07	66.0	96.8	71.2
Bulgarian	403	10.31	20.3	78.2	8.5
Canadian, French	8,164	10.62	79.4	84.1	86.7
Canadian, Other	1,323	14.15	100.0	99.0	90.8
Croatian	4,890	11.37	50.9	70.7	38.9
Danish	377	14.32	96.5	99.2	85.4
Dutch	1,026	12.04	86.1	97.9	81.9
English	9,408	14.13	100.0	98.9	80.6
Finnish	3,334	13.27	50.3	99.1	53.6
Flemish	125	11.07	45.6	92.1	32.9
French	896	12.92	68.6	94.3	70.1
German	11,380	13.63	87.5	98.0	86.4
Greek	4,154	8.41	33.5	84.2	18.0
Hebrew, Russian	3,177	12.71	74.7	93.3	57.1
Hebrew, Other	1,158	14.37	79.5	92.8	73.8
Irish	7,596	13.01	100.0	96.0	90.6
Italian, North	5,343	11.28	58.8	85.0	55.2
Italian, South	7,821	9.61	48.7	69.3	47.8
Lithuanian	4,661	11.03	51.3	78.5	53.8
Macedonian	479	8.95	21.1	69.4	2.0
Magyar	5,331	11.65	46.4	90.9	44.1
Norwegian	420	15.28	96.9	99.7	79.3
Polish	24,223	11.06	43.5	80.1	54.1
Portuguese	3,125	8.10	45.2	47.8	57.5
Roumanian	1,026	10.90	33.3	83.3	12.0
Russian	3,311	11.01	43.6	74.6	38.0
Ruthenian	385	9.92	36.8	65.9	39.6
Scotch	1,711	15.24	100.0	99.6	83.6
Servian	1,016	10.75	41.2	71.5	31.4
Slovak	10,775	11.95	55.6	84.5	60.0
Slovenian	2,334	12.15	51.7	87.3	49.9
Swedish	3,984	15.36	94.7	99.8	87.4
Syrian	812	8.12	54.6	75.1	45.3
Turkish	240	7.65	22.5	56.5	10.0

[a] Able to read.
Source: Immigration Commission, *Report*, I, 367, 474, 439, 352.

speak the language of the country. We therefore propose the hypothesis that, *ceteris paribus*, the greater the proportion of an ethnic group speaking English, the higher were its average earnings. Information is also available on another crucial skill, literacy. We might well question the usefulness of literacy in a foreign language as a skill in America. (In the commission's report "literacy" means literacy in any language.) However, literacy is often a good *proxy* for the existence of skills that are more difficult, or in the present case impossible, to measure. Because the ability to read was typically acquired in schools, literacy is an indication, for example, that the worker also possessed some knowledge of elementary mathematics. We therefore propose the hypothesis that, *ceteris paribus*, the greater the proportion of an ethnic group literate, the higher were its average earnings.

III

To test the two hypotheses we employ the data presented in Table 1. With one exception the groups listed there are all those for which at least one hundred workers, aged 18 and over, reported earnings and for which corresponding data on other group characteristics were available. (The single exception is the Welsh, for whom the reported earnings figure of $22.02 is clearly unrepresentative, probably applying to skilled miners and tinworkers brought over by American companies under special arrangements.)

Using these data we estimate a multiple regression equation in which the dependent variable is an ethnic group's average weekly earnings in dollars (Y) and the explanatory variables are the percentage of the group speaking English (E) and the percentage of the group literate in any language (L). The estimated equation is:

$$(1) \quad Y = 2.55 + 0.0383\,E + 0.0796\,L.$$
$$(0.0105) \quad (0.0195)$$
$$N = 35, \text{S.E.E.} = 1.04, R^2 = 0.78.$$

The two explanatory variables explain almost four fifths of the variance in average earnings among the groups. The coefficients of both variables are highly significant (standard errors are shown in parentheses), and their magnitudes indicate that a percentage-point gain in literacy—our proxy for general skills—was about twice as important as the same gain in the ability to speak English. Obviously these data are quite consistent with the two hypotheses relating earnings differentials to skill differentials.

To obtain a control group for its study of immigrants the commission also obtained information from a large number of native-born workers. A direct test of the ethnic discrimination hypothesis requires a comparison of the actual average earnings of native-born white employees—$14.37 per week for a sample of 41,933 employees—with the figure predicted on the basis of the relation of earnings to skills among immigrant groups as shown by equation (1). The predicted earnings for this group, which was 98.2 per cent literate and 100 per cent English-speaking, is $14.20; the predicted figure is in error by only 1 per cent! This remarkable result casts grave doubt on the notion that ethnic discrimination operated on a wide scale to the detriment of immigrant workers.

This finding does *not* mean that no ethnic prejudice existed, and there is plenty of evidence that such prejudice did exist. Rather, it implies that if some (discriminating) employers offered the immigrant a wage lower than the actual value of his labor services to the firm, another employer could increase his returns by hiring that employee at a slightly higher wage. Of course, with many employers, each attempting to maximize wealth, competition for workers would soon force the wage up to a level at which it equalled the actual value of the worker's labor services to the firm. Not every employer must be a wealth maximizer to obtain this result, however. Just *one* would be enough, for it would pay him to outbid other (discriminating) employers for labor and to expand his business as long as he could continue to obtain workers at less than the going rate for equally skilled native-born workers. The evidence is quite convincing that at least some American employers preferred wealth to the pleasures of discrimination. (Notice that our argument is just the reverse of the common belief that discrimination allows the employer to increase his wealth by "exploiting" his workers; this popular fallacy fails to take competition for labor into consideration.)

From these findings it is only a short step to an explanation of why each new immigrant group came in at the bottom of the economic ladder: it was partly because later groups were less literate, which suggests less skilled generally, than those having arrived earlier, partly because they had less command of English. The ability to speak English was almost perfectly correlated with the duration of a group's residence in America: the simple coefficient of correlation between the proportion speaking English and the proportion having resided in the United States five years or longer is 0.94. Over time the immigrants gained fluency in English and other skills, and in the process their earnings rose; those arriving later merely followed in the footsteps of those arriving earlier. Ethnic discrimination had little or no effect on the process.

Our findings lend systematic corroboration to opinions maintained by well-informed contemporaries long before Hourwich's work appeared. As early as 1890 Jacob Riis heavily emphasized the importance of literacy and a command of English.

The sweater knows well that the isolation of the workman in his helpless ignorance is his sure foundation . . . . But as long as the ignorant crowds continue to come and to herd in these tenements, his grip can never be shaken off.

[The sweater himself, however, is] simply the middleman, the sub-contractor, a workman like his fellows, perhaps with the single distinction from the rest that he knows a little English.

Significantly, even the idioms of the day expressed the importance of speaking English. According to the racial classification commonly used in industrial towns, people distinguished between the "English-speaking man" and the "Hunky." The former, however, "may be neither native American, nor English, nor Irish. He may be one of these, or he may be German, Scandinavian, or Dutch."

IV

"The immigrant," Oscar Handlin has written, "was an exploited unskilled laborer." A glance at Table 1 is enough to convince us that such a statement, not uncommon in the historical literature, is extravagantly oversimplified at best. It is difficult to know what objective meaning can be given to the value-laden term "exploited"; but if it means that earnings were unresponsive to skill differentials among immigrant workers, our findings fail to support the notion. We can sympathize with unskilled people in a labor market where work of relatively low productivity commanded correspondingly low earnings. But having recognized this explanation for the low earnings, it is then much easier to understand how successive immigrant groups managed to escape from the poverty that constituted their first experience in the New World.

FOR FURTHER READING: Handlin's views are reflected in a more specialized context by Moses Rischin, *The Promised Land: New York's Jews, 1870–1914* (Cambridge, 1962). Roland T. Berthoff, *British Immigrants in Industrial America, 1790–1950* (Cambridge, 1953), indicates that British immigrants usually fared better than other nationalities since many were skilled and had no language barriers. That immigrants did not usually depress wage scales is a view expressed in M. A. Jones, *American Immigration* (Chicago, 1960), one of the best general works in the field. Isaac A. Hourwich, *Immigration and Labor: the Economic Aspects of European Immigration to the United States* (New York, 1912), was one of the first writers to indicate that the wages of immigrants were related to skills rather than to ethnicity.

14

ORIGINS OF
THE GREAT
CRASH OF 1929

PROBLEM: *What factors led to the Crash of 1929?*

Few episodes in American history have attracted as much attention from economists and historians as the stock market crash of 1929. Analysis of its causes has ranged within wide extremes, and has focused on major economic trends of the 1920s. Contemporary writers, of whom Yale economist Irving Fisher was among the most popular, believed that a business recession and the overpricing of common stocks between 1925 and 1929 were important reasons, along with increasing disturbances in international trade after 1925. Stressing short-run influences, Fisher also pointed to the boom psychology of the 1920s and the close relations between commercial and investment banks in the decade prior to 1929 as relevant factors leading to the crisis. A generation later another widely read economist, John Kenneth Galbraith of Harvard, re-assessed the origins of the crash, and placed greater stress on long-term dislocations. Galbraith emphasized the maldistribution of wealth in twentieth century America as well as the weaknesses of the corporate structure in the 1920's and earlier. Both men offer concise, provocative analyses that lead their readers into a broad array of problems concerning the origins of the economic crisis of 1929. Were the antecedents of the crash national or international? Was the great crash inevitable? Is there a common ground of agreement among these authors?

The Great Stock Market Crash of 1929

IRVING FISHER

What were the causes of the panic of 1929?

That the stock market crash was "primarily precipitated by foreign liquidation" is the view expressed by John S. Sinclair in the *New York Times* of October 27th. This liquidation accompanied the so-called Hatry Panic on the London Stock Exchange, which resulted in a deeper fall of the London stock price level—45.4 per cent from August 30th to December 27th, according to the British index—than occurred on the New York Stock Exchange between the high point on September 7th and the bottom of November 13th. Few realize today that the greatest fall of stocks in British history, comparable only with the Baring Panic of 1890, preceded and was an actuating cause of the American panic, and that a coincident fall in Paris and Berlin accompanied the British liquidation. It began with the failure of the banking house of Clarence Hatry in August, followed by his arrest in September and subsequent conviction for a gigantic forgery of stock certificates. This started the British liquidation in London and in New York. *Barron's Weekly* of December 9th notes that Britons were extremely active in "distributing" stocks at the high level in New York during September, as seen by the movement in sterling exchange. . . .

LINKING OF COMMERCIAL AND INVESTMENT BANKS

Mr. H. Parker Willis, editor of the New York *Journal of Commerce*, ascribes to the big commercial banks, which had organized speculative pools in the form of investment companies, a causal relation to the crash. I am informed by a country banker in Connecticut that there was a tendency among small banks to copy the big banks in the organization of these investment pools which helped swell the wave of speculation through the country. The big banks, of course, used the funds of their stockholders in speculation under intelligent guidance; the little banks could have no such expert guidance. But in either case there was abuse. The commercial banks are supposed to conduct their operations under close public regulation, but by means of affiliated investment companies, joined as closely as Siamese twins, they have been enabled to act irresponsibly, as is evidenced by the fact that these companies publish no statements and are held to accounting by no public body.

OVERVALUATION OF COMMON STOCKS

That the prime cause was serious overvaluation of common stocks that had previously been undervalued is the opinion of Mr. Carl Snyder, of the Federal Reserve Bank of New York. In correspondence with me Mr. Snyder says, referring to the war inflation of commodity prices:

The long-sustained rise in the level of commodity prices necessarily brought a huge increase in the earnings of common shares, and this naturally forced a valorization of these shares in terms of something like a 57-cent dollar.

On the basis of this higher price level, stocks, through, say, the 1919–1924 period, were, as now seems clear, seriously undervalued. As soon as public confidence in the rate of earnings was established, there began a movement of revalorization that naturally swung to wild extremes, as stock markets always do. With this came a recurrence of the familiar 'new era' theory, which seems to blossom about once in a generation with unfailing regularity. All this brought what appears to have been as serious an overvaluation of common stocks as they had previously been undervalued—overvalued, I should say, because it is clear that we have as yet seen no readjustment of long-term interest rates and bond yields to what look like permanently lower levels. And would not this be inevitable if the high prices attained by the average of stocks were to continue? . . .

There is a measure of truth, also, in the judgment pronounced by another financial expert, who contributes this statement:

BUSINESS RECESSION

In my opinion the basic change was in the business curve and outlook. After nearly two and one-half years of advance at the rate of 1 per cent per month, in July of 1929 business turned downward, and it became evident that a business recession was in prospect. When prices were as high relative to earnings as they were in 1929, the recession outlook pulls the props from the stock market. The profit outlook had changed fundamentally. There were other causes that had been present for a year or more, but these had not broken the market. This downward turn in the business trend was the one new factor in the picture.

With this view the following statement by Mr. Lindsay Bradford, Vice President of the City Bank Farmers Trust Company of New York, is accordant:

Since early in 1929 considerable liquidation and distribution of stocks of various industries had been going on, and but little notice of it was taken due to the fact that the strength in certain other groups, such as the utilities, and certain outstanding industrials gave the whole market the appearance of such strength. This feature of the market was indicated during the Fall by the fact that when certain stocks were daily making new highs other groups were daily making new lows in the weeks before the panic ensued. The reason, it seems to me, that these groups, such as notably the automobile group, were weak was because as early as last June it was apparent that automobile buying was falling off and that the automobile companies as a whole were running into over-production. Similar weaknesses in the building situation were apparent in the early summer and it is such fundamentals as these which, in my opinion, were the real reasons for the decline in prices. . . .

FEDERAL RESERVE POLICY

The *Commercial and Financial Chronicle* also suggested that the market had been sent on a new upward journey by Federal Reserve action during the early part of August, 1929, in sanctioning an increase in the New York Federal Reserve discount rate from 5 per cent to 6 per cent, with simultaneous lowering of the buying rate for bankers' acceptances and the concurrent purchase of acceptances on a large scale. This, the *Chronicle* says, "meant the forcing out of reserve credit by the act of the Reserve System itself, and involved Federal Reserve inflation of a peculiarly objectionable type." . . .

"BOOM" ENTHUSIASM

Senator Robinson of Arkansas declared, and with some real basis in fact, in a formal statement on October 30, 1929, that if the foundation of the belief of ruined investors was faith in the strong position of American industry, it was also true that "no less personalities than a former President of the United States, the Secretary of the Treasury, and the former Secretary of Commerce, now President, contributed by unduly and repeated optimistic statements to the creation of enthusiastic if not frenzied ventures in stocks."

No doubt the "Coolidge boom" and the "Hoover boom" engendered such public enthusiasm, accompanied as they were by repeated statements of the country's prosperity and expected increases in prosperity. These statements led thousands of investors into undue borrowings in order to realize the benefits of this prosperity for themselves. But I cannot entirely agree with Professor Jacob H. Hollander, of Johns Hopkins University, in his view, expressed before the Academy of Political Science in New York on November 22, 1929, that the public by bidding up the price of securities, "ignored yield and earnings in the belief that the country's growth would increase the equity and boost the price" of shares of sound enterprises. No doubt their enthusiasm led them, as Professor Hollander asserts, to make no allowance for business recession, for speculative manipulation, or foreign disturbance.

My own impression has been and still is that the market went up principally because of sound, justified expectations of earnings, and only partly because of unreasoning and unintelligent mania for buying. . . .

The Great Crash, 1929

JOHN KENNETH GALBRAITH

There seems little question that in 1929, modifying a famous cliché, the economy was fundamentally unsound. This is a circumstance of first-rate importance. Many things were wrong, but five weaknesses seem to have had an especially intimate bearing on the ensuing disaster. They are:

1) The bad distribution of income. In 1929 the rich were indubitably rich. The figures are not entirely satisfactory, but it seems certain that the 5 per cent of the population with the highest incomes in that year received approximately one third of all personal income. The proportion of personal income received in the form of interest, dividends, and rent—the income, broadly speaking, of the well-to-do—was about twice as great as in the years following the Second World War.

This highly unequal income distribution meant that the economy was dependent on a high level of investment or a high level of luxury consumer spending or both. The rich cannot buy great quantities of bread. If they are to dispose of what they receive it must be on luxuries or by way of investment in new plants and new projects. Both investment and luxury spending are subject, inevitably, to more erratic influences and to wider fluctuations than the bread and rent outlays of the $25-a-week workman. This high-bracket spending and investment was especially susceptible, one may assume, to the crushing news from the stock market in October of 1929.

2) The bad corporate structure. In November 1929, a few weeks after the crash, the Harvard Economic Society gave as a principal reason why a depression need not be feared its reasoned judgment that "business in most lines has been conducted with prudence and conservatism." The fact was that American enterprise in the twenties had opened its hospitable arms to an exceptional number of promoters, grafters, swindlers, impostors, and frauds. This, in the long history of such activities, was a kind of flood tide of corporate larceny.

The most important corporate weakness was inherent in the vast new structure of holding companies and investment trusts. The holding companies controlled large segments of the utility, railroad, and entertainment business. Here, as with the investment trusts, was the constant danger of devastation by reverse leverage. In particular, dividends from the operating companies paid the interest on the bonds of upstream holding companies. The interruption of the dividends meant default on the bonds, bankruptcy, and the collapse of the structure. Under these circum-

stances, the temptation to curtail investment in operating plant in order
to continue dividends was obviously strong. This added to deflationary
pressures. The latter, in turn, curtailed earnings and helped bring down
the corporate pyramids. When this happened, even more retrenchment
was inevitable. Income was earmarked for debt repayment. Borrowing
for new investment became impossible. It would be hard to imagine a
corporate system better designed to continue and accentuate a deflationary spiral.

3) The bad banking structure. Since the early thirties, a generation of
Americans has been told, sometimes with amusement, sometimes with
indignation, often with outrage, of the banking practices of the late
twenties. In fact, many of these practices were made ludicrous only by
the depression. Loans which would have been perfectly good were made
perfectly foolish by the collapse of the borrower's prices or the markets
for his goods or the value of the collateral he had posted. The most
responsible bankers—those who saw that their debtors were victims of
circumstances far beyond their control and sought to help—were often
made to look the worst. The bankers yielded, as did others, to the blithe,
optimistic, and immoral mood of the times but probably not more so. A depression such as that of 1929–32, were it to begin as this is written, would
also be damaging to many currently impeccable banking reputations.

However, although the bankers were not unusually foolish in 1929, the
banking structure was inherently weak. The weakness was implicit in
the large numbers of independent units. When one bank failed, the assets
of others were frozen while depositors elsewhere had a pregnant warning
to go and ask for their money. Thus one failure led to other failures, and
these spread with a domino effect. Even in the best of times local misfortune or isolated mismanagement could start such a chain reaction. (In
the first six months of 1929, 346 banks failed in various parts of the
country with aggregate deposits of nearly $115 million.) When income,
employment, and values fell as the result of a depression bank failures
could quickly become epidemic. This happened after 1929. Again it
would be hard to imagine a better arrangement for magnifying the
effects of fear. The weak destroyed not only the other weak, but weakened the strong. People everywhere, rich and poor, were made aware of
the disaster by the persuasive intelligence that their savings had been
destroyed.

Needless to say, such a banking system, once in the convulsions of
failure, had a uniquely repressive effect on the spending of its depositors
and the investment of its clients.

4) The dubious state of the foreign balance. This is a familiar story.
During the First World War, the United States became a creditor on
international account. In the decade following, the surplus of exports
over imports which once had paid the interest and principal on loans

from Europe continued. The high tariffs, which restricted imports and helped to create this surplus of exports remained. However, history and traditional trading habits also accounted for the persistence of the favorable balance, so called.

Before, payments on interest and principal had in effect been deducted from the trade balance. Now that the United States was a creditor, they were added to this balance. The latter, it should be said, was not huge. In only one year (1928) did the excess of exports over imports come to as much as a billion dollars; in 1923 and 1926 it was only about $375,000,-000. However, large or small, this difference had to be covered. Other countries which were buying more than they sold, and had debt payments to make in addition, had somehow to find the means for making up the deficit in their transactions with the United States.

During most of the twenties the difference was covered by cash—i.e., gold payments to the United States—and by new private loans by the United States to other countries. Most of the loans were to governments —national, state, or municipal bodies—and a large proportion were to Germany and Central and South America. The underwriters' margins in handling these loans were generous; the public took them up with enthusiasm; competition for the business was keen. If unfortunately corruption and bribery were required as competitive instruments, these were used. In late 1927 Juan Leguia, the son of the President of Peru, was paid $450,000 by J. and W. Seligman and Company and the National City Company (the security affiliate of the National City Bank) for his services in connection with a $50,000,000 loan which these houses marketed for Peru. Juan's services, according to later testimony, were of a rather negative sort. He was paid for not blocking the deal. The Chase extended President Machado of Cuba, a dictator with a marked predisposition toward murder, a generous personal line of credit which at one time reached $200,000. Machado's son-in-law was employed by the Chase. The bank did a large business in Cuban bonds. In contemplating these loans, there was a tendency to pass quickly over anything that might appear to the disadvantage of the creditor. Mr. Victor Schoepperle, a vice-president of the National City Company with the responsibility for Latin American loans, made the following appraisal of Peru as a credit prospect:

> Peru: Bad debt record, adverse moral and political risk, bad internal debt situation, trade situation about as satisfactory as that of Chile in the past three years. Natural resources more varied. On economic showing Peru should go ahead rapidly in the next 10 years.

On such showing the National City Company floated a $15,000,000 loan for Peru, followed a few months later by a $50,000,000 loan, and some ten months thereafter by a $25,000,000 issue. (Peru did prove a highly adverse political risk. President Leguia, who negotiated the loans, was thrown violently out of office, and the loans went into default.)

In all respects these operations were as much a part of the New Era as Shenandoah and Blue Ridge. They were also just as fragile, and once the illusions of the New Era were dissipated they came as abruptly to an end. This, in turn, forced a fundamental revision in the foreign economic position of the United States. Countries could not cover their adverse trade balance with the United States with increased payments of gold, at least not for long. This meant that they had either to increase their exports to the United States or reduce their imports or default on their past loans. President Hoover and the Congress moved promptly to eliminate the first possibility—that the accounts would be balanced by larger imports—by sharply increasing the tariff. Accordingly, debts, including war debts, went into default and there was a precipitate fall in American exports. The reduction was not vast in relation to total output of the American economy, but it contributed to the general distress and was especially hard on farmers.

5) The poor state of economic intelligence. To regard the people of any time as particularly obtuse seems vaguely improper, and it also establishes a precedent which members of this generation might regret. Yet it seems certain that the economists and those who offered economic counsel in the late twenties and early thirties were almost uniquely perverse. In the months and years following the stock market crash, the burden of reputable economic advice was invariably on the side of measures that would make things worse. In November of 1929, Mr. Hoover announced a cut in taxes; in the great no-business conferences that followed he asked business firms to keep up their capital investment and to maintain wages. Both of these measures were on the side of increasing spendable income, though unfortunately they were largely without effect. The tax reductions were negligible except in the higher income brackets; businessmen who promised to maintain investment and wages, in accordance with a well-understood convention, considered the promise binding only for the period within which it was not financially disadvantageous to do so. As a result investment outlays and wages were not reduced until circumstances would in any case have brought their reduction.

Still, the effort was in the right direction. Thereafter policy was almost entirely on the side of making things worse. Asked how the government could best advance recovery, the sound and responsible adviser urged that the budget be balanced. Both parties agreed on this. For Republicans the balanced budget was, as ever, high doctrine. But the Democratic Party platform of 1932, with an explicitness which politicians rarely advise, also called for a "federal budget annually balanced on the basis of accurate executive estimates within revenues . . ."

A commitment to a balanced budget is always comprehensive. It then meant there could be no increase in government outlays to expand purchasing power and relieve distress. It meant there could be no further tax reductions. But taken literally it meant much more. From 1930 on the budget was far out of balance, and balance, therefore, meant an increase in taxes, a reduction in spending, or both. The Democratic platform in 1932 called for an "immediate and drastic reduction of governmental expenditures" to accomplish at least a 25 per cent decrease in the cost of government.

The balanced budget was not a subject of thought. Nor was it, as often asserted, precisely a matter of faith. Rather it was a formula. For centuries avoidance of borrowing had protected people from slovenly or reckless public housekeeping. Slovenly or reckless keepers of the public purse had often composed complicated arguments to show why balance of income and outlay was not a mark of virtue. Experience had shown that however convenient this belief might seem in the short run, discomfort or disaster followed in the long run. Those simple precepts of a simple world did not hold amid the growing complexities of the early thirties. Mass unemployment in particular had altered the rules. Events had played a very bad trick on people, but almost no one tried to think out the problem anew.

The balanced budget was not the only strait jacket on policy. There was also the bogey of "going off" the gold standard and, most surprisingly, of risking inflation. Until 1932 the United States added formidably to its gold reserves, and instead of inflation the country was experiencing the most violent deflation in the nation's history. Yet every sober adviser saw dangers here, including the danger of runaway price increases. Americans, though in years now well in the past, had shown a penchant for tinkering with the money supply and enjoying the brief but heady joys of a boom in prices. In 1931 or 1932, the danger or even the feasibility of such a boom was nil. The advisers and counselors were not, however, analyzing the danger or even the possibility. They were serving only as the custodians of bad memories.

The fear of inflation reinforced the demand for the balanced budget. It also limited efforts to make interest rates low, credit plentiful (or at least redundant) and borrowing as easy as possible under the circumstances. Devaluation of the dollar was, of course, flatly ruled out. This directly violated the gold standard rules. At best, in such depression times, monetary policy is a feeble reed on which to lean. The current economic clichés did not allow even the use of that frail weapon. And again, these attitudes were above party. Though himself singularly open-minded, Roosevelt was careful not to offend or disturb his followers. In a speech in Brooklyn toward the close of the 1932 campaign, he said:

The Democratic platform specifically declares, "We advocate a sound currency to be preserved at all hazards." That is plain English. In discussing this platform on July 30, I said, "Sound money is an international necessity, not a domestic consideration for one nation alone." Far up in the Northwest, at Butte, I repeated the pledge . . . In Seattle I reaffirmed my attitude . . .

The following February, Mr. Hoover set forth his view, as often before, in a famous letter to the President-elect:

It would steady the country greatly if there could be prompt assurance that there will be no tampering or inflation of the currency; that the budget will be unquestionably balanced even if further taxation is necessary; that the Government credit will be maintained by refusal to exhaust it in the issue of securities.

The rejection of both fiscal (tax and expenditure) and monetary policy amounted precisely to a rejection of all affirmative government economic policy. The economic advisers of the day had both the unanimity and the authority to force the leaders of both parties to disavow all the available steps to check deflation and depression. In its own way this was a marked achievement—a triumph of dogma over thought. The consequences were profound. . . .

FOR FURTHER READING: Economic conditions in the 1920's are discussed in William E. Leuchtenburg, *The Perils of Prosperity, 1914–1932* (Chicago, 1958), and John Braeman, Robert Bremner, and David Brody (eds.), *Change and Continuity in Twentieth Century America: The 1920's* (Columbus, Ohio, 1968). Milton Friedman and Anna J. Schwartz, *The Great Contraction* (Princeton, 1965), focus on monetary factors influencing the economy. Notable is Peter Temin, *Did Monetary Forces Cause the Great Depression?* (New York, 1976). This can be read in conjunction with Thomas Mayer, "Money and the Great Depression: A Critique of Professor Temin's Thesis," *Explorations in Economic History*, XV (April, 1978), pp. 127–145.

15

THE NEW DEAL

PROBLEM: *Did New Deal policies revive the economy?*

Whether the economic policies of the New Deal actually fostered a revival of business activity is still a debatable issue among economists as well as historians. Of the financial proposals that President Franklin D. Roosevelt advocated during the first eight years of his Administration, particularly the fiscal measures have been subjected to criticism. These included the manipulation of interest rates, and the creation of budget deficits through the financing of large-scale public works programs. In addition they embraced federal loans to banks, railroads, and home owners. Arthur Smithies, a former official of the United States Bureau of the Budget and an economics professor at Harvard University, argues that federal fiscal policies under the New Deal did not attain an optimum degree of effectiveness, primarily because the very high rate of investment in the 1920's had created a surfeit. This surfeit depressed plant expenditures, residential construction, business inventories and foreign investments in the Roosevelt era, and offset any stimulatory effects which such fiscal manipulation might have had otherwise. Yet the depression would have been much worse, Smithies argues, if the President had not undertaken such large-scale expenditures as he did. From this experience Smithies concludes that the federal government should use fiscal measures as a major tool to combat depressions. However, one of America's most distinguished economists, Gardiner C. Means, takes issue with this view, for he believes that monetary, rather than fiscal, measures were more important in stimulating recovery during the 1930's. Monetary policies included the manipulation of the quantity of money in circulation, as by alteration of the gold standard and the price of gold, by the purchase of silver, and by modification of the Treasury's borrowing procedures. These measures, rather than fiscal policies, Means argues, stabilized prices. Each of these writers presents persuasive evidence that bears on public policies during times of depression. What were alternatives to the New Deal's fiscal and monetary policies? How do political considerations affect the application of large scale fiscal or monetary experiments by government? What standards can be used to measure the effectiveness of the New Deal's economic recovery programs?

The American Economy in the Thirties

ARTHUR SMITHIES

I. INTRODUCTION

Any discussion of the United States economy in the thirties almost inevitably resolves itself into either a general discussion of the business cycle or a discussion of the role of government in economic life. In this paper I am going to place primary emphasis on the role of government, although it will of course be necessary to advert to the nature of the economic problem with which the government had to deal and that will raise the general business cycle issue.

I choose this course because the thirties was the first peacetime period in United States history where the government took positive action, on a wide scale, to control the general level of economic activity. The history of that period must therefore be in the forefront of the minds of those concerned with government policies to forestall depressions in the future.

The policy of the Hoover Administration was to follow the path of orthodoxy and to assume that the situation demanded nothing more than the encouragement and rehabilitation of business. Interest rates were lowered and governmental economies introduced, and the Hawley-Smoot Tariff was enacted. The pressure of events led to the establishment of

Reprinted by permission from the *American Economic Review*, Supplement, XXXVI (May, 1946), pp. 11–27.

the RFC, but the President only very reluctantly agreed to extension of RFC loans to small businesses, to individuals, and to the states for relief purposes. The agricultural policy of the Administration was not so much a product of the depression as a continuation of the policies which had been previously adopted to relieve rural distress, which had continued throughout the whole period of the twenties. Beyond that the President offered good advice and exhortation to business to maintain business and employment. Business responded to an extraordinary degree, but the pressure of events was too strong. The Administration resisted to the end any proposals for direct federal unemployment relief.

It is evident from the political history of the thirties that the United States was no longer prepared to tolerate the privations of a serious depression in the traditional and "capitalist" way. The verdict of the electorate in 1932 testifies to this and the election of 1936 even more so. For the qualified recovery which had been achieved by 1936 can hardly explain the unqualified verdict of approval which was given to the Administration—especially since the great New Deal instrument of recovery —the NRA—had proved a dismal failure and had been pronounced unconstitutional.

But more than relief and recovery were at issue. Social and economic reform—in particular, social security, recognition of the rising political power of labor, and of redistribution of income and economic power— could no longer be delayed. Professor Schumpeter contends that such reforms are inherently anticapitalist in the sense that they impair the effective operation of the capitalist system—and did in fact impair it in the second half of the decade of the thirties. One of my aims here is to examine the force of his contention.

I have said that politically the Administration had no alternative but to do something about the depression. While this cannot be denied, critics have argued that economically it would have been preferable to let nature take its course. My major purpose in this paper is to examine the need for a recovery policy and to evaluate the effectiveness of the recovery policies which were pursued.

II. THE EVOLUTION OF A POLICY

I want now to sketch very briefly the policy objectives of the Administration and the measures taken to reach them.

The First Phase. The President's first inaugural address did not contain many indications of the movement for reform that the New Deal was to be in its heyday, and neither did the legislation of the first "100 days." The first message to Congress requested banking legislation, the second, drastic economies in government, and the third the agricultural adjustment legislation. Recommendations for home and farm mortgage relief, for unemployment relief, for securities and exchange legislation, for emergency railroad legislation, and for TVA followed in quick succession. On May 17 the President transmitted his famous message which requested the Congress to enact legislation to deal with the question of industrial wages, prices, and labor conditions on a nationwide scale and to provide for a comprehensive public works program. This message led to the establishment of NRA and PWA.

Towards the end of 1933 the gold purchase scheme was adopted and this led to the devaluation of the dollar and the Gold Reserve Act of 1934. The Trade Agreements Act of 1934 laid the foundation for future United States co-operation in the international economic sphere.

The Administration, or rather the Federal Reserve Board, continued the policy of cheap money inaugurated during the Hoover Administration. The gold inflow which was partially stimulated by the devaluation of the dollar enabled low interest rates to be maintained throughout the decade and to become a permanent feature of the American economy.

The revenue measures of the first New Deal period consisted of increased liquor taxes following the repeal of prohibition, emergency taxes on corporations and capital stock to provide for interest and amortization on the money borrowed to finance the public works program, the processing taxes to finance AAA, and finally the general but moderate increases in income, estate, and gift taxes incorporated in the Revenue Act of 1934.

That very briefly was the basis for the economic policy of the Administration during its first two years. The most striking characteristic of that program was that it attempted on a national scale to cure the depression by removing specific abuses and dealing with specific maladjustments. Relief was provided to the chief sufferers from the depression, agriculture was dealt with as a special problem, and the main weapon of industrial recovery was to attempt to introduce order in industry and to increase purchasing power by reducing the margin between prices and wages through the operation of NRA. The impression I get from the President's statements on public works is that his motivation in urging the programs was to improve natural resources and to absorb unemployed labor into productive public employment in the absence of private employment rather than to use public works as a pump-priming device.

The point I want to emphasize is that an expansionary fiscal policy played a very minor role in the policy decisions of the period. Reductions of government salaries and veterans' benefits were recommended by the President on grounds of equity and economy. The processing taxes and the liquor taxes can only be described as deflationary. In fact, at a press conference on April 7, 1933, the President said: "So much of the legislation we have had this spring is of deflationary character . . . that we are faced with the problem of offsetting it in some way."

There can be no question in my mind that, despite large deficits, the Administration at this stage genuinely wanted to balance the budget, that it regarded its deflationary fiscal policies as contributions to recovery that it hoped to achieve reflation through price policy rather than fiscal policy, and that it regarded reliance on public works as a last rather than a first resort.

The Second Phase. The year 1935 saw the symptoms of a pronounced change in the political orientation of the Administration. The meagre success of NRA and its ultimate invalidation by the Supreme Court meant that active co-operation of government and business in the process of recovery was at an end; and the mounting opposition from the Right to the New Deal as a whole meant that the Administration would have to enlist its support in other quarters. Moreover, the demand for reform which may have been numbed by the rigors of full depression was excited by the mildness of recovery. While the policies of the first New Deal aimed at relief and recovery those of the second were directed to recovery and reform.

The President refused to separate reform from recovery. In the State of the Union Message for 1935 he said: "The attempt to make a distinction between recovery and reform is a narrowly conceived effort to substitute the appearance of reality for reality itself." He announced his threefold security program: the security of a livelihood through the better use of the natural resources of the land in which we live; the security against the major hazards and vicissitudes of life; and the security of decent homes.

In the State of the Union Message of 1936 the President stepped up the tempo of his attack on "the royalists of the economic order [who] have conceded that political freedom was the business of the government, but . . . have maintained that economic slavery should be nobody's business." The year 1936 was the one and possibly the only year in which the government of the United States could be described as being definitely of the Left.

The second inaugural in 1937 was full of ebullient satisfaction at the progress of recovery, but the President significantly said that "prosperity already tests the persistence of our progressive purpose," and issued his dramatic reminder that one-third of the nation was still ill-clad, ill-housed, and ill-nourished. But that was practically the end of the second New Deal; the onset of depression in the fall of 1937, the changing complexion of the Congress, and the growing preoccupation with international matters barred the further progress of reform.

The legislative and executive action of the second New Deal falls into three main groups: First, measures to give effect to the President's security program and to establish the status of organized labor; second, measures to attack the position of the "economic royalists"; and third, measures to rescue the first New Deal from the shambles created by the Supreme Court.

The great permanent monument to the President's security program is of course the Social Security Act of 1935 which took preliminary steps to free families from poverty in old age and from the hardships of unemployment. Whether or not the principles of the other main security measures of the Administration—WPA and NYA—have become firmly established still remains to be seen. In his 1935 Message, the President had said: "The federal government must and shall quit this business of relief. I am not willing that the vitality of our people be further sapped by the giving of cash, of market baskets, of a few hours of weekly work cutting grass, raking leaves or picking up papers in the public parks."

The third item in the security program—decent homes—ran into legislative and judicial obstacles. FHA insurance contributed to middle-class housing; but it was not until 1937 that provision for low rent housing for slum dwellers was made and that was but a modest attempt.

Labor won its charter under the second New Deal. The National Labor Relations Act of 1935 firmly established the right of collective bargaining and assured that the bargaining would be conducted by representatives of the majority of the workers involved—an assurance which was not provided under Section 7A of the National Industrial Recovery Act. The other great labor measure—the Fair Labor Standards Act— was not passed until 1938, and finally legislated the principles of minimum wages, penalty overtime pay, and the prohibition of child labor.

The "antiroyalist" legislation included the public utilities legislation, but the measures that are of most importance, especially for present purposes, are the tax legislations of 1935 and 1936. The President recommended to Congress imposition of increased estate and gift taxes, increased individual surtaxes, and graduated corporation income tax, and requesting study of other taxes including those "to discourage unwieldy and unnecessary corporate surpluses." With the invalidation of AAA and the consequent loss of processing tax revenues, he recommended an undistributed profits tax in March, 1936.

The 1935 Message was based not on the need for more revenue but on the need for redistributing wealth, plugging evasion loopholes, and reducing concentrations of economic power. Although the 1936 recommendation was based on revenue needs, the particular form of tax chosen was determined on grounds of equity rather than economics. The tax laws of 1935 and 1936 thus differed markedly in their motivation from their New Deal predecessors whose primary objectives had been to increase the receipts of the Treasury. But neither were they motivated by the need for an expansionary fiscal policy.

The Supreme Court decisions removed the processing taxes of AAA and relieved the Administration of the embarrassing necessity of trying to make NRA succeed. The crop control features of AAA were salvaged by the Soil Conservation Act, but NRA had no major successor so far as its prices and wage features were concerned. In fact, the whole spirit of the second New Deal was inconsistent with "self-government in industry" which was the essence of NRA.

As a result of the Supreme Court's surgery and also of the enactment of the Bonus over the President's veto, the government's contribution to recovery after 1935 depended almost entirely on the fiscal effects of its policy; that is, efforts to create purchasing power by attempts to adjust the price-wage structure disappeared and the stimulus to economic activity given by the government was the income-creating effect of the budget deficit. But the deficit was not the result of fiscal plans laid by the government to achieve economic goals. It was rather the net result of the budgetary requirements of relief and reform measures and the political infeasibility of increasing taxation *pari passu* with expenditures. Expenditures depended on the amounts required to provide WPA employment for the unemployed and the new taxes were based largely on the Administration's program to redistribute wealth and income. It was thus a matter of accident rather than design if the fiscal policy actually pursued did in fact promote recovery at the desired rate.

The Third Phase. The third phase of the New Deal period opened with the depression in the second half of 1937. That depression took everyone by surprise—government and public alike. The year 1937 had opened with serene economic optimism. The 1938 budget was to be balanced and the economic instruments of government were to be directed to curbing a boom. The portents in the fall of 1937 were not heeded and it was only in the spring of 1938 that the Administration was convinced that it had a serious depression to contend with.

In April, 1938, the President sent to the Congress his "Recommendations Designed to Stimulate Further Recovery." This document is remarkable in that it was the first outright recommendation by the President designed to achieve recovery through fiscal policy. Increased appropriation for WPA, NYA, Farm Security, and CCC were urged with the frank objective of increasing national income. The government credit agencies were to make cheap credit available to business, and the President recommended a large expansion of the general public works program. The message is noteworthy for the omission of any recommendations for increased taxation. The Treasury had evidently been appeased by recommendations for the elimination of tax-exempt bonds and for federal and state taxation of all government salaries. The goal was a national income of 80 billion dollars, and the President asserted that that goal could be achieved only if private funds were put to work "and all of us recognize that such funds are entitled to a fair profit."

Beyond acting on the President's recommendations, the chief contribution of the Congress to the recovery program was to enact the Revenue Act of 1938 which repealed all but a token remnant of the excess profits tax and substituted a corporation income tax on firms earning more than $25,000.

The other main legislative achievements of the third phase were the Fair Labor Standards Act to which I have already referred and the new Agricultural Adjustment Act of 1938. The latter act instituted the present method of assistance to agriculture through voluntary acreage control and Commodity Credit Corporation price support.

The other noteworthy feature of the third phase was the antimonopoly campaign which found its expression in an aggressive application of the antitrust laws and aggressive investigation through the Temporary National Economic Committee. The NRA policy of recovery through agreement was finally and completely reversed.

Thus through a process of trial and error and of ordeal by Congress and the Supreme Court the Administration wound up its peacetime record and concluded the decade with a clear-cut recovery program of fiscal policy and cheap money. The agricultural policy was the most effective method yet devised to achieve the objective of a floor under agricultural prices. The reforms of the banking and financial system and social security were accepted as permanent, and labor had won its place in the sun. The main unfinished piece of business was the monopoly program. The onset of war postponed the formulation of a comprehensive antimonopoly policy.

III. EFFECTS ON THE ECONOMY

I shall now attempt to analyze the effects of the government's policies on the American economy during the thirties. To do this I shall first consider the behavior of the main determinants of private economic activity —the factors that influence private decisions to invest and to consume. Such a discussion should enable us to decide what effect the government's policy had on the structure of the American economy, and separate the sheep from the goats among the plethora of policies which were pursued.

Let me turn first to the vexed question of private investment. I shall discuss it in terms of the usual division into producers' plant and equipment, residential construction, net additions to inventories, and foreign investment.

Plant and Equipment. Both friendly critics and active opponents have argued that the New Deal policies—at any rate before 1938—were seriously detrimental to private investment in plant and equipment. It has been argued with cogency that the tax policy—the progressive individual income tax, corporation taxes, and especially the undistributed profits tax—diminished the incentives of individuals and corporations to risk their money in venturesome enterprises. It is possible that the antispeculation reforms, while increasing the soundness of investment, diminished its quantity. There is considerable agreement with Professor Schumpeter's argument that anticapitalist attitudes provided a chilly climate for innovation. Finally, there was the all-embracing charge that the mutual distrust of government and business produced a "strike of capital." These arguments lose none of their appeal since something is required to explain why plant and equipment expenditures in the thirties never approached their peak level in the twenties.

On the favorable side, it can be argued that the cheap money policy and the federal loan policy encouraged investment in the traditional way by reducing the cost of borrowing. Also, somewhat to my surprise, I find that Professor Schumpeter includes NRA as a positive recovery factor. He argued that it "pegged weak spots in industries, stopped spirals in many places, mended disorganized markets" and "even Blue Eagles do count for something when, objective conditions for revival being given, it is broken morale that is the matter." While I am quoting Professor Schumpeter, I should like to record his views on the contention that government deficits per se impede business expansion. He says: "Some of the arguments adduced for this possibility fully merit the shrugging of shoulders with which they are usually met; for instance, the argument that the unbalanced budget destroyed confidence."

These arguments are I believe all sound in principle, but, in order to assess their impact on the economy, we need some quantitative measure of their effects. The way for such measurement has been paved by Tinbergen's epoch-making work, but his own study does not extend to the period we are investigating. Tinbergen's work is now being revised, extended, and improved at the Cowles Commission and has resulted so far in a preliminary manuscript by Mr. Lawrence Klein. The Commission and Mr. Klein have generously given me permission to use their results with the caution that they must be regarded only as first approximations. This reservation applies not only to Mr. Klein's results but also to other conclusions based on correlation analysis to which I shall refer.

Mr. Klein has obtained a relation from the data over the period 1921–41 which satisfactorily "explains" the demand for net additions to plant and equipment in terms of the private net output of the economy in the recent past as a positive factor and the existing stock of capital equipment and the price level of capital goods as negative factors. The unexplained residuals are randomly distributed, and, so far as I can see, none of these residuals can be identified as disturbances of the relation due to government policy. For instance, in relation to the values yielded by the formula, investment was abnormally high in 1929, but still higher in 1937. The plausibility of the relation is increased by the satisfactory results which the same method yields for particular individual groups such as public utilities and mining and manufacturing.

I am not satisfied that this relation reveals the whole truth about investment demand in all circumstances. I believe an adequate theory requires the inclusion of net profits after taxes as an explanatory variable.

It has not emerged as such in Mr. Klein's results because net corporate profits (excluding inventory revaluations) have remained very highly correlated with private output. Profits before taxes retained throughout the thirties the same relation to private output, with practically no disturbance, as existed during the twenties. The tax changes of the thirties were not sufficient to disturb greatly the relation between profits after taxes and output. I therefore interpret Mr. Klein's results to mean not that tax changes are irrelevant but that those which in fact did occur had no significant effect.

Mr. Klein's demand function also does not include the rate of interest as an explanatory variable. Although interest rates can be demonstrated to be determining influences in other countries, they are apparently dwarfed by other influences in the United States. Tinbergen reaches the same conclusion and demonstrates that the determinants of investment differ widely from country to country.

The results lead to the conclusion that the underlying factors determining investment in plant and equipment were the same in the twenties and the thirties and that government policy affected investment only insofar as it affected the explanatory variables of the relation.

The large stock of capital which played an important role in depressing investment in the first half of the decade was the inheritance of the twenties and not a product of the thirties. Government policy affected the rate of investment insofar as it influenced national output and capital goods prices. Its influence on output depends on the expansionary effects of all the government policies. Prices of capital goods, and especially construction costs, did rise abruptly and disproportionately between 1936 and 1937. This may be ascribed to wage increases and to increases of world prices of raw materials.

I cannot regard these statistical conclusions as in any way final or definitive, and I am sure the Cowles Commission takes the same point of view. However, until evidence to the contrary appears, I am prepared to enter a verdict of "not proven" to the charge that the political and economic environment of the thirties affected the incentive to invest in plant and equipment through its effect on business confidence.

Residential Construction. The low rate of investment in residential building in the thirties has given rise to explanations involving lack of confidence of the same type I have described in relation to plant and equipment investment. I therefore need not repeat them here, but turn at once to the statistical evidence.

There is a growing volume of reasonably satisfactory attempts—all on the same lines—to explain statistically fluctuations in residential building, and I feel I am here on less treacherous ground than that which I have just left. I refer to the work of Roos, Chawner, Tinbergen and Derksen. Mr. Klein has re-examined the whole question for the period 1921–41 in the light of later statistics than were available to the other writers. He explains expenditure on nonfarm residential building in terms of disposable income, the rent level, construction costs, and net increases in families in the recent past. But the rent level itself depends on conditions in the housing market. Mr. Derksen has given the most satisfactory explanation of rent in terms of the vacancy ratio two years before and nonfarm family income.

These studies give a satisfactory explanation of residential building over the twenties and the thirties, and lead to the conclusion that the major factor accounting for the low level of housing in the thirties was the high rate of construction in the twenties. Higher construction costs also reduced total housing expenditures in the later years of the decade. This was probably reflected, at least partially, in a reduction in the size rather than the number of dwelling units constructed.

Here again I can find little evidence that taxation or lack of confidence in the government was an important explanatory factor. Had it been, surely 1937 and 1938 would have been years of markedly subnormal activity, which they were not. Furthermore, I believe that these factors are less likely to have an adverse effect on residential building than on business plant and equipment expenditures. The main factors which account for the low level of residential construction shown in the thirties appear to be a relatively large supply of housing in relation to the number of families, especially in the first half of the decade, high construction costs, especially in the second half, and a low level of income throughout.

Business Inventories. The behavior of inventories over the thirties requires no particular comment except for two episodes. Inventories were liquidated under the impact of declining production after the onset of the depression and were built up as recovery got under way. The two exceptions to this regular behavior I want to notice are the short-lived inventory spurt in the second half of 1933 and the abnormal accumulations of inventories in the latter half of 1936 and 1937. The 1933 incident must be explained by the prospects of higher costs, especially wages, under NRA, while the accumulations in 1936 and 1937 were largely in response to the expectations of higher prices aroused by the sharp general increases in wage rates at that time—although the prospects for higher world prices for raw materials probably also had significant effects. The 1933 flurry was followed by a mild liquidation. The liquidation of the accumulations of 1936 and 1937 was a major factor in explaining the sharpness of the downswing in 1937 and 1938. These episodes were, I believe, the most important effects of the general behavior of wage rates in the period.

Foreign Investment. Foreign investment as represented by "net exports" reached an average annual rate of about 1 billion dollars in the latter half of the twenties. It did not regain this rate until European war demands expanded American exports at the end of the thirties. What then was the effect of the devaluation of the dollar and the trade agreements negotiated after 1934? It is impossible to isolate the effects of these measures since conditions in the outside world remained by no means static. I believe, however, that devaluation did accomplish some increase in the positive balance of payments in the year or two after it was undertaken, but that restrictive measures taken by other countries, whether in retaliation or for other reasons, very soon offset this effect. It is also an almost impossible problem to isolate the effects of the trade agreements. My own opinion is that the trade agreements negotiated in the thirties laid the foundations of a policy of freer trade in the future and did not have a marked impact on the operation of the economy of the thirties. I must hasten to add that this opinion does not belittle the achievement of those who succeeded in reversing the policy exemplified by the Hawley-Smoot tariff.

I conclude that the net effects of United States economic foreign policy were reflected in the domestic economy rather than in foreign trade Chiefly by reducing confidence in other currencies, devaluation probably accelerated the gold inflow into the United States and thus facilitated the cheap money policy. Secondly, by raising the world dollar prices of agricultural products, the burden of aid to agriculture on the federal budget was somewhat reduced—and after all, was not the real objective of devaluation to raise agricultural prices?

Consumers' Expenditures. It has been widely argued that the government's policies of the thirties, whether designed for the purpose or not, did derive economic justification from their effect in increasing consumption in relation to national income.

NRA was intended by the President to raise wages by more than prices and thereby redistribute income and increase consumption. The anti-monopoly policy of the latter part of the decade was intended to achieve the same result. There was a widespread belief that higher money wages, unassociated with any price policy, would increase mass purchasing power. One of the objectives of agricultural policy was to increase total consumption by improving the lot of agriculture. More progressive income taxes were held to redistribute income after taxes in favor of those more likely to spend on consumption. One of the main economic arguments for the undistributed profits tax was that it would reduce corporate savings and thereby increase income payments to consumers.

Here again the only way to assess the quantitative validity of these contentions is to test the matter statistically. Their quantitative effects would be reflected in the propensities of individuals to spend out of their disposable incomes and of corporations to distribute their incomes as dividends. This evidence can also be reinforced by such evidence as there is on the distribution of incomes.

There is widespread agreement among economists that consumers' expenditures throughout the whole interwar period can be explained as a function of disposable income with a rising time trend representing progress towards higher living standards. Disagreement only exists as to the form the relation should take. Some economists use deflated series, others the money data. Some contend that the regression shifts as between prosperity and depression years. My own belief is that the relation which satisfies both theoretical and statistical requirements best is to relate per capita real consumption to per capita real income for the whole period. But whatever the correct law is, there is no evidence that it changed during the thirties. Thus whatever changes in the distribution of individual incomes after taxes did occur, they had no perceptible influence on consumer spending in relation to disposable income in the aggregate.

The behavior of corporations in distributing their dividends has so far defied systematic explanation, but the figures do enable us to answer the question with which we are mainly concerned. Mr. Hoover's policy of exhortation probably did have some effect in inducing corporations to distribute more than they earned in 1930. But corporations as a whole continued this practice through 1938—though on a smaller scale. Unless it can be argued that Mr. Hoover's advice was still being adhered to it is difficult to explain the behavior of corporate savings except in terms of the depression itself.

The paucity of official data on the distribution of individual incomes does not permit any definitive conclusions. I am impressed, however, with the remarkable stability of the relation between private wages and salaries to private gross product. Throughout the twenties and thirties wages and salaries remained extraordinarily close to 50 per cent of the total. This relation is a dominant factor in determining the distribution of individual incomes. There is some indication that in 1937 labor did succeed in increasing its share of the total product, but these gains were rapidly wiped out by subsequent price adjustments. I am unable to find any identifiable influence of the antimonopoly policies. I infer, therefore, that the redistributive policies of the thirties either did not have their anticipated effects on consumption or were not carried as far as has sometimes been thought.

My survey of the determinants of investment and consumption thus leads to the conclusion that, by and large, during the thirties both businesses and consumers were influenced in making their expenditure decisions by the same factors in the same way as in the twenties. I submit this conclusion with some diffidence since the statistical relations on which it is based are admittedly tentative. But that evidence all leads in the same direction. On the other side there is only a priori opinion however well informed and experienced.

The analysis also enables us to identify the factors which did affect the data on which the decisions of investors and consumers were based. They are as follows:

1. The high rate of construction of business plant and equipment and

residential building during the twenties increased the stock of capital to a high level and thus made for abnormally low investment in the thirties.

2. Declining population growth contributed to the relative abundance of the supply of housing. I should add that I am speaking here of abundance from the point of view of the operation of the private ecomomy and not from any welfare point of view.

3. Increases in construction costs and the prices of capital equipment in relation to the general price level, particularly from 1937 on, contributed to the low rate of long-term investment, as compared with the twenties.

4. The rapid increases in wages contributed to the inventory speculation in 1936 and 1937.

5. The net foreign balance remained at a low level until European rearmament increased United States exports.

These are all factors tending to depress the level of national income. The single factor operating in the opposite direction was the expansionary fiscal policy of the federal government, which considerably more than offset the contraction in the construction programs of state and local governments which occurred after 1929, and afforded a strong positive stimulus to national income and thereby increased the rates of private consumption and private investment.

IV. EVALUATION OF POLICY

I can now attempt to answer the questions which I raised at the beginning of this paper: Was a positive government policy required if full recovery was to be achieved? What were the effects of the policy actually pursued? Did reform conflict with recovery?

We can answer the first question with some confidence. Even if all the disturbing influences that occurred during the thirties had been absent, the high rate of accumulation of capital during the twenties would have made for a low rate of investment and consequently a low rate of income during the thirties. If nature had been left to take its course, there would presumably have been a prolonged period of disinvestment and depression before it would have again become profitable for businesses to undertake the rate of investment expenditures required for full recovery. Our analysis leads to the conclusion that recovery would have arrived eventually, although there is no reason to believe that the "speculative" influences which made 1929 an exceptional year would have recurred. The contentions advanced in the heat of controversy that but for the New Deal full recovery would have been achieved by, say 1935, merit no attention. In fact, I know of no economist who would now argue that if "orthodox" policies had been continued, recovery up to 1937 would have been more rapid than it was.

Whatever the legitimate doubts about the statistical explanations of investment, I do believe the negative correlation between investment and the existing stock of capital is firmly established on both theoretical and statistical grounds. It follows that government action which mitigates depressions by policies which increase the rate of private investment tend to diminish its rate in the following boom. I make this observation, not as an argument against stabilization policies, but merely as a word of warning against the assumption that an effective countercyclical policy will achieve prosperity. Such a policy would tend to eliminate the peaks as well as the troughs. For full employment more is required.

From the point of view of recovery our analysis has shown that the only policies which need to be considered are fiscal policy and wage policy. I have ruled out the vast array of measures such as NRA, AAA, and devaluation, except insofar as they were reflected in fiscal policy and the behavior of wages. For any other effects would have been reflected in changes in the behavior of consumers and investors, which remained substantially unchanged.

I have nothing further to add on wage policy. I am not concerned to debate the extent to which the actual behavior of wages can be regarded as the consequence of the government's policy. I would like, however, to remove one possible misunderstanding. Wage behavior proved disruptive in the thirties, first, because changes were abrupt and, second, because they contributed to an increase in construction costs in relation to other costs. To acknowledge this must not be interpreted as criticism of a wage policy which requires increases in money wages consistent with increased productivity of labor and stability of prices.

I have shown that before 1938 the fiscal policy of the government was a matter of accident and, in detail, was a mass of contradictions. Expansionary expenditure programs were the occasion for the introduction of regressive tax measures. I feel quite convinced that in the early days of the New Deal it was political infeasibility alone that prevented further measures of taxation. We have seen that the tax measures undertaken did not in fact have the desired results on the relation of consumption to income or the feared results on investment. The results of the new taxes must be judged by their over-all effects. These were to reduce private net output in relation to the total. By the end of the thirties it was necessary to rely on a greater rate of government production of goods and services to attain any given national income goal than at the beginning of the decade. On the other hand, the deficit required to attain that goal was smaller as a result of the New Deal taxes. Sometime the United States may have to make up its mind whether it wants to keep private enterprise or hold down the national debt.

The expenditure side of the government's policy was also contradictory. Expenditures were cut to help balance the "regular budget" while the "emergency budget" increased. Expenditures were determined by the need to relieve distress rather than by any consideration of the relation of fiscal policy to economic expansion. Nevertheless, the rate of expansion between 1933 and 1936 was remarkable. But in the light of what was accomplished in 1941, I am inclined to think that rate of expansion could have been greater had the fiscal policy been more ambitious. There were few bottlenecks in 1933, and if they appeared later it was due to the slowness rather than the rapidity of recovery. For instance, prolonged depression in the building industry did impair the skilled labor supply.

It has been alleged that the inflationary situation in 1937 was the consequence of the expansionary fiscal policy. But the expansion from 1938 to 1941 was attended with no phenomena which could be described as inflationary. I therefore cannot accept the explanation for 1937, especially since that inflation can be accounted for on other grounds—particularly the inventory boom which I have already discussed.

The 1937 experience has been used as an argument that an expansionary fiscal policy cannot be tapered off without creating a depression. The year 1937, however, is hardly a fair test since, as we have seen, it contained the seeds of a highly unstable situation not themselves the result of the fiscal policy. But I do agree that tapering off may cause difficulties. I am to some extent reassured on this point by the remarkable way in which the economy has withstood the "tapering off" of war expenditures in the last few months. The government did face a difficult situation in 1937. Full employment had not been achieved but inflation had. Hindsight leads me to the view that it would have been preferable to let the inflation run its course rather than to contribute to a serious depression.

After 1938 fiscal policy again made its full contribution to an unspectacular recovery through 1940. Rearmament and war produced full recovery, but postponed for a later depression the conclusion of the peacetime experiment.

My analysis of investment has led me to disagree with Professor Schumpeter's contention that reforms are per se anticapitalist and therefore depressive. But I do agree that in other ways reform impeded recovery. In the first place the abruptness of the wage increases in 1936 and 1937 can be to some extent attributed to the government's labor policy. In the second place, reform measures gave rise to some of the contradictions of fiscal policy. From the national income point of view, social security meant a highly deflationary tax which was offset to only a trivial extent by disbursement of benefits. But the consequences were accidental and not necessary incidents of reform. My conclusion from the thirties—to say nothing of the forties—is that the American economy can stand a lot of buffeting and that immediate profits can do wonders for business confidence.

V. CONCLUSION

My main conclusion on government policy from the experience of the thirties is that fiscal policy did prove to be an effective and indeed the only effective means to recovery. This conclusion does not, of course, imply that other methods could not have been effective; merely that these would have had to be applied much more drastically and vigorously than they were in the thirties. For instance, if the government were to assume complete control over wages and prices, it might prove possible to achieve recovery by that means alone. If the government were to push far enough the policy of monetary expansion which will be discussed by Mr. Means, I have little doubt that that too would lead to recovery. My own opinion, however, is that a flexible fiscal policy, which pays due attention to flexibility on both the expenditure and revenue sides, would provide the most conservative solution.

I do not mean by this that direct controls have no place in stabilization policy. On the contrary I do believe that a vigorous antimonopoly policy is necessary to prevent abuse of fiscal policy. But I doubt whether such a policy can be relied on to effect major redistributions of income. The evidence of the thirties suggests that the redistributions that did occur in that decade were the direct consequence of fiscal policy.

The thirties have demonstrated that fiscal policy can promote expansion without disturbing the structure of the economy, but as I have said, the last chapter remains to be written; and meanwhile I am left with the impression that the road from depression to enduring recovery is not an easy one.

I am convinced that it is much easier economically to avert depressions than to cure them. My argument leads to the conclusion that the thirties can be explained in terms of the cyclical process and were very largely the product of what had gone before. And that means that a depression of the same order can and probably will recur unless it is arrested by government action. One very eminent observer has described the New Deal as "the price we paid for time to think." At present I am afraid there is danger that we may become impervious to thought in the forties as we were in the twenties.

A Critique of Professor Smithies

GARDINER C. MEANS

We are all familiar with the "economic interpretation of history." I want to speak of Dr. Smithies' paper as a fiscal interpretation of history, for it suffers from the same kind of defect. It leaves out of account what does not fit the theory.

The biggest single omission is the lack of discussion of monetary policy (other than devaluation) and the effects of changes in the stock of money outstanding. Yet there was important action in this field. The government pursued monetary policies between 1929 and 1933 which brought about a reduction of the money stock of 8 billion dollars, or more than 25 per cent. In contrast the New Deal adopted a policy of monetary expansion, bringing about an increase in the stock of money of 14 billion dollars, or over 50 per cent. In our economy, which functions on the basis of money, you cannot increase the money supply by over 50 per cent and have no significant effect. Yet Dr. Smithies has neither mentioned these major changes in his analysis of the thirties nor shown that they are irrelevant.

Actually it would be about as easy to "explain" the level of employment statistically by changes in the stock of money and in the demand for money as by fiscal changes. A decline in the rate of money expansion just preceded the start of the big depression and actually contraction and declining activity went together. Likewise, in recovery, monetary expansion and increased activity went hand in hand with certain exceptions which are consistent with our knowledge of changes in the demand to hold cash. Statistically, as good a case can be made for a monetary as for a fiscal explanation. Or rather, the fiscal explanation is no better *and no worse* than the monetary.

Of course I do not believe that a monetary interpretation of history would be more valid than a fiscal interpretation. The problem is larger then either though I suspect that the monetary has a great deal to do with it. What I am immediately concerned with saying is that Dr. Smithies has given no weight to the major changes in monetary policy and money stocks and that I believe this omission invalidates both Dr. Smithies' major conclusion and much of his analysis. I do not believe he has established "that fiscal policy is the one major instrument for recovery or stabilization in a free society." Nor do I believe that "the United States will have to make up its mind whether it wants to keep private enterprise or hold down the national debt." Theoretically, I believe either fiscal policy or monetary policy alone could produce stability; but in practice we need

Reprinted by permission of the *American Economic Review*, Supplement, XXXVI (May, 1946), pp. 32–35.

to use both, with major emphasis on monetary policy. Through the proper emphasis on monetary policy, we can avoid a policy of cumulative government deficits and yet maintain an economy of full employment. And I believe that the evidence of the thirties if properly interpreted would give support to this thesis. But my immediate object is simply to point out that the evidence Dr. Smithies presents is subject to quite a different interpretation than that which he gives. Let us look at his evidence.

The evidence which he presents is to the effect "that, by and large, during the thirties both businesses and consumers were influenced in making their expenditure decisions by the same factor in the same way as in the twenties." But can you say this if you look at money? In the twenties, businesses and consumers in the aggregate were willing to spend on consumption and investment the whole of the money they received as income provided their "cash on hand" amounted to about 30 per cent of their current income. In the thirties the business and consumer community was unwilling to spend the whole of its current money income even though it held cash on hand equal to half its current income. I submit that this was a major shift and that until it is properly explained, one has not established that businesses and consumers were influenced by the same factors in the same way as in the twenties. And though a part of the difference can be explained by lower interest rates in the thirties the bulk cannot be so explained. So far as I have been able to discover, there was a fundamental shift in the preference of the community to hold money as compared with spending it on consumption or investment goods. If this is true, it means we must examine Dr. Smithies' statistical reasoning more carefully for the two conclusions do not appear to be consistent.

The two main elements in his reasoning are based on evidence (1) that the behavior of businesses with respect to investment in the thirties fitted the same formula which it fitted in the twenties and (2) that the expenditure on consumption in the thirties bore the same relation to disposable income that it did in the twenties. In neither case do I question the evidence involved. I question only the reasoning which leads to the conclusion that the propensities to invest and to consume were stable because of this formula fitting.

I can make the illogic of this position clear most easily in the case of consumption. Dr. Smithies' reasoning assumes, like that of so many other economists, that the regression of consumption on disposable income represents the propensity to consume. Yet it would be perfectly possible to have a propensity to consume which fluctuated from time to time and still have the observations in the time series fall on a smooth regression line. This would be true, for example, if the propensity to invest were a constant. It would also be true if some third factor, say the stock of money outstanding, or the demand for money influenced the propensity to consume and the propensity to invest so that when the stock of money outstanding was high the propensity to invest and consume would be high and when low both propensities would be low. Until these possibilities have been eliminated we cannot accept the time series regression of consumption on disposable income (whether in the aggregate or per capita) as representing the propensity to consume. Some analyses which I have made suggest that if either the investment propensity or the consumption propensity is stable, it is *more* likely to be the investment function. But probably neither is stable. And if the regression of consumption on income does not represent the consumption function then much of Dr. Smithies' evidence to support his exclusive fiscal theory falls by the wayside.

Two recent developments give added weight to the skeptical attitude I am displaying toward this fiscal theory, one in the field of statistical analysis and the other in the field of forecasting. Recent efforts to construct statistical statements of the investment function have produced formulae which give unacceptably high multipliers if the regression of consumption on disposable income is accepted as representing the propensity to consume. One worker whose analysis of investment produced an extravagant multiplier concluded that his statistical analysis must be wrong. He did not even consider the possibility that his theory was wrong.

The other development, that in the area of forecasting, involves the gross underestimates of employment after the war which have been made by many of the protagonists of the exclusive fiscal theory. The forecast of only 46 million employed in the last quarter of 1945 is belied by the actual figures of 51, 52, and 52 employed in October, November, and December. The error in the forecast arose primarily from adherence to the Keynesian assumption that consumer expenditure is a relatively stable function of disposable income. Actually it turned out that while disposable income went down somewhat consumer expenditure on nondurable goods went up by over 10 per cent.

It can be argued that this major departure from the prewar relation of nondurable goods demand to disposable income is a temporary matter resulting from the peculiarities of the transition. It is clear that returned veterans have to restock their wardrobes. The reduction of war tension and war restraint can produce a temporary splurge of spending. Certainly some of the increase in the demand for nondurables comes from this source and must be considered temporary. But is it all temporary? It seems to me likely that an important part is not. Indeed, last summer it was my opinion, as many in Washington can testify, that nondurable demand would increase considerably, relative to disposable income, when the war came to an end, partly because of the temporary factors already mentioned and partly because the huge cash balances and other liquid assets held by the community would have the more or less permanent effect of increasing the propensity to consume. The possession of large cash balances would lead to the spending of a larger proportion of current income on consumption, including the consumption of nondurable goods. This is an effect which is independent of the heavy backlog of demand for durable goods. Since I have taken this position, I naturally interpret the increased propensity to consume as being more than temporary. Indeed I do not think the full rise in the propensity to consume has yet expressed itself. Many nondurable goods are not available in the quantity or in the quality which is wanted. If there were not serious limits on the supply of nondurables at present prices, I believe that nondurable sales would increase considerably relative to disposable income and only a part of the increase would be of a temporary character.

We will have to wait—perhaps a number of years—before we can be sure that there has been a significant and continuing upward shift in the propensity to consume. It is my prediction that events will show such an increase. If this prediction is vindicated it would seem to me pretty clear evidence that the propensity to consume is not fixed but is affected by the volume of money outstanding and can be increased or decreased by increasing or decreasing the total stock.

I have gone into this matter of the employment forecasts in some detail because a very basic issue appears to be involved. If the propensity to consume can be increased by an increase in the real money supply, the Keynesian theory of employment *cannot* be valid and the contribution which monetary policy can make to a program of economic stability is very much greater than the Keynesian theory would indicate. Even a secular tendency to oversave could be overcome without a continuing government deficit. In this case, a fiscal interpretation of history might have to give way to a monetary interpretation or a blend of the two in which monetary elements were dominant.

FOR FURTHER READING: An excellent account is by E. Cary Brown, "Fiscal Policy in the Thirties: A Reappraisal," *American Economic Review*, XLVI (December, 1956), pp. 857–879. Milton Friedman and Anna J. Schwartz, *A Monetary History of the United States, 1867–1900* (Princeton, 1963) touches on the 1930's with a monetary bias. An excellent chapter on the New Deal is in Herbert Stein, *The Fiscal Revolution in America* (Chicago, 1969).

16

BIG BUSINESS
IN THE 1950's:
BIGNESS AND
EFFICIENCY

PROBLEM: *Is big or small business more efficient?*

The steady multiplication of giant business enterprises in the United States during the twentieth century has led to much discussion about the relationship between size and efficiency. Have large industrial units prospered primarily because of the economic advantages which they bring? Economists have divided over the issue and have produced plausible arguments on both sides. In defense of bigness, one of America's outstanding economists, the late Sumner H. Slichter of Harvard University, stressed the economic superiority of large-scale business combinations. He thought their technological efficiency to be especially important. Consequently Slichter believed that federal restraints on corporate mergers should be relaxed to allow greater economies in production. Competition then would actually be increased as scientific research in industries dominated by a few large firms would lead them into more active rivalry. This prescription was viewed rather skeptically by George Stigler of the University of Chicago, another eminent economist. Stigler strenuously opposed the formation of powerful and highly centralized business units. In the first place, he questioned the assumption that Big Business is always more efficient than its smaller counterparts, for evidence reveals that at times just the reverse might be true. Moreover, he argued that the monopolistic behavior of great corporations led them to adopt policies that were socially undesirable, such as the suppression of small competitors. He decried, too, the disproportionately large political influence of Big Business which stimulated the growth of Big Labor and Big Government. For these reasons Stigler believed that mergers should be made more difficult so that a highly competitive economy could be encouraged. Both of these writers provide concise summaries of arguments that are frequently used in the debate over this issue. Why is competition desirable? What are the advantages and disadvantages of Big Business? How can present trends toward greater business consolidation be altered?

The Case for Bigness in Business

SUMNER H. SLICHTER

The 1957 decision of the Supreme Court in the du Pont-General Motors case suggests the desirability of a review and an appraisal of American policy toward competition, monopoly, and bigness in business. The decision reveals the strong determination of the court to prevent competition from being weakened and the court's willingness to resort to controversial interpretations of the law in order to implement the public policy of preventing restraints on competition.

But the decision also reminds us that much thinking on the relation of bigness to competition is out of date and unrealistic. Hence, the adaptation of traditional American antitrust policy to the facts of modern industry requires that we take a fresh look at the role of large enterprises in American business—particularly the role of large enterprises as a source of vigorous and dynamic competition.

When one compares the economy of the United States with the economies of other advanced industrial countries, four characteristics stand out conspicuously.

1. The government of the United States endeavors through broad and drastic laws to prevent restraints on competition and to forestall the growth of monopoly. Most other advanced industrial countries either tolerate considerable restraint on competition or even encourage organizations of business men that are designed to control competition.

2. Competition in American industry is far more vigorous and pervasive

than in the industries of any other advanced industrial country. Indeed, the vigor of competition in the United States almost invariably attracted comment from the European productivity teams that visited this country in the years following the war.

3. The United States has many more huge business enterprises than any other country. Several years ago this country had more than 100 corporations (exclusive of purely financial ones) with assets of more than $250 million each. General Motors produces far more cars than the combined British, German and French automobile industries, and the United States Steel Corporation produces more steel than the entire British steel industry.

4. Production in many American industries (especially those requiring large capital investment) is highly concentrated in the hands of a few large concerns. As a general rule, the concentration of production in other industrial countries is far less than here.

These four characteristics of the American economy are not unrelated. It would be wrong to ascribe the widespread and intense competition in American industry *solely* to the strong public policy against restraint of trade, monopolization and interference with competition. Conditions in the United States—the absence of class lines, the abundance of opportunity, the weakness of tradition—have long made life here highly competitive in all its aspects, and competition in business is just one manifestation of this general competitive spirit. But America's unique and firm public policy against restraints on competition has undoubtedly helped greatly to keep industry here strongly competitive.

This strong policy, however, has paradoxically encouraged the development of giant industrial corporations and the concentration of production in many industries among a few large concerns. The growth of enterprises in Europe has been limited by the practice of forming cartels—a practice which governments have tolerated and even encouraged. The cartel or trade association divides markets among its members, limits the growth of the most efficient concerns, and assures the weak, high-cost concern a share of the market.

In the United States, where cartels are illegal, each concern is pretty completely exposed to competition from all other firms, and business goes to the firms that can get it. This means that in many industries production is gradually concentrated in the hands of a few industrial giants, and only a small part of the business is left for small firms.

The trend toward corporate bigness in industry has led many students of anti-monopoly policy to believe that the American policy of encouraging competition and discouraging monopoly is turning out to be a failure and to conclude that steps need to be taken to limit the influences of large enterprises in American industry. Of many proposals that have been made, two principal ones are of particular interest.

One proposal is that new restrictions be placed on mergers. Some have urged that no merger be permitted which cannot be justified by techno-logical reasons. Some have proposed that mergers involving a corporation above a given size be prohibited unless found by the Federal Trade Com-mission to be in the public interest.

The second proposal deals with the concentration of production in various industries into a few enterprises. It is urged that the government undertake a comprehensive survey of American industry to determine whether enterprises exceed the size required by modern technology and that the government be authorized to break up firms that are un-necessarily large.

Both of these proposals are based on fallacy. They rest upon a mistaken conception of the role of large corporations in American business and particularly upon the relation of large corporations to competition. Each, if put into effect, would weaken rather than strengthen competition. In fact, in order to stimulate competition, existing restrictions on mergers should be relaxed, not tightened, and large enterprises, instead of being threatened with breakup, should be given a clear mandate to grow, pro-vided they use fair means. Let us examine more completely each of these two proposals to restrict the growth of enterprises.

The proposal that new restrictions be placed on mergers arises from the fact that the United States in recent years has been experiencing a great wave of mergers. But recent mergers have not weakened compe-tition. On the contrary, they have indirectly strengthened it because they have enabled managements to build more diversified and better-integrated enterprises—enterprises which are more capable of reaching all parts of the vast domestic market, of adapting themselves to market shifts and changes in technology, of riding out the ups and downs of business, and of supporting technological research and development. Many large firms and firms of moderate size have acquired small firms, but the acquisitions by the very largest firms have not been numerous.

The specific circumstances surrounding each merger are unique, but a case-by-case examination shows how mergers are helping to build stronger enterprises, better able to compete and to hold their own in competition.

Let us consider a few examples. A maker of cans bought a concern manufacturing plastic pipe in order to get a foothold in the plastic pipe business. A maker of railroad freight cars bought companies making electrical equipment, truck trailers and dairy supplies in order to shift from a declining business to expanding businesses. A food manufacturer bought a West Coast manufacturer of salad seasoning in order to give nation-wide distribution to its product. A maker of household ware bought a supplier in order to have a source of pressed wood handles for its appliances.

Unusually competent managements often buy other concerns so that they can spread good administrative methods to less efficiently operated enterprises.

The many advantages produced by mergers show that the proposal that mergers be prohibited unless they can be justified by technological reasons does not make sense. There are good reasons for mergers that have nothing to do with technology.

Moreover, it would be unwise to require government approval of all mergers involving an enterprise above a specified size. That would be substituting the decision of government officials for the decision of businessmen on matters that the businessmen are better able to understand. The public interest is amply protected by the present drastic provision of Section 7 of the Clayton Act.

Indeed, the fact that mergers often make for more vigorous competition by helping managements build stronger and more efficient business enterprises indicates the need for relaxing the present severe restrictions on mergers contained in Section 7 of the Clayton Act. This section prohibits any merger which is likely to lessen competition substantially in *any* line of commerce. The fact that the merger may increase the intensity of competition in *other* lines of commerce makes no difference. As Section 7 now reads, the *total effect* of the merger on competition is irrelevant. If it is likely to lessen competition substantially in any one line of commerce, it is illegal.

Obviously the section, as it now reads, conflicts with the national policy of encouraging competition. It should be rewritten to make the legality of mergers depend upon the *total* effect of competition, thus permitting any merger that has the net effect of increasing competition.

The second proposal—to remake the structure of American industry by breaking up the largest enterprises—rests upon the mistaken view that, where output is concentrated among a few concerns, effective competition does not occur. The error of this view is shown by the vigorous competition in various industries in which most of the output is made by a few firms—in such industries as the automobile, tire, refrigerator, soap, cigarette, paper products, television and many others.

There are two principal reasons why competition tends to be vigorous when production is concentrated among a few large concerns. One is that such enterprises keep close track of their rank in sales and fight hard to move ahead of rivals or to avoid being surpassed by rivals. The second reason, and one that is rapidly gaining in importance, is the fact that competition among large firms is being stimulated by the growth of technological research.

It is only within the last several decades that managements have generally discovered the big returns yielded by technological research. As a result, the outlays by private industry on research and development increased nearly six-fold between 1940 and 1953. In 1957, the total research and development expenditures of private industry, exclusive of the aircraft industry, which is a special case, are running about 71 per cent greater than they were in 1953. By 1960 outlays on research are expected to be 21 per cent above 1957.

No expenditures are more competitive than outlays on research, for the purpose of these expenditures is to improve products, develop new products and cut costs. More than 70 per cent of the outlays on research and development are made by firms with 5,000 or more employees because concerns with large sales can best afford this overhead expense. Hence the rapidly mounting outlays on research indicate both the growing competitiveness of American industry and the increasingly important role large enterprises are playing in making competition more intense.

Incidentally, competition among large firms is superior in quality to competition among small firms and serves consumers more effectively. This is because the greater research by the large firms gives the consumers a wider range of choice over a period of years than competition among a much larger number of small firms that can afford little or no research. In general, the wider the range of choice open to consumers, the more effectively is the welfare of consumers advanced.

In view of the growing importance of large enterprises as a source of competition and the superior quality of this competition, a move to break up large concerns would be a blunder. There is much to be said, however, in favor of incentives for enterprises to split themselves voluntarily, if the managements consider a split desirable. The resulting increase in the number of top managements with independent authority to make policies and to try experiments would be favorable to technological progress—provided the concerns are large enough to support extensive research. A good incentive for voluntary splits would be created by relieving stockholders from liability for the capital gains tax on the appreciation of their holdings from the time they purchased the stock up to the date of the split.

But enforced splitting of enterprises, except as a remedy for flagrant monopolizing of trade by unscrupulous methods, would be another matter. In fact, the present law needs to be clarified in order to encourage a few of the very largest concerns to strive harder for a bigger share of the market. The managements of a few very large and efficient concerns apparently feel that efforts to get more business by cutting prices will be held to be attempts to monopolize. There is need to make clear that efforts to win business by giving consumers the benefits of low costs will not be regarded as monopolistic.

Americans need to understand that a variety of conditions—rapidly changing technology, the growing importance of industrial research, the growing strength of trade unions—tend to increase in many industries the size of the enterprise that is able both to compete and to survive in competition. Hence, we are likely to see a spread of the tendency for production to be concentrated in a few large or fairly large firms.

But this trend, if it occurs, should not disturb us. It will simply represent an adaptation of industry to the conditions of the time.

The Case against Big Business

GEORGE J. STIGLER

. . . Bigness in business has two primary meanings. First, bigness may be defined in terms of the company's share of the industry in which it operates: a big company is one that has a big share of the market or industry. By this test Texas Gulf Sulphur is big because it produces more than half the sulfur in America, and Macy's (whose annual sales are much larger) is small because it sells only a very small fraction of the goods sold by New York City retail stores. By this definition, many companies that are small in absolute size are nevertheless big—the only brick company in a region, for example—and many companies that are big in absolute size (Inland Steel, for example) are small. Second, bigness may mean absolute size—the measure of size being assets, sales, or employment as a rule. Then General Motors and U.S. Steel are the prototypes of bigness.

These two meanings overlap because most companies that are big in absolute size are also big in relation to their industries. There are two types of cases, however, in which the two meanings conflict. On the one hand, many companies of small absolute size are dominant in small markets or industries. I shall not discuss them here (although they require attention in a well-rounded antitrust program) for two reasons: they seldom have anywhere near so much power as the companies that are big relative to large markets and industries; and they raise few political problems of the type I shall discuss below. On the other hand, there are a few companies that are big in absolute size but small relative to their markets—I have already given Macy's as an example. These companies are not very important in the total picture, and I shall also put them aside in the following discussion.

For my purposes, then, big businesses will mean businesses that are absolutely large in size and large also relative to the industries in which they operate. They are an impressive list: U.S. Steel, Bethlehem, and Republic in steel, General Electric and Westinghouse in electrical equipment, General Motors, Ford, and Chrysler in automobiles, du Pont, Union Carbide, and Allied Chemical among others in chemicals, Reynolds, Liggett & Myers, and American Tobacco in cigarettes.

Reprinted from the May, 1952 issue of *Fortune* magazine by special permission; © 1952 Time Inc.

What bigness does not mean is perhaps equally important. Bigness has no reference to the size of industries. I for one am tired of the charge that the critics of the steel industry vacillate between finding the output too large and too small: at various times the industry's output has been too small; for fifty years the largest firm has been too large. Concerted action by many small companies often leads to over-capacity in an industry: it is the basic criticism of resale price maintenance, for example, that it encourages the proliferation of small units by fixing excessive retail margins. Industries dominated by one or a few firms—that is, big businesses—seldom err in this direction. Nor does bigness have any direct reference to the methods of production, and opposition to big business is usually compatible with a decent respect for the "economies of large-scale production," on which more later.

The fundamental objection to bigness stems from the fact that big companies have monopolistic power, and this fundamental objection is clearly applicable outside the realm of corporate business. In particular, big unions are open to all the criticisms (and possibly more) that can be levied against big business. I shall not discuss labor unions, but my silence should not be construed as a belief that we should have a less stringent code for unions than for business.

There are two fundamental criticisms to be made of big businesses: they act monopolistically, and they encourage and justify bigness in labor and government.

First, as to monopoly. When a small number of firms control most or all of the output of an industry, they can individually and collectively profit more by cooperation than by competition. This is fairly evident, since cooperatively they can do everything they can do individually, and other things (such as the charging of noncompetitive prices) besides. These few companies, therefore, will usually cooperate.

From this conclusion many reasonable men, including several Supreme Court justices, will dissent. Does not each brand of cigarettes spend huge sums in advertising to lure us away from some other brand? Do not the big companies—oligopolists, the economists call them—employ salesmen? Do not the big companies introduce constant innovations in their products?

The answer is that they do compete—but not enough, and not in all the socially desirable ways. Those tobacco companies did not act competitively, but with a view to extermination, against the 10-cent brands in the 1930's, nor have they engaged in price competition in decades (*American Tobacco vs. United States, 328 U.S. 781*). The steel companies, with all their salesmen, abandoned cartel pricing via basing-point prices only when this price system was judged a conspiracy in restraint of trade in cement (*Federal Trade Commission vs. Cement Institute, 333 U.S. 683*). The plain fact is that big businesses do not engage in continuous price competition.

Nor is price the only area of agreement. Patent licensing has frequently been used to deprive the licensees of any incentive to engage in research; General Electric used such agreements also to limit other companies' output and fix the prices of incandescent lamps (*U.S. vs General Electric, 82 F. Supp. 753*). The hearings of the Bone Committee are adorned with numerous examples of the deliberate deterioration of goods in order to maintain sales. For example, Standard Oil Development (a subsidiary of the Jersey company) persuaded Socony-Vacuum to give up the sale of a higher-potency commodity (pour-point depressant) whose sale at the same price had been characterized as "merely price cutting."

Very well, big businesses often engage in monopolistic practices. It may still be objected that it has not been shown that all big businesses engage in monopolistic practices, or that they engage in such practices all, or even most of, the time. These things cannot be shown or even fully illustrated in a brief survey, and it is also not possible to summarize the many court decisions and the many academic studies of big business. But it is fair to say that these decisions and studies show that big businesses usually possess monopolistic power, and use it. And that is enough.

For economic policy must be contrived with a view to the typical rather than the exceptional, just as all other policies are contrived. That some drivers can safely proceed at eighty miles an hour is no objection to a maximum-speed law. So it is no objection to an anti-trust policy that some unexercised monopoly power is thereby abolished. (Should there be some big businesses that forgo the use of their dominant position, it is difficult to see what advantage accrues from private ownership, for the profit motive is already absent.)

Second, as to bigness in labor and government. Big companies have a large—I would say an utterly disproportionate—effect on public thinking. The great expansion of our labor unions has been due largely to favoring legislation and administration by the federal government. This policy of favoring unions rests fundamentally upon the popular belief that workers individually competing for jobs will be exploited by big-business employers —that U.S. Steel can in separate negotiation (a pretty picture!) overwhelm each of its hundreds of thousands of employees. In good part this is an absurd fear: U.S. Steel must compete with many other industries, and not merely other steel companies, for good workers.

Yet the fear may not be wholly absurd: there may be times and places where big businesses have "beaten down" wages, although I believe such cases are relatively infrequent. (In any event, the reaction to the fear has been unwise: for every case where big business has held down workers there are surely many cases where big unions have held up employers.) But it cannot be denied that this public attitude underlies our national labor policy, the policy of local governments of condoning violence in labor disputes, etc.

Big business has also made substantial contributions to the growth of big government. The whole agricultural program has been justified as necessary to equalize agriculture's bargaining power with "industry," meaning big business. The federally sponsored milkshed cartels are defended as necessary to deal with the giant dairy companies.

Big business is thus a fundamental excuse for big unions and big government. It is true that the scope and evils of big business are usually enormously exaggerated, especially with reference to labor and agriculture, and that more often than not these evils are merely a soapbox excuse for shoddy policies elsewhere. To this large extent, there is need for extensive education of the public on how small a part of the economy is controlled by big business. But in light of the widespread monopolistic practices—our first criticism of bigness—it is impossible to tell the public that its fears of big business are groundless. We have no right to ask public opinion to veer away from big unions and big government—and toward big business.

Are we dependent upon big businesses for efficient methods of production and rapid advances in production methods? If we are, the policy of breaking up big businesses would lower our future standard of living and many people would cast about for other ways than dissolution to meet the problems of bigness.

A company may be efficient because it produces and sells a given amount of product with relatively small amounts of material, capital, and labor, or it may be efficient because it acquires the power to buy its supplies at unusually low prices and sell its products at unusually high prices. Economists refer to these as the social and the private costs of production respectively. Big businesses may be efficient in the social sense, and usually they also possess, because of their monopoly position, private advantages. But the ability of a company to employ its dominant position to coerce unusually low prices from suppliers is not of any social advantage.

It follows that even if big companies had larger profit rates or smaller costs per unit of output than other companies, this would not prove that they were more efficient in socially desirable ways. Actually, big businesses are generally no more and no less efficient than medium-sized businesses even when the gains wrung by monopoly power are included in efficiency. This is the one general finding in comparative cost studies and comparative profitability studies. Indeed, if one reflects upon the persistence of small and medium-sized companies in the industries dominated by big businesses, it is apparent that there can be no great advantages to size. If size were a great advantage, the smaller companies would soon lose the unequal race and disappear.

When we recall that most big businesses have numerous complete plants at various points throughout the country, this finding is not surprising. Why should U.S. Steel be more efficient than Inland Steel, when

U.S. Steel is simply a dozen or more Inland Steels strewn about the country? Why should G.M. be appreciably more efficient than, say, a once-again independent Buick Motors? A few years ago Peter Drucker reported:

The divisional manager . . . is in complete charge of production and sales. He hires, fires and promotes; and it is up to him to decide how many men he needs, with what qualifications and in what salary range—except for top executives whose employment is subject to a central-management veto. The divisional manager decides the factory layout, the technical methods and equipment used. . . . He buys his supplies independently from suppliers of his own choice. He determines the distribution of production within the several plants under his jurisdiction, decides which lines to push and decides on the methods of sale and distribution. . . . In everything pertaining to operations he is as much the real head as if his division were indeed an independent business.

If big businesses are not more efficient as a rule, how did they get big? The answer is that most giant firms arose out of mergers of many competing firms, and were created to eliminate competition. Standard Oil, General Electric, Westinghouse, U.S. Steel, Bethlehem, the meat packers, Borden, National Dairy, American Can, etc.—the full list of merger-created big businesses is most of the list of big businesses. A few big businesses owe their position to an industrial genius like Ford, and of course future geniuses would be hampered by an effective antitrust law— but less so than by entrenched monopolies or by public regulatory commissions.

We do not know what share of improvements in technology has been contributed by big businesses. Big businesses have made some signal contributions, and so also have small businesses, universities, and private individuals. It can be said that manufacturing industries dominated by big businesses have had no larger increases in output per worker on average than other manufacturing industries. This fact is sufficient to undermine the easy identification of economic progress with the laboratories of big businesses, but it does not inform us of the net effect of monopolies on economic progress.

At present, then, no definite effect of big business on economic progress can be established. I personally believe that future study will confirm the traditional belief that big businesses, for all their resources, cannot rival the infinite resource and cold scrutiny of many independent and competing companies. If the real alternative to bigness is government regulation or ownership, as I am about to argue, then the long-run consequences of big business are going to be highly adverse to economic progress.

Let me restate the main points of the foregoing discussion in a less emphatic—and I think also a less accurate—manner:

1. Big businesses often possess and use monopoly power.
2. Big businesses weaken the political support for a private-enterprise system.

3. Big businesses are not appreciably more efficient or enterprising than medium-sized businesses.

Few disinterested people will deny these facts—where do they lead?

A considerable section of the big-business community seems to have taken the following position. The proper way to deal with monopolistic practices is to replace the general prohibitions of the Sherman Act by a specific list of prohibited practices, so businessmen may know in advance and avoid committing monopolistic practices. The proper way to deal with the declining political support for private enterprise is to advertise the merits of private enterprise, at the same time claiming many of its achievements for big business. Much of this advertising has taken literally that form, apparently in the belief that one can sell a social system in exactly the same way and with exactly the same copywriters and media that one sells a brand of cigarettes.

The request for a list of specifically prohibited monopolistic practices will be looked upon by many persons as a surreptitious attack upon the Sherman Act. I am among these cynics: the powerful drive in 1949 to pass a law legalizing basing-point price systems is sufficient evidence that large sectors of big business are wholly unreconciled to the law against conspiracies in restraint of trade. Even when the request for a specific list of prohibitions is made in all sincerity, however, it cannot be granted: No one can write down a full list of all the forms that objectionable monopoly power has taken and may someday take. Moreover, almost all uncertainties over the legality of conduct arise out of the Robinson-Patman Act, not the Sherman Act, and I would welcome the complete repeal of the former act.[1]

We must look elsewhere for the solution of the problems raised by big business, and a satisfactory solution must deal with the facts I listed at the head of this section. Our present policy is not a satisfactory solution. The Sherman Act is admirable in dealing with formal conspiracies of many firms, but—at least with the Supreme Court's present conception of competition and of the proper remedies for demonstrated restraint of trade in oligopolistic industries—it cannot cope effectively with the problem posed by big business. In industries dominated by a few firms there is no need for formal conspiracies, with their trappings of quotas, a price-fixing committee, and the like. The big companies know they must "live with" one another, and the phrase means much the same thing as in the

---

[1] The prohibition against price discrimination was partly designed to cope with a real evil the use by a large company of its monopoly power to extort preferential terms from suppliers. This exercise of monopoly, however, constitutes a violation of the Sherman Act, and no additional legislation is necessary if this act can be made fully effective. The Robinson-Patman Act, and certain other parts of the so-called "antitrust" amendments, also have another and objectionable purpose: to supervise and regulate the routine operations of businesses in order to ensure that they will display the symptoms of competitive behavior.

relationship between man and woman. Any competitive action one big company takes will lead to retaliation by the others. An informal code of behavior gradually develops in the industry: Firm X announces the new price, and except in very unusual circumstances Y and Z can be relied upon to follow. So long as there are a few big businesses in an industry, we simply cannot expect more than the tokens of competitive behavior. Antitrust decrees that the big businesses should ignore each other's existence serve no important purpose.[2]

This conclusion, I must emphasize, is not merely that of "economic theorists," although most (academic) economists will subscribe to it. It is also the conclusion our generation is reaching, for our generation is not satisfied with the behavior of big business. More and more, big businesses are being asked to act in "the social interest," and more and more, government is interfering in their routine operation. The steel industry, for example, what with congressional review of prices and presidential coercion of wages, is drifting rapidly into a public-utility status. And the drift will not be stopped by slick advertising.

No such drastic and ominous remedy as the central direction of economic life is necessary to deal with the problems raised by big business. The obvious and economical solution, as I have already amply implied, is to break up the giant companies. This, I would emphasize, is the minimum program, and it is essentially a conservative program. Dissolution of big businesses is a once-for-all measure in each industry (if the recent anti-merger amendment to the Clayton Act is adequately enforced), and no continuing interference in the private operation of business is required or desired. Dissolution involves relatively few companies; one dissolves three or four big steel companies, and leaves the many smaller companies completely alone. Dissolution does not even need to be invoked in a large part of the economy: some of our biggest industries, such as textiles, shoes, and most food industries, will require no antitrust action.

A policy of "trust busting" requires no grant of arbitrary powers to any administrative agency; the policy can be administered by the Anti-

---

[2] In the National Lead case (*67 Sup. Ct. 1634, 1947*) this company and du Pont were convicted of violating the Sherman Act. The two companies produced about 90 percent of all titanium, but the Court refused to order divestiture of plants. The Court documented the "vigorous and effective competition between National Lead and du Pont" with the fact that "The general manager of the pigments department of du Pont characterized the competition with Zirconium and Virginia Chemical as 'tough' and that [with] National Lead as 'plenty tough.'" Economists will always find such testimony an inadequate demonstration of competition. Even more unfortunate was the refusal of the Court to order divestiture of foreign holdings of the Timken Roller Bearing Company, which had also been convicted under the Sherman Act (*71 Sup. Ct. 971, 1951*). Here Mr. Justice Reed, the Chief Justice concurring, argues that so "harsh" a remedy as divestiture should be invoked only in extreme cases, perhaps forgetting that inadequate remedies for monopoly are "harsh" treatment of the public interest.

trust Division acting through the courts. It is sufficient, and it is desirable, that the policy be directed against companies whose possession of monopoly power is demonstrated, and that dissolution be the basic remedy for the concentration of control in an industry that prevents or limits competition. Indeed, the policy requires new legislation only to the extent of convincing the courts that an industry which does not have a competitive structure will not have competitive behavior.

The dissolution of big businesses is only a part of the program necessary to increase the support for a private, competitive enterprise economy, and reverse the drift toward government control. But it is an essential part of this program, and the place for courage and imagination. Those conservatives who cling to the status quo do not realize that the status quo is a state of change, and the changes are coming fast. If these changes were to include the dissolution of a few score of our giant companies, however, we shall have done much to preserve private enterprise and the liberal-individualistic society of which it is an integral part.

FOR FURTHER READING: The advantages and disadvantages of Big Business are clearly discussed in Clair Wilcox, *Competition and Monopoly in American Industry*, Temporary National Economic Committee, Monograph #21 (Washington, 1940). Joe S. Bain, "Economies of Scale, Concentration, and Entry," *American Economic Review*, XLIV (March, 1954), pp. 15–39, finds that the evidence does not justify a clear stand on the issue. More positive are Joseph Schumpeter, the great Austrian economist, in *Capitalism, Socialism, and Democracy* (New York, 1942), David Lilienthal, *Big Business: A New Era* (New York, 1952), Adolph A. Berle, *The Twentieth Century Capitalist Revolution* (New York, 1958), and John Chamberlain, *The Roots of Capitalism* (Princeton, 1959). Opposed to the concentration of power are George W. Stocking and Myron Watkins, *Monopoly and Free Enterprise* (New York, 1951), and. George W. Stocking, *Workable Competition and Anti-Trust Policy* (Nashville, 1961). Also useful in this connection is John K. Galbraith, *American Capitalism* (New York, 1952).

17

BLACK
CAPITALISM
IN THE 1960's

PROBLEM: *Was integration or self-sufficiency the best means to improve the economic status of black Americans?*

Out of the heat of the civil rights movement during the post World War II decade came a hard-headed appraisal by black leaders of necessary new policies to secure greater economic equality for black Americans. Throughout the troubled Sixties they proposed various alternative plans to achieve this goal. Two of the most widely discussed proposals are noted below. One possible solution was offered by Dr. Andrew F. Brimmer, a member of the Federal Reserve Board, who was also one of the most distinguished black economists in the nation. Dr. Brimmer was an unabashed advocate of economic integration, arguing that black Americans needed to be fully included in the mainstream of American economic life. At a time when American business enterprise was tending toward centralization and the expansion of large corporations Brimmer felt that it would be futile to expect independent, black, small-scale businessmen to succeed in face of the dominant trend toward bigness. He saw lack of capital, lack of markets, and lack of skill as major obstacles. Where small black entrepreneurs had succeeded in previous years their reliance on segregated markets—due to racial discrimination—had been a prime factor. And with greater racial integration after 1960 black businessmen were even facing discrimination in these fields, of which undertaking was one example. Thus, Dr. Brimmer firmly believed that the path to black economic

315

equality lay in the entry of black Americans into every sector of the American economy, but especially into all levels within large American corporations. Such a solution would be as realistic as it was practical. But Brimmer's analysis was directly challenged by Roy Innis, an advocate of black power who became director of the Congress for Racial Equality (CORE) in 1968. Innis placed great stress on separate, independent, black economic enterprise, and eschewed integration of black Americans into the white economic structure. Thus, he urged the creation of new black economic institutions, black control of business enterprises and consumer markets. The issues raised by these two black leaders were profound. Are their proposals realistic? Which program promises greatest benefits for black Americans? What cultural values affect their economic thought?

The Negro in the National Economy

ANDREW F. BRIMMER

The Negro lives and works in the backwaters and eddies of the national economy in the United States. This has been true since he arrived on these shores long before the colonies became a nation. In recent years, Negroes have made a number of vigorous advances in their efforts to enter the mainstream of economic activity. However, they remain at best a marginal factor in virtually every field, except those protected by the legacy of racial segregation and discrimination. Yet, the winds of change are blowing across the land, shaking old arrangements and creating new opportunities for men with imagination and enterprise. . . .

An appraisal of the Negro's role in the national economy can be approached in a number of ways. One alternative is to chronicle the progress the Negro has made within the long-term development of the economy as a whole. This approach would be primarily historical and descriptive. Since the record of the Negro's progress is impressive, the result might be both a colorful document and a monument to perseverance against great obstacles.

Another alternative is to highlight the strategic factors influencing the conditions under which Negroes participate in the economy and share the

From "The Negro in the National Economy" by Andrew F. Brimmer from *The American Negro Reference Book*, edited by John P. Davis. © 1966 by Prentice-Hall, Inc. Published by Prentice-Hall, Inc., Englewood Cliffs, New Jersey 07632.

benefits of national production. This approach, which is basically analytic and statistical, emphasizes the Negro's adaptation to the malfunctioning of the market place. In general, both resource allocation and income shares are determined by the price system in an economy such as that found in the United States. But the existence of racial discrimination and the mosaic of social disorganization associated with segregation have severely restricted the Negro's opportunities to acquire skills and property and to offer them in exchange for income. Partly because of the resulting limited ability to earn—but also because of additional barriers—the Negro in turn has a restricted access to the market for consumer goods and services.

The effect of these constraints has been essentially the same as that produced by a protective tariff in international trade: two markets have emerged. One is open to the white public virtually without limitations, and whites are free to purchase both goods and services with complete freedom of choice. However, for Negroes entry into this market is extremely circumscribed. While they enjoy considerable freedom of choice in the purchase of goods (except housing), a wide range of services (especially personal services) offered to the general market is unavailable to them. Consequently, a second market has arisen. This is basically a Negro market, and the provision of personal services lies at its core. Thus, the Negro market is entirely derivative; it has evolved behind the walls of segregation to meet a demand left unfilled by business firms operating in the general market. . . .

As mentioned above, segregation has served the Negro businessman in the same way a tariff protects an infant industry. With the removal or reduction of a tariff wall, major adjustments must be made by those who have benefited from its existence. The Negro businessman is faced with such an adjustment. As the process of desegregation permeates the marketplace, Negro-owned businesses (the vast majority of which concentrate on providing personal services in a segregated market) are faced with increased competition from firms catering to buyers with a decreasing reference to race.

The consequences of this process are already evident. Because we have only fragmentary statistics on Negro-owned business, it is difficult to chart these trends with precision. However, since the vast majority of Negro businesses are single proprietorships—rather than partnerships or corporations—Bureau of the Census statistics on self-employed managers, proprietors and officials give a fair indication of the scope of Negro business. These statistics are summarized in Table 1.

Even a cursory analysis of the evidence clearly demonstrates the heavy dependence of Negro businessmen on the segregated Negro market. Where Negro customers have relatively free access to goods and services sold in the general marketplace, Negro businessmen have made little headway against the strong competition of white firms. In 1960, Negroes con-

TABLE 1

SELF-EMPLOYED BUSINESSMEN, BY RACE AND INDUSTRY, 1950 AND 1960

Industry	1950			1960			Annual Average Percentage Rate of Growth 1950–1960		Median Income			
									1949		1959	
	Total[1]	Negro	Negro as % of Total	Total	Negro	Negro as % of Total	Total	Negro	White Males	Non-white Males	White Males	Non-white Males
Construction	191,820	3,390	1.7	222,601	3,978	1.8	1.7	1.6	$3,873	$1,992	$6,756	$3,239
Manufacturing	231,210	1,050	0.4	168,395	1,376	0.8	-3.1	2.7	4,700	2,250*	7,998	3,503
Transportation	50,940	2,430	4.7	38,223	1,241	3.2	-2.9	-6.5	3,535	2,250*	6,638	2,792
Communications, utilities and sanitary serv.	4,260	270	6.3	4,812	82	1.7	1.2	-11.2	3,310	2,500	7,138	3,500*
Wholesale trade	174,240	2,640	1.5	133,607	2,610	1.9	-2.6	-0.1	4,336	1,250*	7,813	2,693
Retail trade	1,349,190	38,730	2.8	994,425	26,303	2.6	-3.0	-3.8	3,277	1,838	5,332	3,511
Food and dairy prods.	376,350	14,520	3.9	214,758	8,740	4.1	-5.5	-4.9	2,875	1,819	4,464	3,487
Eating and drinking places	270,720	15,030	5.5	203,830	11,344	5.6	-2.9	-2.9	3,114	1,870	4,990	3,170
Genl. mdse. and ltd. price variety	63,690	750	1.2	46,406	640	1.3	-3.1	-1.6	3,211	2,000	5,416	2,500*
Apparel and accessories	82,140	600	0.7	56,722	321	0.6	-3.6	-5.9	4,725	1,250*	7,292	4,500*
Furniture and homefurn.	66,210	360	0.5	49,946	182	0.4	-2.9	-6.1	3,931	2,250*	6,923	5,500*
Motor vehicles and access.	58,590	180	0.3	55,476	163	0.3	-0.5	-0.9	6,367	2,000	7,460	3,500*
Gasoline service stations	143,010	1,290	0.9	152,294	2,153	1.4	0.6	5.3	2,906	2,250*	4,657	4,030
Hardware, bldg, materials	79,020	120	0.2	67,002	80	0.1	-1.6	-3.9	4,427	1,750*	6,552	2,500*
Other retail trade	209,460	5,880	2.8	147,991	2,680	1.8	-3.3	-7.5	3,330	1,717	5,794	3,737
Banking and finance	20,910	90	0.4	22,076	41	0.2	0.6	-7.5	8,277	n.r.	14,527	12,500*
Insurance and real estate	44,910	600	1.3	49,232	794	1.6	1.0	2.8	5,727	2,250*	10,393	5,500*
Business services	33,390	570	1.7	37,020	890	2.4	1.1	4.6	4,250	2,250*	7,626	4,500*
Automotive repair and garages	59,610	870	1.5	38,528	1,083	2.8	-4.2	2.2	3,183	2,000	5,237	3,564
Misc. repair services	29,070	450	1.5	19,317	414	2.1	-4.1	-0.8	2,713	1,750*	4,851	3,500*
Personal services	135,720	5,970	4.4	127,356	4,349	3.4	-0.7	-3.1	3,114	2,174	5,060	3,296
Other industries	97,080	2,760	2.8	95,311	3,239	3.4	-0.2	1.6	3,433	1,250*	5,777	2,508
Total	2,422,350	59,820	2.5	1,954,903	46,400	2.4	-2.1	-2.4	3,502	1,860	5,932	3,368

1 White and Negro only.
* Estimated at mid-point of income class interval.
n.r. not reported

SOURCE: U.S. Census of Population, 1950, Special Reports, "Occupational Characteristics," 1956 IB Table 13. U.S. Census of Population, 1960, "Occupational Characteristics," 1963, Table 3.

stituted about 2.5 percent of all self-employed businessmen, but this ratio varied greatly among different industries. Their largest share of a major industry was personal services (3.4 percent); at the bottom of the spectrum was banking and finance, where Negroes represented less than two-tenths of one percent of the total. But behind the array of ratios is an interesting and significant story. If we divide the retail trade sector according to the principal types of stores, we see immediately the importance of segregation in providing opportunities for Negro entrepreneurs. For example, in 1960, Negroes operated 2.6 percent of all retail outlets—but 5.6 percent of the eating and drinking establishments. They also had 4.1 percent of the food stores; this is a reflection of the fact that such stores (especially smaller ones) are typically located in or near segregated residential areas.

In sharp contrast, Negroes owned much less than one percent of the retail establishments selling apparel, furniture, hardware or motor vehicles. In these categories, the meager ownership role played by Negroes can be attributed partly to the fact that few of them can obtain the relatively large amount of capital required for successful operation. Another factor appears to be the sizable volume of sales necessary to sustain such a business. However, the most basic explanation seems to be the freedom Negro customers have to shop for these items in stores catering to the general market. The slightly stronger position of Negroes as operators of gasoline stations is due primarily to the vigorous and competitive efforts of the leading petroleum companies to establish franchise outlets in or near the geographical areas occupied by Negroes in the key population centers. Outside of retail trade, the provision of personal services to Negro customers has been a mainstay of Negro businessmen. The most outstanding examples are owners of barbershops and beauty salons. In fact, this area alone has generated a complex of interrelated activities by Negro businessmen shown under other headings in Table 1. For instance, the majority of the 1,300 Negroes who owned manufacturing firms in 1960 were probably producing cosmetics and barber and beauty shop supplies especially for the Negro trade. Undoubtedly, a fairly large proportion of the 2,600 Negro businessmen engaged in wholesale trade were distributing these items to local shops. Still other businessmen (e.g., insurance and real estate brokers, and those providing a variety of business services) were probably only slightly less dependent on the segregated Negro market. On the other hand, Negroes owning automotive repair facilities, running transportation (such as taxis and local haulage), and doing construction jobs normally would find their customers in the community at large—although Negro customers may provide their ultimate base of support.

But this configuration of Negro-owned businesses is changing drastically. Between 1950 and 1960, the total number of Negro businessmen shrank by more than one-fifth. While there was a similar decrease in the total number of self-employed businessmen during the decade, the proportion was smaller. Moreover, much of the decline in the overall number was accounted for by the change to the corporate form of organization. This was much less true for Negroes.

Furthermore, with few exceptions, the incidence of decline was greater for Negroes, compared with the total, in those fields where segregation and discrimination imposed the least constraints on Negro customers. For instance, the annual average percentage changes between 1950 and 1960 in several key areas for Negroes and the total self-employed, respectively, were: communications, utilities and sanitary services, —11.2 vs. +1.2; transportation, —6.5 vs. —2.9; furniture and housefurnishings, —6.1 vs. —2.9; apparel and accessories, —5.9 vs. —3.6; hardware and building materials, —3.9 vs. —1.6. It is difficult to account for the causes underlying these specific decreases, but several considerations can be cited. The sharp drop in the number of Negroes in the private sanitary services (and the growth in the total number of businessmen engaged in this activity) probably reflects the increased competition from large firms which move trash for restaurants, department stores and similar establishments on a contract basis. A similar explanation probably applies in the case of transportation. In the past, numerous small Negro businesses were formed around one or two trucks, with the owner and a few helpers providing local moving and job-by-job transportation services. However, with the growing unionization of the trucking industry, even extending into purely local transportation, the rising wage levels have made such opportunities increasingly attractive to white men. The trend toward the use of more sophisticated equipment (such as refrigerator trucks and other specialty vehicles) has also necessitated the accumulation of considerably more capital than most Negro truckers could raise. In addition, the number of Negro taxi owners in the major cities (with the possible exception of Washington, D.C.) has shrunk as gigantic corporations have acquired franchises to operate fleets of several thousand vehicles. The decline in the retail outlets undoubtedly reflects the diffusion of mass marketing throughout the economy; this has made it exceedingly difficult for the small Negro retailer (along with similarly situated white merchants) to compete with the super market, large department stores and discount houses.

Several other types of traditional Negro businesses, although not shown explicitly in Table 1, also experienced absolute decline or a severe slackening in the rate of growth. For example, the number of funeral directors dropped by 6 percent between 1950 and 1960, and the number of barbers decreased by over 16 percent. While the number of Negro-owned hotels and motels has continued to expand, they have lost a sizable proportion of their most desirable clientele—a loss only partly made up by the growth of luxury and semiluxury resort and vacation sites.

On the other hand, Negro businessmen made significant strides in several new or revitalized fields. The number of self-employed in construction climbed by more than 17 percent, about the same rate achieved by this category as a whole. Substantial gains were also registered in the ownership of gasoline service stations, automotive repair shops and garages. In manufacturing, modest expansion occurred. This gain was made despite the capture by large corporations of a fairly sizable share of the cosmetics market among Negro customers, which traditionally accounted for virtually all of the output of Negro manufacturing firms. Many of the more recent ventures in manufacturing include plastics, apparel, food processing and other relatively new areas.

In analyzing these general trends in Negro-owned businesses during the last decade or so, the intention is not to paint a bleak picture of total stagnation and decline. On the contrary, a great number of individual Negro businesses have been launched and have achieved considerable success. Moreover, many established firms have made substantial progress. Indeed, without much difficulty, one can find exceptionally prosperous businessmen whose enterprises stand out against the general trend in any of the areas described here. Nevertheless, when the basic trends are viewed against the panorama of the overall business landscape, one cannot escape concluding that Negro businessmen taken as a group have lost considerable ground and are facing an uncertain future. . . .

If the fields in which Negro businessmen have traditionally concentrated are less promising than in the past, what alternative opportunities are likely to appear in the future? For Negroes, as for other citizens in the business world, such opportunities are likely to be found primarily as managers and officials employed by our medium and large corporations and public enterprises. That Negroes have made little progress in this field is common knowledge. For example, in 1960, about 8 percent of the total civilian labor force of 68 million was engaged as non-farm managers, officials and proprietors. Less than 1.5 percent of the 6.6 million Negroes in the labor force were so engaged. If the percentages had been approximately equal, there would have been about 525 thousand—rather than the actual 191 thousand —Negroes in the managerial class. Furthermore, over half of the Negro managerial group was self-employed, compared with just over one-third of all managers in the country.

Thus, from these data a clear inference can be drawn: with a change in aspirations among potential Negro businessmen, better preparation on their part and a genuine commitment to equal opportunity by leaders in the corporate business community, the future could be promising for a number of Negro businessmen.

Some progress is already being made in this direction, although few corporate executives would claim that the pace has been rapid. A rough indication of the current trends is given by the experience of those companies which participate in "Plans for Progress." This is a voluntary program to expand access to jobs, operated in conjunction with the President's

Committee on Equal Opportunity. In a report covering the period when the companies joined Plans for Progress through mid-July, 1964, 103 of these firms reported that their total employment increased by 300,796 or 7.6 percent. Just over two-fifths of this gain represented an expansion in white collar employment. During the same period, these companies added 40,938 employees from minority groups. This represented about 13.6 percent of the expansion in total employment. On the other hand, nonwhites filled about 11.0 percent of the increase in white collar jobs.

When these companies joined Plans for Progress, nonwhites constituted about 5 percent of their total labor force, and they represented approximately 1.2 percent of those in the managerial group. In the subsequent expansion in employment, nonwhites obtained about 3,000 (or 2 percent) of the new jobs in the management category. While this gain is obviously very small, it does represent about 1,000 more managerial and technical positions for nonwhites than might have been expected on the basis of the companies' traditional employment practice.

Simultaneously, many corporations are making a special effort to recruit and train Negroes and other minority group citizens for corporate positions. Some of this effort undoubtedly can be written off as "image-making" by some firms, who would like to point to their recruiting efforts which have—unfortunately—failed to produce "qualified" candidates. On the whole, however, the vast majority of corporate recruiters seem to be making a genuine effort to identify and to enroll promising minority group candidates. On the other hand, given the criteria which the typical corporation uses in selecting its managerial personnel, most corporate recruiters are undoubtedly finding it difficult to locate qualified personnel. The sources of these difficulties are widely known. They spring from the vicious circle created by a history of discriminatory employment practices; poor undergraduate training provided by the archaic curricula of basically segregated institutions attended by many Negro college students; a resulting peculiar pattern of occupational preferences stressing medicine, law, teaching and the ministry; a reluctance to venture into the expanding fields of business administration and related social sciences, engineering and other technical areas—which result in only marginal preparation for management careers in business.

In the meantime, it may be helpful to provide a profile of the types of skills for which corporations are searching among Negroes and other minority group members. A rough outline can be sketched by an analysis of the recruiting visits which corporations are currently making on predominantly Negro college campuses. For this purpose, the experience of Howard University may be taken as a prototype. (Of course, the Howard University experience is undoubtedly biased because its curricula are most varied and its program in engineering and the physical sciences probably far surpasses that of all other predominantly Negro schools; its program in business administration also ranks high among the three or four genuine programs to be found on Negro college campuses. But, if we keep in mind these limitations of the Howard data, we can gain an insight into the types of professions demanded by corporations.)

. . . Howard University . . . for the academic year 1963–64 . . . received visitors from about 160 corporations and about 20 government departments and independent agencies. These companies represented a variety of industries, but the heaviest concentration was in chemicals, transportation equipment, and communications and utilities. Among government agencies, the Defense Department was the most frequent visitor.

Together, these potential employers made more than seven hundred requests about some forty-odd occupational categories. The engineering field accounted for about two-fifths of the total, with electrical and mechanical engineering being most frequently specified. Somewhat over one-fifth of the inquiries sought graduates in the physical sciences, with chemists and physicists taking the lead. Thus, more than three-fifths of all of the requests were concentrated in the engineering and technical fields. If the closely related field of mathematics is added, about 70 percent of the total inquiries were for candidates with highly technical undergraduate training.

In contrast, requests for personnel in the field of business administration represented only 15 percent of the total. General business administration and accounting each attracted 5 percent, and marketing about 4 percent. If we add inquiries for graduates in the social sciences—which frequently serve as a pool of skills that can be reshaped for business administration purposes—the share accounted for by the business area would rise to only one-sixth of the total.

A number of inferences can be drawn from these data, but one implication seems clear: if we can generalize the Howard experience, corporations (and to some extent government agencies) have directed their recruitment efforts on Negro campuses more to the technical and scientific fields and less to those which lead directly into key managerial functions in corporate enterprise. While engineers, chemists and other technicians (with years of experience) do frequently move into positions of general management responsibility, the more likely routes through the corporate hierarchy typically begin in the nontechnical fields, such as financial administration, accounting and marketing.

Of course, the chance to go into business for themselves is an option which will remain open to Negroes along with other citizens. However, before this option is taken up in the future, potential Negro business should give careful consideration to several factors that are rapidly reshaping the environment in which they will have to operate. While the majority of Negro businessmen are correct in assuming that (within the foreseeable future) they will have to rely primarily on Negro customers for their patronage, they apparently do not realize that in the future they will have to compete in a wholly different type of market. As mentioned above, the desegregation of places of public accommodation, such as restaurants, theaters, hotels and similar establishments, will have a serious impact on many of the sheltered businesses which most Negro businessmen have operated behind the barriers induced by segregation. With greater access to facilities provided for the public in general, Negro customers will increasingly demand that Negro businesses compete in terms of quality of services provided at competitive prices.

Further, there is a prime need to shift from the single proprietorship form of organization, which is so dominant among Negro businessmen, to the corporate form which is the key to financing business expansion. The superiority of the corporation over unincorporated enterprises as a medium for expanding business has been clearly demonstrated, and growth as opposed to stagnation has always been a measure of business health. Recent data on the distribution of firms by type of organization and the relative share of receipts and profits show that relatively few companies account for the major share of the nation's business, and these are the large and ever-growing corporations. For example, in 1960, corporations constituted about 10 percent of the total number of businesses in existence. However, the total receipts of corporations were $803 billion, representing over three-quarters of the total. Their net profits, after allowing for losses, amounted to $44 billion, or three-fifths of the total net profits of business enterprises.

But whatever form of organization a businessman chooses for his operation, several conditions must be met if success is to be realized. In the first instance, a businessman must perceive a market for a product or service. Next, steps must be taken to translate this idea into a practical production process. Thirdly, technical and managerial know-how must be sufficient to establish and conduct an enterprise. Financial resources, especially equity capital, must be available or acquired. A skilled labor force must exist or must be trained. Finally, the businessman must possess enough marketing know-how to find and maintain customers in the face of competition from other products and services. As we all know, the typical Negro-owned firm is deficient in all or most of these vital requirements.

While there is no shortage of potential Negro businessmen, there is a severe shortage of technical know-how outside the traditional areas of trade and personal services. This lack of mastery over technical requirements may well be an obstacle as great as the lack of equity capital. To help fill this gap, a number of economic development and business service centers (including centers at Atlanta University and Howard University) were established in 1964. The objectives of these projects include:

—The provision of technical and management assistance to establish or expand businesses, particularly those that are Negro-owned or managed and have a preponderance of Negro employees.

—The provision of technical training and services to groups and communities, particularly Negro, in the field of economic development which will enable them to take a more active role in the creation of new enterprises and new job opportunities.

Such centers could become the locus of the kind of economic and technical research and guidance so necessary for economic development and successful business enterprise. Finally, they would provide for both students and faculty exposure to the variety and complexity of managerial problems with which virtually every future businessman must deal.

The above observations focus on only a few of the growing opportunities for Negro businessmen to participate in the future growth of the country. Above all, there will undoubtedly be a variety of ventures engaged in the production and distribution of goods and services for the community as a whole. Moreover, there will undoubtedly be growing opportunities for Negroes to participate in the management activities of large corporations which are also oriented to the general market. It should be emphasized again that desegregation of the marketplace which is already well under way will require desegregation in the ownership and management of business enterprises as well. While the future of a segregated Negro-owned business, existing in a segregated market, appears not to be bright, the future of Negroes in the business life of the country in general does appear to be more promising than ever before.

Separatist Economics: A New Social Contract

ROY INNIS

There exists today a crisis of immense proportions within the boundaries of the United States of America. This crisis is the direct result of the breakdown of the relationship between black and white people in our society. It was scarcely a good relationship to begin with. For blacks it has been degrading and dehumanizing; for whites, it has been abrasive, guilt-ridden, and a perpetual thorn. Over the decades, the problem has festered and spread to the point where it now threatens to destroy the entire political organism in which it is rooted.

Even at this late date, we can provide an alternative to the collision course of whites and blacks in this country. But to do so, we must develop entirely new solutions to the massive problems of the past. The present

From Roy Innis, "Separatist Economics: A New Social Contract" in William F. Haddad and G. Douglas Pugh, Eds., *Black Economic Development,* © 1969 by The American Assembly, Columbia University. Reprinted by permission of Prentice-Hall, Inc., Englewood Cliffs, N.J. 07632.

programs and plans offered by well-meaning agencies, groups, and individuals are entirely insufficient. Aside from the fundamental lack of understanding in the past of the nature and degree of racism in this country, there has been a failure to coordinate the multiplicity of suggested "solutions." Such solutions, in any case, have never been structured by black people. They have always been structured by whites who interpreted our needs and in many cases designed these solutions to accommodate their own needs.

Where the collision of black and white is concerned, we have falsely assumed in America that a contract or constitution designed for a dominant majority, with distinct attributes, self-interests, and needs, could simply be adapted, by minor modifications, to fit the needs of a significant minority with different attributes, interests, and needs. Obviously, this has not worked. A crucial weakness has been the lack of control by black people over the institutions that surround them: institutions that not only establish imposed values for them but also control the flow of goods and services within their communities, thereby shaping the quality of their lives. The black community sees these institutions in the hands of people with interests too often at odds with their own. Thus, schools in black neighborhoods too often do not teach, sanitation departments do not protect, employment departments do not find jobs, welfare departments do not give adequate relief, housing departments do not give decent housing. Most ironic of all, human rights departments do not guarantee human rights.

The obvious solution, then, is a *new social contract*, to be drawn in the mutual interest of both parties. This contract must redefine the relationship between blacks and whites, to the extent that black people are recognized as a major interest group. While this redefinition is in progress, there are palpable changes to be implemented.

Large, densely populated black areas, especially in urban centers, must have a change in status. They must become political sub-divisions of the state, instead of sub-colonial appendages of the cities. Blacks must manage and control the institutions that service their areas, as has always been the case for other interest groups. There is an immediate need in the institutions of education, health, social service, sanitation, housing, protection, etc. Black people must be able to control basic societal instruments in the social, political, and economic arenas.

Definitions

In short, black people must seek liberation from the dominance and control of white society. Nothing less than this liberation will allow black people to determine their own destinies.

Perhaps, at this point, a few definitions are in order. There is always a controversy as to whether our tactics, our objectives, are reformist or

revolutionary. In my own view, black people at this state of their development are not and should not be talking about some romantic thing
called revolution, but rather a more pragmatic and necessary step called
liberation. There is a difference between the two. A revolution, of course,
occurs where one class of a national group rebels against another class
of that same group, as in the Russia of 1917, the France of the late 18th
Century. Liberation come about in a setting of two distinct groups, where
one is suppressing the other. Jews caught in Egypt in the time of the
Pharaohs did not talk about revolution against what was the most powerful
and formidable military machine of the time. They talked about liberation
—separating themselves from Egyptians.

We black nationalists, too, must speak of separating ourselves. We live
in a setting where one group—not our own—controls the institutions, and
the flow of goods and services. We can change our condition by liberating
ourselves and placing these vital instruments of social and economic destiny
in our own hands. This is what we mean by separation—quite a different
matter from segregation, which is the condition that now exists, in fact,
throughout the United States.

Separation is a more equitable way of organizing the society. The
important distinction is that in such a society the control of goods and
services flowing through a distinct geographical area inhabited by a
distinct population group would be in the hands of those indigenous to
the area. In other words, if we have a clearly defined sociological unit
called Harlem, New York City, the people of Harlem will control the flow
of goods and services there. The same would hold true for the white areas
of New York City: the whites would control their own "action."

In the struggle toward self-determination, there has been a great deal
of argument about the order of steps to be taken. Should we be talking
first about politics, about culture, or should we be talking about economics?
Let me suggest that we can resolve this dilemma by understanding first of
all that these three stages of liberation are virtually inseparable. There must
be some sort of socio-cultural renaissance if there is to be movement in any
other direction. There must be some sort of politico-economic development if the cultural movement is to have any base on which to acquire
significance.

My feeling is that we have already begun part of this movement. That
is, black people have begun revitalizing their culture, recreating their
values. We must now phase in the element of economic growth. The failure of many of the past economic measures—community action, training
and hiring programs, and the like—is that they have been little more than
board games, depending on some sort of arithmetic progression. What we
need to do now is to find the geometric factor that can speed up this
process. And that is why we turn to the control of institutions. But some
further definition is needed.

Capitalism or Development

In the new focus on economic control, there has been much talk about something called "black capitalism." Many of our people have been deluded into endless debates centered around this term. There is no such animal. Capitalism, like socialism, is an economic and political philosophy that describes the experience of Europeans and their descendants—Americans. Blacks must innovate, must create a new ideology. It may include elements of capitalism, elements of socialism, or elements of neither: that is immaterial. What matters is that it will be created to fit our needs.

So then black people are not talking about black capitalism. Black people are talking about economic development. We are talking about the creation and the acquisition of capital instruments by means of which we can maximize our economic interests. We do not particularly try to define styles of ownership; we say that we are willing to operate pragmatically and let the style of ownership fit the style of the area or its inhabitants.

The question of autonomy is critical. Any reliable sociological analysis will indicate that we live in natural units called communities. Where whites are concerned, these natural sociological units then become natural political units—political subdivisions of county, state, or federal government. This does not happen with black communities, so that extensive areas like Harlem in New York, Roxbury in Boston, Watts in Los Angeles, exist as colonial appendages of the urban center. In fact, government programs almost always deal with us as part of urban centers, and in terms of the overall condition of those centers. This is something we must resist strenuously, for there is a fundamental conflict of interest between our communities—the so-called ghettos—and the urban centers in which they are situated. The urban centers are managed by political and institutional barons who include our piece of "turf" in their domain. And we see that whenever we make any attempt to change that relationship—political, social, or economic—we meet the massive resistance of these barons. This sort of frustration has led and will continue to lead to disastrous confrontations between blacks and whites.

We understand also that the urban setting, throughout history, has been the energizer of mankind, thus the cradle of change. It is there that blacks, too, will have to find their solutions. We cannot go off to conduct a masquerade of change in newly created little rural centers. But if we are to develop in the urban centers, our position must be newly understood.

There is a very striking similarity between the so-called underdeveloped countries and our underdeveloped black communities. Both have always been oppressed; almost always there is an unfavorable balance of trade with the oppressors or exploiters; both suffer from high unemployment, low income, scarce capital, and we can point to a series of other similarities. But let me point to at least one vital difference. In every so-called underdeveloped country, the people have a measure of sovereignty. They have a vastly greater amount of autonomy compared with the black communities across this country. It seems to me, then, that a natural impetus for our communities is to move to gain that missing ingredient—sovereignty, or at least a greater degree of autonomy and self-determination.

In other words, I am saying there is no way we can divorce economic development from political imperatives. You cannot have economic development unless you have certain supportive political realities, one of which is some degree of self-determination.

The Dividends

What economic gratuities would flow from self-determination? Let us consider the massive budgets provided to pay for the goods and services of a single black community (which are then almost always poorly distributed in that community). Take the schools, for example. In a community like Harlem, close to a hundred million dollars is spent yearly for goods and services to supply the schools. We must assume, in fact we know, that in almost every instance those goods and services are purchased from sources outside the community. Now we in the black community pay taxes that are intended to be used to pay for these commodities, so that nominally, all tax monies are returned to us in this form. But what really happens is that our tax monies are returned to agents of the urban centers— the mayor and his commissioners and department heads—who will then use that money to enhance the economic interest of the white-dominated urban center by buying goods and services outside the black communities they are meant to serve.

That same hundred million dollars could have gone, let us say, to a corporation in Harlem put together by two or three black entrepreneurs and awarded a contract to supply books for the Harlem schools. It is immaterial that this hypothetical corporation does not own a publishing house or a printing plant. Neither do the white corporations that presently supply books to the public school system in Cleveland, or New York, or any place else across this country. They are merely middlemen. They buy from someone else and sell to the schools. They move paper from one side of their desk to the other and turn a handsome profit. That kind of profit could be turned just as easily within the black community, to increase its income by the millions. Multiply the massive budgets for the schools by the massive budgets in health and hospital services, sanitation, and all the other urban services, and you get a massive amount of money that represents a guaranteed market.

The name of this in economics is guaranteed market. That is what you have when you are selling to your own institutions: there will always be a demand for your goods and services. If you have control of these institutions you are able to determine who will get the contracts, and you can direct them back to your own people.

So here we see at least one route by which the black people can get a running start in economic development without huge investments in machinery, materials, technical expertise, and without most of the other impediments that are immediately cited when we talk about economic development. And it is a way in which we could secure a maximum return to our community from those precious tax dollars that we pay year after year.

Of course, this same division of interest and diversion of profit has social as well as economic consequences. We must control our schools if we are to upgrade education and pass on positive values to our children. We must control health facilities if we are to cut down our mortality rate. We must control the law enforcement in our areas if the police are to serve their proper function—which is protection, not oppression. In short, we must control every single institution that takes our tax moneys and is supposed to distribute goods and services equitably for us.

VEHICLES FOR SELF-DETERMINATION

The Congress of Racial Equality has been working to develop vehicles and instruments for black self-determination at both the local and national levels.

The Harlem Commonwealth Council

The first group in America to formalize the advance of black business beyond the "Mom-and-Pop" stage was the Harlem Commonwealth Council in New York. With a controversial grant from the Demonstration Office of the Office of Economic Opportunity, the HCC was organized as a non-profit, tax exempt corporation which invests in profitmaking businesses and uses the accumulated income to re-invest in other businesses. The National Association of Manufacturers and McKinsey and Company agreed to provide help, along with two universities.

The HCC's first brochure notes that Harlem's half million people can spend half a billion dollars for consumer goods every year—a sum larger than the gross national product of many underdeveloped nations. Yet, says the brochure, "the economic sickness of Harlem" is that most of this capital is siphoned off from the community by the outsiders who own 80 per cent of Harlem's business volume. "One root problem of Harlem is that almost no one who lives there owns anything."

Accordingly, the goal of HCC is to "bring back to Harlem that internal economic vitality which is essential to social development . . . . It is not enough to attract white-owned industry. Finding jobs for blacks is not enough either, critical as that is. Both of these become enough only if we can also develop Harlem's capital."

To implement its plans, HCC set up a community-based Board of Directors who, with help from the outside consultants, quickly developed their own ability to pick and choose among business opportunities. As objectives they selected those businesses which would meet community needs (e.g., a 24-hour pharmacy selling prescription medicines by their generic names, thus permitting prices considerably lower than those for brand name medicines), and modern businesses which capitalize on Harlem's strategic location in Manhattan (e.g., an Automotive Diagnostic Center near the Triborough Bridge which feeds in traffic from two other boroughs).

The HCC is not looking for yesterday's businesses but tomorrow's opportunities. They are utilizing the most modern market instruments to determine markets and potenials; helping locate business opportunities in Harlem and then finding the potential businessmen to run them; designing training and apprenticeship programs to prepare a black man to run his own business; and providing the technical services to train managers.

The Cleveland Plan

In Cleveland, Ohio, CORE has projected the development of a consortium of black economic institutions designed to significantly broaden the base of ownership by the black community of productive capital instruments. The Cleveland program is seeking $10 million of funding for a two-year operational budget, to establish sustaining economic institutions through which black residents could be both owners of capital instruments and wage earners. An excerpt from the formal summary of the proposal states this general concept:

CORENCO (CORE Enterprises Corporation) contends that the way to correct (the economic imbalance between black and white communities) is to effect institutional changes which increase the productive power of under-productive households and individuals so that they may legitimately receive enough income to satisfy their reasonable needs and desires. Although it is a method which would tend to protect existing private property, it would also tend to build a "New Black Economy" in the black community, so financed that it becomes owned in moderately-sized holdings by the great majority of households and individuals who own no productive capital in the existing economy. . . .

New financing techniques can enable the man without capital to buy it, and to pay for it out of the wealth it produces, and therefore to enjoy a new stream of income, if there is a demand for his employment—and the only full employment possible in our advanced industrial economy must result from the building and operation of a second economy producing humanly useful and desirable goods—he will then have two sources of income with which, on the one hand, to erase his poverty and, on the other hand, to provide the market—the effective market—for the expanded output by industry and business.

CORENCO will establish research and development teams to promote a wide range of economic projects aimed at creating a black economic infrastructure and increasing black ownership and employment in the institutions that purchase and distribute goods and services in the black community.

The Federal Bill

Most of the problems we have discussed in this chapter we have tried to deal with, to some degree, in the Community Self-Determination Bill. This bill, created by CORE with a wide spectrum of expert assistance, was introduced before the Congress of the United States in July of 1968, receiving support from all political corners. (Ironically, but not surprisingly, most of the opposition came from labor, from the leadership of the AFL-CIO, which used to proclaim itself the great friend of the black man. In the current history of the civil rights movement and the black power movement, we have had to fight our biggest and toughest battles against the labor unions. More recently, the AFL-CIO has declared itself opposed to so-called black capitalism and thus, by implication, to black self-determination. Meanwhile, of course, they continue to endorse programs advocating jobs for blacks—jobs that the unions themselves consistently prevent us from getting.)

The Community Self-Determination Bill can serve as a social, political, and economic tool by means of which the black communities can make giant strides. Through it, we can create community instruments that can in themselves create community industries; these in turn would produce jobs for men. It would provide for a variety of types of ownership, for community boards in black areas to coordinate economic development and the control of indigenous institutions.

These community boards would be the sole agencies in the black community responsible for both social welfare and economic development. They would give contracts to community industries and raise sound financing for them with the help of a new banking system—community development banks.

As projected, the program will provide incentive for broad-based community ownership. It will contain provisions for research, development, and training, for the development of innovations in health, welfare, education, and other community services. It will provide performance bond guarantees to enable existing industries that cannot now meet bonding requirements to compete for a fair share of contracts for the black communities. It contemplates providing incentives for outside industry to come into our areas—though not to stay. Unlike other programs, we do not want to bring white industries into the black community to create jobs. We want industries to come into the community to create *instruments*, to sell them to us, and then move out.

WILL IT WORK

So what we are talking about, in the final analysis, is not jobs, but instruments that create jobs. We are not talking about bringing white businesses into black communities, but about building economic instruments that themselves can hire blacks. Nor are we talking merely, as some people seem to construe it, of substituting black ownership of a pants-pressing business for white ownership of a pants-pressing business, for that is looking at the economics of the community on the lowest scale. We are talking about the acquisition of capital instruments on a major scale, to maximize the flow of money in the community and begin that geometric progression toward economic well-being.

This separatist economics, as I choose to call it, is not essentially different from the basic principles of developmental economics employed by any people—for example, the Americans of post-Revolutionary period. It is the manipulation of the economy of black areas in a preferential way to obtain an edge and protect the interests of the community; to place a membrane around the community that allows full commercial intercourse with outside business interests while setting pre-conditions and guidelines advantageous to the community for those who may seek to operate within the community. This principle is known by many names, one of the more familiar being *tariff*.

Will whites go along with this? I must be honest—I do not have an unshakable faith in white people; I have no experience that would support such a faith.

But the underlying assumption of all I have said here is that whites who have the most power (real power) and the most to lose from chaos *will* go along with it; that the Community Self-Determination Bill will become the high-powered vehicle of the new black economy. What I assume is that an enlightened self-interest will head off the impending collision in this country—and I am talking about the enlightened self-interest of black people and white.

For we are past the stage where we can talk seriously of whites acting toward blacks out of moral imperatives. That does not work. Yet we can still talk of change coming about through enlightened self-interest, the prime motivator of orderly change in society throughout the history of mankind. That is the only thing that works without destroying what it seeks to save.

FOR FURTHER READING: One of the best surveys of diverse views concerning Black Capitalism is by William L. Henderson and Larry C. Ledebur, *Economic Disparities: Problems and Strategies for Black America* (New York, 1970). See also Ralph H. Kinzer and Edward Sagarin, *The Negro in American Business: the Conflict Between Separatism and Integration* (New York, 1960). Essays that reveal some skepticism about Black Capitalism include Eli Ginzberg (ed.), *The Negro Challenge to the Business Community* (New York, 1964), and by the same editor, *Business Leadership and the Negro Crisis* (New York, 1968). Similar reservations are expressed by the president of Hampton Institute, Jerome H. Holland, *Black Opportunity* (New York, 1967). The case for Black Capitalism is aptly described by C. Eric Lincoln, *The Black Muslims in America* (New York, 1961). E. U. Essien-Udom, *Black Nationalism* (New York, 1964), Harold Cruse, *The Crisis of the Negro Intellectual* (New York, 1967), and James Boggs, *Manifesto for a Black Revolutionary Party* (Philadelphia, 1968).

INDEX